VINTAGE CHAMPAGNE

CHAMPAGNE

1899 to 2019

Charles Curtis MW

WineAlpha

Editor: Harriet Bell

Copy editor: Trevor Wisdom

Art direction and design: Madeleine Curtis

Published by WineAlpha 106 West 32nd Street 2/F #151

New York, NY 10001 ISBN 978-0-9906844-2-8

Table of Contents

Producer Index (Alphabetical)...1

Producer Index (Geographical)...6

Preface..10

Introduction..13

Part I: The Leading Producers

Hors classe..26

Four-star producers..32

Three-star producers..61

Two-star producers...126

One-star producers...202

Part II: The Vintages

Chapter I: 1899 – 1909 Luxe, Calme, et Volupté?...277

Chapter II: 1910 – 1919 Riots & War...288

Chapter III: 1920 – 1929 Les Années Folles...299

Chapter IV: 1930 – 1939 Depression & Innovation.......................................308

Chapter V: 1940 – 1949 War & Postwar...318

Chapter VI: 1950 – 1959 Les Trentes Glorieuses Begin.................................330

Chapter VII: 1960 – 1969 Goodbye to All That..342

Chapter VIII: 1970 – 1979 Dawn of the Modern Era 356

Chapter IX: 1980 – 1989 Mergers, Acquisitions, and Growth.......................374

Chapter X: 1990 – 1999 Pricing & Pressing...390

Chapter XI: 2000 – 2009 The Green Revolution...409

Chapter XII: 2010 – 2019 Limits to Growth..430

Part III: The Glossary & Appendices

Glossary..451

Appendix I: Specifications of the AOC Champagne
("Cahier des Charges")..479

Appendix II: Article D645-7 of the Rural Code
("Code Rural et de la Pêche Maritime")..507

Appendix III: Article D645-15 of the Rural Code...................................509

Appendix IV: Article D645-18 of the Rural Code...................................510

Appendix V: Decree of 17 October 1952..511

Appendix VI: Timeline of Champagne..513

Appendix VII: Champagne Villages..520

Bibliography..530

General Index...536

Index of Producers & Cuvées...540

Alphabetical Index of Producers

Agrapart..61

Yann Alexandre...202

L. Aubry...203

Ayala..205

Paul Bara..206

Bérêche et Fils...64

Billecart-Salmon...126

Bollinger..32

Francis Boulard et Fille...208

Emmanuel Brochet...68

Etienne Calsac...210

Vincent Charlot...211

Chartogne-Taillet..70

Chevreux-Bournazel..213

Gaston Chiquet..128

La Closerie...73

Coessens..214

Ulysse Collin...216

Corbon..217

Vincent Couche...218

Marie Courtin...76

R.H. Coutier..219

De Sousa...220

Dehours et Fils..130

Benoît Déhu..133

Delamotte..135

Deutz..221

José Dhondt..222

Diebolt-Vallois...78

Dom Pérignon..37

Pascal Doquet..80

Doyard,,,...223

Drappier..82

Egly-Ouriet..84

Fallet-Dart..225

Nathalie Falmet...136

Fleury...226

Val Frison..228

Gatinois..229

Geoffroy..138

Pierre Gerbais...141

Pierre Gimonnet..86

Philippe Glavier...230

Gonet-Médeville...231

Gosset..233

Alfred Gratien..143

Maurice Grumier..145

Guiborat...234

Marc Hébrart...147

Charles Heidsieck & Piper-Heidsieck............................149

Henriot...153

Olivier Horiot..89

Huré Frères..155

André Jacquart...92

Jacquesson...94

Jeaunaux-Robin...236

Juillet-Lallement..159

Krug...26

Lacourte-Godbillon..238

Benoît Lahaye..157

Laherte Frères..162

Philippe Lancelot...239

Lancelot-Pienne...240

Lanson...165

Larmandier-Bernier..97

Jacques Lassaigne..99

David Léclapart..102

Leclerc Briant..167

Marie-Noëlle Ledru..170

Pierre Legras...171

A.R. Lenoble..104

Lilbert-Fils..106

Joseph Loriot-Pagel...241

Nicolas Maillart...173

Mailly Grand Cru...242

Sadi Malot...244

A. Margaine...245

Marguet..247

Serge Mathieu...249

José Michel....................175

Christophe Mignon....................250

Jean Milan....................251

Moët & Chandon....................177

Pierre Moncuit....................252

Robert Moncuit....................180

Moussé Fils....................253

G.H. Mumm....................182

Bruno Paillard....................186

Pierre Paillard....................108

Hubert Paulet....................189

Penet-Chardonnet....................254

Perrier-Jouët....................190

Laurent-Perrier....................256

Pierre Péters....................110

Philipponnat....................42

Piollot Père et Fils....................258

Pol Roger....................112

R. Pouillon....................259

Eric Rodez....................114

Louis Roederer....................46

Roses de Jeanne....................116

Ruinart....................118

Ruppert-Leroy....................261

Denis Salomon....................262

Salon....................50

Savart....................121

Camille Savès...263

J.M. Sélèque...265

Jacques Selosse..53

Soutiran...267

Stroebel...268

Suenen...193

Taittinger..57

Tarlant..194

Vazart-Coquart & Fils..196

Jean Velut...269

J.L. Vergnon...270

Veuve Clicquot..197

Veuve Fourny..271

Vilmart & Cie. 200

Vouette et Sorbée...123

Geographical Index of Producers

Champagne Towns

Epernay

Dom Pérignon, Gosset, Alfred Gratien, Leclerc-Briant, Moët & Chandon, Perrier-Jouët, Pol Roger

Reims

Charles Heidsieck, Henriot, Krug, Lanson, G.H. Mumm, Bruno Paillard, Louis Roederer, Ruinart, Taittinger, Veuve Clicquot

Montagne de Reims

Grande Montagne (North) :

Ludes: Bérêche et Fils, Huré Frères, Mailly, Mailly Grand Cru;
Rilly-la-Montagne: Hubert Paulet, Vilmart & Cie.; *Verzy:* Juillet-Lallement, Penet-Chardonnet, Villers-Allerand, Stroebel

Grande Montagne (South) :

Ambonnay: R.H. Coutier, Egly-Ouriet, Marie-Noëlle Ledru, Marguet, Eric Rodez, Soutiran; *Bouzy:* Paul Bara, Benoît Lahaye, Pierre Paillard, Camille Savès

Grande Montagne (Perle Blanche) :

Trepail: David Léclapart; *Villers-Marmery:* Sadi Malot, A. Margaine

Petite Montagne

Ecueil: Nicolas Maillart, Savart, Lacourte-Godbillon;
Gueux: Champagne La Closerie (Prévost); *Jouy-lès-Reims:* L. Aubry Fils;
Villers-aux-Nœuds: Emmanuel Brochet

Ardre Valley :

Courmas: Yann Alexandre

Massif de Saint-Thierry

Merfy: Chartogne-Taillet; _Faverolles-et-Coëmy:_ Francis Boulard et Fille

Côte des Blancs

Côte des Blancs:

Avize: Agrapart, Etienne Calsac, Corbon, De Sousa, Selosse; _Chouilly:_ Pierre Legras, Vazart-Coquart & Fils; _Cramant:_ Diebolt-Vallois, Philippe Glavier, Guiborat Fils, Philippe Lancelot, Lancelot-Pienne, Lilbert-Fils, Suenen; _Cuis:_ Pierre Gimonnet; _Le Mesnil:_ Delamotte, Pierre Moncuit, Robert Moncuit, Pierre Péters, Salon, J.L. Vergnon; _Oger:_ José Dhondt, Jean Milan; _Vertus:_ Pascal Doquet, Doyard, André Jacquart, Larmandier-Bernier, Veuve Fourny

Montgueux:

Jacques Lassaigne, Jean Velut

Val du Petit Morin:

Congy: Ulysse Collin; _Talus-Saint-Prix:_ Jeaunaux-Robin

Marne Valley

Grande Vallée:

_Aÿ:_ Ayala, Bollinger, Gaston Chiquet, Deutz, Gatinois, René Geoffroy; _Bisseuil:_ Gonet-Médeville; _Damery:_ A.R. Lenoble; _Dizy:_ Jacquesson; _Mareuil-sur-Aÿ:_ Billecart-Salmon, Marc Hébrart, Philipponnat, R. Pouillon; _Tours-sur-Marne:_ Laurent-Perrier

Coteaux Sud d'Epernay:

Chavot-Courcourt: Laherte Frères; _Moussy:_ José Michel; _Pierry:_ J.M. Sélèque

Right Bank:

Mareuil-le-Port: Dehours et Fils; _Venteuil:_ Maurice Grumier; _Vandières:_ Denis Salomon; _Cuisles:_ Moussé Fils

Left Bank:

Festigny: Joseph Loriot-Pagel, Christophe Mignon; *Mardeuil:* Vincent Charlot; *Œuilly:* Tarlant

Western Marne (Aisne):

Fossoy: Benoît Déhu; *Connegis:* Chevreux-Bournazel; *Charly-sur-Marne:* Fallet-Dart

Côte des Bar

Barséquanais:

Avirey-Lingey: Serge Mathieu; *Buxières-sur-Arce:* Vouette et Sorbée; *Celles-sur-Ource:* Pierre Gerbais; *Courteron:* Fleury; *Essoyes:* Ruppert-Leroy; *Gyé-sur-Seine:* Vincent Couche; *Landreville:* Roses de Jeanne (Bouchard); *Les Riceys:* Olivier Horiot; *Polisot:* Marie Courtin, Piollot Père et Fils; *Ville-sur-Arce:* Coessens, Val Frison

Bar-sur-Aubois:

Rouvres-les-Vignes: Nathalie Falmet; *Urville:* Drappier

Preface

I began to explore the subject of Champagne as a young man in my twenties while attending the Cordon Bleu in Paris. My girlfriend at the time and I were both training to be chefs. During that year, we made the first of many trips to the Champagne region. Our daughter was born shortly after we returned to the United States upon the completion of our studies. Rather than continuing to work as a chef, I began selling wine to restaurants. In 2001, I began a seven-year stint working for Clicquot, Inc., the U.S. subsidiary of Veuve Clicquot, while halfway through my studies in the Master of Wine program. I completed my dissertation for the program on a topic related to Champagne, and just before receiving the Master of Wine title, I was given the opportunity by Moët-Hennessy to set up their educational program in the United States. My time at Moët-Hennessy was an intense period of involvement in Champagne for me, traveling to the region five to six times each year with trade groups as well as by myself to deepen my knowledge of the category and promote my employer's brands. In 2008, I began to work in the auction business as Head of Wine for Christie's in New York, and at the end of 2012, I ventured out on my own to form WineAlpha, a fine wine consultancy for collectors buying and selling at auction. During these peregrinations, however, I never lost my enthusiasm for Champagne and its wines and have continued to visit the region frequently.

As an instructor on the Master-Level Champagne course for the Wine Scholar's Guild, I realized that while there were English language books on vintage conditions in Burgundy and Bordeaux, a similar volume for Champagne did not exist. *Vintage Champagne 1899 - 2018* is the first volume in English to focus exclusively on this topic. The book is intended for those who are already familiar with the basics of Champagne. My hope is to help wine lovers choose which vintages and which producers of vintage Champagne they enjoy. The volume also shares my great enthusiasm for the topic, which I hope will come through. I would like to thank (in alphabetical order) those who helped initiate me into the world of Champagne: the collectors Bruce Fingeret, Charles Lin, and Joe Tsai, with whom I have enjoyed many rare bottles, and with my friends and fellow journalists Essi Avellan MW, Brad Baker, Dominik Betschart, Nieke Beute, Gerhild Burkhart, Ada Chan, Peter Crawford, Peter Dooman, Tim Hall, Richard Juhlin, Robin Kick MW, Jeannie Cho Lee MW, Peter Liem, Christine Mayr, Ed McCarthy, Kat Morse, Tuomas Rahkamaa, Carl Edmund Sherman, Tim Triptree MW, and, of course, with the following producers and members of the wine trade: Pascal Agrapart, Raphaël Bérêche, Cécile Bonnefond, Marc Brevot, Cyril Brun, Julie Cavil, Laurent Champs, Jean-Hervé Chiquet, Hervé Dantan, Guy de Rivoire, Jacques and Isabelle Diebolt, Marie Doyard, Michel Drappier, Jean-Baptiste Geoffroy, Richard Geoffroy, Didier Gimonnet, Mireille Giuliano, Benoît Gouez, Fabien and Hélène Grumier, Christian Holthausen, Olivier and Marie Horiot, Michel Jacob, Nicolas Jaeger, Remi and Olivier Krug, Jean and Virginie Lallement, Pierre and Sophie Larmandier, Eric Lebel, Vincent and Marcelline Legras, Steve Lewin, Antoine and Anne Malassagne, Dominique Moreau, Jean-Philippe Moulin, Antoine, Quentin and Benoît Paillard, Frédéric Panaiotis, Jacques Péters, Rodolphe Péters, Charles Philipponnat, Kevin Pike, Christian Renard, Anselme Selosse, and Jean-Mary and Mélanie Tarlant.

Charles Curtis
New York, 2020

INTRODUCTION

What is Vintage Champagne?

To define "vintage Champagne" as Champagne produced only from grapes grown in one specific vintage year and aged three years from bottling is correct as far as it goes. As a definition, however, it is certainly incomplete (a full copy of the regulations is translated into English in the first appendix). Unlike most other types of wine, vintage-dated Champagne is the exception rather than the rule. At first blush, this may strike the neophyte as odd, since nearly all of the world's great wines bear a vintage date. The only category with a similar indifference to vintage dating is sherry. As with sherry, the blending process is central to the production technique for Champagne, and there are other categories such as Port and Madeira, where blending across vintages is an accepted practice.

The 2019 newsletter of the Comité Interprofessionnel du Vin de Champagne (CIVC) concerning 2018 champagne shipments informs us that the categories of "Vintage" and "Prestige Cuvée" together[1] comprise 6.1% of shipments by volume and 17.7% by value. These figures translate to the equivalent of 18.4 million bottles worth € 513.3 million at the cellar door – a significant category by any measure. And while these wines account for 4.2% by volume and 12.8% by value of shipments to other EU member countries, in non-Eurozone markets, they are even more critical. The United States is the most valuable export market for Champagne, and here vintage wines account for 8.4% by volume and 20.5% by value.

In some ways, vintage Champagne runs counter to the essence of Champagne. The art of blending is at the heart of Champagne, which is most often a blend of grapes, a blend of wines from different years, and a blend of fruit from different sub-regions within Cham-pagne. It can be a blend of different

---

[1] There is no official definition of "prestige cuvée" at the CIVC. Instead, they rely on a self-reported list of what each correspondent feels is their "prestige cuvée." In reality, most of the cuvées thus reported are vintage also, although there are certainly examples, such as Krug Grande Cuvée and Laurent-Perrier Grande Siècle, which are multi-vintage blends.

winemaking techniques and a blend of wines of different colors. In one sense, however, vintage Champagne is in fact the soul of Champagne since it tries to capture the region's superlatives. Vintage Champagne will always be a snapshot, showing one particular moment in time and one specific winemaker, but these moments can be exhilarating.

The reason for this practice in Champagne is unique and stems from the terroir itself. It is a region of such a northerly location that grapes ripen with difficulty. It is only because of the chalky, water-bearing soils, and the region's well-aligned hillside slopes that grapes can ripen at all. Grapes here seldom reach the minimum alcoholic strength of most other appellations and often retain notably high acidity. Because of the soil and the slopes, however, the resulting wines' fruit character is usually well-developed, even if the potential alcohol remains low and the acidity remains high. The Traditional Method of producing Champagne is a response developed over centuries by the Champagne winemakers to the raw materials that nature provides. Even the method of putting in the bubbles was a response to these characteristics of the terroir. The process of making the wine sparkling (which the French call the "prise de mousse") is essentially a process of enrichment. It is carried out today by adding sugar and yeast (known as liqueur de tirage, or bottling liqueur) to finished wine before bottling. The yeast begins a second fermentation in the bottle, increasing the alcoholic strength of the wine while it adds depth of flavor as well as the characteristic bubbles.

There are other elements of the Traditional Method that are tied to the innate character of the base wines produced in the region. These base wines, quite thin and sharp before the secondary fermentation in the bottle, are often given a bit of sweetening before shipping to balance out the acidity. The agent of this sweetening, either in the form of concentrated, unfermented grape juice or cane sugar, is known as the shipping liqueur (liqueur d'expédition in French) or dosage, another long-standing adaptation of the Traditional Method to the raw materials available in Champagne. Sweetening Champagne with sugar began in the 17th Century, but the mastery of the bubbles came later. The particular sparkling character of Champagne, however, can only be preserved by the use of bottles (as distinct from bulk storage in cask), and the widespread use of glass bottles for long term storage also dates to the 17th Century. The use of bottles leads to a final element of the method that arose from the same needs: the tradition of blending across vintages to minimize the difficulties posed by a poor vintage. Wines produced in great years would be uncorked and added to the wines produced in lesser years to improve the blend. Dr. Jules Guyot explains this process in his seminal work *"Culture de la Vigne et Vinification"*:

"Not only does one add shipping liqueur to the wine, but when the bottling has been done in poor or mediocre years, one also adds a proportion of wine from a great year which has been set aside for this purpose. This is called recoulage[2]. One blends, for example, the mediocre wine from 1874 with 10% or 15% or 20% of wine from the great vintage of 1846. Through this blending, the wines of Champagne may present each year and everywhere in the world characteristics that differ very little and are generally very acceptable. Also, the great and rich [négociant] houses buy at any price the most significant quantity of wine from the great years. This wine is their treasure, their essence, used to enrich and perfume the wines of the miserable years. A house deprived of old wines of the first quality during a series of mediocre years is a house undone, lost to the market."

This blending was called "recoulage" because the reserve wines that Dr. Guyot mentions were stored in bottles (or magnums) and literally "repoured" into the blend. Guyot also mentions the reason for this: to maintain the consistency of the blends. As the method became codified, this type of blending became the accepted practice, and in time, no other way was known. François Bonal explains in his excellent book *"Le Livre d'Or de Champagne"*:

"If one blends only wines from a single year, one has what one would call today a vintage. In the 19th Century, this

---

2   Literally "re-pours." This term is no longer used.

word did not exist[3], and the notion was somewhat hazy. At the beginning of the 1830s producers began to date some labels, but rarely, and only to signal a year that was truly exceptional, notably for the British and American markets[4]. Simultaneously, however, wine merchants and connoisseurs, particularly in England, often refer to the years of production, even when they are not indicated. It was only from 1865 that Champagne that in principle did not contain any reserve wine began to be marketed, every two or three years in France and more frequently in England. Nevertheless, the vintage only occasionally featured on the label, at least until the 1870s."

George Saintsbury makes a further reference to the 1865 vintage in his *"Notes on a Cellar Book"*, published in 1920: "And, taking well-known brands all round, I do not know that I was more faithful to any than to Krug. I began my fancy for it with a '65, which memory represents as being, though dry, that "winy wine," which Champagne ought to be, but too seldom is. And when, just fifty years after that vintage, I drank farewell to my cellar before giving up housekeeping, it was in a bottle of Krug's Private Cuvee, 1906."

In addition to documenting the 1865 vintage, Saintsbury's comment is interesting because it speaks to another characteristic of vintage Champagne – its vinosity. When Saintsbury praises it as a "winy wine," he is referring to precisely that quality that sets vintage Champagne off from non-vintage blends. The non-vintage blends are crafted on purpose to reduce the differences between vintages. Just the opposite is the case with vintage wines, where the differences between vintages are their very raison d'etre. Most often, a vintage wine is made when wines have greater ripeness than usual. Usually, the base wines also have firm acidity and abundant dry extract. It is this combination that endows a wine with vinosity. This character makes vintage Champagne a "winemaker's wine" in the words of Frédéric Panaiotis, Chef de Caves at Champagne Ruinart.

---

3   Bonal's footnote here reads, "The 19th Century term in England for Champagne constituted of wines from a single year was vintage wine, or one said more simply, vintage."
4   Bonal's footnote: "One finds labels of sparkling Sillery crowded with the mention "Celebrated vintage of 1834."

André Simon has given us invaluable information regarding the origin of vintage Champagne in his 1905 work *"History of the Champagne Trade in England."* He explains:

"Shippers used to sell their wine in very small lots to suit the requirements of their customers, whether they had only a blend of several years to show or an exceptional vintage wine such as the 1834, 1842, 1846, 1857. In this last case, there was nothing to indicate the vintage, either on cork or label[5] and wine merchants bought it in very small parcels, and during as long a period as the size of the cuvée, and the amount of the demand allowed."

He goes on to note: "The vintage which was sold at the highest figures ever paid for Champagne in London was that of 1874, probably the first strictly speaking vintage and Brut or Nature Champagne shown in England," and that "Messrs. Perrier Jouët were one of the first to indicate the year of the vintage on their labels, and Messrs. George Goulet did so when they showed their 1870 vintage. The branding of the corks with the year of the vintage was only adopted universally later on, the last shipper but one to do so being Messrs. Heidsieck, who never branded any of their wines before the 1889s; the last were Messrs. Pommery, whose 1892 was the first cuvée bearing the date of the vintage on the corks and labels."

Bonal, citing Henry Vizetelly, who wrote several works on Champagne in the late 19th Century, documents which vintages were sought after during the 19th century "Here are the very good years of the 19th Century, according to his [Vizetelly's] research and observations, and according to other, later witnesses: 1802, 1806, 1811, 1815, 1818, 1819, 1822, 1825, 1834, 1840, 1842, 1846, 1848, 1857, 1865, 1868, 1874, 1880, 1884, 1889, 1892, 1893, 1898, 1899. One must add that 1875, which gave the largest harvest of the Century, has sometimes been praised for its quality..." In contrast, André Simon sees the matter somewhat differently and discerns top honors on these 19th Century vintages : 1802, 1804, 1811, 1818 and 1819, 1822, 1825, 1832, 1834, 1842, 1846, 1857, 1862, 1865, 1868, 1870, 1874, 1880, 1889, 1892, 1893, and 1899.

---

5   Simon's footnote: "In most cases, there were no labels whatever, but simply a small foil round the cork and the top part of the neck of the bottle."

Among the oldest surviving bottles that still exist today were found in a shipwreck off the coast of Finland in 2010. It is thought that the wreck occurred in the 1840s. Among the cargo were 168 bottles of Champagne attributed to the house of Juglar. This house existed between 1804 and 1829 when they merged with Jacquesson. There were several bottles sold as "circa 1820", which sold for up to €24,000. The same wreck contained bottles of 1841 Clicquot, which sold for €24,000.

Another instance of "shipwreck" champagne was that from the wreck of the Jönköping, a Swedish vessel torpedoed by a German U-boat in 1916. In 1997, divers recovered an estimated 3,000 bottles of Heidsieck "Goût Américain" 1907 from the wreck. These bottles of Heidsieck have been described in the press as selling for "$275,000 per bottle," although this price stems from a private transaction between anonymous parties at the Ritz Hotel in Moscow at an undisclosed date. Several bottles of 1907 Goût Américain traded at documented commercial auctions, and it commonly sells for $2,000 - $4,000 per bottle. I have been privileged to taste the wine twice in my career at Christie's, in 2008 and in 2009. I remember the first bottle as a total loss, and the second as pleasant, at least "interesting." The problem, however, is that as is often the case, these old bottles can fail to live up to expectations. As one would expect, the wine is mature and may well be oxidized. Most often, they have no bubbles. Finally, they usually are very sweet, since before the 20th Century, Champagne was served as a dessert wine. Tests indicate that the dosage of the Heidsieck "Goût Américain" 1907 was 165 g/l, and analysis of the 1841 Clicquot showed a dosage of 149 g/l. (For a discussion of sugar levels in Champagne, see the glossary entry under Brut).

The combination of this level of sugar with a complete lack of mousse and an evolved nose makes the wine a beverage completely unlike Champagne today. For me, it is difficult to compare these very old wines with the ones I enjoy today. For this reason, I rely on contemporary authorities to inform my opinion of some of the early years of the century. My experience of other venerable vintages suggests that the quality of the bottles that remain today is highly variable. I have found bottles as old as 85 years of age that still have bubbles, while in other instances bottles only 30 years of age have begun to lose their mousse and to show definite signs of aging. Whether you find these bottles enjoyable or even acceptable depends on your frame of reference. If you come from a long experience of tasting old white Burgundy, you will probably like these wines more than if you approach them from a background of drinking youthful wines.

As champagne ages, it goes through several changes, some of which are unique to itself. As with many white wines, the non-rosé champagnes gradually deepen in color, changing from straw yellow or light lemon yellow to gold, and then to amber and ultimately to brown. Rosé champagnes also deepen in color, varying from pink to salmon to copper and finally to umber, with the rim losing color more quickly than the core.

Next is the evolution of the aromas. I feel there are two parts to this. The first is an evolution as with the wines of Burgundy that moves from fresh fruit aromas gradually take on more lactic character, moving toward cream and butter, and eventually to butterscotch and caramel. With even more time, the wines will develop a bouquet of truffle and forest floor (which the French call sous-bois). Distinct from this is the change in the character of the aromas coming from the yeast. This aspect, called the autolytic character, is a smoky type of aroma. At the outset, it resembles lightly buttered toast, then brioche, and finally, smoke and ground coffee appear. If it goes too far, there is a suggestion of soy sauce. This autolytic trans-formation is a complex process since it depends both on the length of time on lees before disgorgement and on bottle age.

Next comes the changes in texture. The first to be re-marked is the change in the bubbles or mousse. The pressure overall decreases with time, and the size of the bubbles dimin-ishes. Smaller bubbles change the texture of the mousse from one of "fizziness" like sparkling water or soda to one of "cream-iness," bringing the wine more of a velvety texture. At the same time, the wine goes through a deceptive transformation as it appears to lose acidity and gain sweetness. In fact, the amount of acid declines imperceptibly in chemical terms, and there is no additional residual sugar over time. This change is instead the result of what is called the "Maillard Reaction" occurring in the aging Champagne. This reaction is an interaction between an amino acid and a non-reducing sugar molecule, similar to the browning of steak or other food during cooking. It is essentially a form of caramelization, but in Champagne, it happens without heat.

Mature Champagne is not for everyone. I hope, however, that the readers of the present volume will join me in its appreciation. With time and tasting experience, you will learn what age Champagne best suits you – do you prefer bright, newly disgorged Champagne, or do you start to swoon only when it reaches twenty, or thirty, or forty years from the vintage date? Do you prefer champagnes with extra time on the lees or those that have much post-disgorgement aging and relatively less time on the lees? I hope the present volume will help you to know your preferences and to better appreciate vintage Champagne.

PART I

The Producers

In this section I discuss the leading producers who are at the forefront of making vintage Champagne. I have evaluated them on several criteria and rated them from one to five stars. There are some caveats. First, some of the criteria (as with nearly all wine writing) are subjective in nature. These include my personal assessments of quality and of ageability, formed through countless tastings over more than two decades. I have tried to temper my assessments with objective information about the value of the wines on the secondary market. This is an issue of some importance to wine lovers who are laying down wines for aging, sometimes for decades. If two like Champagnes both improve with aging, but one goes up in value and another declines in value, many collectors will prefer the former to the latter. For collectors, the second caveat is an important consideration: the top two tiers of classification are reserved for Champagnes that enjoy a robust secondary market.

Finally, *Vintage Champagne* and its classifications are not intended to be an encyclopedic guide to everyone who is producing vintage wine. Such an undertaking would be daunting to say the least and of minimal value. My main goal in writing this book has been to identify what I feel are the best and/or most interesting Champagnes and to explain why I think so. I have little interest in tasting large quantities of mediocre wines. Even when I do so (it happens!), I do not feel compelled to write about them. Time is short —let's spend it discussing what is best. My criteria for evaluation of these producers follow. At the outset, the reader will notice that I have one producer that is outside the classification system – this is literally the meaning of the term "Hors Classe".

In this section I explain my rationale at length, but the short explanation is that these wines surpass those of other producers in terms of power, balance, complexity, intensity, ageability, and collectability.

HORS CLASSE

Krug

✳✳✳✳

An outstanding producer, many of whose wines are often extremely good, and who often produces wines of great depth, intensity, balance, and complexity that are capable of aging and improving for more than fifty years. These wines are sought after on the secondary market, trade for fairly high prices, and appreciate in value.

Bollinger, Dom Pérignon, Philipponnat, Louis Roederer, Salon, Selosse, Taittinger

✳✳✳

An excellent producer, whose wines can be extremely good, and who can produce wines of depth, intensity, and complexity as well as wines capable of aging and improving for more than twenty years. These wines either trade infrequently on the secondary market or they do not consistently appreciate in value.

Agrapart, Bérêche et Fils, Emmanuel Brochet, Chartogne-Taillet, La Closerie, Marie Courtin, Diebolt-Vallois, Pascal Doquet, Drappier, Egly-Ouriet, Pierre Gimonnet, Olivier Horiot, André Jacquart, Jacquesson, Larmandier-Bernier, Jacques Lassaigne, David Léclapart, A.R. Lenoble, Lilbert-Fils, Pierre Paillard, Pierre Péters, Pol Roger, Eric Rodez, Roses de Jeanne, Ruinart, Savart, Vouette et Sorbée

A very good producer, whose wines can be delicious, and who has produced wines of quality and elegance, capable of aging and improving for at least a decade. These are not usually wines that trade on the secondary market, or do not appreciate consistently in value.

Billecart-Salmon, Gaston Chiquet, Dehours et Fils, Benoît Déhu, Delamotte, Nathalie Falmet, René Geoffroy, Pierre Gerbais, Alfred Gratien, Maurice Grumier, Marc Hébrart, Charles Heidsieck, Piper-Heidsieck, Henriot, Huré Frères, Benoît Lahaye, Juillet-Lallement, Laherte Frères, Lanson, Leclerc-Briant, Marie-Noëlle Ledru, Pierre Legras, Nicolas Maillart, José Michel, Moët et Chandon, Robert Moncuit, G.H. Mumm, Bruno Paillard, Hubert Paulet, Perrier-Jouët, Suenen, Tarlant, Vazart-Coquart et Fils, Veuve Clicquot, Vilmart & Cie.

A notable producer, but either one who is just starting out and does not have the track record to be rated higher, or one whose wines can be very good but are not as consistent as one might hope. They produce interesting wines of intrinsic quality, have the potential to move to a higher category, and stand out for their special merit. These wines usually do not trade on the secondary market, and do not appreciate consistently in value.

Yann Alexandre, L. Aubry, Ayala, Paul Bara, Francis Boulard, Etienne Calsac, Vincent Charlot, Chevreux-Bournazel, Coessens, Ulysse Collin, Corbon, Vincent Couche, R.H. Coutier, De Sousa, Deutz, José Dhondt, Doyard, Fallet-Dart, Fleury, Val Frison, Gatinois, Philippe Glavier, Gonet-Médeville, Gosset, Guiborat Fils, Jeaunaux-Robin, Lacourte-Godbillon, Philippe Lancelot, Lancelot-Pienne, Joseph Loriot-Pagel, Mailly Grand Cru, Sadi Malot, A. Margaine, Marguet, Serge Mathieu, Christophe Mignon, Jean Milan, Pierre Moncuit, Moussé Fils, Penet-Chardonnet, Laurent-Perrier, Piollot Père et Fils, R. Pouillon, Ruppert-Leroy, Denis Salomon, Camille Savès, J.M. Sélèque, Soutiran, Stroebel, Jean Velut, J.L. Vergnon, Veuve Fourny

HORS CLASSE

Champagne Krug

Location: Reims | Terroir: Blended

In my opinion, Champagne Krug stands above all others as the best and most consistent producer in the region. The reason for this, however remains a bit of a mystery to me. It cannot be due to any one specific technique of winemaking: other producers ferment exclusively in cask, others block the malolactic fermentation, and others blend large numbers of individual lots to achieve a harmonious whole. It also isn't due to the raw materials, since Krug sources most of their grapes throughout the entire region and no one at Krug will tell you that the vintage wine is produced only from *grand cru* slopes. Quality at Krug is due to what Olivier Krug (and his uncle Rémi before him) have always attributed to their success: an unquenchable dedication to excellence handed down from fathers to sons for six generations.

As a young man, I trained as a chef and apprenticed in Michelin-starred kitchens. Each recipe had several techniques, often time-consuming, that needed to be used to arrive at the desired result. It was difficult to say precisely what each technique added, but if you changed or left one out, the dish would not be the same. To get the perfect texture for the salmon soufflé in the style of Auberge de l'Ill, it is essential to rub the chopped salmon painstakingly through a very fine tamis. In the same way, the magic of Krug depends upon not only the quality of the fruit, but also the nature of Krug's relationship with the growers, how they handle the fruit, the winemaking techniques employed, the length of time on the lees, and the many other small steps taken along the way.

The house was established in 1843 in Reims by Joseph Krug, who had emigrated from Mainz, Germany, in 1834. He began his Champagne career with an eight-year stint at

Jacquesson, which was at the time the largest Champagne firm. It was the ambition of Joseph Krug to create a firm that produced only the finest luxury Champagne. The base was meant to be a blend of vintages, "Champagne No. 1" in his original iteration, as he intended to present the best possible wine each year. In his mind, the second wine was a vintage, "Champagne No. 2," which would reflect the character of the year. The house flourished, both under Joseph and his son Paul. Joseph II, the founder's grandson, took over the reins in 1910, and after a rough patch during and after WW I, Krug went on to produce some of its most legendary vintages in the 1920s. Paul Krug II joined the family house in 1959.

In 1973 Paul Krug sold the house to Cognac producer Rémy Martin although he remained at the helm until 1977. Rémy Martin wisely decided to leave Krug's sons Rémi and Henri in charge, with Henri doing the winemaking and Rémi handing commercial affairs. The merged Rémy-Cointreau, in turn, sold Krug to LVMH in 1999 for the sum of one billion francs. This was equivalent to $175 million at the time, a price that many thought high. Henri retired in 2002. In 2006 Olivier Krug was appointed Director of Champagne Krug, and the following year Rémi Krug retired. Current president Margareth (Maggie) Henríquez assumed her post in 2009. After Henri's retirement, the winemaking team was led by Chef de Caves Eric Lebel from his appointment in 1998 until 2020. From 2006 he worked alongside Julie Cavil, and in 2020 Cavil took over the as Chef de Caves.

On my first visit to Krug in 2002, they were making between 400,000 and 500,000 bottles, and vineyards that they owned in Le Mesnil, Oger, Avize, Ambonnay, and Aÿ provided up to 40% of the fruit. Primary fermentations are were (and are) all carried out in used casks (ideally 10 to 15 years of age). The malolactic fermentation is neither blocked nor encouraged. Vintage wines spend approximately a decade on the lees before being disgorged. The dosage has always been low. These, however, are merely the technical details, which are among the least important factors in understanding the wine. Most of these facts, and others, are available through the "Krug iD" code on the back of every bottle that allows Krug lovers to research their bottle through Krug's website. Many appreciate the fact that the house has become more transparent over the years with production details. To truly understand Krug, however, it is necessary to taste the wines.

The oldest vintage that I have enjoyed was 1926, which I describe in the section on that year (p.304). The oldest wines are rare. My research shows there is only a single transaction for the '28, one for the '38, and two for the '43. No vintage before 1959 has traded hands more than three times. Some of these older vintages have been released as Krug Collection, including 1928, which sold most recently at Sotheby's London for just a bit more than $19,000 per bottle. It is with the 1949 Collection that the wine begins to trade more frequently, but it is only after 1959 that the late-disgorged "Collection" program gained in importance. Of more recent vintages, several bottles of '66 traded hands in 2019 at an average of $1,980; two different six-bottle lots of the legendary '73 made an average of $1,240 per bottle net of premium, and 90 bottles of the '88 (one of my personal favorites) averaged $527 per bottle in 2019.

The vintages that Krug has released since 1900 include 1900, 1904, 1906, 1914, 1915, 1920, 1926, 1928, 1929, 1932, 1937, 1938, 1942, 1943, 1945, 1947, 1949, 1952, 1953, 1955, 1959, 1961, 1962, 1964, 1966, 1969, 1971, 1973, 1975, 1976, 1979, 1981, 1982, 1985, 1988, 1989, 1990, 1995, 1996, 1998, 2000, 2002, 2003, 2004, and 2006.

The vintages that have been released as Collection to date include 1928, 1929, 1937, 1938, 1943, 1947, 1949, 1952, 1953, 1955, 1959, 1961, 1962, 1964, 1966, 1969, 1970, 1971, 1973, 1975, 1976, 1979, 1981, 1982, 1985, 1988, 1989, and 1990.

For me, the style of a Krug vintage is vinous and powerful, but never heavy. The wine has a deep complexity of flavor, lots of structure, and a fine balance. There are numerous examples of my tasting notes for Krug throughout the text describing the characteristics of each vintage. I feel it is a benchmark indicator for the potential of a vintage, and when I am evaluating the quality of a year, that I always take into consideration how I felt about the Krug in that year. As an example here I take the 1996, tasted in 2008: *"Explosive aromas of super-ripe exotic fruits including passion fruit, guava, and coconut slowly reveal a firm, minerally, smoky side. With time, notes of lime peel and Granny Smith apple appear. The wine is tightly wound and powerfully structured, with lots of density and an important component of acidity that will take some time to resolve. A wine of immense potential."* ***** (2019 auction average, $436)

How does a newly released bottle taste? In the fall of 2019, I attended the release party for the Krug 2006 creations, both the '06 vintage and the Grande Cuvée based on that year. The wine was accessible and pleasure-giving, right from the start, yet showed potential for future improvement: *"Forward and lush, this initially presents aromas of toasted brioche, ripe apple, and white flowers. On the palate, the wine had a silky, soft texture, yet it retained a fresh balancing acidity that carried the finish with impressive length."* **** (2020 retail average, $264)

As wonderful as the vintage wine is, the Krug Clos du Mesnil has always impressed me as being on an entirely different level. I have always felt that it is the "Romanée-Conti of Champagne." Like Romanée-Conti it is a small, ancient vineyard enclosed by walls. The 1.84 hectare (ha) Clos du Mesnil vineyard was established in 1698, while the 1.81 ha Romanée-Conti was leased in 1584 under its original name as the Cros des Cloux. The Clos du Mesnil vineyard in the 19th century was owned by Champagne Tarin. In the early years of the 20th century, the cellar master at Tarin was named Marcel Guillaume, who was the brother-in-law of Eugène-Aimé Salon. Although not specifically identified as such, Tarin was a longstanding supplier to Salon, including the grapes from this clos until it was sold in 1971 to Krug. Krug replanted the vineyard, and the first vintage of the new vines was 1979, released in 1986. Subsequent vintages include 1980, 1981, 1982, 1983, 1985, 1986, 1988, 1989, 1990, 1992, 1995, 1996, 1998, 2000, 2003, and 2004. 1999 was produced but not commercially released.

Yes, Clos du Mesnil is expensive, yet it is much less expensive than Romanée-Conti, for example. The most costly vintage is the first, which trades less and less frequently these days.

Five have changed hands in 2019, and four in 2018. The price at auction in both of these years hovered near $5,200 per bottle. This price is up from an average of nearly $3,600 per bottle in 2009, and an average near $1,000 per bottle in 2006. By way of comparison, the 1978 Romanée-Conti (a similarly lustrous vintage) averaged over $22,000 in 2019. Other vintages of Clos du Mesnil are even more affordable. Bottles of the 1985 vintage traded at $2,000 per bottle in 2019, and the superb 2002 cost just over $1,400 that year. The price of the current 2004 vintage was around $1,000 in 2020. As with Krug vintage, the text is replete with tasting notes for Krug Clos du Mesnil, so they are not repeated here.

Krug also produces another single-vineyard vintage wine called the Krug Clos d'Ambonnay, a blanc de noirs produced from a 0.68 ha parcel located within the village of Ambonnay. Krug acquired the parcel in 1994, after having purchased the fruit for several vintages for use in their blends. The first vintage was 1995, released in 2007. Further vintages have included 1996, 1998, 2000, and 2002. Since the parcel is approximately one-third the size of the Clos du Mesnil, the price is accordingly higher. The current 2002 vintage in the U.S. costs an average of roughly $2,700 in 2020. Curiously, the inaugural vintages of 1995 and 1996 sold for the same price or less at auction in 2019, including premium. This trading history suggests to me that the wine is fully valued upon release and does not have the same ability to appreciate as does the Clos du Mesnil (or the "regular" vintage). I am a lover, not a doubter of Krug, yet the Clos d'Ambonnay has yet to prove itself fully. On release and in the decade following release, the wine has been frustratingly slow to open.

In 1996, I was less impressed with the Clos d'Ambonnay than with the other wines from this house. From my note: *"A bit of a disappointment. Closed on the nose, without the depth or complexity of the Clos du Mesnil. One hopes that with time it will open up. On the palate, there was a lot of acidity and a lot of extract. The wine, however, had not yet come together."* **** This is consistent with my experience of the other releases.

My reaction may be simply because it is Pinot Noir and thus more vinous and more slow to open. Until the earlier vintages begin to show their full potential, I am going to continue to buy Krug Vintage and, for special occasions, the Clos du Mesnil. I can think of no more luxurious a drink.

5 rue Coquebert 51100 Reims | 03 26 84 44 20
http://www.krug.com/

✳ ✳ ✳ ✳

Champagne Bollinger

Region: Marne Valley | Terroir: Grande Vallée

In some ways Bollinger, represents the soul of Aÿ. This grand cru lies at the center of the section of the Marne Valley known as the Grande Vallée. Unlike many of the houses of this stature that came later to the towns of Reims or Epernay, Bollinger has always been located here. The house was formed in 1829 by an alliance of three men. The first of these was Athanase Louis Emmanuel Hennequin, comte de Villermont, whose family had significant landholdings in and around Aÿ. Hennequin teamed up with Paul Renaudin and Jacques Bollinger. The Renaudin family had been active for generations in the Champagne region, but Jacques Bollinger was an emigrant from Württemberg. He arrived in Champagne in 1822 and worked at Müller-Ruinart, the house formed by the former Veuve Clicquot Chef de Caves who had married into the Ruinart family. At Müller-Ruinart, Bollinger and Renaudin became friends and the three began to collaborate to produce the wine we know today as Bollinger.

The house they formed grew in renown in the 19th Century and obtained the Royal Warrant from Queen Victoria of England in 1884. The following year Joseph and Georges, the sons of Jacques, the founder, took over and led the company through the Belle Epoque and the First World War. In 1918, Georges' son Jacques joined the family firm and married Emily Law de Lauriston Boubers, known as Lily. Following Jacques' untimely death in 1941, Lily took over the running of the house, expanding the vineyards and promoting the brand throughout the world. She stepped down in 1971 and was succeeded first by her nephew Claude d'Hautefeuille, director from 1971 to 1978, and then by another nephew, Christian Bizot, who ran the company from 1978 to 1994. Bizot was in turn succeeded by Ghislain de Montgolfier, great-great-grandson of Jacques. Ghislain de Montgolfier retired in 2008, and since then the president has been Jérôme Philippon, the first non-family member to run the estate. In 2018 he was promoted to the COO of the holding company Société Jacques Bollinger, and Charles-Armand de Belenet replaced him as managing director. However, in 2019 it was announced that Philippon would leave his role at Bollinger altogether, while de Belenet remains as managing director. Giles Descôtes is the Chef de Caves, and Guy de Rivoire, formerly of Ruinart, handles commercial matters.

Today Bollinger owns 178 hectares of vines, which provides more than half of the fruit necessary for its production. The majority of the Bollinger-owned vineyards provide Pinot Noir, and the character of this grape marks the wines of this house perhaps more than any other. Bollinger produces three vintage wines: Grande Année, RD, and Vieilles Vignes Françaises. The house started referring to the vintage wine as Grande Année with the 1976 vintage; before this, it was simply vintage-dated. I have had two different bottlings of the 1975 vintage: one was labeled *Année Rare*, with an ornate label, and one was labeled simply Brut Vintage. I drank them both in 2019, the latter out of jeroboam, and it was particularly delicious. From my note: *"To consider that this is "just" a vintage wine makes it impressive indeed, although the quality shows that with Bollinger, it's never "just" a vintage wine. There was so much mousse here that the wine started by literally shooting out of the bottle. The color was extraordinary. The aromas were very fresh, given its age and the vintage. There was a predictable maturity and a pronounced yeasty-toasty character that gave the impression of a bit of truffle around the edges. On the palate, the wine was rich, with a creamy texture, but there was certainly enough acidity to balance the wine, which combined with an impressive depth of flavor to carry it to a lingering finish. Very good indeed."* **** (Three jeros sold at auction in 2017 for an average $1,834)

More recent vintages of Grande Année have also shown well. The 1996 vintage has been consistently delicious. In 2010: *"A pronounced lemony fruit, a bit of oak, some mineral notes and a lovely scent of toasted brioche on the nose. Very structured, with a rapier-like acidity and great length. This is a concentrated, vibrant Champagne that is still years from being ready to drink, but it is tremendous wine nonetheless."* **** (2019 auction average, $183)

Grande Année is usually produced from a blend of about 70% Pinot Noir and 30% Chardonnay, with all of the fruit fermented in cask and aged under cork (*agrafe et liège*) following the secondary fermentation, instead of being aged under crown caps as most Champagne is. Although the science behind this practice does not explain its advantages, it is undeniable that the results obtained by Bollinger (and by others who employ this system) are delightful indeed. Grande Année is a minimum of five years on the lees before disgorgement.

Vintages released in the 20th century include 1900, 1904, 1906, 1911, 1914, 1919, 1926, 1928, 1929, 1934, 1937, 1941, 1943, 1945, 1947, 1949, 1952, 1953, 1955, 1959, 1961, 1962, 1964, 1966, 1969, 1970, 1973, 1975, 1976, 1979, 1981, 1982, 1983, 1985, 1988, 1989, 1990, 1992, 1995, 1996, 1997, 1998, 1999, 2000, 2002, 2004, 2005, 2007, and 2008

Lily launched the emblematic cuvée called R.D. (*for Récemment Degorgé*, or recently disgorged) in 1961, with a late-disgorged version of the 1952 vintage. A bottle of '82 R.D. drunk in 2019 was a massive, ripe vintage holding well. *"The color is surprisingly light, and the wine is still incredibly fresh. There is a certain biscuit-y, yeasty edge to the wine but nothing tending toward caramel or soy on the nose. On the palate, the wine is lush and full-bodied but lively and fresh, with plenty of mousse and an impressively youthful vivacity on the finish."* ***** (2019 auction average, $672) Perhaps even better was a bottle of the '85 R.D. consumed in 2014: *"Disgorged in 1999 and then aged another 15 years on the cork, this is a stupendously beautiful Champagne drinking at its peak, with a smoky edge to the roast pear and walnut fruit. It shows the contradictions of 1985, with great ripeness balanced by tense acidity and a wonderful lingering finish."* ***** (2019 auction average, $293)

Vintages released as R.D. include: 1952, 1953, 1955, 1959, 1961, 1964, 1966, 1969, 1970, 1973, 1975, 1976, 1979, 1981, 1982,

1985, 1988, 1990, 1992, 1995, 1996, 1997, 1999, 2000, 2002, and 2004.

Another of Lily's innovations was the cuvée called Vieilles Vignes Françaises, known to fans simply as VVF. This exceptional cuvée is produced exclusively from ungrafted vines planted in two small vineyards in Aÿ, in the lieux-dits of the Clos-Saint-Jacques (21 ares[6]) and Chaudes Terres (15 ares). The vineyards have long survived despite being planted in the old way. All of these vines are ungrafted, and much of the vineyard is planted "en foule" (in a heap). This term refers to the system of planting known as provinage or layering, as explained in the glossary. For years the fruit was blended with the rest of the production of Bollinger, but in 1969 the English wine writer Cyril Ray convinced Lily Bollinger to bottle them separately. The first vintage was the 1969 (the year of her 70th birthday), which Bollinger released in 1974.

There had originally been a third vineyard, located in Bouzy, that was 16 ares in size in the lieu-dit of Croix Rouges, but this section was not enclosed with walls and eventually succumbed to phylloxera, which began to invade the vineyard in 1998. The last vintage that included fruit from the site in Bouzy was 2004. Vintages released have included 1969, 1970, 1973, 1975, 1979, 1980, 1981, 1982, 1985, 1986, 1988, 1989, 1992, 1996, 1997, 1998, 1999, 2000, 2002, 2004, 2005, and 2006.

I have not had the opportunity to taste many of the older vintages, but more recent versions seldom fail to please. Perhaps the most magnificent bottle of VVF that I have ever drunk was the 1996 vintage, consumed at a dinner in 2010 next to a Krug Clos du Mesnil of the same vintage. *"Spectacular -- the antithesis of what the Clos du Mesnil is about -- toasty and rich on the nose, with an almost red berry fruit character. On the palate, the wine was creamy, dense, very vinous, and astonishingly long. More about power than finesse, it is undeniably one of the great Champagne experiences out there."* ***** (2019 auction average, $1,960)

The vinosity of the VVF is something that takes quite some time to resolve. I have recently shared a bottle of the 1998 and found it not quite ready: *"Intriguing wine, if somewhat the*

---

6   An *are* is 1/100 of a hectare, i.e. 100 square meters or 0.0247 acres

odd man out in this tasting. The wine was too youthful to drink, but interesting all the same. The nose had a pronounced savory character. Not in the way of evolution, but in an almost meaty way. Aggressive, powerful. The wine was bursting with mousse, and on the palate, it was so palpably dense that one almost wanted a fork. Balanced acidity, a ton of extract. The wine went on forever, but it is perhaps more to be admired than loved. I was a fan on the night, although it was too much for several other tasters. With time it should be superb." **** (2019 auction average, $670)

16, rue Jules Lobet 51160 Aÿ | 03 26 53 33 66
https://www.champagne-bollinger.com/

Dom Pérignon

Location: Reims | Terroir: Blended

The wines created under the Dom Pérignon label are among the finest from the region and satisfy connoisseurs as well as casual drinkers. For many, it is perhaps the myth and the legend of Dom Pérignon that are the most compelling. The biography of Pierre Pérignon, the Benedictine monk and contemporary of Louis XIV, who was the cellar master at the Abbey of Hautvillers at the dawn of the 18th Century, has intrigued generations of wine lovers. However, most of the things that people associate with Dom Pérignon are false. He didn't "invent" Champagne. He didn't introduce the use of cork. He didn't blend wines from throughout the region (instead, he blended grapes before pressing). He wasn't blind. He was, however, a superb winemaker and an able administrator. Accounts written by his contemporaries during his lifetime comment on the high price commanded by the wines from his abbey. When he passed away in September 1715, he was given the honor of being buried next to the abbots in Hautvillers. Finally, there is not exactly a direct link between the monk of Hautvillers and the house of Moët & Chandon. By coincidence Claude Moët founded his winery a few decades after the death of Dom Pérignon in 1743. He passed the business on to his grandson Jean-Rémy Moët, and it was Jean-Rémy's son-in-law, Pierre Gabriel Chandon de Briailles, who purchased the abbey and its vines in the 1820s.

The birth of the cuvée named for Dom Pérignon is even more interesting, however. Paul Chandon-Moët, the great-grandson of Pierre Gabriel, married Francine Durand, granddaughter of Eugène Edouard Mercier (founder of Mercier Champagne). Francine had been given the rights to the Dom Pérignon trademark by her grandfather. Mercier had trade-marked the name but had never developed it into a brand. The first to take advantage of the Dom Pérignon legend was Robert-Jean de Vogüé. He was a decorated officer from the First World War, and a distant cousin of Paul Chandon-Moët who had been hired in 1930 as a marketing director for Moët. The origin of Dom Pérignon began with the 1926 vintage. According to Tom Stevenson in his *World Encyclopedia of Champagne*, 300 bottles of 1926 vintage Moët were transferred into the iconic antique bottle with the shield-shaped label and shipped in 1935 to Simon Brothers, the Moët agent in Great Britain. This bottling was labeled "Champagne specially shipped for the Simon Brothers & Co's Centenary 1835-1935." Simon Brothers distributed the bottles to their best customers, who clambered for more. The second bottling, which was the 1921 vintage, shipped in 1936 to Simon Brothers' customers, and de Vogüé had the idea to label the wine Cuvée Dom Pérignon. It is from these uncertain beginnings in the midst of the Great Depression that the modern-day commercial legend of Dom Pérignon was born.

While working at Moët-Hennessy, I was told that the vineyard sources include the vines around the Abbey of Hautvillers, the lieux-dits of Saran and Les Buissons in Cramant, Les Moulins and Les Joyettes in Le Mesnil, and Les Assises and Les Dames in Bouzy. However, these are no more than the highlights, as we were also told that there were 25 to 50 different origins that were assembled and blended to make Dom Pérignon. As with all great Champagnes, the sublime secret of Dom Pérignon is not in the vineyard sources for the grapes, but the synthesis of fruit, winemaking, and time on lees.

One of the key elements that defines Dom Pérignon is a marvelous purity of fruit and the delicate and elegant texture of the wine. This can be attributed in part to the mastery of the techniques of the reductive winemaking. Oxygen can play an important role in developing the complexity of a wine, but it also changes the character of the fruit dramatically. At Dom Pérignon, winemakers strive to preserve the original beauty of the fruit. To do this, they emphasize a series of techniques to reduce the influence of oxygen. These techniques, collectively known as reductive winemaking, work to protect the grapes and the fermenting juice from exposure to oxygen.

The net effect of this strategy is that the wines are deceptively approachable when first released. I have long felt that they only show their true potential with some bottle age. The

2008 tasted in 2019 vintage shows an example of the youthful wine: *"Great wine, but too young to appreciate fully. The nose has pleasant floral and stone fruit aromas with a suggestion of toasty brioche notes; on the palate, the wine is elegant and balanced, sufficiently fresh but round and supple, with a hint of the substance that will develop with time. For now, the wine is eminently pleasant but not yet profound. If experience is any gauge, however, this will be one for the ages."* **** (2019 retail average, $170)

At twenty years of age, the wine shows more depth: *"The 1998 Dom Perignon opens with ripe apple and floral fruit colored with a smoky, mineral edge, and underpinned by a substantial, almost savory depth. On the palate, there is a crisp, citrusy fresh-ness, a silky texture, and a lingering finish."* **** (2019 auction average, $195)

At thirty-five years, more mature aromas begin to show: *"Still fairly youthful for an '85, this shows subtle notes of ripe apple, toasted brioche, fresh and dried flowers, and a hint of black truffle. The texture is silky and very fine, with a soft mousse, balanced acidity, and a lingering finish."* ***** (2019 auction average, $353)

It is only at fifty years that the wine begins to taste fully mature. From a note taken in 2008 on a bottle of the original disgorgement of the 1966: *"Amazingly, freshness and youth still dominate this forty-year-old Champagne. The nose shows a softly delicate floral aroma along with a verdant and lush stone fruit and honeydew melon character. Some developed forest floor aromas on the finish are well-integrated into the whole. Wonderful."* ***** (2019 auction average, $817)

Vintages that have been released thus far (other than the one-off for Simon Brothers) include: 1921, 1928, 1929, 1934, 1943, 1947, 1949, 1952, 1953, 1955, 1959, 1961, 1962, 1964, 1966, 1969, 1970, 1971, 1973, 1975, 1976, 1978, 1980, 1982, 1983, 1985, 1988, 1990, 1992, 1993, 1995, 1996, 1998, 1999, 2000, 2002, 2003, 2004, 2005, 2006, 2008, and 2009.

Like the original 1926 vintage, the first Dom Pérignon Rosé was also a special request: 306 bottles of the 1959 vintage were produced for the Shah of Iran and served in 1971 at the 2500th anniversary of the founding of the Persian Empire by Cyrus the Great. In my view the Dom Pérignon Rosé is every bit the equal of the blanc version, but very different. While the blanc is elegant and delicate, the rosé has always struck me as reasonably vinous and robust. There is still a striking purity of fruit, but the red wine component adds a vinous character and concentration. From my notes on the 2002 (tasted in 2012): *"Marvelously fresh and packed with lots of cherry fruit accented by a smoky note and a mineral undercurrent. A vibrant mousse and a lush mouth-filling texture with plenty of substance to sustain it for several decades in the cellar."* ***** (2019 auction average, $350)

The Rosé also ages well. From a note on the 1988 tasted in 2008: *"Approaches perfection in a glass. This copper-colored wine has a nose that is rich and complex – it retails a plum and blackcurrant primary fruit, but has developed notes of ground coffee and black truffle as well. Complex, almost savory and still vibrant and fresh, with a wonderful balance and elegance."* ***** (2019 auction average, $548)

Dom Pérignon Rosé has been produced in the following years: 1959, 1962, 1964, 1966, 1969, 1971, 1973, 1975, 1978, 1980, 1982, 1985, 1986, 1988, 1990, 1992, 1993, 1995, 1996, 1998, 2000, 2002, 2003, 2004, 2005, 2006.

Dom Pérignon introduced their late-disgorged line of Champagne in 2000, calling it Œnothèque after the French word designating the cellar where old wines are stored in the winery. Since the inception of the program, the same wine would be released after different amounts of aging. The initial release is usually 6 to 7 years after bottling, the second release is typically 10 to 12 years after bottling, and the third release can be anywhere from 25 to 50 years after bottling. These wines were referred to by Cellar Master Richard Geoffroy as plénitudes[7]," and in 2014, the name was changed from Œnothèque. Now the second and third stages are simply called P2 and P3 to indicate the second and third plenitude.

These late-disgorged wines have distinctive characteristics. Late-disgorged Champagne, and Dom Pérignon in particular, seem to show a pronounced smoky aroma that reminds me of ground coffee. This aroma comes from the toasty-brioche element brought by the yeast being carried to its ultimate

---

7   "fullness": apotheosis or ultimate development. This term is used in Champagne to mean a wine that has fully realized its potential. Richard Geoffroy had the insight that there may be more than one level of "potential

extension as the wine spends much more time in contact with the lees. The wines are typically fresh, with a vigorous mousse. They also have a lower dosage than the same vintage disgorged upon the initial release, as the industry moves inexorably toward lower dosage.

The other difference, of course, is the price of the wine. Late-disgorged versions are invariably more expensive. This differential is justified by the fact that a winemaker checks each bottle, and one has a reasonably strong assurance that it will be in good condition. I wondered if that assurance was worth the premium in price, and I often felt that buying the original disgorgement at auction was a better option. In reviewing my notes for the preparation of this manuscript, however, I noticed that over the course of decades of tasting both I often preferred the late-disgorged version.

From a comparison of the 1995 vintage in both versions, tasted in 2011: *"The original disgorgement of Dom Pérignon '95 has always provided pleasure and is now starting to open now, showing a fresh, yeasty richness to the floral fruit character on the nose. If anything, however, the Œnotheque is even more pleasant, creamy and rich, with a softness that almost disguises the firm mineral side of the wine. On the palate, the wine fills the mouth and continues on to a long finish. Classic."* ***** (2019 auction averages: $406 for Œnotheque, $237 for the original disgorgment)

Some collectors wonder how late-disgorged versions will age if it is even older when it is released. How can it last? My experience has been that if anything, it matures even more slowly. I suspect this is because the lees are a reductive (oxygen-scavenging) element in the wine, and as it is on the lees much longer, it will also last longer. 1996 Œnothèque, tasted in 2010 after some years on the cork: [8]*"Consistent with previous tastings and seems not to have evolved at all over the last five years. The nose has notes of toast, truffle, and ground coffee. On the palate, the mousse is fine but persistent, the acidity is balanced, and the texture is smooth. This is a wine for the ages."* ***** (2019 auction average, $342)

---

[8]   i.e., with some post-disgorgement aging in addition to the time on lees

The '85 Œnotheque averaged \$692/btl at auction this year, while the 1969 vintage averaged \$2,124. Rarest of all, however, is the Rosé P3; only one bottle of the '85 changed hands at auction, and it sold for \$4,800 including premium.

MHCS, 9 avenue de Champagne 51200 Epernay | 03 26 51 20 20
https://www.domperignon.com/

Philipponnat

Region: Marne Valley | Terrroir: Grande Vallée

Philipponnat is a four-star producer because of the majestic wine they produce from the stunning vineyard called the Clos des Goisses. This vineyard is composed of four lieux-dits that the house has divided into fourteen different plots. It was cobbled together in a series of transactions made by Pierre Philipponnat beginning in 1935. He and his firm purchased the blocks from all of the various owners, the last as recently as 2019. The vineyard is a 5.83 ha site on steep slopes facing due south in Mareuil-sur-Aÿ. Because of the dramatic slope, which reaches 45° in some places, this is an exceptional place to grow grapes. It is appreciably warmer than the rest of Mareuil and much of the Marne. Because of these conditions, a vintage wine can be produced almost every year. Since the purchase of these plots by Pierre Philipponnat, they have only missed a dozen vintages.

The entire list of vintages produced include: 1935, 1936, 1938, 1939, 1940, 1942, 1943, 1945, 1946, 1947, 1948, 1949, 1950, 1951, 1952, 1953, 1955, 1956, 1957, 1958, 1959, 1961, 1962, 1964, 1966, 1969, 1970, 1971, 1973, 1975, 1976, 1978, 1979, 1980, 1982, 1983, 1985, 1986, 1988, 1989, 1990, 1991, 1992, 1993, 1994, 1995, 1996, 1997, 1998, 1999, 2000, 2001, 2002, 2003, 2004, 2005, 2006, 2007, 2008, 2009, and 2010; all of the vintages from 2010 have been declared as such with the CIVC, and the house plans to release them all. However, the decision has been taken in the past (with the 1994 vintage) to "declassify" a poor vintage and not release it in the normal course of events. Interestingly, the 1994 Goisses has just been released in 2019 as a *Long Vieil-lissement* (late-disgorged) bottling.

Philipponnat was incorporated in 1910, although the roots of the family in the Champagne region date to 1522. They produced wine under their own label from the 1850s, but the volumes increased in 1910 once they took over an existing house called Albert Valet and moved from Aÿ to Mareuil-sur-Aÿ. Monique, the daughter of Pierre Philipponnat, married Michel Collard when he returned from the war, and Michel went to work for his father-in-law, replacing him as the head of Philipponnat in 1963. The Collard family sold to Gosset in 1980, but the new owners kept Michel on board until selling to Marie Brizard in 1987. Philipponnat did not prosper under Marie Brizard, and in 1998 it changed hands again, with Marie Brizard selling to BCC, whose president Bruno Paillard was keen to own the Clos des Goisses vineyard. Paillard was so eager, in fact, that he endured monumental struggles and court battles with the labor unions over staffing levels at Philipponnat. Paillard appointed Charles Philipponnat director and confirmed Thierry Garnier as Chef de Caves – both of whom have remained in the intervening twenty years and have provided steady growth and improvement for this iconic wine.

This team has put together a seductive profile for its flagship wine. Two and one-half hectares of the vineyard are planted to Chardonnay, and three hectares are planted to Pinot Noir. The grape blend varies from year to year, with a strict selection being made for the Clos des Goisses bottling. In the 2010 release, only five of the fourteen vineyard plots went into this wine. In 2008, the blend was 45% Pinot Noir, 55% Chardonnay, rather the inverse of the proportion of the vineyard. In 2009, it was 61% to 39% of these varietals, and in 2010 it was 71% to 29%, which is closer to the original blend of previous years. A proportion of the base wines are fermented in cask or *foudre* (75% in 2008, but only 53% in 2010). After the primary fermentation, the malolactic fermentation is blocked, and the wines are dosed in the extra brut range, between 4 to 4.5 g/l.

Dosage levels at Philipponnat have changed over time, just as they have at nearly every house. I have enjoyed wines made under the older style as well as those made by the current team. A recently disgorged magnum of '76 Clos des Goisses drunk in 2015 was exquisite: *"Stunningly fresh. From a recently disgorged and released bottle, the bouquet showed with a lovely aroma of fresh flowers, lightly toasted almond, toast and butter, and a fine minerality. On the palate the wine was fresh as well, with a lively acidity, a graceful balance, and a subtle, lingering finish. Really spectacular."* ***** (One magnum sold in 2019, $2,032)

The 1996 produced at the end of the Marie Brizard tenure has been consistently superb. From my note in 2010: *"Ripe apples, brioche and the suggestion of truffle and smoke. Loads of extract, a finely balanced acidity, and good length. The wine has moved into a phase where it is beginning to show and should last for decades beyond that."* ***** (2019 auction average, $558)

The 2002 vintage from the present team has shown consistently well over the years: *"A lovely sweet fruit character, notes of toasted brioche and almond and a smoky note at the end. Rich, almost sweet, with a lively mousse and balanced acidity. The overall impression was perhaps a bit soft, but it was drinking quite well, and will hold."* **** (2019 auction average, $231)

There are a wealth of distinctive vintage wines produced in addition to the Clos des Goisses. I have enjoyed many examples of their vintage Blanc de Blancs, back to the '80s, at least. A representative note from the '82: *"...an exotic nose, with notes of eucalyptus, passionfruit, petrol, and grapefruit. On the palate, the wine still retained a balancing acidity, but the richness dominated..."* **** (trades rarely) Since 2008, there is also a vintage-dated Blanc de Noirs, an assemblage of Pinot Noir from the Montagne and their vineyards in Mareuil-sur-Aÿ. From 2009: *"A lovely and accomplished wine. This shows pronounced notes of almonds, cream, and spice; there is a dense texture here, but the wine retains an essential freshness that is attractive. Half of the base wines are fermented in cask, and malo is blocked for this half, while the tank-fermented wines do their malo. The wine was bottled in May of 2010, and disgorged in November of 2016 and dosed at 4.5 g/l."* **** (2020 retail average, $54)

Next comes the Cuvée 1522 range, both of which are roughly two-thirds Pinot Noir from the Le Léon site in Aÿ, which has been in the family since 1522, and one-third Chardonnay from Oger or Le Mesnil. As with the rest of the vintage line, only the cuvée is used, and it is fermented half in cask, half in tank, with the malolactic fermentation inhibited for the cask ferment. The 2007 Cuvée 1522 was dosed at 4.5 g/l. *"The wine shows a nice density while avoiding any hint of heaviness. There are some mature aromas of truffle and sous-bois, but there is enough substance here to sustain it and a pleasantly waxy texture."* *** (2020 average retail, $80) Even more impressive was the rosé version of the same wine: *"A similar blend to the blanc, but 8.5% of the Pinot is in the form of still red wine, fermented from the fruit of the Clos des Goisses. The balance is from Le Léon. Here there is a rewarding red fruit expression, but unlike the NV Rosé, there is also a more substantial, vinous side with a hint of ripe plum and an earthy note and a slightly chewy texture."* **** (2020 retail average, $78)

A relatively new introduction at Philipponnat is what they call the Parcellaires series. At the peak is the super-cuvée from the Clos des Goisses called Les Cintres. It comes from two lieux-dits within the Clos, Les Grands Cintres and Les Petits Cintres. The wines are fermented entirely in cask, the malo is blocked, and they are dosed at 4.5 g/l. There is also another wine from Mareuil called La Rémissonne, an assemblage from the lieux-dits Valofroy and Dessus des Goisses that lie right next to the Clos des Goisses. This is fermented 44% in cask, and the malolactic fermentation is partially blocked. Finally, there is a selection from the Philipponnat holdings in the Le Léon lieu-dit in Aÿ that is 45% fermented in cask without malolactic fermentation. From my notes on the inaugural 2006 vintage, tasted in 2015: *"Eight years on the lees before disgorging and then dosed at 4.5 g/l. The nose shows creamy apricot, and butter notes with a hint of almond or marzipan touched with honey and a hint of yeasty brioche – truly a beguiling nose. On the palate, the wine is fresh but accessible, with a supple texture, plenty of weight, and good length. An impressive debut."* **** (2020 retail average, $154)

13 rue du Pont 51160 Mareuil-sur-Aÿ | 03 26 56 93 00
http://www.philipponnat.com/

Louis Roederer

Location: Reims | Terroir: Blended

The origins of Champagne Louis Roederer lie in a négociant business founded by Pierre-Joseph Dubois in 1765 with his partner Jean-Baptiste Dussaulois. The two separated the following year, and Dubois, in turn, established Dubois Père et Fils. This house would be inherited in 1833 by his nephew Louis Roederer. Roederer was the fifth cousin of the Count Pierre-Louis Roederer of Metz. He re-named the business after himself, and it continued to grow throughout the mid 19th Century. The house was taken over upon his death in 1870 by his son, also named Louis Roederer, who ran it for a decade before launching a career in politics. It was during the administration of the younger Louis Roederer that the house reached its initial apogee, with sales of 2.5 million bottles by 1872, more than a quarter of which were shipped to the Imperial Russian market that had been opened by his father's commercial director, Hugues Krafft. In 1876, Roederer created a special bottling solely for Tsar Alexander II and the Russian court. The wine was bottled in crystal bottles with no indentation in the bottom of the bottle (called a punt). This original bottling of Cristal is said to have been sweet, typical of many wines destined for Russia. The Russian market (and the post-Civil War American market) would remain important to Roederer. This special Roederer bottling pre-dates all of the other prestige cuvées by a considerable margin.

Upon the premature death of the younger Roederer in 1880 at the age of 34, the house passed to his sister Léonine, who ran it with her husband, Jacques Olry. Their son Léon Olry-Roederer ran the house from 1903 until his death in 1932, when it was taken over by his widow Camille. She ran Roederer for forty years, and amid the Great Depression, brought it once again to prominence. In 1973, ownership passed to her daughter Marcelle, and her grandson Jean-Claude Rouzaud took the reins in 1979. In 1989, Rouzaud hired Jean-Baptiste Lecaillon, who became Chef de Caves in 1994, a role which he retains as of this writing.

Roederer owns 410 distinct plots which stretch over 240 ha of vineyards, producing a quantity of fruit sufficient for nearly four-fifths of their supply, including all of the vintage wines. This total represents a much higher percentage than is common among négociants of this size. It is even more impressive because it is composed exclusively of premiers crus and grand crus in the Marne. All of the vineyards are sustainably farmed, and more than 60 ha are biodynamically-farmed, with more than 20 ha worked in the traditional way with horses.

At Roederer, all the wines except the nonvintage brut (Brut Premier) and the demi-sec are vintage-dated, including the Brut vintage[9], the Rosé, the Blanc de Blancs, a Brut Nature and Brut Nature Rosé, as well as Cristal and Cristal Rosé. The range is superb throughout, although in terms of reputation, it is clearly led by Cristal. Cristal blanc is typically about 60% Pinot, 40% Chardonnay, and approximately 15 to 25% of the blend is barrel fermented. The malolactic fermentation is normally blocked.

The first commercially available vintage of Cristal was the 1921, sold only in Europe. Distribution was expanded with the 1945 vintage, available from 1949 in the rest of the world. The complete list of vintages produced since this time includes 1947, 1949, 1953, 1955, 1959, 1961, 1962, 1964, 1966, 1967, 1969, 1970, 1971, 1973, 1974, 1975, 1976, 1977, 1978, 1979, 1981, 1982, 1983, 1985, 1986, 1988, 1989, 1990, 1993, 1994, 1995, 1996, 1997, 1999, 2000, 2002, 2004, 2005, 2006, 2007, 2008, 2009, and 2012.

A recent bottle of the 1990 Cristal tasted in 2019 typifies everything I love about the style of this wine: *"A marvelous bottle of Cristal, definitely the best one from the 1990 vintage that I have had because of its bright, youthful appeal. The biscuit notes come to the fore, but there is no lack of ripe apple fruit. The wine is still fresh, and the development is restrained but beginning to show just now, and the wine is drinking well at present. On the palate, there is plenty of mousse and impressive density; the wine is open, but not overly so, the acid balance is beyond reproach, and the length is very satisfying. In my view, it is just moving into its peak, although it can doubtless be cellared for up to another twenty years if you want to wait."* ***** (2019 average auction, $412)

---

9   For the sake of clarity, we will refer to a vintage-dated cuvée that has no further indication in the name as "Brut Vintage"

CHARLES CURTIS

The 1996 Cristal and Cristal Rosé were both spectacular. Cristal, on numerous occasions, has seemed subtle and under-stated and yet packed with flavor: *"A charming success, this seems open and toasty, with youthful notes of almond, apple, and flaky pastry on the nose. It is only with a bit of reflection that one notes how stylish and fine the wine is – this is a Champagne with a glorious future."* **** (2019 auction average, $395) The Rosé was a bit more forward: *"Lush, forward aromas of ripe but not overly sweet red berry fruit, notes of toast, yeast, just a hint of hazelnut. Round and full, with plenty of acidity but nothing sharp or tight. The wine is opening nicely now but should be able to last for years to come. Marvelous!"* **** (2019 auction average, $715)

Cristal Rosé was introduced with the 1974 vintage that was launched in 1980. The following years have also appeared: 1975, 1976, 1978, 1979, 1981, 1982, 1983, 1985, 1988, 1989, 1990, 1995, 1996, 1999, 2000, 2002, 2004, 2005, 2006, 2007, 2008, 2009, and 2012.

Today Cristal Rosé is produced using 45% Chardonnay and 55% Pinot Noir, with the Pinot Noir coming from biodynamically-farmed vineyards in Aÿ. Color is produced using the *saignée* method; 20% of the blend is aged in cask.

Among the older vintages, the 1979 vintage tasted in 2010 was a highlight: *"The '79 Cristal Rosé showed a crazy nose with smoky, ripe black cherry fruit character, hints of baking bread, and a ripe, vinous edge that distinguishes it here. On the palate, all is soft elegance and finesse – the wine isn't lacking power, but the ripeness has given everything a subtle glow. Lovely."* ***** (One bottle sold in 2019, $1,984)

Roederer Brut vintage is also reliably excellent. I was reminded of this in the fall of 2019, drinking the recently-released Brut Vintage 2012: *"Superb. The nose shows lush notes of toasted brioche yet remains eminently fresh with primary notes of ripe apple, red fruits, and a hint of fresh flowers. On the palate, the wine has a lively but discreet mousse and a rich, velvety texture balanced by crisp acidity, carrying it to a pleasantly lingering finish. This is a 2012 with a long life ahead of it. More stuffing than most."* **** (2019 retail average, $69)

Vintage Rosé was no less compelling. From the 2008 vintage, tasted in 2018: *"An appealingly pale pink, this has a surprising volume of black cherry fruit touched with mineral, smoke, and a hint of spice. There is fresh acidity to keep it lively, yet this wine is meaty enough to accompany the main course to perfection."* ****

The same is true of the Vintage Blanc de Blancs. I think in general that Roederer perhaps doesn't get enough attention for this lovely, consistent offering. My note on the 2009, tasted in 2019: *"Fresh and crisp, with a fine citrusy fruit character supplemented by pleasantly notes of mineral, toast, and almond. On the palate, the wine showed a fine, persistent mousse, elegant balance, and nice length."* ****

The only wine that is not yet performing at the same level is perhaps the Vintage Brut Nature. From my note on the 2009 vintage, tasted in 2019: *"Somewhat closed at first, there is a bit of almost sulfury reductive quality on the nose. While there is abundant lemony fruit and a mineral, saline edge, it lacks a bit of concentration at this point. The texture is suitably racy and yet not lacking in warmth, but it somehow fails to carry through convincingly on the finish."* *** (2019 retail average, $85 for all three wines)

21 boulevard Lundy 51722 Reims | 03 26 40 42 11
http://www.louis-roederer.com/

Salon

Region: Côte des Blancs | Terroir: Côte des Blancs

Salon is a mythic wine. One might even call it a wine of destiny, since it seems that the founder, Eugène-Aimé Salon, was destined to return to his Champenois roots, and that Bernard de Nonancourt was destined to pur¬chase it and elevate it to its present preeminence. Eugène-Aimé Salon was born in 1867 in the village of Pocancy just to the east of Le Mesnil-sur-Oger on the poor land on the "wrong side of the road." His father was a wheelwright, and his parents longed for their son to become a schoolteacher. Eugène-Aimé had bigger dreams and fled to Paris and found work at a furrier called Chapal, later famous for producing the Bombardier jackets worn by pilots.

During his Parisian sojourn, Eugène-Aimé kept in contact with his family. His brother-in-law Marcel Guillaume was the Chef de Caves for Champagne Tarin, a small house that vinified grapes produced in several locations, including the vineyard later renamed the Clos du Mesnil. Eugène-Aimé purchased a country house in Le Mesnil that eventually became his gastronomic retreat and a place to entertain his Chapal clients. The smallish vineyard attached to this home called Le Jardin became the nucleus of Champagne Salon.

Initially, Champagne Salon was created for Salon's personal use. It was blended from Chardonnay produced in twenty parcels, all within the village of Le Mesnil. These parcels have remained unchanged since Salon's time, with one exception: there is no longer any fruit from the Clos du Mesnil. Initially, Salon was a private and discreet brand: the first four vintages were reserved for the personal use of Salon and his friends and clients. The first vintage offered outside this select circle was the 1921. Eugène-Aimé also was a member of the exclusive gastronomic club called *Club des Cent*, which met at Maxim's. Through this tie, the Salon became the house wine of Maxim's in 1928.

Eugène-Aimé Salon passed away in 1943, and ownership of the house passed to his sister and then to her son, named Marcel Guillaume after his father. Due to the heavy burden of French inheritance taxes, Marcel was forced to sell. The winery was purchased by Besserat de Bellefon, owned at the time by Compagnie Générale des produits Dubonnet-Cinzano-Byrrh, known as CDC. CDC, in turn, was acquired in 1976 by Pernod-Ricard. At the time of the sale to CDC, Paul Bergeot was named president. In his *World Encyclopedia of Champagne,* Tom Stevenson tells the following story: Bergeot was eager to re-launch Salon in its current Cuvée S bottling with its antique bottle. According to Stevenson, he had stocks of the 1971 and 1973 decanted and rebottled in the new bottle shape with additional liqueur de tirage, provoking a third fermentation.

Pernod-Ricard sold Salon to Laurent-Perrier in 1988. Since this time, the brand has consistently grown in renown. The Chef de Caves at Laurent Perrier responsible for its production at the time of the acquisition was Alain Terrier. His second-in-command Michel Fauconnet took over in 2004. Didier Depond is the president of Salon and Delamotte.

In the bottle, Salon seems to start closed and reticent, and then to blossom suddenly. The 2007 vintage was at this stage in 2019: *"Mineral and saline notes open on the attack, but after a decade on the lees, this is still not showing its full expression. There is a pleasant, almost bracing, lemony fruit but little in the way of toasty character. On the palate, there is a beautiful, almost frightening tension and tons of potential, but the wine is lacking generosity and not showing the length it should."* (2019 average retail, $587)

Early in its life, the '96 had a similar beginning. From a tasting in 2008: *"A bit tight, with a nose that showed hints of lemon peel, mineral, green almond, and wood smoke. On the palate, the wine showed a biting acidity and a lean, racy structure. The wine was certainly not lacking in substance, however, and there is little doubt that this is a wine for the ages."* **** (2019 auction average, $744)

With time, however, the Salon becomes truly exuberant. From my notes on the 1990 tasted in 2010: *"Thrilling, with a crazy profusion of aromas that ranged from coconut and pineapple to toast, smoke, flint, freshly roast coffee beans, and a hint of caramel. Impeccably fresh, with a lively yet silken-textured mousse,* *crisp acidity, and a substantive finish. Drinking well now, this Champagne has the stuffing to age for the long haul."* ***** (2019 auction average, $1,164)

Forty years on it reaches its apogee: *"A 1979 Salon was drinking near its peak, with exotic notes of ripe mango, truffle, mineral, smoke, and brioche on the nose. On the palate, the wine was lively and vital, and despite its maturity, the wine was showing supremely well, with a lingering finish that was impressive.* ***** (2019 auction average, $2,552)

Vintages released to date (including those reserved for private use) include 1905, 1909, 1911, 1914, 1921, 1925, 1928, 1934, 1937, 1942, 1943, 1946, 1947, 1948, 1949, 1951, 1952, 1955, 1956, 1959, 1961, 1964, 1966, 1969, 1971, 1973, 1976, 1979, 1982, 1983, 1985, 1988, 1990, 1995, 1996, 1997, 1999, 2002, 2004, 2006, 2007, and 2008 (released in magnum only).

5 rue de la Brèche d'Oger 51190 Le Mesnil sur Oger | 03 02 57 51 65
https://www.champagne-salon.fr/

Jacques Selosse

Region: Côte des Blancs | Terroir: Côte des Blancs

Anselme Selosse – son of Jacques Selosse – is a genius. Of his genius, we can be sure, although we may not agree about his wines. We may not even be able to make up our minds about the wines. During a visit to Selosse, the first impression is that of eloquence. Tastings can run long – two hours is not unusual – and Anselme is discursive. He is one of Champagne's most profound thinkers about winemaking, viticulture, and the environment. Each thought that Selosse spins off in these free-wheeling monologues is a gem, and he expresses them in a rapid-fire stream of consciousness narrative that is nearly impossible to transcribe. Perhaps it is his nature as something of a trickster that throws wine lovers into confusion. When describing his methods, he begins with his version of the Hippocratic oath: "First, do no harm." Then he moves on to Sermon-on-the-Mount territory, "I am a servant of the wine;" before changing into Wodehouse mode, "I am a butler – each week I see what I can bring to the wine."

As opaque as his epigrams can be at times, it is possible to gather some thoughts about his working style. The characteristic most visible to the uninitiated is the use of oak barrels of various sizes. The use of oak and other Burgundian techniques date to Anselme's formation at winemaking school in Burgundy as well as his internships at Coche-Dury, Comtes Lafon, and Domaine Leflaive. As with great white Burgundy, the wines are vinified parcel by parcel. He ferments using native yeasts without a long settling to clear the juice. He makes the wine in an oxidative way that can include lees-stirring in the event of reduction, sometimes until the July following the harvest. Malo is neither blocked nor encouraged, although the natural acidity of the wines tends to inhibit the transformation, and he would prefer to avoid it. The second fermentation is done to the extent possible with native yeasts that he has cultured from grape must from his vineyards. There is a largish range of wines, many involving the fractional blending technique referred to as *réserve perpetuelle* or solera. Since this book focuses on vintage Champagne, I do not address them here. However, all of them are worth seeking out; particularly the single-vineyard wines that called the "Lieux-Dits" collectively. This series includes Les Carelles from Le Mesnil, Chemin de Chalons from Cramant, Les Chantereines from Avize, La Côte Faron from Aÿ, Bout du Clos from Ambonnay, and Sous le Mont from Mareuil-sur-Aÿ.

Champagne Jacques Selosse at this time is a house in transition since Anselme and Corinne's son Guillaume has taken over. Guillaume has worked alongside his father since 2011, in addition to making his own wines, a Blanc de Blancs from Cramant (lieu-dit Au Dessous de Gros Mont), and a Blanc de Noirs from fruit purchased from Jérôme Coessens' vineyard Largillier. From the recently launched 2007, he is also responsible for the vintage wine at Jacques Selosse.

Unlike the producers discussed until this point, Champagne Jacques Selosse is a récoltant-manipulant. This is denoted by the code "RM" on the label, and it means that they grow the grapes and make the wine themselves[10]. It is thus truly a domaine in the Burgundian sense. The history is fairly straightforward. Anselme's father, Jacques, settled in Avize after World War II. He began to purchase vineyards in 1947 and founded the domaine in 1949. At first, he sold the fruit and then began to bottle wine under his own name in 1964. Anselme returned from his studies in Burgundy in 1974 and worked alongside his father until 1980 when he took over with his wife Corinne. He was declared "Winemaker of the Year" by La Revue du Vin de France (RVF) in 1993, and by Gault-Millau the following year. In an unprecedented move, the RVF named him "Winemaker of the Year" again in 2017.

There is only one vintage wine from Champagne Jacques Selosse, the aptly named Millésimé (French for "Vintage"). Selosse does not produce every year, and when it is made there are only about 500 cases. Under Anselme, it was made exclusively from two lieux-dits in Avize planted with old vines, Les Maladries du Midi and Les Chantereines. This latter site is a steep, mid-slope, east-facing parcel, and one of the emblematic

---

10   See Glossary entry for "Professional Declaration" for more information.

vineyards for the domaine. The initial holding was purchased by Jacques just after WW II and then expanded in 1960. At present, Selosse holds 0.8 ha in Les Chantereines. In addition to the vintage wine (when made), he blends the grapes into the wine called Substance, and it also appears as one of the rare lieu-dit bottlings described above. Les Maladries du Midi is a south-facing parcel at the foot of the slope. Fruit from Les Chantereines brings tension and structure, while Les Maladries du Midi suppleness and softness. Under Guillaume, the direction of the vintage wine has changed. Now it will be composed from the best parcels across the domaine, including their holdings on the Montagne and in the Grande Vallée. For the moment, the Selosse family is a bit coy about the exact parcels, but they do inform visitors that the 2007 vintage is 30% Pinot Noir. The average retail price for the 2007 vintage in 2019 was $540.

Anselme is a classic raconteur, and it is difficult to dislike him. The wines, for some, can be otherwise. I do not count myself among the haters, but neither am I entirely convinced. There have been issues with oxidation and the use of oak. When I first tasted the wines, I felt they were rather right at the edge. From my first note on the 1996, tasted in 2009: *"A profusion of aromas from truffle and toast to ground coffee, mineral, and soy along with perhaps a hint of volatility. Vigorous mousse, a trenchant acidity, and wonderful length. Delicious Champagne, with the substance to age for at least another decade."* **** (2019 auction average, $1,255) It was complex and intriguing, but the touch of soy sauce that left a question mark.

My most recent tasting in 2019 was a bottle of the 1995 vintage. This vintage seemed oddly fresher and more youthful. Here, however, the oak still stood out: *"A vigorous and youthful Champagne...One of the first impressions here was a rather dominant note from the oak casks used for fermentation. Behind this, certainly was plenty of fruit (more pear and apple than citrus), and lots of toast. On the palate, there was a vigorous mousse, plenty of freshness, and lots of extract. The wine carried itself superbly well, made a powerful statement, and lingered seductively on the finish. However, even at the end there was still a bit of wood present and it makes one wonder how long it will take to integrate."* **** (2019 auction average, $827)

Among the most exuberant vintages I have had was the 2005, tasted in 2013: *"Spectacularly good; approachable now. On the attack there is a profusion of exotic tropical notes with hints of passion fruit and coconut. With a bit of time this is complemented by earthy undercurrents and a savory note and a firm toasty yeast character. The aromatic palette unfolds with time in the glass to give the impression of great richness. Picked at 14.2% potential, this is undeniably rich, but there is balance here as well, with the Chantereines bringing a mineral, citrus freshness to the blend that is essential to its success. With loads of extract and a super-long finish, this is undeniably a special bottle of wine."* ***** (2019 auction average, $485)

Finally, In 2013 I tasted the inaugural 1986 vintage from a private collection, but the wine had not weathered the years well: *"The 1986 Selosse was a rare treat that I had never tasted before. The wine was complex, mature and truffley, but unfortunately lacking mousse of any kind. More of a history piece than a lively wine, more interesting than compelling."* ** (One bottle sold in 2019, $1,683).

There is much to love at Selosse and much to discuss. It will be fascinating to see the direction that the estate takes under Guillaume and what we will drink in the coming years. Vintages released to date include 1986, 1988, 1989, 1990, 1993, 1995, 1996, 1997, 1998, 1999, 2002, 2003, 2005, and 2007.

22 rue Ernest Valle 51190 Avize | 03 26 57 53 56
https://www.selosse-lesavises.com/en/le-domaine-jacques-selosse/

Taittinger

Location: Reims | Terroir: Blended

Taittinger is modern and ancient, forward-looking, and tradition-al. The house traces its roots to the firm of Jacques Fourneaux, founded in 1734 as only the third firm to produce sparkling Champagne (after Ruinart in 1729 and Chanoine Frères in 1730). Initially, though, the firm focused on still wines due to the risk inherent in sparkling wine production at that time, but eventually, they also produced sparkling Champagne. Little is known about the firm of Fourneaux, but it was important enough to be included in the 1870 work by Charles Tovey *Champagne: Its History, Manufacture, Properties, &c*. The house owned both Château de la Marquetterie in Pierry and the ancient building called the Demeure des Comtes de Champagne (on the Rue de Tambour in Reims). This building was once owned by Theobald the Troubadour, Comte de Champagne, and King of Navarre from 1234.

Pierre Taittinger had been billeted in the Château de la Marquetterie during World War I while he was attached to the command of Marshal Joffre, who made his headquarters there. Frère Jean Oudart originally constructed the château. Oudart was a Benedictine monk close to Dom Pérignon and the developments of Champagne during the 17th Century. The name La Marquetterie derives from the checkerboard pattern of the Pinot Noir and Chardonnay vines planted in the vineyards surrounding the château. In 1932, Pierre Taittinger acquired the firm of Forest-Fourneaux (along with the Château de la Marquetterie) and changed the name to Champagne Taittinger.

Pierre Taittinger was active in politics between the two wars. He was elected President of the Municipal Council of Paris in 1943 under the German occupation and held this role until the Liberation. From the end of World War II, the firm was directed by François Taittinger, his third son by his first wife, along with his brother Jean and half-brother Claude. It was during this period that Taittinger became established in the Abbaye de Saint-Nicaise and adjoining *crayères*, or caves. After the untimely death of François in a 1960 car accident, the firm was directed by Claude, since Jean was increasingly occupied with his political career. He served as a member of Parliament, was Mayor of Reims for 18 years, and France's Minister of Finance under Georges Pompidou.

It was during the administration of Claude Taittinger that the firm came to international prominence. Some credit him with the conception of the prestige cuvée Comtes de Champagne, the first vintage of which was 1952. However, others have suggested that the idea for the Comtes de Champagne came from a conversation between Rudy Kopf, founder of Taittinger's American importer Kobrand, and François Taittinger. The family firm expanded gradually. Champagne sales grew, particularly in the U.S., and in 1954 Pierre Taittinger also became the president of the hotel chain Société du Louvre, an activity expanded by Pierre's son Guy. By the turn of the millennium, the group included Champagne Taittinger as well as luxury hotels, including the Crillon, Lutetia, and Martinez, budget hotels such as Kyriad, Première Classe, and Campanile, and the crystal manufacturer Baccarat. The forty-five descendants of Pierre Taittinger voted in 2004 to sell their holdings for €2.4 billion to Starwood, who were less interested in making Champagne than in running hotels. Pierre's grandson Pierre-Emmanuel was able to put together a successful bid to buy back the Champagne house with the assistance of Crédit Agricole and the support of the unions. Today, he works alongside his son Clovis and his daughter Vitalie.

Under the guidance of Pierre-Emmanuel, the house has gone from strong to stronger. Comtes de Champagne is an exceptional prestige cuvée and the epitome of *grande marque* eloquence (and one of the most well-priced at this level). Most years, the Blanc de Blancs is produced exclusively from fruit from the five grands crus of the Côte des Blancs: Chouilly, Cramant, Oger, Avize, and Le Mesnil. Only the first press juice is used. The first fermentation is mostly done in stainless steel tanks, with the exception of about 5% of the base wines that are fermented in cask. The malolactic fermentation is normally done. The typically ages ten years or more on the lees before it is disgorged, and the dosage is typically in the range of 9 to 10 g/l. The 2007, tasted in 2019, is a perfect case in point: *"Impressively rich for the vintage, this opens with an aroma of ripe golden delicious apples, fresh flowers, and the scent of toasted brioche, with an undercurrent of spice and butter, yet it is never too far from the citrus/mineral realm as well. On the palate, the wine is approachable and silky-textured, with a lively mousse and rich, mouth-filling, plumpness. There is, however, enough freshness to balance all of this substance -- the pH is 3.04 -- and in the end, the wine is in lovely equilibrium."* **** (2020 retail average: $141)

The wine evolves remarkably over time. Perhaps the greatest vintage in my experience is the 1996; I have tasted it many times and given it five stars each time, yet the character was different each time. My first note from 2008 calls out *"...primary floral and mineral notes over lime peel and green apple fruit character. On the palate there is a very fine acidity and nice length. Needs time, but will definitely be one of the greats."* By 2013: *"Superb. A very exotic bouquet, with notes of papaya and passion fruit, mineral and smoke. Rich, with a sexy satiny texture and great finesse. There is no lack of acidity or structure, but the wine is highly approachable now."* ***** (2019 auction average, $397)

Older vintages, however, have not always shown well - bottles from 1961 and 1971 tasted in 2019 were past their prime. When the wine is in its prime, it is truly superb. Perhaps my favorite among the older vintages I have tasted was a bottle of 1979 shared among friends in 2011: *"Rich and pungent on the nose, this shows an incredible depth of aromas, with an interplay of smoke, truffle, and candied lemon peel on the nose with a strong mineral, almost salty note at the end. On the palate, the wine is rich, almost oily, yet there is certainly enough freshness to balance the substantial structure and carry it to an elegant, lingering finish. Truly lovely."* ***** (2019 auction average, $573)

Vintages of the Blanc de Blancs released to date include: 1952, 1953, 1955, 1959, 1961, 1962, 1964, 1966, 1969, 1970, 1971, 1973, 1975, 1976, 1979, 1981, 1982, 1983, 1985, 1986, 1988, 1989, 1990, 1993, 1994, 1995, 1996, 1997, 1998, 1999, 2000, 2002, 2004, 2005, 2006, and 2007.

Taittinger also produces a Rosé version of Comtes de Champagne. The style here is equally regal and elegant, but the Rosé version is more full-bodied and vinous, made for aging. Its substantial nature comes from the red wine that is used for color and body; the fruit comes from the crus of Bouzy and Ambonnay on the Montagne de Reims, and these ripe, lush Pinots add power and structure to the blend. Even in a lighter year such as 2007, this substance is apparent. From my note, tasted 2018: *"Among the rosé wines, the Taittinger Comtes de Champagne was among the most successful, with an exquisite balance and an expressive fruit character showing lovely floral aromas. On the palate, there is plenty of density and structure, but there enough freshness that the wine never seems heavy despite its vinous nature."* **** (2019 retail average, $166/btl)

The rosé ages extremely well. My notes on Comtes de Champagne Rosé 1973 are consistent, even if tasted on multiple continents over several years. A representative note from 2009: *"The '73 Comtes Rosé was tremendous at a recent vertical tasting, with sweet cherry fruit and a rich, toasty, truffley character. The mousse was still very vigorous given the age, and the acid balance was terrific."* **** (2019 auction average, $772)

It would be a mistake to overlook the "regular" vintage Taittinger, which can provide an extraordinary value, delivering the depth, power, and elegance of vintage Champagne at a very reasonable price. The recently released 2012, tasted in 2019, is a good example: *"Lovely concentration, with aromas of ripe apricot and pear on the initial attack with subtle, well-integrated hints of smoke and yeast. Lush on the palate but fresh enough to bring the wine a superb balance, this should age very well."* **** (2020 average retail $72)

9 place Saint-Nicaise 51100 Reims | 03 26 85 45 35
http://www.taittinger.com/

Agrapart

Region: Côte des Blancs | Terroir: Côte des Blancs

The wines of grand cru Avize are noted more for steely depth and concentration than for their effusive fruit character. Pascal Agrapart, in many ways, is a reflection of this cru where he is based. He can be quiet when you first meet him—not taciturn, but not forward. Like his wines, however, he is endlessly fascinating. He is the fourth generation of the Agrapart family to direct the estate, which was founded in 1894. From the beginning, Champagne Agrapart was bottling wine from its own vineyards, which was relatively uncommon at the time. Today, Agrapart works 12 hectares of vines spread over 62 parcels, concentrated in the grand crus of Avize, Oger, Cramant, and Oiry, with additional parcels in Coligny (now Val-des-Marais, part of the Val du Petit Morin in the southern Côte des Blancs), and also Vauciennes and Avenay-Val-d'Or in the Marne Valley. Chardonnay accounts for 90% of the fruit produced.

The holdings in Avize, however, form the heart of the estate. The vintage wines come mostly from Avize, as does one non-vintage blend called Complantée. This wine features six grape varieties (Pinot Noir, Meunier, Chardonnay, Arbanne, Petit Meslier, and Pinot Blanc) planted together in the lieu-dit Les Fosses.

Pascal Agrapart's skill truly becomes evident with the top three vintage wines: Minéral, Avizoise, and Vénus. The first of these is from the lieux-dits of Bionnes in Cramant and Champbouton in Avize. Here, the thin topsoil over chalk gives a mineral result, hence the name of the cuvée. The vines are forty years of age; half of the base wines are fermented in tank and half in old 600-liter casks. The second cuvée, Avizoise, is produced from the lieux-dits Robarts and Gros Yeux in Avize from vines more than fifty years of age. Although they are planted further up the slope, there is a deeper layer of clay here over the chalk. This cuvée is bottled under cork. The third vintage wine, called Vénus, is produced from a single lieu-dit in Avize called Fosse aux Pourceaux ("Pig Hollow"). Roughly half of this vineyard is directly on the chalk, and the other half has more clay topsoil. The vineyard is worked using a horse, and the cuvée is named for the original horse who worked the vines named Vénus. The plot that produces Vénus was planted in 1959; this wine is also aged under cork and disgorged without dosage.

There is also a fourth vintage wine called Expérience. This special cuvée is produced from old vines from Avize, and nothing is added to the wine – no sulfur, no yeast for either of the fermentations, and no dosage. It is bottled by hand and aged under cork. It is only be made when conditions make it possible to conserve unfermented must from one vintage to produce the second fermentation in the bottle the following year. The wine is blended from the plots whose grapes produce Minéral and Avizoise. The first commercial release was 2007.

The terroir determines the method of working the vines, but respect for nature is a common thread: no herbicides or other systemic products are used, although Agrapart feels organic cert-ification is too constraining. He believes in tilling the soil, and in many of the vineyards, this is done manually using a horse. In the winery, most of the *vins clairs* are fermented in cask on native yeasts. The wines mature over the winter following the harvest before being blended. No new wood is used; the youngest barrels are five years old. Some hold 600 liters, others 300 liters. Agrapart says that he is looking for minerality more than acidity. He picks fairly ripe for the region and does not chaptalize his musts. No sulfur is used, and there is no inoculation with yeast for either of the fermentations. The wines receive no dosage.

A comparative tasting of the 2002 vintage done in 2008 shows just how successful Agrapart is in teasing out the com-plexities of his terroirs. *"The 2002 Minéral, dosed at 4 to 5 g/l, is aptly named, as the mineral notes are prominent on the nose, along with smoke and citrus fruit. On the palate, the wine is crisp,*

structured, and verging on tart. Very clean and focused, there is a firm line here and an almost thrilling sense of structure." ****
The 2002 Avizoise was entirely fermented in cask and aged under cork. *"On the initial attack, there are aromas of ripe golden apples that almost veer into something a bit more tropical, under-pinned with notes of minerals, smoke, and spice. On the palate, this wine is a bit fatter and richly textured; although it is also dosed at 4 to 5 g/l, richness is from its maturation, and has a rounder feel and a longer finish."* ****

The 2002 Brut Nature Vénus also is aged under cork. *"In a way, this is the culmination of the work at Agrapart. A delightful complexity of tropical fruit, buttered toast, smoke, sous-bois, and spice on the nose, although there is a certain overt oak element that will likely resolve with time. On the palate, there is a fine balance between textural richness and crisp acidity. The finish goes on forever."* *****

57 avenue Jean-Jaures 51190 Avize | 03 26 57 51 38
http://www.champagne-agrapart.com/

Bérêche et Fils

Region: Montagne de Reims | Terroir: Grande Montagne North

Ludes is one of the north-facing premier cru villages on the
Montagne de Reims. A solid terroir, capable of producing
thrilling wines, it is less well-known than its grand cru neigh-
bors to the east, Mailly, Verzenay, and Verzy. It is the first in
a series of premiers crus that extend to the east and include
Chigny-lès-Roses, Rilly-la-Montagne, and Villers-Allerand.
Champagne Bérêche was founded in Ludes in 1846. Despite the
relative lack of visibility for Ludes, Bérêche has risen to become
one of the brightest stars of the new generation of growers.
New, but not too new: the first vintage bottled under their name
was the 1928. Brothers Raphaël and Vincent Bérêche have
been working with their father Jean-Pierre since 2004 and represent the fifth generation of the house. The Bérêche family are
proprietors of 11.5 hectares between three main sites and are
now adding additional parcels. The vines are spread between
Ludes, Ormes in the Petite Montagne, and Mareuil-le-Port on
the Left Bank of the Marne. There are also plots in the premier
crus Trépail and Rilly, supplemented by a recently acquired
parcel in grand cru Mailly. Ten people work the vineyards full
time. The vineyards have been grassed over for more than
fifteen years now, and although they are not seeking certification, they work with as few synthetic compounds as possible
and some biodynamic principals are applied. The estate works
with much lower yields than those officially permitted by law.
In some years, growers will receive an authorization for 10,000
to 11,000 kg/ha but the harvest at Bérêche will be a maximum
of 7,000 kg/ha. Raphaël and Vincent believe this adds to the
depth of the wine.

In the winery, Raphaël has introduced cask fermentation.
At the beginning, they used the traditional 205-liter Champagne casks, but now they prefer larger 300-liter or 600-liter
barrels. The vins clairs are normally left on the lees until the
end of June. Little sulfur is used, and although the ferments are
done in cask, care is taken to limit oxygen uptake, and so the

wine is moved using peristaltic pumping. Most cuvées spend at least three years on the lees before being disgorged with and extra-brut dosage, usually around 3 g/l. Everything except the nonvintage wines is aged under cork. The Bérêche lineup features six vintage Champagnes, and a Coteaux Champenois.

The top vintage wine is called Le Cran, a blend of fruit from two parcels from the same area, at 220 meters at the top of the hill, up against the forest in Ludes. The grapes from the lieu-dit Les Hautes Plantes is from a west-facing parcel at the top of the slope planted to Chardonnay in 1969, while Les Vignes Saint-Jean is a nearby plot of Pinot Noir that faces the other direction, planted in 1973. Both feature very thin soil over chalk and limestone. They are considered by the Bérêche brothers to be among the top parcels of the property. The wine has been produced each year since 2007. The cuvée was originally called Vieilles Vignes Selectionnées but then became Le Cran in 2004. I have notes with both names from that vintage -- luckily, they are consistent. I loved both of them, tasted in 2010: *"Opened with a bit of wood yet retains a fresh lemony fruit with fairly complex notes of yeast, toast, mineral, and spice on the nose. Crisp acidity, a silken, satiny texture, nice density, and good length. Lovely."* *****

Rive Gauche is produced from Meunier planted in sandy-clay soils over chalk from two steep parcels in Mareuil-le-Port, Maisoncelles, and Côte aux Chataîngers. The parcel is 0.4 hectares, and the vines are more than 40 years of age. The Rive Gauche produces an accessible, friendly wine, but one that lacks the punch of Le Cran. From the 2012 vintage tasted in 2019: *"The nose opens with attractive floral notes and a pretty fruit aroma of ripe peaches. On the palate, the wine benefits from a silky texture and a supple, approachable feel, but there is not the tension and depth that one finds in Le Cran."* ***

A single vineyard vintage is produced in Mailly from the parcel Les Chalois, 0.4 hectares in reasonably flat, deep clay soils planted to old vine Pinot Noir. Although I have yet to taste the finished wine, a vin clair from the warm 2018 vintage had an admirable freshness and should make a wine of structure and charm. Also, a single vineyard vintage wine is produced from Les Sablons in Rilly using the same methods. The parcel is .45 ha, and the vines are more than 30 years of age. I tasted the 2013 vintage in 2019: *"This Blanc de Noirs is from a small parcel in Rilly with sandy limestone soils. The wine is silky and expressive, with no hint of heaviness. Still very primary, it should continue to drink well for years to come."* ***

Beaux Regards is a Blanc de Blancs produced from Chardonnay in two lieux-dits in Ludes: Beaux Regards (planted in 1964), and Les Clos, planted in 1970 by the great-grandfather of Raphäel and Vincent. The vines are close to the village, on the Chigny side in a stony vineyard that provides their oldest Chardonnay fruit. The 2013 vintage is a wine of real character: *"...the result of an October harvest. The wine, dosed at 3 g/l, is creamy and rich, accessible and drinking well now. The 2012 vintage is a bit more angular and built more for long aging."* **** (Tasted in 2017)

The Rosé is called Campania Remensis (since 2009) after the name given by the Romans to the region. The fruit comes from a south-exposed vineyard with deep, sandy soils called Les Montées in the Petit Montagne village of Ormes. The fruit ripens well: the 2012 vintage was picked at 10.5°. The grapes come from the same site used for the Coteaux Champenois. The blend for the rosé is 60% Pinot Noir, 30% Chardonnay, 5% Meunier, and 5% Coteaux Champenois. The 2012 vintage was impressive during my visit in 2017: *"On the initial attack, the wine screams its Pinot Noir character, with immense red berry fruit aromas with a violet floral edge that verges on the herbal. The grapes underwent a long press for a bit of color. On the palate, it is lively and vivacious, fresh and structured without being tannic. Rewarding length and substance."* ****

The Coteaux Champenois Rouge is aged in barrels from the Domaine de la Romanée-Conti. It is 75% Pinot Noir and 25% Meunier; 70% of the fruit is fermented as whole clusters. The wine is bottled by hand (in part because they only make 500 bottles). An engaging wine, more cerebral than substantial. The 2015 vintage, tasted 2017: *"...spicy, silky, and fine, this has a lovely red fruit expression and a subtle perfume but in a high-toned register. Approachable young, should do quite well with food."* ****

A Coteaux Blanc called Les Monts Fournois was produced from old Chardonnay vines until 2013, but this fruit is now blended into the nonvintage wine. In addition to the domaine parcels, in 2014 Bérêche launched their négociant line called "Crus Selectionés," which allows them to purchase small lots of wine that reflect the specific characteristics of a given village. The villages are intended to change over time, but the current lineup features a 2005 vintage from Le Mesnil and a 2002 vintage from Rilly.

33 Route de Louvois 51500 Le Craon de Ludes | 03 26 61 13 28
www.bereche.com

Emmanuel Brochet

Region: Montagne de Reims | Terroir: Petite Montagne

To leave Reims, one takes the main road to the south, and then the autoroute, driving through an urban sprawl that leads past the suburb of Bezannes, where the TGV terminal is located. Driving through roundabout after roundabout, one passes what must rank among the largest supermarkets in Northern France, the E. Leclerc in Champfleury. A few kilometers on the other side of this massive shopping agglomeration, however, is one of the most dedicated producers of artisanal Champagne, Emmanuel Brochet, and his vineyard Le Mont Benoit. The Brochet family has owned vines here for several generations, but until recently, the land was leased. In 1997, Emmanuel took the lease back and began to produce his own Champagne. His 2.5 hectare vineyard, all in one single parcel, has been farmed organically since 2008. He gradually reduced the use of all synthetic products beginning in 2002 and released his first certified organic Champagne in 2011, labeled with the name of the vineyard, and his attention to detail in the vineyard is legendary.

He is just as careful in the winery. He uses a small press he purchased in 2006 to press each lot separately and ferments in cask after a short settling. He uses only the cuvée and sells off the tailles. In recent vintages, he has used native yeasts exclusively for the alcoholic fermentation and is experimenting with doing the second fermentation with native yeasts as well. The wines are kept on the fine lees until bottling, which is done without fining or filtration. Le Mont Benoit is a non-vintage, and the malolactic fermentation is done. He reserves the fruit from the old vines, taking only the heart of the cuvée, to produce two vintage wines where the malo is blocked. The parcel of old vine Meunier that he bottles separately in some years is known as Les Hauts Meuniers. These vines were planted in 1962, and today give concentrated wines with character. From 2012, tasted in 2017: "*...from fruit on the top of the hill planted in 1962, this has notes of pomelo and tangerine, and a fresh, floral background which enchants while the structured, yet silky and* *expressive texture is supported by fresh acidity that leads to a lin-gering, subtle finish. No dosage, but the wine never loses its ele-gance or finesse."* ****

There also is a block of Chardonnay that has been isolat-ed and is bottled in some years as Les Hauts Chardonnays. The 2009 vintage was a triumph: *"...creamy, and seductive, this old vine cuvée in chalky soil has exotic notes of tropical fruit as well as refreshing citrus. On the palate, it is ethereal and crisp, yet there are surprising persistence and depth."* **** (Tasted 2015)

7 Impasse Brochet 51500 Villers-aux-Nœuds | 03 26 06 99 68
[No Website]

Chartogne-Taillet

Region: Montagne de Reims | Terroir: Massif de St.-Thierry

Merfy is located in the Massif de Saint-Thierry, which seems to lie almost in the suburbs just north and west of Reims itself in the subregion known as Val de Reims, planted in mostly sandy soils. Grape growing here dates to the 7th Century, and while Chartogne-Taillet was formed in 1920, the Chartogne family traces its roots here to the 19th Century, and the Taillet family goes back to the 17th Century. The family owns just over 11.5 hectares of vines spread over thirteen plots. Although Meunier dominates the village overall, the Chartogne-Taillet holdings are 50% Pinot Noir and 40% Chardonnay, with only 10% Meunier. Due to the sandy soils, three of these plots are planted with own-rooted vines.

Philippe and Elisabeth Chartogne took over the estate in 1978 and built a reputation for the reliable quality of their domaine-bottled wines. The prestige cuvée of this couple was named Cuvée Fiacre, after their ancestor Fiacre Taillet, born in 1700. The assemblage was a blend of Pinot Noir from the lieu-dit Orizeaux and Chardonnay from the Chemin de Reims vineyard, with a slight dominance of the latter. The 2005 vintage was particularly delicious: *"...fresh floral aromas and a nice bit of minerality. On the palate, the texture is creamy and there is real density and length. This substantial Champagne is a classic, delicious now, will also age for years to come."* **** (Tasted 2010)

Philippe and Elisabeth's son Alexandre worked with Anselme Selosse and returned to the family estate in 2006. He took full control the following year, and his influence has elevated the domaine to the top ranks of grower-producers in the region. In the vineyard, there is an acute sensitivity to the soil and to biodiversity, but there is no attempt at certification. No synthetic pesticides or herbicides are used, and Alexandre either plows or grasses over the vineyards. In the winery, all the ferments are done with native yeasts. After an early period of experimentation, most of the wines are fermented in old casks of various sizes, although there are concrete and stainless steel tanks at his disposal as well. The wines stay on their fine lees for extended aging before the bottling.

The Brut Millésime is a blend of Chardonnay and Pinot Noir, but all of the fruit comes from their vines in the lieu-dit Les Couarres. The 2008 vintage was superb: *"Pinot Noir dominates here, giving the wine a floral note to complement the crisp, citrus fruit and the mineral and almond notes. From a single vineyard called Les Couarres, this shows a fresh, lively character that pairs well with the tender, supple fruit expression."* **** (Tasted 2015)

One of the innovations of Alexandre has been to introduce a series of single-site Champagnes. Champagnes made from only one vineyard are known in French as *parcellaires*; some producers use this general word in the name of their cuvée. I tasted these in 2015. The first is from a vineyard called Orizeaux. Chartogne-Taillet owns a bit more than a one-half hectare here, planted to Pinot Noir in 1961. The 2010 was impressive: *"A bit closed initially, with time it shows real complexity and depth, presenting a bit of gunflint, floral aromas, and a hint of smoke over a ripe marzipan-inflected fruit character. On the palate, the wine is firm and structured, but impressively long.* **** (Tasted 2015)

Another well-known site is the lieu-dit Chemin de Reims, which has produced noted Champagnes for centuries. The Chartogne family has nearly two hectares here, mostly planted to Chardonnay, with a bit of Meunier and just a few rows of Arbanne. The Blanc de Blancs from 2008 was compelling: *"Creamy and rich with a lovely depth of flavor and complexity—there are notes of ripe apple and a hint of tropical fruit, white flowers, and a hint of brioche. The vines are planted on what is essentially a red vine terroir, and this gives the wine a savory character on the palate along with impressive weight and power."* ****

To complement the Chardonnay and Pinot Noir, there is a varietal Meunier from Les Barres, although Alexandre discounts the impact of the varietal to focus on the site. Here the vines are 60 years of age and planted ungrafted in deep sandy soils over a bedrock of chalk that is nearly two meters deep. The 2012 was spectacular: *"There is a lovely balance of creamy, truffley richness and fresh floral notes on the initial attack. On the palate the wine is lively and fresh, with a vigorous mousse and a dynamic, zesty texture, although it is not lacking in substance and holds well through the lingering finish. Dosed at 2 g/l."* **** (Tasted 2018)

Finally, there is a site called Couarres Château (different from Les Couarres). This site produces both Pinot Noir and Chardonnay; the 2010 was a vinous assemblage of 60% Pinot and 40% Chardonnay: *"Grown on cool clay soils over tuffeau* (sandy limestone more common in the Loire Valley) *provides firm acidity and lots of structure. The wine is disgorged without dosage, producing a somewhat strict wine and a bit closed on the attack initially. With time the wine begins to reveal itself first with hints of mineral, citrus, and white almonds and then a more pronounced and expressive lemon peel/saline character. There is plenty of substance, but the wine will reveal itself with time."* **** (Tasted 2015)

In addition to these, there is a holding of more than a hectare planted to Chardonnay in Les Heurtebise, which produces a single vineyard Chardonnay that I have yet to taste.

37-39 Grande Rue 51220 Merfy | 03 26 03 10 17
http://chartogne-taillet.com/

La Closerie

Region: Montagne de Reims | Terroir: Petite Montagne

The restless, experimental Jérôme Prévost continues to produce exquisite Champagnes from a terroir that has not always been highly prized. He creates his Champagne La Closerie from a 2 hectare plot of Meunier above the town of Gueux, near Vrigny, outside of Reims. The vines, inherited from his grandmother in 1987, are planted in layers of sand interspersed with layers of firmer marine deposits. At the end of the Cretaceous period this was a tidal zone, and the sea retreated and repeatedly advanced. There is chalk at a depth of 25 meters, too deep to be of use to the vines. The sandy soil presents its advantages of its own, however, because it is a reasonably warm terroir that also drains quickly. The parcel was planted in the early sixties, even though the region was not yet highly esteemed. For reasons that are still unclear, the parcel was planted on 3309C, a root-stock that was well adapted both to the terroir and to the vari-ety, even though it is often overlooked in Champagne. Prévost feels he has been lucky with his vineyard because this rootstock is one that limits vigor and increases fruit concentration. His vineyard is also among the last at this time that was planted using massale selection. Finally, he is happy that *boues de ville*[11] were never spread on his parcel.

In 1998 Prévost began to work the soil to improve its life and cause the vine roots to plunge to greater depths to find nutrients. He intentionally prunes the spurs long so he can arrange the foliage for the greatest possible photosynthesis. The Prévost philosophy is to pick as late as possible to have the greatest aromatic potential in the grapes. He contends that this aromatic potential is produced by the action of enzymes on the sugars contained within the grapes.

In the winery, Prévost avoids excessive settling of his must and does not add cultured yeast at all. He ferments in oak and leaves the vins clairs in barrel until the time from May to July when the work in the vineyard slows. During this time, the lees are not stirred, and the barrels are not topped up. The

---

11   Urban compost from Paris, spread on the vineyards until 1995 to enrich the soil.

wine is bottled without filtration or fining. Prévost does not believe in allowing his Champagne to stay a long time on the lees of the secondary fermentation because this is a cultured yeast and not indigenous to the vineyard. He usually leaves his wines on the lees 15 to 18 months, and thus cannot be labeled with the vintage. Nonetheless, each of his wines are made with grapes grown only in one single year, a practice called informally "millésime non-revendiqué". None of the wines receives dosage. The wine is called "Les Béguines" after the name of the parcel. Prior to 2002, Prévost made the champagnes at the winery of his friend Anselme Selosse, moving to his own premises in 2007. I tasted through the first three bottlings from that winery at the estate in 2007. The bottling from the 2002 harvest disgorged in 2004 was a wine of complexity and length. From my notes: *"The is a superbly elegant floral note on the nose here, but the aroma has taken on a bit more fullness and a rich, toasty character. On the palate the wine is balanced and not at all heavy. A brilliant effort from a fantastic year."* ****

The wine from the 2004 harvest was the lighter, but still lovely: *"There is a remarkable purity of ripe apple fruit and floral notes on the nose. As with all the wines there is no dosage, yet it is crisp but not severe. There is a nicely creamy texture good weight and length."* ****

The wine from the 2003 harvest was bottled at the same time, and thus was left an extra 12 months in cask prior to the prise de mousse. The name "d'Ailleurs" ["elsewhere"] was given to the wine with extended aging. From my note: *"The aromas here are ripe apricot, beeswax and toast overlaying exotic tropical notes. On the palate it is dense, but shows remarkable balance given the year. Perhaps the single greatest effort I have seen in this anomalous year. Prévost recommends decanting."* *****

Ten years on I again tasted through the range with Prévost. The wine based on the 2013 harvest was lovely – again a very nice success in a difficult year. *"Mineral and saline notes accent the citrus fruit on the nose. On the palate there is freshness and tension but the wine is not thin and retains a marvelous balance."* **** The experiment with extended aging on the lees had been repeated with the wine based on the 2012 harvest. *"Ripe apple and richer notes of apricot and orange blossom on the nose. On the palate there is a silky texture and noticeably more weight although the essential finesse still comes through."* ***** Prévost also showed a Rosé made from the same parcel. This wine, called "Fac-simile" is exquisite: *"Perhaps the lightest, finest rose ever. On the nose there are barely hints of rose petal and no red fruit aromas to speak of. The finesse and elegance on the palate are superb."* ****

These are lovely wines that are unfortunately produced in tiny quantities but well worth seeking out.

2 rue de la Petite-Montagne 51390 Gueux | 03 26 03 48 60
http://champagnelacloserie.fr/en/

Marie Courtin

Region: Côte des Bars | Terroir: Barséquanais

Dominique Moreau is one of the standard-bearers for the renaissance of the Aube. Her label Marie Courtin (named for her grandmother) was established to vinify the fruit from her single 2.5 hectare parcel of vines in Polisot. The vines are all located in the lieu-dit Le Tremble, planted in Kimmeridgian marls, with yellow Portlandian soil at the top of the hill reserved for the Chardonnay. As is common in the Aube, the majority (2.3 hectare) is planted to Pinot Noir, with the balance planted mostly to Chardonnay with a bit of Pinot Blanc. The estate is run according to biodynamic principles, both in the vineyards and in the winery, and Moreau is certified organic and biodynamic. After fermentation, the base wines stay on their lees and are normally bottled in Mid-July, since Moreau feels that the lees nourish the wine. No reserve wine is used, which means that all of the Champagnes come from one vintage year. Sometimes the vintage is not noted on the label when the aging of the wine on the lees is not long enough. Dosage is not used outside of the rosé.

From her single parcel, Moreau produces a variety of wines. Much of the focus here is on Pinot Noir, and three of the wines are Blancs de Noirs. The first, called Resonance, is tank fermented. From my visit in 2017: *"The 2013 shows the wonderful results Moreau regularly achieves. This has a lovely richness and body, but there is great clarity and freshness as well. A thrilling introduction."* ****

The next, Efflorescence, is produced from the old vines in the vineyard, and the fruit is entirely fermented in cask. From the same visit: *"The 2014 Efflorescence opens with bright, concentrated fruit aromas of white flowers with hints of mineral, apple, and lime. On the palate, the wine has a silky texture but firm acidity and impressive length. There is no dosage, but there is also no acerbity here, just silky, luscious fruit."* ****

Perhaps the most technically impressive wine is the Concordance, done entirely in tank without any addition of sulfur. From the 2013 vintage: *"There is a superb purity of fruit* *for a wine done without sulfur. To avoid complications, the malo-lactic fermentation is carried out. The wine is rich and expressive, yet not heavy at all, with a suggestion of marzipan and fresh white flowers that linger on the delightful finish. A tour de force of wine-making technique as well as of terroir."* ***** (Tasted 2017)

There are also two Blanc de Blancs. The wine called Eloquence is fermented half in tank, half in cask, with the malolactic done. The 2013 vintage was superb: *"Very pleasant, the wine shows an impressive ripeness and body for a Blanc de Blancs without dosage, with floral and almond notes, and a slightly fat texture that lacks just a bit of tension."* **** There is another wine called Presence, which is a blend of Chardonnay and Pinot Blanc. I have not yet tasted the finished wine, but a 2017 vin clair tasted in 2018 was surprisingly silky and dense for the vintage, with a waxy texture and plenty of finesse.

Finally, there are also rosés made in special years. The 2011 Indulgence is 100% Pinot Noir crushed by foot and macerated for four days to produce a vinous, delightfully playful wine: *"Lovely and tender with an accessible, silky fruit up front, a hint of toast, and a creamy, silky texture on the palate,"* *** (tasted 2015) Another rosé, called Allégeance, was also produced in 2013. Like the Concordance, no sulfur was added. From my visit in 2017: *"Another wine of superb clarity, this is a fantastic showcase for red berry fruit as well as a gentle note of roast almonds and cream. This is a rosé de saignée with 30 hours of maceration, and yet no sulfur is used in the production. Dosed at 3 g/lit."* ****

13 rue du Tonnerre 10110 Polisot | 03 25 38 57 45
[No Website]

Diebolt-Vallois

Region: Côte des Blancs | Terroir: Côte des Blancs

Based in Cramant, Diebolt-Vallois is indisputably one of the top growers in the Côte de Blancs. The reputation of the estate was built through the hard work and dedication of Jacques Diebolt, and today it is run by his children Isabelle and Arnaud. The family owns 11 hectares, mainly in Cramant and Cuis, with a bit in Chouilly and Epernay, and a tiny plot in Le Mesnil. The jewels here are the marvelous holdings in Cramant, which include the lieux-dits Les Pimonts, Les Buzons, Les Fourches, Gouttes d'Or, Rouilles, and Gros Mont, as well as choice parcels in Cuis, Chouilly, and Epernay. In the vineyard, the Diebolt family eschews organic certification but works in a sustainable way ("meticulous *lutte raisonné*," according to Isabelle), either grassing over between the rows or working the soils manually to aerate them and employing sexual confusion for pest control. In the winery, there is close attention to detail in the vinification the wines, as they are made parcel by parcel. The vins clairs are fermented in a combination of tank and barrel, and the malolactic fermentation is normally finished. The top wine, Fleur de Passion is fermented exclusively in cask and the malolactic fermentation is not done. The wine is bottled unfiltered.

The "regular" vintage wine can be long-lived. This is produced from an assemblage of Cuis, Chouilly, and the younger vines from Cramant, fermented in tank. In 2012, the somewhat modest 1997 vintage was maturing but still youthful: "...*this shows great aromatics as it opens, with notes of coconut, hazelnut, almond, and buttered toast. On the palate, the wine had a waxy mineral feel with a long, structured finish. There is sufficient substance here to age the wine for another decade.*" **** The same tasting included a revelatory taste of the 1976, mature, but very much alive: "...*there is a coffee/truffle nose here, with notes of game, earth, and leather. Creamy and nutty, long and complex, this wine still retains a vibrant freshness. On the palate, it has remarkable (especially considering the year) acidity and a vinous texture. Superb.*" *****

While the vintage is reliable year in and year out (and produced in reasonable quantities up to 1,000 cases), the real showstopper at Diebolt-Vallois is the cask-fermented Blanc de Blancs prestige cuvée Fleur de Passion. In a top vintage such as 2008, it can be among the best wines of the Côte des Blancs. *"Truly spectacular wine. Produced from the seven best parcels with the oldest vines, all from Cramant, this starts with pronounced tropical aromas of coconut and passion fruit touched with exotic spices and a bit of brioche. The sense of substantial wet chalk minerality comes out on the palate, but the wine never loses its charm and elegance. Marvelous intensity and concentration: the wine has more substance, but there are a balancing freshness and the extract to sustain a long and lingering finish. One of the greats, this will age for decades to come."* ***** (Tasted 2018)

84 rue Neuve 51530 Cramant | 03 26 57 54 92
www.diebolt-vallois.com

Pascal Doquet

Region: Côte des Blancs | Terroir: Côte des Blancs

The legends surrounding Le Mont Aimé go back to the castle that Blanche of Navarre built there in 1210 AD where her son Thibault IV burned 183 suspected Cathar heretics at the stake before leaving for the Crusades. Today, Pascal Doquet is creating legends of a much more appealing nature. Doquet is based in Vertus, just north of Mont Aimé; his family holdings go back several generations to the founders of the Jeanmaire brand. Pascal's grandfather André Jeanmaire began bottling his own wine during the Great Depression, and his uncle produced champagne under this label until it was sold to Oudinot in 1978. Jeanmaire's daughter married Michel Doquet and the couple formed Doquet-Jeanmaire in 1982. Pascal directed the family estate from his father's retirement in 1995 until he and his sister divided the estate in 2003. Since 2004, he bottles under the Pascal Doquet label.

Doquet owns a total of 8.69 hectares. 60% of the vines are located in the Côte des Blancs with 40% in the Vitryat, or the Côte du Perthois as Doquet refers to the region. Chardonnay accounts for 95% of the vineyard area. Doquet has been certified organic since 2010, although he has been working without herbicides since 2001. He believes deeply in the life of the soil, has cover crops planted between the rows in all vineyards, and tills the soil as needed. Yields are modest. In the winery, Doquet uses native yeast for the fermentation, and since 2016, he has employed a yeast cultured in-house for the secondary fermentation. Approximately one-third of the base wines are fermented in cask overall, but a slightly higher proportion is customary for the vintage wines. Malolactic fermentation is normally finished, and dosages are low across the board.

The first of the vintage wines is the Vertus Cœur de Terroir, produced from a blend of fruit from mid-slope parcels in Vertus, where Doquet owns more than two hectares. These sites produce a fresh result, even in warm years such as 2005: *"...presents a concentrated, lemony fruit on the attack with saline mineral notes that develop with time. There is a fine, toasty autolysis that lends complexity to the aromas. On the palate, the wine is ripe but not flabby and retains a reassuring taut acidity that leads to a lingering finish."* **** (tasted 2018)

As with the Vertus bottling, the Mont Aimé can be superb. It is structured, and fine even in warmer years. Doquet has 1.2 hectares of vines here. The 2006 has impressed me on numerous occasions: From 2017: *"50% cask fermentation; 8 years on the lees. The wine is marked by oak spice on the initial attack, but then a lovely tropical fruit appears with time. The palate is lushly dense and wonderfully silky, with a lovely, lingering finish. Dosed at 4 g/l."* **** (Tasted 2017)

Doquet also has a generous holding of vineyards in Le Mesnil, including parcels in Champ d'Alouettes and Les Migraines. This fruit produces a different style than the wines in Vertus, but equally impressive. From my notes on the 2008 Le Mesnil Cœur de Terroir, tasted in 2019: *"Spectacular density, concentration, and minerality, with a creamy texture. The aromas open with citrus and spice and moves on to smoke, salt, and fresh brioche. Produced from old-vine fruit from the lieux-dits Champ d'Alouettes and Les Migraines, dosed at 3 g/l"* ****

44 chemin du Moulin de la Cense Bizet 51130 Vertus | 03 26 52 16 50
www.champagne-doquet.com

Drappier

Region: Côte des Bars | Terroir: Bar-sur-Aubois

Urville is at the edge of the Champagne universe. It is scarcely moments from Burgundy and can seem like light-years from the heart of the Marne. Yet, the Champagnes produced here at Drappier are comparable to or better than most similarly-sized operations anywhere in the region. Champagne Drappier was founded in 1808 and makes excellent use of the cellars initially built in 1152 by Bernard of Clairvaux and his Cistercian monks. Today Michel Drappier is the seventh generation to develop his family's estate located on the eastern edge of the Aube départe-ment. Drappier owns 57 hectares, and they purchase fruit from another 50 hectares to produce approximately 1.4 million bottles per year. Pinot Noir accounts for 70% of the planted surface. Chardonnay and Meunier are also present, but so are Arbanne, Petit Meslier, Pinot Blanc, and Pinot Gris. The vines are tended using organic methods where possible, although the house is not certified.

In the winery there is minimal use of sulfur. Fermenta-tions are done in a combination of stainless steel and in cask – either small *barriques* or larger foudres. For the vintage wines, only the cuvée is used. Base wines for some wines see a year in cask on the lees before bottling. The juice is pressed in four Coquard presses using very low pressure. There is no filtration, the wines are moved by gravity and static settling is used. The liqueur for the dosage is aged in special wooden casks for 15 to 25 years and in some cases for an even more extended period in demi-johns.

The house's reputation for its vintages rests upon two foundations, the first being its Brut Millésime Exception. True to the tradition of the Aube, the wine is often 60% Pinot Noir. Because of the structure that this Pinot Noir brings, the wine can be long-lived. A magnum of the 1979 vintage drunk in 2018 was showing well: *"The wine is still fresh and youthful. Despite some hints of truffle on the nose, it is dominated by toasty brioche and fresh-baked Tarte Tatin, with just a suspicion of sous-bois.*

The mousse is vigorous, and the texture on the palate is at once rich, silky, and fine. There is enough freshness here to carry the wine to a lovely, lingering finish." ****

There is also a late-disgorged version of the vintage wine that is released later. I was with the 2002 Œnothèque, drunk in 2019. *"A blend of 90% Pinot Noir and 3% Meunier with 7% Chardonnay, disgorged after more than 15 years on the lees and dosed at 3 g/l. The nose is Pinot Noir, with ripe red fruits, toasted almonds, fresh and dried flowers, and a suggestion of ground coffee. On the palate, the wine is rich and vinous, slightly soft but approachable, with a delightful edge of truffle at the end."* ****

The real Drappier showstopper is their prestige cuvée Grande Sendrée. It is produced from one single vineyard that had been devastated by fire in the early 19th century. Approximately one-third of the base wine is fermented and aged in cask. The 2008 was particularly successful: *"The nose starts off with prominent notes of exotic tropical fruit touched with a suggestion of freshly ground coffee and buttered toast. On the palate, the texture is creamy and rich, with lovely finesse and impressive length. There is enough substance here to carry it to a long finish, but there is no heaviness at all. This is a sumptuously good prestige cuvée that should not be overlooked. 55% Pinot Noir, 45% Chardonnay, dosed at 5 g/l, and bottled with <30mg SO2."* **** (Tasted 2017)

Rue des Vignes 10200 Urville | 03 25 27 40 15
http://www.champagne-drappier.com

Egly-Ouriet

Region: Montagne de Reims | Terroir: Grande Montagne South

Vinous is the first adjective that comes to mind when describing the wines produced by Francis Egly at Egly-Ouriet. While there are other superb growers on the south face of the Montagne, these wines have ascended to the top level of prestige among connoisseurs because of this richness. And yet, there is nothing overdone here: Egly does everything to ensure that the wines are balanced and elegant. It is the juxtaposition of a deft balance with the power and richness that come from the warmest part of the Montagne and the use of old vines that makes these wines so compelling. Although there is only one vintage-dated Champagne in the range (and one Coteaux), this estate proves that less can be better.

The domaine traces its origin to 1930 but initially little of the wine was bottled under their own label, and the bulk of the fruit was sold to négociants. As the domaine passed from father to son, more property was acquired. Francis took over the domaine in 1980, and recently added vineyards that bring the total to 17 hectares of vines, 8 of which are located in Ambonnay. The Vintage Brut and the Coteaux are both made exclusively with old vine fruit from Ambonnay. Part of the secret at Egly-Ouriet is that the vine age is relatively high, with an average of 40 years across the domaine and some parcels that are much older. The fruit is picked late, and the must is fermented in cask on native yeasts. The malolactic fermentation is sometimes blocked (as with the current vintage release of 2009), but this is not uniformly the case. The base wines stay on the lees usually for more than six months until they fall bright on their own, and then they are bottled without fining or filtration. Aging on the lees is long – the 2009 was nine years before being disgorged. Dosage may vary slightly according to the conditions of the year, but it is always Extra Brut.

The old vine Blanc de Noirs is a parcellaire from a lieu-dit called Les Crayères with old vines. From 1989 until 2007 this was made from a single year, although it was not vintage-dated. Since the release based on 2007, however, reserve wines from previous years have been added to the mix. The current release, for example, is 60% from the 2012 vintage and 40% from 2011.

The Brut Grand Cru Millésime 2009 tasted in 2019 was almost absurdly luxurious: *"A blend of 30% Chardonnay and 70% Pinot Noir fermented on native yeasts in cask (30% of which were new), this is not a Champagne for the faint of heart. On the initial attack, the wine is marked by oak, but with time a spicy, ripe fruit character evolves that combines tropical notes, ripe apple, and almost a suggestion of red fruit with hints of roast almond, toast, and a suggestion of coffee. On the palate, the wine is powerful and full-bodied, yet it retains a lively, fresh acidity to balance out the extract and lingers almost imposingly on the palate. This is a wine of great depth that should age well for decades in a proper cellar."* ****

The Coteaux was oddly perhaps less sumptuous on the palate but sang in a Burgundian fashion. Tasted in 2011: *"The 2008 Coteaux Champenois from Egly-Ouriet showed lovely ripe, juicy cherry aromas on the nose, a spot-on ringer for a Burgundy from the same vintage. There is an exuberant fruitiness, and none of the thin, tart feel that one fears from this category. The wine is balanced and surprisingly full-bodied. Although it drinks well now, this is a wine that will improve with a bit of time in the cellar."* ***

15 rue de Trepail 51550 Ambonnay | 03 26 57 00 70
[No Website]

Pierre Gimonnet

Region: Côte de Blancs | Terroir: Côte des Blancs

Didier and Olivier Gimonnet produce Champagnes that stand out for their purity of the fruit. The Gimonnet family has lived in the village of Cuis since the middle of the 17th century, and began to bottle wines under their own label in the early 20th century. Today the estate includes 29.4 hectares, much of it in Cuis, but also three hectares in the lieu-dit Montaigu in Chouilly planted in 1951, and other old vines in Cramant that came from Michel's wife, a member of the Larmandier family. Notable Gimonnet old vine parcels are two plots of 100-year-old vines: one in Fond du Bateau in Chouilly and another in Buissons in Cramant. Of their grand cru vineyards, 80% of the vines are more than 50 years of age, and the oldest were planted in 1911. The vineyards are sustainably farmed, with some parcels grassed over and others tilled according to their needs; herbicides are not used. Almost without fail, the vintage will start early chez Gimonnet, and yet, it will be picked very ripe - at an average of 11° potential alcohol, with the oldest parcels picked closer to 12°. In the winery, the fermentations are done in stainless and carried out in small tanks to enable parcel-by-parcel vinification. The must is so rich that chaptalization is rarely required. Malolactic fermentation is usually done, and following this, the pH is generally between 3.00 and 3.05, with total acidity between 6.5 to 7 g/l.

Among the vintage wines, the Cuvée Gastronome is special. Less yeast is added during the prise de mousse, resulting in a level of pressure between 2.5-3 bars, half that of regular Champagne. This particular cuvée tends to be about 70% grand cru fruit – mostly Chouilly, with a bit of Cramant, and some from Oger -- with the balance coming from premier cru Cuis for freshness. I like the style very much. The recent 2004 vintage was delightful: *"A minerally, bright, lemony fruit character on the nose and a soft, lovely mousse, a silky texture, and a lingering finish."* **** (Tasted 2012)

The next vintage wine in the Gimonnet lineup is called the Cuvée Fleuron, which is considered the flagship of the line.

It is usually a complex blend of fruit from many different villages. For example, the 2009 was based on Chouilly, assembled with more fruit from Cramant and a bit from Oger and Cuis: *"Plenty of substance but there is still freshness and minerality here to complement the ripe apple fruit. Dosed at 4.5 g/l."* **** (Tasted 2019)

The Cuvée Oenophile is the same blend as the Fleuron, but there is no dosage. I was particularly taken with the 2008: *"Superb. This opens with a lime peel nose and hints of mineral and gradually opens up with time to show a smoky, mineral side. The fruit character continues to open on the palate with notes of passionfruit. The wine is supremely fresh and concentrated, almost massive, yet it never becomes acerbic or loses its engaging, silky texture. Wonderful length, marvelous wine."* **** (Tasted 2019)

Another important cuvée at Gimonnet is the Special Club bottling. It is usually assembled from different villages, as is the Fleuron, but the vineyard breakdown is different. I was charmed by the 2010: *"...mostly old vines from the Cramant lieu-dits of Buisson and Fond du Bateau along with some fruit from Mont Aigu in Chouilly planted 1951 and some bits from Cuis and Vertus. The result is lovely -- creamy, toasty, and rich without heaviness. Ripe pear and brioche aromas and a sensuous texture on the palate."* *** (Tasted 2015) The wine holds very well. My notes on the 1982 vintage: *"Complex, with abundant tropical fruit still on the nose touched with a bit of smoke, a touch of honey, and some aromas of crème brûlée, The texture is creamy and very fine, no doubt aided by the extra brut dosage at 3 g/l"* ***** (Tasted 2016)

Recently, the house began to produce separate mono-cru versions of the Special Club, with one from Oger and one from Chouilly. Both were marvelous. Didier remarked that they usually don't do single cru and that the version from Chouilly was not his favorite. Still, it demonstrated what he wanted to showcase – the genius of the fruit from the Montaigu lieu-dit. The house has 3 hectares in Mont Aigu, commonly considered among the best in Chouilly, and this is from vines planted in 1951 (67%) and in 1991 (33%). My notes on the 2012: *"White flowers and a gentle, soft pear fruit character. The texture is silky and very fine, but not lacking underlying tension."* *** (Tasted 2017)

The mono-cru from Oger produced in the same year was equally delightful in 2017 but quite different: *"2012 Oger Grand Cru Special Club has lovely lemony fruit with a soft, creamy floral note. The wine is silky and supple and shows great delicacy and finesse. Produced from the lieux-dits Terres de Noël and Brulis, Champs Nérons, and Fondy. The fruit was picked at 11.5% potential alcohol, and dosed at 3 g/l."* ****

Finally, there is the Cuvée Millésime de Collection, an impressive wine. In 2006, for example, it was one of the wines of the vintage: *"Still youthful, but the lemony tropical fruit is starting to take on a discreet note of ground coffee. Still opening up, but with massive potential for future development. Intensely structured and very long. 45% old vine fruit from Cramant, 25% old vine fruit from Chouilly, with the balance from Cuis, dosed at 3 g/l."* **** (Tasted 2016)

1 rue de la Republique 51530 Cuis | 03 26 59 78 70
www.champagne-gimonnet.com

Olivier Horiot

Region: Côte de Blancs | Terroir: Barséquanais

A tasting with Olivier Horiot and his charming wife Marie is always a delight. He is one of the top growers in the Aube and the leading light in Les Riceys, the village with the largest vineyard in the Champagne region. Located on the border with Burgundy, Les Riceys itself is three tiny hamlets: Ricey Bas, Ricey Haut, and Ricey Haute Rive; the oldest, Ricey Bas, dates to Gallo-Roman times. Olivier's father, Serge Horiot, was the co-founder of the Coopérative Viticole de Ricey-Bas, and Olivier still sends some of his production to the co-op and produces Champagnes under the Serge Horiot brand. After assuming control of the winery from his father in 2000, his initial focus was the production of still wines, including the notable single parcel Rosé des Riceys from En Valingrain and En Barmont, as well as a Coteaux Champenois from each also: a red from En Barmont and a white from En Valingrain. In 2004 he also began to make vintage Champagne under his own name, fermented in cask and aged on the lees for a year (with *bâtonnage*), which he believes shows the character of the vintage to its fullest.

Olivier and Marie work 8.7 hectares of vines with a meticulous respect for nature. They began to implement biodynamic practices in 2002, although the process of certification was started in 2007, and they received the official certification in 2017. All of the vines are in Les Riceys, but the jewels of the estate are the parcels in En Valingrin and En Barmont. En Barmont is an east-facing site with deep, dark clay over Kimmeridgian marl, while En Vaulingrin has a southern exposure but a lighter white clay on the same Kimmeridgian base. All seven authorized grape varieties planted: 75% Pinot Noir, 10%, and 5% Pinot Blanc, with the remaining 10% is divided between Meunier, Arbanne, Petit Meslier, and Pinot Gris.

The newly expanded winery, completed in 2012, incorporates gravity-flow production and allows experimentation with a variety of fermentation vessels such as concrete tanks, eggs, and amphorae. Most of the wines, however, are fermented and aged in cask in an almost Burgundian fashion. For example, the reds and rosés use whole cluster fermentation, and the winemaking is as natural as possible: no added yeast, little sulfur, and no fining or filtration. Horiot also works without temperature control to make the wines adapt to the natural cycles of the terroir. They are blended and then allowed to rest in cask for another six months before bottling.

To fully understand the Horiots' work, it is best to start with the Rosé des Riceys. This still rosé wine made by a maceration of whole bunches in carbonic maceration is produced only in Les Riceys. Although not well known outside the region, the style is important here—this is the only village where it is possible to produce red, white, and pink still wine as well as Champagne. My comparative tasting of these at the estate in 2015 was enlightening. En Valingrin: *"En Valingrin in 2011 shows a pronounced red fruit character with a hint of smoke and a savory element, almost a whiff of bacon on the initial attack. The trademark softness of the terroir shows itself on the palate with a lovely complex finish."* **** En Barmont from the same year: *"En Barmont opens with forward, light-toned raspberry notes on the initial attack. The vines are planted in clay soil and produce a wine that is typically more polished and less rustic than the En Valingrin. On the palate the wine is fresh and perhaps more direct, if less complex, with a silky texture and a marvelous floral note at the end."* **** (Tasted 2015)

These same distinctions also show up in the Champagnes. From my note for the Sève Rosé 2011: *"Produced exclusively from fruit from En Barmont, this shows beautiful floral and berry aromas on the nose and a light, elegant mousse. On the palate, there is a delightful freshness and elegance. A real treat."* **** And of the Blanc from the same year: *"...fresh and a bit soft, with a supple, silky texture and a delicate elegance."* **** (Both tasted 2017)

Perhaps most interesting among the Champagne is the 5 Sens, made from one barrel each of wines fermented from the old vine fruit from five grapes: Arbanne, Pinot Blanc, Pinot Meunier, Pinot Noir, and Chardonnay: *"The result is lush and dense, with hints of spice, smoke, and brioche on the nose. The texture is supple and velvety, with impressive concentration and length."* **** (tasted 2017)

It would be a mistake to leave Horiot without tasting the Coteaux Champenois. The red from En Barmont produced exceptional results in 2015: *"The Coteaux Champenois is produced using semi-carbonic maceration, with the clusters loaded into the tank and fermented with the juice that is naturally expressed from the grapes. Ferments are done with wild yeast, and the wines are aged on the lees without racking, fining or filtration. The wine does a year in cask and then another six months in concrete. In 2015, this vineyard produced a Coteaux that shows an exquisite ripe cherry fruit but also plenty of earthy complexity. The texture is silky and fine, and there is an impressive length to the finish,"* **** (tasted 2017) In En Valingrain, there are about 500 vines producing white grapes, split evenly between Chardonnay and Pinot Blanc. The vines, however, are co-planted in a field blend with the rest of the fruit. Olivier's solution is to pick the reds first and allow the whites to sit on the vines for approximately two additional weeks, which gives a style he loves. The 2015 was beguiling: *"...rich and exotic, with aromas of peach and ripe pear colored with a bit of spice and smoke as well as a hint of licorice or fennel. The fruit was pressed and run directly into cask for fermentation. The texture is solid and dense but the wine never loses its elegance."* **** (Tasted 2017)

25 rue de Bise 10340 Les Riceys | 03 25 29 32 16
www.horiot.fr

André Jacquart

Region: Côte de Blancs | Terroir: Côte des Blancs

Marie Duval-Doyard is doing superb work with her family's vineyards. Family on both sides have been in the champagne industry for generations. Her father is descended from Doyard family who have been growers in Vertus since the 17th century, and her paternal great-grandfather was Maurice Doyard, one of the co-founders of the CIVC. The Doyards have been domaine bottling some of their production since the 1920s. Marie's maternal grandfather was André Jacquart, a grower from Le Mesnil, who began to domaine bottle in 1958. During Marie's youth, her mother, Chantal Doyard-Jacquart, and her father, Pascal Doyard, both worked in their family's respective houses in Le Mesnil and Vertus. In 2004 they decided to join their family holdings producing an exceptional estate that includes 24 hectares in all: 16 hectares split between Chardonnay from Vertus and Le Mesnil, 3.5 hectares in the Aube, and 4.5 hectares in the Aisne devoted to Pinot Noir and Pinot Meunier. Champagne André Jacquart is a *récoltant-manipulant* and no relationship to the Jacquart brand produced by the Alliance Champagne co-op.

The estate is today run by Marie and her brother Benoît, who moved the operations to Vertus to allow an expansion of the cellars. Benoît looks after the vineyards, Marie the commercial matters, and they collaborate on the winemaking. The fruit is pressed in Vertus using two Coquard PAI presses (see glossary). While their grandparents' style was traditional and featured ferments entirely done in stainless, the new method employs mostly fermentation in used Burgundian barrels. Malolactic fermentation is blocked, and the dosage is kept low. Currently, the house is producing approximately 100,000 bottles/year, employing only fruit from the Côte de Blancs and keeping only the cuvée. The remaining must is sold off to négociant houses. The vins clairs are left for five to eight months on the lees before bottling. The wines age for five (for the non-vintage) to eight years (for the vintage) and are disgorged with low dosage levels done with concentrated grape must made from their own fruit.

The one vintage Champagne is produced from pure Mesnil fruit issuing from 50-year-old vineyards. It is fermented fully in cask and dosed at 3 g/l. The results for the '06 , were fantastic: *"...a nose that begins with a gourmand note of ripe, fresh Golden Delicious apples, flaky pastry, crème fraiche, and brioche and with time shows the smoke, toast, and minerality of the appellation. On the palate, the wine is rich but not soft, with plenty of structure and concentration and yet a velvety and luxurious texture and a lengthy finish."* **** (Tasted in 2017)

63 avenue de Bammental 51130 Vertus | 03 26 57 52 29
[No Website]

Jacquesson

Location: Marne Valley | Terroir: Blended

As Jacquesson moves into its third century of winemaking, it is one of the oldest Champagne houses in existence and at the same time one of the most innovative. The house was founded in Châlons-sur-Marne in 1798 by Claude Jacquesson and his son Maurice, known as Memmie. Memmie's son Adolphe joined the firm in 1832 and assumed ownership in 1835 upon the death of his father. He worked alongside Johann-Joseph Krug, who began with the firm in 1834, and gradually became the general manager of the firm. In 1841, Krug married Emma Jaunay, Adolphe's sister-in-law, and in 1843 he left to form his eponymous firm. With Adolphe at its head, sales at Jacquesson reached one million bottles. In 1844, he trademarked the invention of the *muselet* or cage that holds the cork in the bottle. In the 1860s, however, business fell off, and by 1873 the house was nearly bankrupt.

Following Adolphe's death, Jacquesson was sold several times, ultimately becoming the property of the wine broker Léon de Tassigny in 1925. De Tassigny improved both the reputation and landholdings of the house before eventually selling to Jean Chiquet in 1974. Jean's sons Jean-Hervé and Laurent direct the house today. Under their thoughtful administration, Jacquesson has made a continual improvement, producing less wine, but better quality. Formerly, there were 15 hectares of house-owned vineyards and 30 hectares of contracts for a total production of 450,000 bottles. The Chiquet brothers have increased the vineyard holdings to 17 hectares in the Grande Vallée and 11 hectares in the Côte des Blancs. They also purchase fruit, but only from growers located near the house-owned parcels, which means that the house controls all of the grapes that it presses. Jacquesson only uses the cuvée, and they sell off the tailles as well as the first 50 liters to come off the press to ensure the purity of the must. Although the total production has declined, Jean-Hervé believes that quality has increased. Few wine lovers would disagree.

In the vineyard the Chiquet brothers believe in the use of cover crops wherever possible. Where this causes too much competition for the vines, the soil is tilled instead of using herbicides. And in recent years, they have employed two different grape growing strategies: for one-third of the vineyards, they have opted entirely for organic grape growing, and for the remaining two-thirds, they do two treatments, one before the flowering and one after. This allows them to use less copper sulfate when treating the vines later in the season. Although copper sulfate is permitted for organic grape growing, at Jacquesson they try to limit its use as much as possible.

Jean-Hervé gave an interesting explanation of the technique for pressing used at Jacquesson. He explained that process of *retrousser*, which literally means "to roll up," as in rolling up one's sleeves. In winemaking, it translates more as "forking-over" and describes the action of using a pitchfork to pile the pressed grapes upon themselves once they have been pressed. Three retrousses can give anywhere from 17 hl to 23 hl; this is what Jacquesson takes for the cuvée (technically it is 20.5 hl). Everything afterward is regarded as tailles and not used in the Jacquesson blends. Although by law they are obligated to press the full 20.5 hl from the marc, this juice is sold off to other négociants. Nearly 90% of the base wines are fermented in large oak fermenters. The malolactic fermentation is done for all wines. The wine is racked but is kept in contact with the fine lees, and 60% is aged in large casks. The wines are bottled without fining or filtration. Jacquesson to ages all Champagnes on the lees for at least three years, and the dosage is uniformly light. Although most of the wines receive no more than 5 g/l they are not explicitly labeled as Extra Brut.

In addition to their admirable Cuvée 700 Series of non-vintage wines (not discussed here), the house produces several compelling vintage wines. The flagship wine at Jacquesson used to be the *Grand Vin Signature*, entirely fermented in cask and aged for seven years or more prior to disgorgement. The 1995 showed a complex and nuanced nose: *"...real substance and depth of flavor, leading with fresh flowers, apple tart fruit character and a hint of brioche. Concentrated and fresh, it lingers satisfyingly on the palate."* **** (Tasted 2019)

In 1995 Jacquesson began to experiment with single-vineyard wines, starting with a Blanc de Blancs from the Corne Bautray vineyard in Dizy. The 2007 was one of the most compelling wines from the vintage. My notes from a visit in 2017: *"Produced from Chardonnay planted in 1960 high on the slope in Dizy with a southwest exposition in clay with limestone pebbles; 'Chardonnay from the wrong place,' according to Jean-Hervé. Quite simply, this is among the richest of the '07s I have had. The nose has a bit of ripe orchard fruit and spice along with a pleasantly toasty autolytic character. On the palate, the wine is dense and concentrated—more than one would expect from 2007. Disgorged without dosage in January 2016."* ****

Historically, Jacquesson has had a long history of producing Blanc de Blancs. One of the first was a mono-cru version from Avize, a practice that dates to the time of de Tassigny, who purchased land there in 1925. Before the Chiquet Family, this wine was a blend of vintages, but they transitioned it in the 1990s to the vintage wine it is today (latest vintage being the 2000). Starting with the 2002 vintage, one of the elements that had gone into the Avize blend was isolated for use as the single-vineyard Champ Caïn. I tasted the 2008 in 2017: *"Lovely. More exotic tropical fruit than the Corne Bautray bottling, this also shows a distinct mineral/saline note. On the palate, the wine is firm, with crisp acidity and a tightly wound structure, but the final impression is silky, and the finish is long."* ****

The second wine to be isolated (in 1996) was the Vauzelle Terme in Aÿ, from 100% Pinot Noir. The fruit from this vineyard produces a lush, dense, vinous wine as one might expect from a south-facing site in this sunny commune. From my notes on the 2002 vintage: *"A complex and compelling nose that opens with aromas of apricot and honey and then moves on to marzipan and toast, with a deep undercurrent that has just a hint of truffle and caramel at the end. On the palate it is rich and vinous, with full body, balanced acidity, and a finish that goes on forever."* ***** (Tasted 2017)

They also have produced several rosé wines over the years. Most recently, there was a version produced from the

Terres Rouges site in Dizy, but starting with the 2012 vintage, this will be produced as a blanc de noirs, not as a rosé. I look forward to tasting this, and even more to what the future will bring.

68 rue du Colonel Fabien 51530 Dizy | 03 26 55 68 11
www.champagnejacquesson.com

Larmandier-Bernier

Region: Côte des Blancs | Terroir: Côte des Blancs

The Larmandier family has long roots in the Côte des Blancs. Larmandier Père et Fils was established in 1899. In the 1970s, brothers Philippe and Guy split off from the family business. The domaine created by Philippe is now run by his son Pierre Larmandier. Together with his wife Sophie (aided by their son Arthur since 2017), they are producing some of the most thought-provoking wines in the Côte des Blancs. (The other branch, Champagne Guy Larmandier, is run today by Guy's widow and their children François and Marie-Hélène.) Larmandier Père et Fils was purchased by the Gimonnet family in 1987.

Based in premier cru Vertus, the wines here are some of the most exceptional work done in the region. The Larmandier-Bernier vineyards include 15 hectares in Vertus and another 3 hectares in Cramant, along with small parcels in Avize and Oger. Pierre abandoned the use of herbicides in 1992, and by 1999 he was working the entire estate biodynamically. The estate was certified organic in 2003. The vineyards are spread over 50 parcels located throughout the Côte de Blancs. The vines average 33 years of age, but some vines are much older. The fruit is pressed in a pneumatic press and settled for one to two days before being fermented on natural yeasts. Most of the ferments are done in casks with the option to use stainless steel tanks and experiments with eggs, amphorae, and other fermentation vessels. Base wines are left on the lees without racking for eleven months before being bottled without filtration.

There are three vintage wines. The first is Terre de Vertus. Initially, this was an assemblage of vins clairs fermented in both cask and in tanks. Today, however, Terre de Vertus is produced from a single lieu-dit, Les Barillers, and fermented entirely in casks. It spends five years on the lees prior to being disgorged and is shipped without dosage. The most recent vintage (2013) tasted in 2017 showed *"...abundant aromas of ripe apple and lemon peel with an underpinning of mineral notes and a well-integrated toasty yeast character. On the palate, it is certainly fresh, but also super-rich and still silky. Impressive harmony and length."* ****

The second vintage wine began life in 1988 as Vielles Vignes de Cramant; today, it is called Vieilles Vignes du Levant. The wine has always been produced from one parcel, Bourron du Levant, that has a southeast exposition that catches the rays of the rising sun (*levant,* the French term referring to the rising sun). The site is superb, and the vines are aged 56 to 80 years. The wine is usually dosed at 2 g/l. I found the 2008 vintage to be particularly delicious during my visit in 2015: *"Absolutely lovely, with an impressive density of toasted hazelnut, butter, and brioche over a ripe apple fruit on the nose. On the palate, the wine is dense and compact but still elegant and silky, never heavy. A marvel of balance and finesse."* *****

Their third and most recently created vintage cuvée is the Chemins d'Avize. This is produced from grapes from fifty-year-old vines in two lieux-dits from Avize called Chemin de Plivot and Chemin de Flavigny, whose combined area is 0.7 hectares. The first vintage (which I did not taste) was 2009. By 2010, however, I was on board. The wine, tasted in 2010, was fantastic: *"...ripe and lush with a nose redolent of coconut, ripe apricot, and honey, with a floral edge and a suggestion of toasty brioche-like notes. On the palate, the wine is expressive and approachable, with a supple texture and impressive length. While immediately enjoyable, this has the stuffing to age for the long term."*

19 avenue du Général de Gaulle 51130 Vertus | 03 26 52 13 24
www.larmandier.fr

Jacques Lassaigne

Region: Côte de Blancs | Terroir: Montgueux

There are few Champagnes that I associate more closely with eating and drinking in Champagne than those of Montgueux producer Jacques Lassaigne. When I first discovered these wines, they were difficult to procure outside of the region—a situation that has now considerably improved. Montgueux is thought to be the location of the battle of the Campus Mauriacus, where the Roman Emperor Flavius Aetius allied with the Visigoth King Theodoric I to turn back Attila the Hun in 451 AD. Although the village is located in the Aube, it is often grouped with the Côte de Blancs. This makes wine sense, however, because of the similarity of the Turonian chalk subsoil to what is found in the Marne even if it is located nearly 100 km to the south of Vertus. Montgueux has a long history of grape growing, but it languished after phylloxera and was only replanted to its current extent beginning in the 1960s. It was at this time that Emmanuel's father planted vines with the intention of selling the fruit to the négociant houses. They began to bottle *vin nature*[12] in the '70s and a bit of Champagne from the '80s. His first *parcellaire* (although it was not designated as such) was made with fruit from the lieu-dit Le Cotet, which Emmanuel still uses to produce a single-vineyard wine.

Emmanuel joined his father in 1999, and his first solo vintage was 2002. His father worked the vines using organic principals, and he has continued with this method as well, using nothing synthetic in the soil. The rows are grassed over and the grass is not mowed, creating competition for the vines and reducing yields. Minimal intervention also is the rule in the winery. Lassaigne prefers the traditional Coquard press, since it allows direct observation of the pressing process and the must. There is a small amount of sulfur added at this point, and no more after that. All of the alcoholic fermentations are done with native yeasts. Dosage was always low, but in recent years all the cuvées have been released without dosage.

---

12 Still wine, a forerunner of Coteaux Champenois

The Brut Vintage range is particularly rare. The regular vintage bottling comes from parcels selected by Emmanuel every year, as he believes it increases the "traceability" of his production. He ferments the must in stainless and ages it for eight years before release. My notes on the 2008, tasted in 2017: *"Concentrated and rich as one would expect from the vintage. This wine opened with green apple and mineral notes on the nose, and the aromas expanded on the palate to show more creamy depth and complexity, with a bit spice and some autolysis developing with time. The texture is dense, and while the wine is fresh, there is an exquisite balance between the freshness and the ripeness. This is top-notch Champagne and should last for decades in a proper cellar."* *****

The 2009 vintage tasted in the fall of 2018 had a lovely freshness: *"Superb tension, depth, and length. Surprisingly structured for a 2009, this opens with ripe apple and citrus notes, and a floral edge as the autolysis has yet to show itself. It seemed tightly wound on the palate, with plenty of crisp acidity, a powerful yet silky structure, and a ringingly good finish that ended with a salty exclamation point. Lovely with food but will probably be better in a couple of years."* ****

In addition to the nonvintage wines and the annual vintage, Lassaigne has produced a series experimental cuvées that he calls Cuvées Ephémères. He identifies them as "scenes" belonging to different "acts." Acte I Scène II was a 2010 Coteaux Champenois produced from a single lieu-dit called Haut Revers du Chutat. *"The Coteaux Blanc from Lassaigne was similar to a grand cru Chablis, with bright, lemony fruit and a mineral undertone on the attack, accented with spice notes from the cask ferment. On the palate, the wine was intensely concentrated and fairly full-bodied, with enough substance and stuffing to balance out the structure and carry it to a lingering finish. To be taken with food!"* ****

Acte II was a series of nonvintage rosés that are not discussed here. Acte III is a series of vintage-dated wines fermented in different types of casks, including some purchased from natural wine producer Jean-François Ganevat in the Jura and others purchased from Cognac. Acte III, Scène I was from a vineyard called the Clos St. Sophie in 2010. This Clos has more of an eastern exposure than many of the southern-facing vineyards in Montgueux and gives a structured wine with great depth and complexity. *"Explosively aromatic from the beginning, this shows notes of lemon peel, pomelo, and passion fruit at the outset, giving way to notes of gingerbread and toast. On the palate, the wine is fresh and concentrated, but there is a silky texture that has nothing exotic about it."* I have had (in 2016) a version of this wine labeled as *Autour de Minuit* with the Acte III, Scène I designation, and another version (tasted in 2019) of the same vintage that was labeled as the Clos Sainte-Sophie. The clos has been the property of the Valton family for more than 100 years. Formerly all the fruit was sold to Charles Heidsieck, whose former Chef de Caves Daniel Thibault said: "...if there is a Montrachet in the Aube, it will be found in Montgueux." Today Lassaigne receives a portion of the fruit from this clos for this marvelous cuvée.

Acte IV is consecrated to single-vineyard wines from the site La Grande Côte. Scène I is titled Soprano, and there was a single pressing vinified in a 500-liter demi-muid and aged on the lees for eight months. Scène II, called Alto, was produced precisely the same way but left on the lees for 20 months. Scène III, Tenor, was identical, save that it spent 32 months on the lees; it will be released in the spring of 2020. All three – Soprano, Alto, Tenor – were produced from the 2012 vintage, and each was five years on the lees after the second fermentation before being disgorged. I tasted Soprano and Alto side-by-side in 2019: *"Soprano was perhaps most marked by the cask, with notes of spice over fresh ripe apple and citrus peel on the nose. On the palate, the wine is high-toned and bright with markedly fresh acidity and a magically silky texture. The Alto is deeper and richer, with a creamy texture and much more density on the palate. There are more tropical nuances and floral notes to the fruit character here, and it seems that the additional elevage of the vins clairs has absorbed some of the cask character, which is still present but seems to be more in the background. Both are exquisite, compelling wines, and the entire experiment is fascinating to all who love Champagne."* *****

As of March 2020, the Tenor has not yet been released but is scheduled, according to my sources at Aux Crieurs de Vin in Troyes, and hopefully, it will be out in time for my next visit.

7 chemin du Aube 10300 Montgueux | 03 25 74 84 83
[No Website]

David Léclapart

Region: Montagne de Riems | Terroir: Perle Blanche

Trépail is an interesting terroir – the "Perle Blanche" of the Montagne, where the focus is more on Chardonnay than on Pinot Noir. David Léclapart was one of the first to bring this region to broader attention and is producing marvelously well-crafted wines with a personal, authentic style matched by few producers in Champagne. He began bottling under his own name with the 1999 vintage after wine school and a stage at Leclerc-Briant. He was one of the earlier converts to biodynamic production in Champagne, and has been certified biodynamic by Demeter since 2000. He farms his family's three-hectare holdings in Trépail himself, strictly observing biodynamic principles.

He vinifies partly in enameled steel tanks and partly in neutral casks using native yeasts, and all wines complete their malolactic fermentation. They are bottled unfiltered, disgorged without dosage, and sulfur levels are very low. This light hand with the sulfur led in early years to issues with oxidation in my view. In recent years, however, Léclapart has mastered this challenging way of working to produce elegant, accomplished champagnes. The only problem with the wines now is finding them, as he is very popular, and the wine from this small production is incredibly tricky to find.

Although the wines are not vintage-dated, they are produced from grapes from a single harvest, and the vintage is coded into the lot number on the bottle.

The Blanc des Blancs called Artiste is fermented half in stainless-steel tank, half in cask. My notes on the wine from the 2011 harvest: *Blended across different sites in Trépail, this features aromas of fresh and dried apricot with hints of smoke and a firm, chalky grounding to the fruit. On the palate, it is supple and elegant with a silky texture and a lingering finish."* ***

The Blanc de Noirs called Astre used to be vinified as a rosé, but now the fruit is vinified without maceration. The bottling from 2011 was beautifully expressive despite the difficulties of the vintage: *"This blanc de noirs from old vine Pinot Noir is structured tense with a mineral expression and notes of fresh flowers and gunflint on the attack. It is a new cuvée for this domaine and among the more approachable cuvees from Leclapart."* ****

The prestige cuvée from Léclapart is a Blanc de Blancs called l'Apotre, produced from vines in the lieu-dit La Pierre St. Martin planted in 1946. My notes on the wine produced from the 2009 harvest: *"This is the most compelling Champagne from David Leclapart. 100% cask fermented old-vine Chardonnay from Trepail, it has a richly truffly aroma and a dense, creamy texture that leads to a lovely lingering finish."* ****

10 Rue de la Mairie 51380 Trépail | 03 26 57 07 01
[No Website]

A.R. Lenoble

Location: Marne Valley | Terroir: Blended

A.R. Lenoble is perhaps the archetype of a small, quality-focused négociant house, where in recent years, the fourth-generation siblings Antoine and Anne Malassagne seem to do everything right. The house was founded in 1915 by Armand-Rafaël Graser, an Alsatian wine merchant. His son Joseph continued to expand the business. Grandson Jean-Marie, a doctor, sold most of the fruit from the estate to négociants, principally Bruno Paillard and Jacquesson. He also almost sold the business, but Antoine and Anne took over the reins in 1993 and are producing a lovely series of wines.

The foundation of the house is the fruit from their own holdings: 10 hectares of Chardonnay in Chouilly, 6 hectares of Pinot Noir in Bisseuil, and 2.5 hectares of Meunier in Damery, where they are based. Chouilly is the driving force with its pure chalk soils, while Bisseuil, with its chalk and clay, produces structured Pinot Noir base wines. The winery is run in a completely sustainable way with no pesticide or herbicide use and a strong commitment to biodiversity. Beehives house 70,000 bees in the vineyards to pollinate the apple trees, and grass grows between rows, reducing yields by 10% but improving the health of the soil. In 2012 they received certification as *Haute Valeur Environnementale* Level 3 (HVE), the highest of three levels of accreditation by the French government for sustainable agriculture.

All of the fruit is pressed in Damery with three 45-year-old presses since Antoine dislikes new presses. Only the cuvée is used, and the primary fermentation takes place in a combination of stainless-steel tanks, casks, and foudres. Reserve wines are fermented and stored in cask. In recent years they have begun to occasionally block the malolactic to retain freshness in the face of global warming.

There are three vintage wines. The first is the Grand Cru Blanc de Blancs from pure Chouilly fruit. The 2008 vintage, first tasted in 2015, is tremendous: "*...an intense concen-*

tration of lemon peel and bright green apple on the nose colored with mineral and saline notes and a pleasant toasty autolysis and a suggestion of black truffle; 10% of the vins clairs are fermented in cask, and the wine dosed at 3 g/l." ****

The complement to the Blanc de Blancs is the Blanc de Noirs, produced from 100% Pinot Noir from Bisseuil originating with the vines coming from Anne and Antoine's mother. I found the 2009 vintage a bit heavy, but the 2012 was superb. My note on the latter, from 2019: *"On the initial attack there are notes of fresh flowers, marzipan, toast, and spice. On the palate, the wine was silky and fresh, not at all heavy, with an extraordi8anary balance that carried straight through to the lingering finish. 35% fermented in cask, dosed at 3 g/l. Lovely."* ****

My favorite vintage wine in the line-up is the consistently rewarding old vine cuvée from Chouilly called Gentilhomme. The 2009 tasted in 2019 was one of the great successes from that sunny vintage: *"From three small parcels representing some of the best of Chouilly: Mont Aigu, Les Aventures, and Les Vallons. The wine shows lovely candied lemon peel fruit with a strong mineral note and hints of smoke and honey. It is lush, ripe, and round on the palate but never loses its lively vivacity. The finish is lingering and gentle. 22% fermented in cask and dosed at 3 g/l."* ****

Lenoble also releases late-disgorged versions of previous vintages called Collection Rare. The 1973 vintage was holding well when tasted in April 2017: *"There are mature notes of coffee, truffle, and butterscotch, but this is showing well. On the palate, it is rich and mouth filling, with a balance kept in check by a well-integrated note of bitterness. Delicious."* *****

35 rue Paul Douce 51480 Damery | 03 26 58 42 60
https://champagne-arlenoble.com/

Lilbert-Fils

Region: Côte des Blancs | Terroir: Côte des Blancs

For me, the phrase that most sums up the northern portion of the Côte de Blancs is gentle elegance, and there are few winemakers that embody this more than Bertrand Lilbert. The Lilbert family has been involved in viticulture in Cramant since 1746 and have bottled their own wine since 1900. The house was founded by Bertrand's great-great-grandfather. The estate today consists of 3.5 hectares, mostly in Cramant, with a few parcels in the neighboring areas of Chouilly, and Oiry, divided among 15 plots, ranging in size from 3 ares to 50 ares. There are a variety of exposures and soils amongst the parcels, and the wines are a blend of early- and late-picked sites. The fermentations are carried out in stainless or enameled steel vats on cultured yeasts after a settling period of about one day. After the primary fermentation, the malolactic conversion is done for all wines. The base wines are filtered lightly, if at all. All the bottles are riddled by hand, and until quite recently disgorged by hand as well. The dosage of the vintage is usually 4 g/l.

Cramant has a complex topography, with some vineyards that wrap around the Butte de Saran in the northern part of the village, and others that face east and southeast on the border with Avize. The parcels owned by the Lilbert family are in a range of locations, including a large holding in the southeast-facing Terres des Buissons. Parts of this vineyard were planted in 1936, and this is the portion that provides the majority of the fruit for the vintage bottling. The balance of the fruit comes from the southwest-facing Les Moyens du Levant, which tempers the powerful wines from Buissons and gives the bottling the elegance that is all-important to Lilbert. Among recent vintages, the 2007 was exemplary: *"Lovely and rich wine but very fine. The nose shows bright a lemony fruit with a bracing saline note on the initial attack, with hints of smoke and toast that develop with time. On the palate, the wine is fresh but still subtly powerful and hauntingly memorable."* **** (Tasted 2017) A marvelous success for this vintage. The 2008 vintage, however, showed the heights that this bottling could reach: *"...opens with super-ripe aromas of apple, Wiliam pears, fresh white flowers and cream, and with time begins to show pleasantly yeasty autolysis. On the palate, it is concentrated and rich but always with a firm mineral note that gives it strength and power through the lengthy finish."* ***** *(Tasted in 2018)* Vintage after vintage, this is one of the references for a style of elegance and finesse in the Côte des Blancs.

223 rue du Moutier 51530 Cramant | 03 26 57 50 16
www.champagne-lilbert.com

Pierre Paillard

Region: Montagne de Reims | Terroir: Grande Montagne South

Pierre Paillard is a reference for their powerful, luxurious style produced exclusively from fruit from the village of Bouzy, located in the heart of the south face of the Montagne de Reims. This particular subregion is known above all for superbly ripe Pinot Noir, yet paradoxically Pierre Paillard has 40% of their holdings here planted to Chardonnay. Benoit Paillard explained his vision on a visit in 2003: "Chardonnay is planted mainly around the village and between the village and the road, while the Pinot Noir is largely planted on the slopes". The Paillard family have been growers for eight generations in Bouzy, and Benoit's father began bottling under his own label in 1946. Benoit took the reins in 1973, and his sons Antoine and Quentin are now in charge. They are in the vanguard of young, intelligent, and thoughtful winemakers in Champagne today.

Although they are not certified organic, the brothers are deeply committed to sustainability. No herbicides are used. Grass has been planted between the rows of the vineyard for many years. The domaine is composed of 11 hectares in total with ten in production currently, including three hectares in Chardonnay. The estate's holdings stretch over 22 parcels, all located in Bouzy grand cru. The average age of these vines is 31 years, and work continues in the vineyard to perfect the raw material. Antoine gives increasing importance to the massale selection of vines for replanting. There are two sites used for single-vineyard wines and also for the massale selection: Les Maillerettes for Pinot Noir and Les Mottelettes for Chardonnay. Similarly, the Pinot Fin clone used in Burgundy is used to improve the red wine for the Bouzy Rouge and the rosé. At harvest, Antoine prefers to pick ripe fruit and then avoid chaptalization. Fermentations are done mainly in stainless steel and malolactic fermentation is completed.

Pierre Paillard produces a range of vintage cuvées. The first two of these are named for the parcels from which they come. Les Mottelettes was planted to Chardonnay in 1960, co-planted with a small proportion of Pinot Blanc, while Les Maillerettes is the mid-slope, southeast facing parcel of Pinot planted in 1970. Both can produce superb results. On the 2008 vintage: *"Les Mottelettes shows great finesse, with lemon peel and mineral aromas and a hint of yeast. On the palate, there is an elegantly soft and creamy texture since the wine has been produced with slightly less fizz (5 bar instead of 6) than other Champagnes, giving it a tender character on the palate."* **** And of the Blanc de Noirs Les Maillerettes: *"A floral edge with pear fruit and notes of smoke and mineral, great purity and elegance, and no heaviness at all in spite of considerable extract. Fresh, silky and fine, with a finish that is clean and long. Very impressive."* **** (Both tasted 2013)

In addition to these two wines, there is La Grande Récolte, a fifty-fifty blend of Chardonnay and Pinot Noir from the oldest vines of the domaine. From my notes on the 2006 vintage: *"This is always a wine of both concentration and elegance. The 2006 today is approachable with a delicate, silky texture. Still, there is also a density of toasted, nutty aromas, ripe orchard fruit, and a subtle minerality that testify to its ability to age."* **** (Tasted 2017)

To complete their production, Paillard also releases a Coteaux Champenois, both in red and white. In the past, the red Coteaux has been assembled from different lieux-dits, but in 2015 it was a parcellaire from Les Mignottes. *"The still red wine from Pierre Paillard in 2015 showed a superbly expressive cherry fruit aroma with notes of violet and spice -- perfumed, yet also powerful and ripe. This is a classic Coteaux that can stand with top Burgundy."* **** (Tasted 2017)

2 rue du XX Siècle 51150 Bouzy | 03 26 57 08 04
www.champagne-pierre-paillard.fr

Pierre Péters

Region: Côte des Blancs | Terroir: Côte des Blancs

Rodolphe Péters is among the most charismatic personalities of the Côte des Blancs, and his wines reflect this character. They are easily loved and accessible, yet they harbor deep reserves of concentration and the complexity to age for years. Rodolphe is the sixth generation to head this family firm, which is based in Le Mesnil. The family has been growing grapes in Le Mesnil since the mid-19th century, and bottling under the family name since 1919 with the label Camille Péters. Camille's son Pierre changed the name of the domaine after the Second World War. Pierre's second son François took over the direction of the estate in 1967, while his eldest son Jacques led a long career as the Chef de Caves at Veuve Clicquot. In 2007, François' son Rodolphe took over for his father with the blessing of his uncle and now leads the charge to bring the estate to a new generation of wine lovers.

More than ten hectares of the Péters vineyards are located in Le Mesnil, with other parcels in Avize, Oger, and Cramant. Among the jewels of the estate are the three parcels in the Le Mesnil vineyard called Les Chétillons that were acquired by the family in 1930. The vines in Chétillons average 45 years of age, and have been vinified separately since 1971. Originally this wine was called the Cuvée Spéciale, but it has been labeled with the name of the parcel since the 2000 vintage.

According to the "seasonal" philosophy of Rodolphe Péters, Le Mesnil represents winter, and gives wines with minerality and purity. Some of the plots have only ten cm of topsoil covering the chalk. Oger represents spring, and the warmer climate delivers pleasant floral aromas. Avize represents summer, and the 40 to 60 cm of topsoil here help to produce fruity wines, while Cramant represents autumn and delivers spicy aromas. In total, the house farns nearly 20 hectares spread over 70 parcels. Sustainable agriculture adapted to each parcel is adopted in the vineyard, including cover crops where appropriate. In the winery, the philosophy is to use a partial malolactic fermentation. The must is run directly into the tank to avoid pumping, and for now, Rodolphe uses cultured yeast, although he is experimenting with producing one that is a culture from his own vineyard.

There are a variety of vintage wines. L'Esprit is the first to be released. It is a blend of the old vine parcels from Le Mesnil, Oger, Avize, and Cramant. The 2012 was particularly lovely: *"Rich, dense, and complex with ripe apple, cream, and brioche on the nose, a dense texture, and richness on the palate that yet do not take away from the lively acidity, finesse, and delicacy on the finish. The wine is a blend of Le Mesnil, Oger, Avize, and Cramant, and represents a selection of best wines from these terroirs. 4 years on the lees, dosed at 6 g/l."* **** (Tasted 2019)

This same wine is also released without a vintage date and with a lower dosage as the Extra Brut. In this instance, it is three years on the lees and dosed at 3 g/l: *"Here the minerality of Le Mesnil comes to the fore, and the wine shows sleek notes of citrus peel and sea salt. On the palate, it is less forward and somewhat austere, but there is deep concentration, wonderful balance, and impressive length."* **** (Tasted 2019)

The top vintage wine is Les Chétillons. The 2012 is compelling: *"Yield was low as the vineyard froze on the left side. The remaining fruit produced a wine of great complexity and density, with notes of citrus and tropical fruit, a hint of flowers, and well-integrated autolysis. Density and power on the palate, but the wine isn't heavy. A delight."* **** (Tasted 2018)

9 rue de l'Église 51190 Le Mesnil-sur-Oger | 03 26 57 50 32
www.champagne-peters.com

Pol Roger

Location: Epernay | Terroir: Blended

Many Champagne lovers think of Pol Roger as the house be-loved by Englishmen. After all, it holds the royal warrant as the supplier of Champagne to Queen Elizabeth II, and their prestige cuvée is named for Sir Winston Churchill. The house dates to the middle of the 19th century. Born in 1831 in Aÿ, Pol Roger formed his company in Epernay at a young age and directed it for 50 years. He was succeeded by his sons Georges and Maurice, who in 1900 legally changed the family name to "Pol-Roger" in honor of their father. Maurice became the mayor of Epernay during the First World War. In 1927, Maurice's son Jacques joined the firm. The friendship of Maurice's wife Odette, a legendary beauty, converted Winston Churchhill to a life-long support of the brand. In the postwar years, the leader-ship transitioned to the next generation as Maurice's grandson Christian de Billy joined the firm. Christian Pol-Roger arrived in 1963, and his son Hubert de Billy joined the house in 1988. Since 1997 Patrice Noyelle has been President of the Board of Directors. Although he is not a member of the family, the supervisory board is still dominated by family members. The house today is the proprietor of 92 hectares spread over pre-miers and grands crus throughout the region.

Pol Roger produces four vintage wines. The base wines are all fermented in stainless steel tanks at low temperatures, and the malolactic fermentation is routinely done. The Brut is produced from a blend of Pinot Noir (60%) and Chardonnay (40%) from 20 different premier cru and grand cru sites and aged for seven years prior to release. The 2004 was particularly lovely: *"Imposing, almost regal, this opens with aromas of fresh flowers, toasted brioche, and fresh cream. On the palate, the wine fills the mouth with a velvety richness and lingers invitingly on the palate."* *** (Tasted 2015)

The vintage Blanc de Blancs is produced using only fruit from the Côte des Blancs, and only the cuvée is used in order to create an elegant result. The wine is aged seven years before release. Although the wine ages marvelously, it is particularly attractive in its youth, particularly in a year such as 2008: *"This is a wine of lovely concentration, yet still there is an exquisite restraint. The nose mingles aromas of lemon peel, mineral, and cream with abundant finesse. The texture is fine and filigreed despite the power developed over seven years of aging."* *** (Tasted 2016)

The vintage Rosé is produced with a similar 60/40 blend as the Brut, but 15% of the blend is red wine from Pinot Noir from the Montagne de Reims. The wine is aged six years before release. From the same 2008 vintage: *"This is a powerful, vinous rosé with a bright red fruit expression, but nothing sweet or cloying. This is a vinous wine with touches of marzipan, fresh flowers, and smoke. On the palate, it is bone dry and fairly full-bodied, with lots of structure and impressive length on the finish."* **** (Tasted 2016)

The prestige cuvée, Cuvée Sir Winston Churchill, was launched in 1984. The exact proportions are not revealed by the house, but Pinot Noir dominates the blend. All of the fruit comes from Grand Cru vineyards that were planted during the time of Churchill. This ages superbly well. From my notes on the 1990 vintage: *"...showing aromas of truffle, yeast, and biscuit with a mineral undercurrent. The mousse was fine with a great deal of elegance and finesse on the palate. The wine is vinous but not heavy. Although this is drinking near its peak it should continue to improve for years to come."* ***** (Tasted 2014)

1 rue Henri Le Large 51200 Epernay | 03 26 59 58 00
http://www.polroger.com

Eric Rodez

Region: Montagne de Reims | Terroir: Grande Montagne South

The engaging, ebullient Eric Rodez is a multi-faceted producer of Champagne. The estate is located on 6 hectares in grand cru Ambonnay spread over 36 parcels. Before his first vintage here in 1984, Rodez worked in Burgundy and, for a time, at Krug. He feels that it is both a privilege and a responsibility to tell the story of Ambonnay where he is based. Rodez is very attuned to the environment. He began moving towards organic production in 1989, and was certified organic in 2002 and biodynamic in 2008. In 2012, his domaine also received the certification as Haute Valeur Environnementale Level 3. He calls this his "work for the regeneration of Ambonnay terroir." He now uses essential oils to treat the vines as well as biodynamic preparations. He is a deeply reflective and thoughtful winemaker, and produces a dizzying number of wines, including many vintage-dated cuvées to show the complexity of the Ambonnay terroir.

The first, simply called Cuvée Millésime, is an assemblage of roughly 60% Pinot Noir and 40% Chardonnay blended from parcels across the village all fermented in cask. There is also the wine called Empreinte in both Blanc de Blancs and Blanc de Noirs versions, which Rodez see as the reflection of a single variety blended across different old vine parcels located in Ambonnay. The Blanc de Blancs includes fruit from the lieux-dits of Le Noyer Saint Pys, Les Genettes, Les Crayères, and Les Agusons. The 2002 has aged extremely well : *"Ambonnay is known for Pinot Noir, but this delicious Chardonnay shows a different expression with a ripe apple and pastry crust aroma and a rich, velvety texture. It is substantial yet very elegant and taking on now a burnished glow."* **** (Tasted 2012) The Blanc de Noirs version is blended from lieux-dits that include La Pierre aux Larons, Le Moulin, Les Fournettes, and Les Secs. Typical of the Empreinte bottling was the 2005 vintage: *"Rich and structured, with a dense and vinous texture and lots of yeasty bread dough aromas and just a hint of black truffle make this an immediately impressive wine. It is blended from across the Rodez holdings in*

Ambonnay. The fruit is fermented in cask and lightly dosed at 2.5 g/l. Ten years on the lees, it will doubtlessly age well over the next two decades. Fabulous quality." **** (Tasted 2016)

In addition to these wines, there is a series of parcellaires. Les Beurys is most often a Blanc de Noirs from a single lieu-dit of the same name, planted with vines of more than 35 years of age. The parcel is in Ambonnay, but on the border with Trépail in a site with an eastern exposure and a scant 35 cm of soil on top of the pure chalk. The parcel is located close to the lieu-dit Les Secs, with which it is blended in some vintages. The wine has been made in both blanc and rosé versions and is entirely fermented in cask, bottled without malolactic fermentation, and dosed at approximately 3 g/l. The 2010 was typical: *"Exuberant and exotic tropical notes are complemented by a hint of marzipan on the nose with elements of toast and chalky minerality. Despite the substance and weight, the structure is very silky and elegant. Perfectly balanced and supremely elegant."* **** (Tasted 2017) The Rosé from the same terroir is equally compelling: *"This blanc de noirs rosé is made with a maceration of three days to give it a lovely fruit expression. It strikes a marvelous balance between an abundance of cherry and floral notes along with a pleasant autolytic character and a slightly vinous feel on the palate."* **** (Tasted 2017)

Les Genettes is another parcellaire, from a site with vines of more than 40 years of age. This has been done in both Blanc de Blancs and Blanc de Noirs versions. The base wine from the super-rich 2018 vintage showed ripe tropical fruit still enough acidity to balance it on a 2019 visit to the winery. Next among the Pinot Noir parcellaires is Les Fournettes, from a site with a southeast exposure. It is fascinating to taste the differences of terroir among the different sites. In a 2017 domaine visit, I tasted the 2009 Les Fournettes: *"Rich and generous, this has a bit more buttered brioche and ripe apple fruit, with notes of white flowers on the nose, and a silky, velvety texture on the palate that is rich without being cloying or heavy. Fermented in cask without the use of cultured yeast, and then aged on the lees another 6 to 7 months before bottling. Dosed at 2 g/l."* ****

4 rue de Isse 51150 Ambonnay | 03 26 57 04 93
http://en.champagne-rodez.com/

Roses de Jeanne

Region: Côte des Bars | Terroir: Barséquanais

Cédric Bouchard is among the most sought-after growers in the Aube, and he is a man with rules: Work in the vines is organic. Yields in the vineyard are low, between 4,000 to 8,000 kg/ha (about one-third to two-thirds less than usual). Only the cuvée is used. Only native yeasts are used for the fermentation, which are done in stainless, and the malolactic fermentations are done. There is no blending of grapes or of sites or of multiple vintages (thus, everything here is both a parcellaire and a millésime non-revendiqué). There is no dosage. Bouchard's philosophy can be summed up as grapes turned into wine with nothing added and as little intervention on his part as possible.

He began making wine fairly recently after beginning his career as a sommelier in Paris. In 1999 he returned to assist his father in his vineyard. In 2000, he launched his own label, which he named Roses de Jeanne after his grandmother. Initially, Bouchard worked a 0.9 hectare plot called Les Ursules belonging to his father. Later he added another 1.5 hectare vineyard site in nearby Polisy, called Côte de Val Vilaine. Initially, the Val Vilaine bottling was called Inflorescence and was meant as a second label to Roses de Jeanne. In 2003 it produced one of my favorite wines in that rather odd vintage: *"Racy and fine even in '03, the Inflorescence from Cédric Bouchard has pleasant toasty aromas on the nose and a bit of butter and cream, yet on the palate, the wine is still crisp – an achievement in '03. Well done."* **** (Tasted 2011) Since 2012, however, this has been labeled with the name of the vineyard, thus Côte de Val Vilaine. And since 2014, all of the Champagne from Cédric Bouchard is bottled under the Roses de Jeanne label.

To this initial structure, he began to add more single-vineyard wines. The first was called initially La Parcelle, a 1.5 hectare plot planted to Pinot Noir, which is now known by the vineyard name, Côte de Béchalin. The 2008 was superb: *"...this shows the possibilities of the Blanc de Noirs with no dosage in the Aube. It goes through malolactic fermentation, but receives no dosage and thus retains a crisp, fine edge and an almost citrus/ saline cast despite grape variety. The wine is produced from tiny yields with minimal intervention and is aged in bottles six years before release to give a stunning complexity and depth of flavor despite the fine, racy profile."* **** (Tasted 2017)

In 2004, Bouchard began to produce a Chardonnay from a 0.12 hectare vineyard called La Haut-Lemblé. There is also a tiny production of rosé from the 0.07 hectare vineyard Le Creux d'Enfer, and a Blanc de Blancs made from Pinot Blanc from the 0.22 hectare vineyard La Bolorée. From my notes on the 2009: *"Delicious and refreshing, this shows elegant floral and toasty notes and a creamy texture with a lively mousse. Well balanced and very fine, this is an elegant wine, and drinking now."* **** (Tasted in 2015)

The newest edition is a Blanc de Noirs from the 0.25 hectare vineyard called Presle, which I have not yet tasted. One can only imagine that like all wines from this young talent that all are worth trying.

4 rue du Creux Michel 10110 Celles sur Ource | 03 25 29 69 78
[No Website]

Ruinart

Location: Reims | Terroir: Blended

Ruinart, the first Champagne house founded to make sparkling Champagne, is still producing wines at the highest level. Before May 25, 1728 the wine of Champagne could not be transported in bottles until a decree by Louis XV changed the rules. It was customary at the time to ship red wine in barrels, but this was not possible for the newly fashionable sparkling Champagne. Nicolas Ruinart was a prosperous cloth merchant based in Reims and ideally placed to take advantage of the new decree. His uncle was a Benedictine monk, Dom Thierry Ruinart, based at the abbey in Hautvillers and a student of the scholar Dom Mabillon. More importantly for our story, Dom Ruinart was a colleague of Dom Pérignon. Dom Ruinart learned the art of making Champagne and transmitted his knowledge to his nephew Nicolas, who began to make Champagne in 1729.

The innovations of the Ruinart family did not stop there. They were the first to use the Gallo-Roman chalk pits, called *crayères*, for aging Champagne wines, and by the end of the 18th century, their wines were found throughout Europe. Irénée Ruinart, the grandson of Nicolas, was made Vicomte de Brimont by Charles X. By the first decades of the 19th century, the popularity of Ruinart Champagne had spread to the U.S. The house flourished throughout the 19th century and into the 20th, although it suffered during the First World War while under the direction of André Ruinart de Brimont, who passed away in 1919. His widow Charlotte managed the business until her son Gérard assumed leadership in 1925. It was Gérard who led Ruinart during the difficult years between the wars and then during the Second World War. After the war, he passed charge of the house to his cousin, Bertrand Mure, whose famous quote was "I like my Champagne from 9 a.m. until 9 a.m. the next day." In 1947 the house produced its first vintage Blanc de Blancs, and the first prestige cuvée Dom Ruinart was created from the 1959 vintage and released in 1966. In 1963, Ruinart merged with Moët & Chandon, and Robert-Jean de Vogüé of Moët was named president. In 1971 Ruinart was absorbed into LVMH. The early 1970s also saw the launch of the first vintage of Dom Ruinart Rosé, the 1966.

The Blanc de Blancs from Ruinart has always relied in part on Chardonnay from the Montagne de Reims. In the north-facing premier cru villages, it accounts for 21.5% of the planted area. In the northeastern-facing grand cru villages (a group that includes Verzenay and Sillery), it accounts for 20.8%. There is a group of villages that face east/southeast that is sometimes known as the *Perle Blanche* (White Pearl); Trépail and Villers-Marmery are the two largest villages, both premiers crus, and here the proportion of Chardonnay is above 98%. Only in the villages that face south, such as Bouzy, Ambonnay, and Tours-sur-Marne, does it dip to 16.5%. This Chardonnay gives a tension and a vinous character that complements perfectly the lush, almost exotic nature of the wines from the Côte des Blancs.

Over the years the Ruinart style has become more elegant and focused. I have had several wines from the '60s and early '70s, but they have not survived into the modern era. The first electrifying vintage was the 1988, which I have enjoyed on many occasions. From one note: *"An enormously seductive complexity, with notes of toasted walnuts, marzipan, orange peel, brioche, and black truffle. Surprisingly lively acidity and a fairly soft mousse, but certainly sufficient. Light in body, yet remarkably persistent on the palate, the wine was wholly satisfying."* ***** (Tasted 2006)

The 1989 and 1990 were similarly rich. By 1996, the style had more precision: *"Beginning to show developed smoky notes over the citrus and pear drop fruit character on the nose. Still very structured with crisp acidity but also a mouth-fillingly rich texture and exquisite length. Subtle but profound."* **** (Tasted 2006)

Frédéric Panaïotis was appointed Chef de Caves in 2007. He is a gifted winemaker with a strong focus on aromatic freshness. Panaiotis ferments in stainless and pays close attention to oxygen uptake. The wines do their malolactic fermentation, but he doesn't like the creamy lactic flavor, which he attempts to control with the yeast, the fermentation temperature, the number of rackings, and other techniques. Panaïotis spares no effort to achieve his vision: from the 2012 vintage, all of the wines are bottled under cork for the aging process. His personal style can be seen with the 2007 vintage, his first as Chef de Caves: *"Produced from an assemblage of 63% Côte de Blancs (Chouilly, Le Mesnil, Avize) and 37% Montagne (Sillery, Puisieulx), this is a lightning bolt of a wine, with aromas that start with fresh citrus peel and green apple and gradually reveal smoke, toast, mineral, and saline notes. On the palate, the wine is thrillingly fresh, but still not lacking in richness. There is a vibrant acidity, but no lack of substance and the finish goes on and on. 6.5 g/l total acidity; malolactic done, dosed at 4.5 g/l."* **** (Tasted in 2015)

The vintages to date of Dom Ruinart include: 1959, 1961, 1964, 1966, 1969, 1971, 1973, 1975, 1976, 1978, 1979, 1981, 1982, 1983, 1985, 1986, 1988, 1990, 1993, 1996, 1998, 2002, 2004, 2005, 2006, and 2007.

Today the Chardonnay focus at Ruinart is so relentless that even the Dom Ruinart Rosé is at least 80% Chardonnay and often more, with the addition of a small amount of Pinot Noir done as still red wine. Panaïotis believes in keeping the maceration short for the nonvintage wine. For the Dom Ruinart Rosé, the maceration can last a full two weeks in the Burgundian style to give more structure and backbone to the wine. In 2007, Ruinart produced a delightful Dom Ruinart Rosé on the lees from bottling in early 2008 until early 2017: *"Dosed at 5 g/l. The profile on release was concentrated and focused, with more emphasis on floral notes than on juicy red fruit. On the palate, there was plenty of firm structure, lots of freshness, but also enough substance to age gracefully."* *** (Tasted 2018)

Vintages produced of Dom Ruinart Rosé: 1966, 1969, 1971, 1973, 1975, 1976, 1978, 1979, 1981, 1982, 1983, 1985, 1986, 1988, 1990, 1996, 1998, 2002, 2004, 2005, and 2007.

4 rue des Crayères 51100 Reims | 03 26 77 51 51
https://www.ruinart.com/

Savart

Region: Montagne de Reims | Terroir: Petite Montagne

Frédéric Savart has a larger-than-life personality and a somewhat smaller vineyard. Smiling, generous, *"rigolo,"* as they say in French, he is also intensely passionate about his terroir and his art. Based in Ecueil, he owns four hectares here and in Villers-aux-Nœuds. He is one of the few people to put "Petite Montagne" on the front label, along with his name. The labels did not always look this way. The domaine was founded by his grandfather René after the second world war, and expanded by his father Daniel who took over in the '70s. When I began to drink these wines, they were still named after his father. Frédéric took over in 2005, and for several years the labels read "Champagne Savart." The newest ones, however, specify "Champagne Frédéric Savart," as well as the motto *"vins singuliers, identitaires."* He explains on his website that these are wines that are "...far from the standardization of taste, a wine in which the winegrower is intimately involved, and where technique and knowledge are placed at the service of his intention."

His winemaking has evolved over the years. A common thread, however, has been his racy, intense style of winemaking. The vineyards are sustainably farmed, and he stopped using pesticides and herbicides shortly after taking over in 2005. The vineyards are either grassed over or manually tilled. Vines are replaced using massale selection from his grandfather's vines.

When he began, he was doing most of his fermentation in stainless steel and then aging the wines on the fine lees in cask. Today, he is mostly doing more of the fermentation in large barrels, some made from oaks from the forest of Ecueil. The wines still spend almost a year on the fine lees. Although he used to practice bâtonnage, today he avoids it to preserve the straight, lemony line of the wines. Malolactic fermentation is blocked, and the wines are bottled without fining or filtration. The dosage is uniformly low.

One fact is incontestable: the wines make a statement. The first vintage wine, called "l'Année," comes typically from the lieu-dit Les Rosets in Ecueil and Le Mont Benoit in Villers-aux-Nœuds. It is a blend of Chardonnay and Pinot noir, which Savart presses and ferments together. It is fermented in large casks, and the malolactic fermentation is blocked. The wine normally spends six years on the lees before being disgorged with a dosage around 3 g/l. On my initial visit in 2013, I tasted the 2005 vintage: *"...exuberantly floral on the nose with hints of cream, almond, and toast. On the palate, the wine is tightly wound and structured yet crisply refreshing and well balanced."* ****

We also tasted the 2008 vintage of a wine called "Dame de Cœur". It was a Blanc de Blancs produced from several different parcels in Ecueil. The equivalent wine is now called "Mont des Chrétains" since it is now a made exclusively from the lieu-dit of the same name in Ecueil. The 2008 vintage was a Brut Nature, but later vintages have had an extra brut dosage added: *"There are racy lemon and mineral aromas here with hints of fresh flowers – not at all closed down. On the palate, the wine is crisp yet shows admirable finesse and delicacy, leading to a lingering, elegant finish."* **** (Tasted 2013)

Next, we tasted the 2008 vintage of a wine called "Calliope," which used to come exclusively from fruit from the lieu-dit Derrière Moutier in Ecueil. These grapes are now blended with other lieux-dits, including Les Aillys, Les Gillys, and Les Chaillots, and the resulting wine is called "Expression." The 2008 vintage was delicious: "Seductive notes of green papaya and lemongrass on the nose with a bit of toast and a hint of spice. The wine is fermented in large casks and bottled unfined and unfiltered. Superbly crisp and fine on the palate, yet structured and long. Superb." **** (Tasted 2013)

1 chemin de Sacy 51500 Ecueil | 03 26 84 91 60
http://champagne-savart.com/

Vouette et Sorbée

Region: Côtes des Bar | Terroir: Barséquanais

"You don't drink a wine because it's biodynamic, you drink it because it's good." This quote, attributed to vigneron Bertrand Gautherot on the Rare Wine Company website, would be truthful in an ideal world. There are wine lovers who ascribe to this philosophy. Others do, in fact, drink wine because it's biodynamic. An even more significant proportion, perhaps, will drink wine because it is fashionable. The Champagnes of Vouette et Sorbée will satisfy all three motivations, which explains why the wines are tough to track down. The Gautherot family are growers based in Buxières-sur-Arce in the Côte des Bar.

According to French lexicographers Dauzat and Rostaing, "Bar" is a Gallic word meaning summit or height, referring here to an outcropping of Kimmeridgian marl topped with Portlandian limestone that has been eroded by the river Arce as it winds into the Seine. Bernard inherited two vineyards here from his father in 1986. Initially, the fruit was sold to négociant houses, but he gradually took back the leases and stopped using pesticides and herbicides, and the domaine was certified biodynamic by Demeter 1998. Today Gautherot owns 5 hectares, mostly in Buxières-sur-Arce, with one parcel in neighboring Ville-sur-Arce. Vouette is the parcel immediately behind Gautherot's house on south-facing Kimmeridgian slopes. This vineyard (like much of the Côte des Bar) was initially planted to Pinot Noir. Encouraged by his success with Chardonnay, however, Gautherot budded the vineyard over to Chardonnay in 2014. At the top of the slope where the bedrock transitions to Portlandian limestone, there is a wooded break in the vineyards, which continue further upslope as they flatten out towards the summit. This site is where Gautherot's parcel in the lieu-dit of Sorbée is located, planted to old vine Pinot Noir. Briaunes is located next to Sorbée, where the slope of the hill swings around to face west. The site is planted to both Pinot Noir and Chardonnay. Gautherot has another vineyard on the other side of the village in lieu-dit Fonnet, planted to a mix of Pinot Noir, Chardonnay, and Pinot Blanc. There are also two additional vineyards for Pinot Noir: one called Tirmy and the another in neighboring Ville-sur-Arce called Chatel.

The vineyards are farmed according to the principles of biodynamics. In the winery, similar natural, non-interventionist techniques are used. The must is not chaptalized, and fermentation is carried out with native yeasts. For the most part, casks are used for fermentation, but some of the Pinot Blanc is fermented in amphorae. The wines are bottled without filtration or fining, and there is no dosage added during disgorgement. All of the wines except Fidèle come from a single vintage year, although most are not vintage-dated – it is necessary to look at the code on the cork to find the year of the harvest.

The largest production is Fidèle. It is 100% Pinot Noir from Briaunes, Fonnet and Tirmy. It receives 5 to 7% reserve wine and thus is not a vintage wine, yet it is delicious. There is a Blanc de Blancs, 100% Chardonnay, called Blanc d'Argile, whose fruit comes from Briaunes and Fonnet. A bottle of the wine from the 2015 harvest (non-revendiqué) was superb when tasted in 2020: *"The nose had gentle aromas of toast and smoke, ripe apricot fruit, and a suggestion of hay and beeswax. Acidity was balanced, and the texture was silky and soft, yet not lacking substance. The mousse gently fills the mouth and leads to a lingering finish."* ****

There is another wine called Textures. This wine is also a Blanc de Blancs but made from 100% Pinot Blanc from Fonnet, fermented in amphorae. The wine from the 2015 havest was delicious: *"Ripe aromas of fresh white flowers and ripe peach with a toasty edge. On the palate, the wine is sturdy, rich, and broad, with a substantial, almost chewy character, balanced acidity, and a long, harmonious finish."* **** (Tasted 2018)

Next comes the Rosé, called Saignée de Sorbée. This is done in a sturdy, vinous style. The color is invariably deep pink, almost red, and the wine is exceptionally vinous on the palate. It almost resembles a Rosé des Riceys with bubbles. In recent years, it has has been without the use of sulfur. My notes on the wine from the 2014 harvest, tasted in 2020: *"Looks like a light red wine with bubbles. This wine is an outlier in many ways, but the wine is superb. The nose is restrained but has an elegant aroma of roses. On the palate, the wine is vinous but there is a very fine balance and a lovely, fresh balancing acidity. The whole is harmonious and elegant."* ****

Finally, there are two wines with a minute production—noted Champagne authority Peter Liem relates that they are limited to approximately 200 bottles each year. Extrait is a vintage-dated Blanc de Noirs from Pinot Noir, aged ten years on the lees before being disgorged. My notes on the 2008: *"Deep gold in color, this radiates pronounced aromas of toasted brioche and smoke, toasted almond, and ground coffee. On the palate the wine is vinous and concentrated, with a rich, creamy texture, but also a strong balancing acidity. Definitely a wine to make a statement."* **** (Tasted 2020)

The final wine is called Sobre, which I have yet to taste. It is a Blanc de Blancs that produced without the addition of a liqueur de tirage. In its place, unfermented grape must triggers the second fermentation in the bottle. Given the tiny number of bottles, I imagine that it will have to wait until my next trip to the Côte des Bar. My advice is to enjoy these when you find them -- these are unique and delicious Champagnes.

8 rue de Vaux 10110 Buxières-sur-Arce | 03 09 79 70 32 70
http://www.vouette-et-sorbee.com/

* *

Billecart-Salmon

Region: Marne Valley | Terroir: Blended

Billecart-Salmon is an impeccable source of Champagne from the Marne Valley. The house was established in 1818 following the marriage of Nicolas-François Billecart and Elisabeth Salmon, and has been family-owned for seven generations. Today, Billecart owns or has sharecropping (*métayage*) contracts for 100 hectares of vineyards, and they purchase grapes and from a further 200 hectares, mostly in the area surrounding Epernay. Only the cuvée is utilized, and the tailles are sold. In the winery, most base wines are fermented in stainless-steel tank at very low temperatures. Exceptions to this rule include the Brut Sous Bois, the Clos Saint-Hilaire, and a portion of the vintage Blanc de Blancs.

The vintage Blanc de Blancs has always been very attractive. From my notes on the 2004 vintage: *"There is a lovely lemon peel aroma with floral notes and a saline edge on the initial attack. The grapes for this bottling comes from old vines in Avize and from Les Chétillons in Le Mesnil and other grand cru sites. One-third is vinified in cask, which is evident on the nose in the aromas of coconut and melted butter. There is a lovely richness here as well as impressive length. Dosed at 6 g/l."* **** (Tasted 2015)

The Clos Saint-Hilaire is the Billecart prestige cuvée. A Blanc de Noirs, the wine was first created in 1995 from a vineyard planted in 1964. Of the 1999 vintage: *"...only 3,000-5,000 bottles are produced of the pure Pinot Noir coming from old vines. The vineyard is cultivated using organic methods (including using a horse for vineyard work and a sheep to eat the grass), even if the Billecart has not pursued certification. Yields are absurdly low for the region. The wine is vinified in small cask and shows notes of tropical fruit and orange zest with hints of smoke and toast and almost a suggestion of ground coffee. Initially, this vineyard served to* make red wine, but now it is vinified on its own. *The fruit is picked late and very ripe, and thus it was not chaptalized and received no dosage."* **** (Tasted 2015)

One of the best values in the Billecart range is the Cuvée Nicolas-François, created in 1964 as a tribute to the houses' founder. This is on par with many more expensive prestige cuvées, yet costs the same as an average vintage wine. The 1982 vintage was notable: *"...the Billecart-Salmon Cuvée Nicolas-François opens with toast, mineral, citrus, and roasted hazelnut, although with time a more tropical note developed in the glass. Undoubtedly fresh but also concentrated and tightly wound, with crisp acidity and great density of flavor, leading up to an impressive finish."* ***** (Tasted 2011)

Finally, the Rosé Cuvée Elisabeth Salmon should not be overlooked. My notes on the 1996 vintage: *"...a copper color, with a pronounced nose of fresh and baked cherries, fig, and truffle with a strong yeasty character. On the palate, the wine shows crisp acidity, a high level of extract, and a mouth-filling, creamy texture."* **** (Tasted 2010)

40 rue Carnot 51160 Mareuil-sur-Aÿ | 03 26 52 60 22
https://www.champagne-billecart.fr/en

Gaston Chiquet

Region: Marne Valley | Terroir: Grande Vallée

The Chiquet Family had been growers since the mid-18th century when Gaston and his brother Fernand took the bold move in 1919 to become a récoltant-manipulant and keep their grapes, bottle their own Champagne, and sell it themselves. In 1935, the brothers went their separate ways, and Gaston established his own brand. Today his grandsons Antoine and Nicolas direct the estate. The house owns 23 hectares, including parcels in the lieux-dits of Vauzelles and Haut-Crohauts in Aÿ (used for the Blanc de Blancs d'Aÿ), in the lieux-dits Crohauts-Guillemoine, Cerisières, Sous-Chienne, and Moque-Bouteille in Dizy, and the lieux-dits La Grange de Dizy and Colombier around the village of Hautvillers. Chardonnay and Meunier each represent about 40% of the plantings. The Chardonnay (cultivated in all three villages) has long been a specialty; the Meunier is mostly used for the non-vintage. The vineyard the rows are either grassed over or tilled manually, and they have received certifications for both sustainable viticulture (Viticulture Durable en Champagne, or VDC) and high environmental quality (Haute Valeur Environnementale Level 3, or HVE). Fermentations are done in small stainless tanks to allow them to vinify parcel-by-parcel, and the malolactic fermentation is always done.

There are three vintage wines. The first, called "Or Millésime", is made from grapes grown in Hautvillers, Dizy, and Mareuil. Pinot Noir normally dominates the blend. The 2008 vintage was delicious: *"Beguiling notes of fresh flowers and citrus on the nose, this is an ethereal wine of very subtle finesse that charms with its upfront accessibility but then impresses with its hidden power and concentration. 60% Pinot Noir and 40% Chardonnay, dosed at 8 g/l."* **** (Tasted 2018)

The Special Club usually is 70% Chardonnay from the same villages, dosed at 8 g/l. Because of a dosage that seems high today, recent vintages can sometimes seem soft and lacking in tension. However, the wine can age well. The 1982 was particularly attractive more than thirty years after the vintage:

"Lovely, mature aromas of coffee and mocha, yet the wine is still very fresh, with a pleasantly sweet character to the lingering finish." **** (Tasted 2016)

Finally, there is the house specialty, the Blanc de Blancs d'Aÿ. The 2013 showed exceptional richness given the vintage: *"Dense and almost vinous, the Blanc de Blancs d'Aÿ from Gaston Chiquet has a ripe apple and brioche nose with a suggestion of honey. On the palate, it is dense and creamy, leading to an elegant finish."* *** (Tasted 2018)

906 avenue du Général Leclerc 51530 Dizy | 03 26 55 22 02
www.gastonchiquet.com

Dehours et Fils

Region: Marne Valley | Terroir: Left Bank

Based in Cerseuil on the left bank of the Marne, Dehours et Fils is definitely among the up-and-coming producers in champagne. With his array of single-vineyard wines, proprietor Jérôme Dehours has come to typify the new quality-conscious, terroir-driven generation. No one who has visited his tasting room with its *très chic* iPod selection piped in would dispute the description of him as one of the rock stars of Champagne. Jérôme Dehours is a perfectionist and bottles only the very best of his crop, with one-third to one-half sold off as grapes. He feels that 85% of the work is done in the vineyards, not only caring for the vines during the growing season, but picking fruit at the right harvest date. In the winery, the focus is on maturation on the lees until disgorgement, and on fermenting the wine without a preliminary settling. And, as a general principle, Dehours intervenes as little as possible in the process and reduces sulfur to the lowest possible level – he points to a three-fold decrease over 10 years. Dehours quotes Émile Peynaud, the noted 20th century French oenologist: *"On ne fait pas de grand vin sans prendre de grandes risques"* ("One doesn't make great wine without taking great risks").

Dehours works 14 hectares spread over 42 parcels in the Marne Valley premiers crus of Mareuil-le-Port, Cerseuil, Troissy, and Œuilly, with an emphasis on single-vineyard plots. The estate has recently completed their organic certification although many of the sustainable practices have long been in place, including grassing between the rows or plowing the soil as appropriate to eliminate herbicide use. Another leitmotif of Dehours' work is the emphasis on Meunier. Given its dominance in the Marne Valley, this seems appropriate, and Dehours feels that his sites give an ideal expression to the grape. The vineyards are on the southern or left bank of the Marne, and so have a northern exposure, but this cooler location is fine with Dehours, who values the racy character it gives the wine.

In addition to a number of different non-vintage cuvées, Dehours produces several vintage-dated vineyard designates called The Collection. Since 1999, all have been fermented in cask, with a long maturation on the lees. Côte en Bosses is located in Mareuil-le-Port. From my notes on the 2005: *"Issued from a hot year, the Côte en Bosses is an old vine parcel of approximately a half-hectare, co-planted to Pinot Noir, Pinot Meunier, and Chardonnay, all harvested together. The base wine is fermented in cask and aged on the lees until the July following the vintage. It was disgorged in December 2012, and dosed at 2 g/l. This is a big, powerful wine of extraordinary scope. It shows a very vinous character with notes of smoke, roasted nuts, and mineral on the nose. On the palate, the wine is structured, fresh, and concentrated, with lots of extract and an incredibly long finish. This is a wine with a great presence."* **** (Tasted 2013)

Nearby lies the lieu-dit Maisoncelle. My notes on the 2004: *"2004 was a year of high volume and high quality. Although the Maisoncelle plot is near the Côte en Bosses, the character is quite different. The blend is nearly 100% Pinot Noir, with just a few Meunier vines co-planted in the same parcel. The wine was fermented in cask and bottled in July 2005, disgorged in August 2010, and dosed at 3 g/l. The wine is charming and fresh on the nose, with notes of cherries, red berry fruit, nuts, truffles, and violets. On the palate it is supple and silky, with a fine mousse and great elegance. In spite of its elegance and finesse, there is a lot of substance here, and the wine finishes long and complex at the end. Wonderful."* ****

Also in Mareuil-le-Port, the lieu-dit Brisefer has produced exciting results. From my notes on the 2008: *"Old vines planted in 1947 at the base of the slope in clay soils, this site has produced an exemplary wine with a crisp, lemony fruit upfront and some more subtle marzipan notes that expand on the palate along with a well-integrated toasty autolytic character. The texture is crisp and fresh, but the wine lingers in an engaging way."* **** (Tasted 2017)

Les Genevraux is in the next village over, Troissy. The 2005 was very expressive: *"From an old-vine parcel of Pinot Meunier planted in 1979, this champagne was bottled in July 2006, disgorged in April 2012, and dosed at 3 g/l. The wine shows a complex nose of hazelnut, fresh and dried white flowers, mineral,* and cream with a smoky note at the end. On the palate the wine is very crisp but not tart, with a supple texture, nice extract, and a creamy mousse carrying through to a lovely finish." **** (Tasted 2013)

Finally, there also is a vintage-dated rosé from lieu-dit La Croix Joly called Oeil de Perdrix. The 2009 showed great delicacy: *"Pretty red fruit and floral aromas open this wine crafted mostly from Meunier that has undergone a slight maceration on the skin, giving it a very faint color. The wine is among the most delicate of roses and a beautiful expression of terroir."* (Tasted 2017)

2 rue de la Chapelle 51700 Mareuil-le-Port | 03 26 52 71 75
https://champagne-dehours.fr/en/cuvee#nos-cuvees

Benoît Déhu

Region: Marne Valley | Terroir: Marne Valley West (Aisne)

Benoît Déhu is one of the bright stars of the new generation of champagne producers. He is hardly newly arrived; however. The Déhu family have been vignerons for eight generations (since before the French Revolution), and Benoît trained at Bollinger. He directs operations of the family Champagne Déhu Père et Fils and oversees the estate in Fossoy. The village is located on the on the left bank of the river in Château Thierry on the western edge of the Marne Valley. Importantly for wine lovers, he also has his side project called La Rue des Noyers. Named after the vineyard where he applies cutting-edge techniques to produce impressive wines from this 1.7 hectare parcel, which has been certified organic since 2014. He makes four wines from this parcel under the Benoit Déhu label: a blanc and rosé Champagne, and red and white Coteaux Champenois.

The parcel is planted to Meunier and biodynamically farmed. The Champagnes are fermented in casks made of wood sourced from the local forest of Meilleray and coopered in Champagne. Malolactic fermentation is avoided, and the wines are not racked before bottling. The Coteaux Champenois lots are destemmed and fermented in stainless. By the 2014 vintage, Benoit was hitting his stride with the Rue de Noyers and making wines of real substance: *"...opens with forward floral and spice aromas upfront; tropical notes and hints of coconut develop with time. The wine is tightly wound with plenty of structure, but this has the substance to age for years."* **** (Tasted 2018)

At the bottom of the hillside vines for Rue de Noyers lies another 1.5 hectare parcel that is planted to Pinot Noir which Déhu uses for the Brut Vintage L'Orme. Because the soils are sandy, the fruit ripens quickly, and the wine is accessible at an earlier point in its evolution. The 2015, was easy to love: *"Elegant and a bit restrained, within a few moments this opens up to show floral notes and a delicate apricot fruit character with a hint of spice. On the palate, the wine is supple and approachable yet ultimately very well balanced and easy drinking."* *** (Tasted 2018)

The red Coteaux has always impressed me. Made from 100% Meunier, it is serious wine. Although Benoit said that it was "not his best vintage," I thoroughly enjoyed the 2013: *"...open and forward there is a lovely expression of bright cherries and violets on the nose. The palate is fairly structured, as no malo-lactic fermentation was done. This is taken from a portion of the vineyard located at mid-slope, and it shows. Twenty-two months in cask."* **** (Tasted 2018)

The white Coteaux is the same, except it is pressed beforefermentation. From my notes on the 2013: *"Here the floral element dominates the nose, with accents of smoke and beeswax. On the palate it seems weighty and dense, with a complexity to the flavors that linger on the finish. 24 months in cask."* **** Definitely one of the new producers to watch.

3 rue Saint Georges 02650 Fossoy | 03 23 71 90 47
www.champagne-déhu.com

Delamotte

Region: Côte des Blancs | Terroir: Blended

Delamotte is a byword for elegance and finesse in the Côte des Blancs and is among the most historic Champagne houses. The house was founded in Reims in 1760 by François Delamotte, who was joined by his son Alexandre in 1786. Alexandre's younger brother Nicolas-Louis joined the business in 1798. After their father's death in 1799, the brothers moved the house to Le Mesnil, and in 1828 Nicolas-Louis offered Jean-Baptiste Lanson a minority stake in the business. When Nicolas-Louis died in 1837, Lanson ran the company with Delamotte's widow Marie-Pierrette, but when she passed away in 1856 without heirs, the Lanson family took complete control and changed the house name to Lanson. However, the Delamotte trademarks passed through the female line to the great-granddaughter of Jean-Baptiste, Marie-Louise Lanson de Nonancourt. Her son Charles de Nonancourt led Delamotte back to prosperity. In 1988, the house joined with Champagne Salon under parent company Laurent-Perrier, led by his brother Bernard de Nonancourt. Today, Delamotte and Salon are under the direction of Didier Depond.

Delamotte produces both a non-vintage Blanc de Blancs and rosé, and its vintage wine is a Blanc de Blancs. The 2008 vintage is particularly brilliant just now, tasted most recently February 2020: *"It takes a moment for the Delamotte '08 to show its potential. With time, however there is a bright, lemony fruit with a mineral/saline edge and a well-integrated autolysis. On the palate the wine is very fresh, yet the texture is creamy and very fine. The wine was nine years on the lees and represents 20% each of Le Mesnil, Avize, Oger, and Cramant. Disgorged in the autumn of 2017."* ****

The wine ages well and the slightly reductive tendency of its youth is counteracted by gentle aging in the late-disgorged release of the same wine, called Collection. The 2002, recently disgorged, was sumptuous. From a tasting at the winery in 2019: *"Delamotte Brut Blanc de Blancs 2002 showed well with a bit of age, with a bouquet of ripe orchard fruit, toasted brioche, and mineral on the nose and a creamy yet dense mousse on the palate with a lingering finish. There was more concentration here than expected – a very nice surprise."* ****

5 Rue de la Brèche d'Oger 51190 Le Mesnil-sur-Oger | 03 26 57 51 65
https://www.champagne-delamotte.com/en/

Nathalie Falmet

Region: Aube | Terroir: Bar-sur-Aubois

Nathalie Falmet originally studied chemistry at Paris XI University before returning to Champagne to study winemaking in Reims. Ultimately, she returned to her home in the Côte des Bar to set up a winemaking analysis laboratory in 1994 and began to work with her father on the family's 3.2 hectares in Rouvres-les-Vignes in the Aube department. This village is at the south-east extremity of the Champagne region, on the border with the Haute Marne. It lies next to Colombey-les-Deux-Eglises, famous as the home of Charles de Gaulle. Winemaking, however, has played an important role since Burgundian abbot Bernard de Clairvaux arrived in the 11th century to found nearby Clairvaux abbey. Falmet's vineyards include 2.1 hectares planted to Pinot Noir, 0.5 hectares planted to Chardonnay, and 0.6 hectares planted to Meunier. The vines are all sustainably worked, and the farming employs many organic techniques, although she is not certified.

Her work is modern, with a small pneumatic press that allows her to vinify parcel-by-parcel. However, she is also restlessly experimental and ferments in cask, stainless steel tanks, and amphorae. A réserve perpetuelle provides reserve wine for the Brut non-vintage, but the other wines all come from just one year, including the Brut Nature. From my notes on the 2014 Brut Nature: *"100% Pinot Noir, this shows pronounced floral and marzipan notes on the nose. The ripeness is exemplary but not overdone, and the fruit is overlaid with a well-integrated yeasty character. The texture is creamy and long. This Champagne shows why the Aube can often be* *so successful with the Blanc de Noirs done in a Brut Nature style."* *** (Tasted 2019)

The Rosé de Saignée called "Tentation Rosée" is also a millésime non-revendiqué, produced from a blend of half Pinot Noir and half Meunier. My notes on the 2012: *"Pressed off the skins after a 48-hour maceration, this has a fairly deep salmon color. The aromas and flavors are vinous and concentrated, with notes of raspberry and violets and a certain earthy character. Dosed at 5 g/l, it lacks the vibrancy of some of her other wines."* *** (Tasted 2019)

Falmet also produces a vintage-dated parcellaire from the lieu-dit Le Val Cornet. My note from the 2012: *"This Blanc de Noirs is approximately 50% Pinot Noir and 50% Meunier from 2012. Plenty of ripe, buttered apples on the nose with a hint of smoke and toast. The texture on the palate is silky and dense, with a slight hint of bitter almond on the finish to provide a lovely balance. A producer to watch."* **** (Tasted 2018)

Finally, there is a series of wines, each produced in tiny quantities produced from specific vineyard blocks within Le Val Cornet. The one that I have tasted most often is named ZH 302, named for the specific parcel within the lieu-dit. My notes on the 2010 vintage: *"This comes from very old Meunier vinified completely in cask and disgorged without dosage in 2013. The overall impression is of classic Meunier floral aromas, but there is a toasty edge here. On the palate, the wine is incredibly fresh and lively, but there is also a round, rich texture and lovely length. Only 1000 bottles produced."* **** (Tasted 2015) In addition to this wine there are two other varietal wines produced from contiguous vineyard blocks within Le Val Cornet: ZH 303 is made with fifty-year-old Chardonnay, and ZH 318 from Pinot Noir planted at the same time. All are produced in the same fashion, and all are Brut Nature. In addition to this, Falmet's experiment with fermentation in clay amphorae, called Terra, is a Blanc de Blancs that comes from the same old-vine plot ZH 303. The current vintage is 2012, dosed at 1 g/l, but I have yet to taste the wine. Falmet makes interesting and delicious wines and is well worth following.

1 Rue Saint-Maurice 0200 Rouvres-les-Vignes | 06 07 02 74 27
https://www.champagne-falmet.com/en/

Geoffroy

Region: Marne Valley | Terroir: Grande Vallée

The Geoffroy family traces its roots to the 17th century and has long been associated with Cumières, though today they are based in Aÿ. Réné Geoffroy was joined by his son Jean-Baptiste at the end of the 1980s. In 2008 he brought the cellars to Aÿ and installed a gravity-fed winery. The Geoffroy holdings include 14 hectares spread over 50 parcels. The majority of vineyards are located in Cumières, with other parcels in Hautvillers, Damery, and Fleury-la-Rivière. The vineyards are planted to 42% Pinot Noir, 34% Meunier, and 24% Chardonnay. The situation of the plots around Cumières is particularly favorable, with southern exposure, a warm microclimate, and the moderating influences of the Marne and the woods at the crest of the hill, all of which help assure grapes of great maturity. The vineyards are farmed using sustainable practices. Cover crops are used where possible, and where this is not practical, the ground is manually tilled.

Pressing is done with an old vertical press. 18 hectoliters of juice are pressed for the cuvée, with one retrousse (re-mixing of the grapes) after the second *serre* (tightening) of the press[13]. Vinification is by parcel-by-parcel as much as possible, using large and small casks (although new casks are avoided) in addition to enameled or stainless steel tanks of differing sizes. The base wines are aged on the lees, fined, and filtered before bottling. Because of the generally high level of ripeness, Geoffroy avoids malolactic fermentation when possible. He does not make any unbreakable rules, but instead adapts his work to the conditions of the vintage. He ferments on cultured yeast after a light sulfuring, and the wines are dosed "as little as possible."

There are several vintage cuvées, including the flagship of the house, Terre Millésime. This bottling is made from vines more than 50-years-old and is a blend of 70% Pinot Noir and 30% Chardonnay. The base wine is fermented in large wooden foudres and aged on the lees before bottling. Only the best barrels are selected for Terre, and the prise de mousse takes

---

13   See the Glossary entry for Press and Pressing for a further explanation.

place under cork. My notes on the 2005 vintage: *"Ten years on the lees. As one might expect, the nose opens with plenty of toasty autolytic character, but there are still plenty of ripe apple and pear fruit and aromas as well as hazelnut, dried flowers, and ground coffee. On the palate, the wine has a silky, creamy texture but enough freshness to carry it to a delightfully long finish."* ***** (Tasted 2015)

The next cuvée is called Empreinte. This is a Blanc de Noirs, composed mostly of Pinot Noir, with all the grapes coming from Cumières. The 2008 vintage was fantastic: *"79% Pinot Noir, 15% Meunier, and 6% Chardonnay, coming from south-facing, early-ripening sites above Cumières, from the lieux-dits of Barremonts, Demoiselles, and Houtrants. 80% of the base wine was fermented in cask. Disgorged in December 2014 and dosed a 6 g/l; the result was softly spicy on the nose with a ripe Tarte Tatin fruit character of baked apples and pastry that is beginning to open up. On the palate, it is pleasantly ripe but deftly balanced. Bravo!"* **** (Tasted 2017)

The counterpart to Empreinte is called Volupté, a 100% Chardonnay made from selected sites in Cumières: Montagne, Chênes, and Tournemidi. As with Empreinte, 80% of the base wines are fermented in cask. I have not had the finished Champagne, but I have tasted this as a vin clair from the 2016 vintage. I was dazzled by the voluptuously ripe, textured nature of the fruit with its many layers of tropical fruit and spice. The wine seemed to be pleasant enough to drink as a Coteaux Champenois, but I am eager to taste it after the prise de mousse.

Next in the line-up is a 100% Meunier from single lieu-dit in Cumières, Les Tiersaudes. The 2013 was impressive: *"The problem with some 100% Meunier Champagnes is a lack of structure, but here the wine is concentrated and firm, and yet still has all of the pretty floral aromas typical of the grape. There is a lot of backbone here, with a clean, straight line, plenty of minerally undertones, and power. Impressive."* **** (Tasted 2019)

Another charming wine is the Blanc de Rose, a rosé de saignée of 50% Pinot Noir and 50% Chardonnay. My notes indicate that it is a millésime non-revendiqué. The bottling from the 2012 harvest was not your typical rosé: *"This was served at the annual Printemps des Champagnes trade tasting decanted, and it showed more like a light red Burgundy with bubbles. The aromas opened with a rich, dark cherry fruit character and pronounced earthy notes. The mousse was soft due to the decanting, and the feel on the palate was seductively rich. Enormously successful, but take with food."* **** (Tasted 2015)

Finally, it would be a grave error to leave off without considering Geoffroy's delicious Coteaux, bottled as Cumières Rouge. It is consistently one of the best Coteaux produced in the region. The 2015 was particularly successful: *"Lovely, expressive red fruits on the nose with a profusion of cherry and violet notes – very Pinot Noir. On the palate, the fruit is sweet but not cloying. It does 24 months in cask and has both freshness and a slight tannic edge that carry it far beyond the norm. Should last a decade at least in a proper cellar."* **** (Tasted 2019)

4 rue Jeanson 51160 Ay | 03 26 55 32 31
https://www.champagne-geoffroy.com/en

Pierre Gerbais

Region: Côte des Bar | Terroir: Barséquannais

The Gerbais family have grown grapes for eight generations and bottled their own wine since 1930, and today Aurélien Gerbais is infusing the wines with passion and precision. The estate was begun by Ulysses Gerbais, Aurélian's great-grandfather and continued under his grandfather Pierre, and his father, Pascal. Champagne Pierre Gerbais has been using organic principles in the vineyard since 1996 and is certified Haute Valeur Environnementale Level 3. The house works 20 plots, nearly all within Celles-sur-Ource in the Côte des Bar. Holdings total 18 hectares, with ten hectares of Pinot Noir, four hectares of Chardonnay, and four hectares of Pinot Blanc, making this estate the single biggest source of Pinot Blanc in Champagne. The average age of the vines is 30 years.

The domaine is still fairly traditional, but young Aurélien also is at the forefront of the revolution underway in the Aube. He took us to the hillside slopes where their vineyards are planted overlooking the terrain, where the Laignes, the Ource, and the Arce flow into the Seine. Gerbais produces two cuvées that are a blend of all the sites in addition to single-varietal champagnes from Chardonnay, Pinot Blanc (from vines that were planted in 1904), and two different cuvées from Pinot Noir, one produced without sulfur. Among the vineyard sites farmed by the Gerbais family are the Champ Viole (a south-facing slope planted to Chardonnay), Envers (a very cool, west-facing site that gives minerality to the vines), and Sainte-Marie (a plot of 60-year-old Pinot Noir used for their blanc de noirs l'Audace). The grapes are generally harvested a week after the rest of the nearby producers. Gerbais uses both a traditional Coquard press and a pneumatic press, and the grapes are pressed and vinified parcel-by-parcel. Fermentations are done in tank, and the malolactic fermentation is always finished. The wines are all produced from a single vintage. The Blanc de Blancs is called l'Osmose, made using grapes from two sites, Champ Viole and Envers. The former is a south-facing slope that gives very ripe grapes, and the latter is a cool, west-facing site that gives minerality to the vines. The bottling from the 2013 harvest was delicious: *"This intriguing cuvée is blended from two distinct plots of Chardonnay, one that faces south and one that faces north. Both are planted with old vines. The 2013 is dosed at only 2 g/l. This is a wine that leads with mineral, showing a hint of reduction, yet there is also ripe yellow apple and citrus notes. Fresh, clean and long on the palate."* **** (Tasted 2018)

The use of Pinot Blanc is not widespread in Champagne, and the majority of it is planted in the Côte des Bar. Gerbais explains that it is resistant to rot, a frequent plague in Celles-sur-Ource with its very moist and humid microclimate at the juncture of the four river valleys. The Pinot Blanc cuvée is called l'Originale. *"This is produced from the oldest plots of Pinot Blanc that date to 1904 in a lieu-dit called Les Proies. The bottling from the 2013 harvest was dosed at 3 g/l. The result shows lovely ripe, clean pear and floral notes with just a bit of beeswax and a touch of honey. There is a nice aromatic complexity here and a lush, sensuous feel on the palate, with balanced acidity and impressive length."* ***** (Tasted 2018) There is also a second cuvée called l'Unique, produced from the same lieu-dit, but without sulfur. To my taste, it shows a bit more oxidation and lacks some of the tension of l'Originale.

The old vine Pinot Noir "l'Audace" also uses no sulfur in its production. This cuvée has made strides in recent years, and, for me, the oxidation in early iterations was a bit of an obstacle. Now it is much fresher and cleaner. From my notes on the bottling produced from the 2015 harvest: *"...slightly closed initially, this opens up with firm notes of almond, wood smoke, and earth. On the palate, the wine is structured and tense but not lacking in depth."* *** (Tasted 2019)

The Coteaux Champenois at Gerbais are often a high point. The white from 2015 was nothing short of spectacular: *"At the end of the tasting, almost as an afterthought, we were offered a stupendous Coteaux made from 100% Pinot Blanc. Unlike the rest of the production, it is fermented in cask. No new wood, but one used (600-liter) demi-muid. The results were intense* *and concentrated, with aromas that ranged from citrus to apricot and stone fruit, pear and apple, all with a trimming of fresh white flowers. The texture was dense, almost meaty, and the finish was very long. Truly special."* ***** (Tasted 2017)

13 rue du Pont 10110 Celles-sur-Ource | 03 25 38 51 29
http://www.gerbais.com/en

Alfred Gratien

Location: Epernay | Terroir: Blended

Founded in 1864, Gratien is a traditional Champagne négociant in the best sense of the term. They have employed members of the same family as their chefs de cave for four generations. The first was Gaston Jaeger, who began in 1905. Today's winemaker, Nicolas Jaeger, began working with his father Jean-Pierre in 1990 and took over the reins seventeen years later, although Jean-Pierre still helps maintain contacts with the growers. The German firm Henkell purchased the house in 2004, but Gratien has been allowed to keep its identity as a small family producer. Henkell has made significant investments in Gratien without in any way detracting from its charm.

The house purchases the quasi-totality of their fruit since they own only 1.56 hectares of vines, but this is an area where the Jaegers excel. Gratien sources nearly all the fruit in the area around Epernay where they are based, and none comes from the Aisne or the Aube. All of the base wines are fermented in cask. There are over 1,000 used oak casks on the premises – the third largest collection after Krug and Bollinger. Wines are kept on the lees until the spring following the harvest, but no bâtonnage is done, as Jaeger feels it can make the wines heavy. Only the cuvée is used, and the tailles are vinified in a separate process for a different brand entirely that is only sold in Germany (home to parent company Henkell). Malolactic fermentation is not done. The dosage is moderate, and it is done using a liqueur made from the Cuvée Paradis blend, held in solera (with 10% renewed each year).

A tasting of the vintage range at Gratien begins typically with the vintage Blanc de Blancs. The 2007 was a classic, too often overlooked, even though Chardonnay from 2007 was pretty successful: *"Using only grand cru fruit from Le Mesnil, Avize, Chouilly, Oger, and Cramant, the Blanc de Blancs is always a vintage. The 2007 shows notes of pear and lemon peel with an edge of mineral and an almost saline note. On the palate, a well-integrated note of toasted brioche develops; the texture is silky and soft yet not insubstantial."* ***

The Millésime is always a standout. Aged under cork and disgorged with a moderate dosage, it is consistently rewarding. The 2004, however, was a standout: *"Wonderful wine; fresher and more vibrant than the 2005. This is a blend of 68% Chardonnay and 13% Pinot Noir blended with 19% Meunier sourced from a treasured site at Leuvrigny. There are aromas of ripe apples colored with toasty yeast notes and a hint of minerality. The texture is fresh and silky, with a creamy density, lovely weight and persistent finish."* ***** *(Tasted 2018)*

The bottling known as Cuvée Paradis is the Gratien prestige cuvée, produced in both blanc and rosé versions, and well worth seeking out. The 2008: *"This is a blend of 65% Chardonnay and 35% Pinot Noir from grand and premier crus, dosed at 8 g/l. The combination of the cask ferment, long aging under cork, lively acidity (from the blocked malolactic fermentation), and the delicate, creamy texture brings both an incredible density and concentration but as well as a uniquely rewarding finesse."* **** (Tasted 2018)

The wines also can last a very long time indeed. From my notes on the 1985 Vintage, tasted at the winery in 2016: *"76% Chardonnay, 24% Meunier – this is mature but holding well. The nose brings gusts of truffle, ground coffee, toffee, and caramel. In spite of the deep, complex aromas, the wine is still very fresh, and the finish is deceptively long."* ****

30 rue Maurice Cerveaux 51201 Epernay | 03 26 54 38 20
www.alfredgratien.com

Maurice Grumier

Region: Marne Valley | Terroir: Right Bank

A member of the Grumier family has been growing grapes in the Marne Valley village of Venteuil since at least 1743. For nearly 200 years, they sold their grapes, but in 1928 Amand Grumier began to bottle wine under his own label. The current generation, Fabien, began to work at the family estate in 1999. Today, he and his wife Hélène farm 8.5 hectares of vines spread over 29 parcels in five different villages: Venteuil and Reuil on the Right Bank of the Marne, and Dormans, Festigny, and Nesle-le-Repons on the Left Bank. The vineyard's soul is in the home base of Venteuil, with its slopes exposed to the south. The vineyards are 55% Meunier, 25% Pinot Noir, and 20% Chardonnay, all sustainably farmed, with some rows tilled and some rows grassed over. Chemical products are rarely used.

Much of the fermentation is done in small stainless steel tanks suited to the size of the parcels, although Fabien is increasingly fond of cask fermentation. Some of the casks used are from the Argonne forest just east of the Champagne region. These are produced by the local Tonnellerie de Champagne. Other casks are made of wood from Festigny, where the family owns vines. They choose the oak carefully and age the staves for three years before the barrels are coopered. After the fermentation, there is bâtonnage every 12 to 15 days. A small amount of sulfur is used at the press and nothing more until the bottling. The wines are kept at 6 to 8°, minimizing the need for sulfur and naturally blocking the malolactic fermentation.

There are two vintage wines. The first is a parcellaire called Les Plates Pierres, named for a lieu-dit in Venteuil. My notes on the 2011: *"The wine is an assemblage of 62% Chardonnay and 38% Pinot Noir, fermented partly in stainless steel tanks and partly in cask. The result is crisp, lemony, and bright, with plenty of structure and a beautiful line. Although 2011 was a warm year, the wine has retained a marvelous freshness. Dosed at 3 g/l."* **** (Tasted 2018)

The top Grumier vintage wine is Armand, a parcel selection of the best vines in the home village of Venteuil. The base wines for this tribute to Fabien's great-grandfather is fermented entirely in cask, aged on the lees with bâtonnage, and then bottled without fining or filtration. My notes on the 2008: *"...still youthful more than ten years after the vintage, with creamy apricot and hazelnut aromas, a touch of smoke, and just a hint of black truffle. On the palate, the wine shows a lovely, spicy side, and a rich texture. Despite the complexity and power of this wine, it retains a deft balance and lovely persistence."* **** (Tasted 2015)

13 route d'Arty 51480 Venteuil | 03 26 58 48 10
http://www.champagne-grumier.com/en/

Marc Hébrart

Region: Marne Valley | Terroir: Grande Vallée

Jean-Paul Hébrart has something in common with his wife: they both make fantastic Champagne. He is married to Isabelle Diebolt (see Diebolt-Vallois), but they each run their estates independently. Jean-Paul took over from his father Marc Hébrart, who had been domaine-bottling wine since 1964. Champagne Marc Hébrart owns 13.80 hectares based in Mareuil-sur-Aÿ, with other parcels in Aÿ, Oiry (2 parcels totaling 17.5 ares), and Chouilly. The vineyards are very scattered, with a total of 65 parcels varying from 2.10 ares to 80 ares. Some are very impressively sited, including vines in two lieux-dits that abut the Clos du Goisses: Noyer La Ville and Les Côtes. The overall varietal blend across parcels is 70% Pinot Noir and 30% Chardonnay. Sustainable viticulture practices are used everywhere, and yields are kept in check by rubbing out every other bud rather than by green harvest. In the winery, Hébrart uses two membrane presses, and most wines ferment at cool temperatures in stainless and enameled steel tanks, with each parcel vinified separately. A small proportion of fruit from the old vine parcels is fermented in cask. Malolactic is routinely done, and the wines are disgorged six months before shipping.

There are three vintage cuvées. What used to be the Millésimé now is labeled as Special Club. This has always been a standout wine for the estate. I was entranced by the 2002: *"...produced from 60% Pinot Noir from forty-year-old vines in Mareuil (lieux-dits: Faubourg d'Enfer, Côte, Haut de Varille, Croix Blanches, Sente des Demoiselles), and 40% Chardonnay vines more than forty-years-old in Oiry (La Justice) and Chouilly (Montaigu). The wine is wildly aromatic with notes of tropical fruit, licorice, and spice, along with fresh cream, toast, and hot pastry. On the palate, it has the particular aspect of lightness alongside great complexity and very subtle length."* **** (Tasted 2016)

In 2004 he began to produce a new cuvée called Rive Gauche Rive Droite, entirely fermented in cask. The 2012 was riveting: *"Half Pinot Noir from Aÿ (lieux-dits of Pruche,*

Cheuzelles, Longchamps, and Chaffour), and half Chardonnay from Oiry, Chouilly, and Avise, this is entirely fermented in cask and dosed at 4 g/l. The nose shows brioche, ripe apple, and well-integrated spice from the cask ferment, although this does not dominate the wine. On the palate, it is lovely and fresh with elegance and power but also with a sense of playfulness." ****
(Tasted 2016)

The most recent addition is called Noces de Craie, a Blanc de Noirs from Aÿ. My notes on the 2015: *"100% Pinot Noir from Ay (lieux-dits Cheuzelles, Longchamp, Pierre Robert, Pruche, and Chauffour). The result is sublime, and not at all heavy. On the initial attack, the wine shows hints of hazelnut, toast, and cream, and a ripe red apple and white blossom perfume emerge with time. On the palate, the wine is rich and structured but sufficiently refreshing to maintain a superb balance through to the lingering finish. Only the cuvée is used, and the wine is dosed at 5 g/l."* **** (Tasted 2019)

8 rue du Pont 51160 Mareuil-sur-Aÿ | 06 07 52 55 61
[No Website]

Charles Heidsieck & Piper-Heidsieck

Location: Reims | Terroir: Blended

The case of the Heidsiecks is complicated. The history of the three houses that include "Heidsieck" in the name is deeply intertwined, and even today Charles Heidsieck and Piper-Heidsieck are under the same ownership. I have placed both here. They merit inclusion at least in the "two-star" category; some of the wines are even better than this. For the sake of brevity, I discuss Piper-Heidsieck and Heidsieck Monopole here as well. First, the history. In 1785 Florens-Louis Heidsieck formed a company called Heidsieck & Cie. to trade in cloth and wine. He was joined by his nephew Christian Heidsieck in 1800, and his other nephews Frédéric-Auguste Delius, Charles-Henri Heidsieck, and Henri-Louis Walbaum joined him in 1814. His cousin Henri-Guillaume Piper arrived at the firm in 1815. Christian Heidsieck took over upon the death of his uncle, with Piper in charge of sales. Upon Christian's death in 1838, Piper married his widow, giving rise to the house of Piper-Heidsieck. In 1851, Heidsieck took a partner named Jacques-Charles Théodore Kunkelmann, while the cousins continued to operate their firm as Walbaum Heidsieck & Co. In 1860, the cousins trademarked the name Heidsieck Monopole, but this name does not appear to have been used until the firm was acquired in 1923 by grocer Édouard Mignot.

Kunkelmann's granddaughter married the Marquis Jean de Suarez d'Aulan in 1926, and Piper Heidsieck remained in the Suarez d'Aulan family until it was sold by them to Rémy-Martin in 1987. The two firms continued side-by-side through much of the 20th century. Heidsieck Monopole was eventually purchased by Mumm in 1976, and in turn Mumm was purchased by Seagram's, who held Heidsieck Monopole until 1996 when it was sold to Paul Vranken.

The third Heidsieck line also begins with one of Florens-Louis Heidsieck's great nephews, Charles-Camille Heidsieck. Charles-Camille founded the négociant house Charles Heidsieck in 1851 in partnership with his brother-in-law Ernest Henriot. After Charles-Camille's death, the firm was run by his sons, and it stayed in the family until it was sold in 1975 to Joseph Henriot. By a twist of fate, Henriot was a descendant of Charles-Camille's brother-in-law and original partner. Henriot appointed Daniel Thibault, his cellar master at Champagne Henriot, as the new Chef de Caves. Ultimately, Henriot sold Charles Heidsieck to Rémy-Martin, and Daniel Thibault ended up as Chef de Caves for both Charles Heidsieck and Piper-Heidsick when Rémy acquired Piper-Heidsieck in 1987. Thibault is credited with resurrecting the fortunes of Charles Heidsieck through his use of large quantities of reserve wines to bolster the non-vintage blend. He also originated the innovative *"Mise en Cave"* program that labeled a non-vintage wine with the year of bottling and the date of disgorgement. This let consumers know how long a wine had aged on the lees. He also dramatically changed the style of Piper by reversing the policy of blocking the malolactic fermentation which had long been the Piper style. After his death, supervision of both brands assumed by another notable Chef de Caves, Régis Camus. In 1990 Rémy-Martin and Cointreau merged to form Rémy-Cointreau, who continued to hold the brands until 2011 when they were sold to French conglomerate EPI. Today, the Chef de Caves at Charles Heidsieck is Cyril Brun, formerly of Veuve Clicquot, while Emilien Boutillat, formerly of Cattier/ Armand de Brignac presides over Piper-Heidsieck.

So much for the history; now to the wines. Charles Heidsieck is the place to begin. As mentioned above, this brand is renowned for its non-vintage blend. However, the vintage wines deserve some discussion. The 2005 and 2006 have both seemed a bit heavy to me. From my notes on the 2006: *"Aromas of ripe apricot and apple with a floral edge. On the palate the text- ure is silky, but the acidity is a bit soft and the finish is very ripe, almost sweet. A blend of 60% Pinot Noir and 40% Chardonnay."* *** (Tasted 2018) They also release a late-disgorged series called La Collection Crayères that I find much more compelling. My notes on the 1989: *"Pungent aromas that range from honey to toffee and butterscotch and finally to roasted coffee - mature but balanced. On the palate, despite this richness, the wine is still* surprisingly fresh, and the length is very good. A blend of 60% Pinot Noir and 40% Chardonnay, disgorged in 2012." **** (Tasted 2019) Champagne Charlie is from the same series despite the different name. My notes on the 1982 was consistent with this note when I tasted it in 2011.

The best from Charles Heidsieck, however, has been the Blanc des Millénaires. This wine was introduced with the 1983 vintage, and there have been few vintages since then -- only 1985, 1990, 1995, and 2004 have been released. The 1990 is good, if mature now, but I have enjoyed the 1995 on many occasions and it continues to show well. A typical note: *"This wine shows much more autolysis than previous bottles of the same, with a pronounced smokiness, good lemony fruit, and mineral notes on the nose. On the palate the wine has crisp acidity and a very long finish. Extremely successful."* **** (Tasted 2015)

Piper-Heidsieck for its part is of note more for the future potential than it is for recent efforts. They have enjoyed a better reputation generally in recent decades. To me the range seems designed to appeal to everyone and thus to lack distinctiveness at the high end. The regular vintage wine has always been well-made. My notes on the 2004: *"Dominated by Pinot Noir, this is a firm, masculine Champagne with an edge of truffle and marzipan. Rich, yet not lacking in finesse or elegance, it is a very attractive offering. Lovely complexity and depth."* *** (Tasted 2015)

The top of the range has been known as Rare, but now Piper is launching "Rare Champagne" as a stand-alone brand, similar to the way in which Moët & Chandon markets Dom Pérignon. The new vintage is 2008, which I have yet to taste. I enjoyed the 2002 very much: *"There is superb aromatic complexity here, with aromas of apricot, confit fruit, and tropical fruits, all accented with a bit of truffle. On the palate the texture is silky, if a bit soft, and the finish is elegantly long. The blend is composed of 70% Chardonnay from the Côte des Blancs along with some from the "Perle Blanche," notably Trepail, and Villers-Marmery for minerality. These are blended with 30% Pinot Noir from the Montagne."* **** (Tasted 2016) This is the best of the house, but with the name change it seems that the rest of the Piper-Heidsieck range will not benefit from the reflected glory.

As for Heidsieck & Co. Monopole, some of the oldest champagnes I have enjoyed were Heidsieck Monopole. This includes the 1907 vintage and the 1929, both described in the sections relating to those years (pages 285 and 307). The other mature vintage of Heidsieck Monopole that I have enjoyed is the 1961 Sec, found on page 345. These were very well-made champagnes, and collectors seeking out truly mature Champagne should not hesitate to acquire old bottles of Heidsieck Monopole, which can be quite affordable. However, the wines produced under the current regime have not held up to the same scrutiny and I would not seek them out.

For Charles Heidsieck, Piper-Heidsieck, and Rare Champagne:

12 Allée du Vignoble 51100 Reims | 03 26 84 43 00
https://www.charlesheidsieck.com
https://www.piper-heidsieck.com
https://www.rare-champagne.com/en

For Heidsieck & Co. Monopole:

5 place du Général Gouraud 51100 Reims | 03 26 61 61 64
https://www.heidsieckandco-monopole.com/

Henriot

Location: Reims | Terroir: Blended

Champagne Henriot was founded in 1808, and today it is run by 8th generation Gilles de Larouzière. The house has come to greater prominence in recent years due to the energy and vision of late proprietor Joseph Henriot. Henriot was one of the legendary dealmakers in Champagne. He engineered the purchase of Charles Heidsieck (as outlined in the previous section), along with the Champagne houses of Trouillard and de Venoge. All of these houses, along with Henriot, were all sold in 1985, and Henriot took a seat on the board of LVMH. He was installed as the president of Veuve Clicquot, but resigned in 1994 and negotiated a return to his family house, without the vineyards, which LVMH retained.

Since retaking control of the family brand, the house has embarked on an ambitious vineyard purchase program and relies on contracts for the rest of their needs for Champagne Henriot. Purchases are dominated by fruit from the grands crus, especially Chardonnay from the Côte des Blancs and the north of the Montagne. The house emphasizes a style led by Chardonnay, although there is almost an equal quantity of structured Pinot Noir from the north face of the Montagne in the villages of Mailly, Verzy, and Verzenay. These characteristics are tempered with fruit from the Aube and Montgueux, and given these sources, Cellar Master Laurent Fresnet placed a strong emphasis on freshness and elegance. In 2019, it was announced that Laurent Fresnet would leave Henriot to take up the post of Chef de Caves at G.H. Mumm and would be replaced by former Krug winemaker Alice Tétienne.

At Henriot fermentations are traditionally done in stainless steel tanks and all of the base wines undergo malolactic fermentation. Aging on the lees is long, and the vintage wine typically sees six to eight years of aging before being disgorged. The current vintage release from the house is the 2008. Aged six years on the lees and another three after disgorging, it is superb: *"extremely well, with a superb fruit ripeness and lots of smoky, toasty notes from the yeast, although it is very well integrated and does not give the impression of heaviness at all. On the palate, the wine is rich and velvety, but there is plenty of freshness. Despite the vintage, this is exceedingly fresh, and although it shows well now, it will undoubtedly hold for another decade or more."* ****

The prestige cuvée was until recently called Cuvée des Enchanteleurs, and in a fresh vintage such as 1996, it was reliably top quality. Even a bottle of 1979, tasted in 2019, showed very well more than thirty years after the fact: *"A '79 Enchanteleurs from Henriot was mature, with aromas of cream, toast, and truffle coming to the fore. On the palate, there was still a good amount of mousse, however, and a crisp acidity backed the fruit aromas. Perhaps not a wine to keep forever, it is drinking very well now."* ****

This cuvée, however, has been phased out to re-align as a more Chardonnay-driven wine with more freshness and elegance rather than the luxurious, occasionally somewhat heavy richness of the Enchanteleurs. The new cuvée is called "Hemera"; the inaugural 2005 vintage is showed well at its 2018 launch: *"Powerful and dense, but not heavy, with notes of lemon, toast, and ripe apricot on the nose, and a lovely silky texture with admirable freshness."* ****

81 rue Coquebert 51100 Reims | 03 26 89 53 00
www.champagne-henriot.com

Huré Frères

Region: Montagne de Reims | Terroir: Grande Montagne (North)

Pierre and François Huré are third-generation growers based in Ludes who are bringing their family estate to the notice of a new generation of Champagne lovers. The domaine has 10 hectares of vineyards, mostly in Ludes, where vines are planted in chalk and clay soils. The vineyards in Ludes used to be planted to a majority of Pinot Meunier, but today the mix is 45% Pinot Meunier, 15% Chardonnay, and 40% Pinot Noir. Although the family loves Meunier, the yields and quality can be variable. The benefits are apparent, however, in the sandy terroirs at the bottom of the slope. These areas are more susceptible to frost, and since Meunier buds out later it is less prone to frost damage. Other vines are located in Villedommange, where the sandier soil produces charming, accessible wines. This same soil type is found in the Ardre Valley village of Brouillet, where the vineyards were replanted from Pinot Meunier to Pinot Noir in the 1970s. The vines in Brouillet usually are about a week behind the others, since they are located at the top of the hill in a cooler terroir based on calcium-rich clay and sand over limestone. The family loves the results, however, which give a wine scented with mirabelle plums and honey. The last site is Vavray le Grand in the Vitryat. Here there are 1.5 hectares of Chardonnay vines planted on pure limestone. This is a fascinating terroir, but the fruit must be picked ripe or risk a thin and tart result. Finally, Huré Frères is buying a bit of Chardonnay in Rilly-la-Montagne from the lieu-dit Les Blanches Voies, a terroir with a south-facing exposition and abundant limestone. Sustainable practices are used throughout the vineyards. Most of the rows are grassed over, organic compost is used, and no synthetic herbicides are employed.

Fermentation is mostly done in stainless steel tanks, but there is an increasing proportion of it done in cask. Malolactic fermentation is normally not done for the base wines fermented in cask, and the proportion of the base wines that undergo malolactic is steadily decreasing. Dosage is low. The first of the vintage wines is a classic vintage wine called "Instantanée," meant to reflect the character of each year. It has been made every year since 1985. The grape blend is approximately one-third each Meunier, Chardonnay, and Pinot Noir. The 2006 was fresh and lively: *"...notes of apple, citrus peel and smoke on the nose with a slightly lifted character to the fruit and a note of cream at the end. On the palate, the wine has a lively acidity and tightly structured texture on the palate that leads to a rich, lingering finish."* **** (Tasted 2013)

There is also a series of wines called "4 éléments" – there is a version that is 100% Chardonnay, and one for Meunier, and another for Pinot Noir. The wines share four characteristics: they are each made with one grape from one parcel in one harvest, fermented in large 600-liter casks. In addition to each of those "elements," the wines are all done without malolactic fermentation and aged under cork. I tasted through the current 2014 range at the importer's trade tasting in the fall of 2019. *"Each of these shows their grape variety to its best advantage. The Chardonnay is from the lieu-dit Les Blanches Voies in Rilly, and the nose shows hints of lemon peel, smoke, wet chalk, and a hint of spice. On the palate, the wine has vivacious acidity, yet there are substance and density as well. The Meunier is from the lieu-dit La Grosse Pierre in Ludes. Here the wine is fresh and floral on the first approach, with just a hint of spice from the cask ferment. On the palate, there is a supple, silky feel and surprising length. The Pinot Noir is also from Ludes, from the lieu-dit La Perthe. This is the most vinous and substantial wine, with aromas of brioche, marzipan, and fresh white flowers. On the palate, the mousse is very creamy, and the wine feels almost plump, yet there is still an excellent balancing acidity."* ****

The top wine at Huré Frères is named Terre Natale ("Homeland"), and is made solely from fruit grown in Ludes. The blend is 40% Chardonnay from the lieu-dit Les Sentiers, 35% Pinot Noir from the Chemin d'Amis, and 25% Pinot Meunier from La Grosse Pierre, all planted using a massal selection from their existing sites. My note on the inaugural 2000 vintage: *"Disgorged in February 2013 and thus twelve years on the lees. The nose opens with pronounced autolytic notes of smoke, ground coffee, and mineral along with toasted brioche and an underlying fruit character that is almost tropical. On the palate, there is a creamy, dense texture, good balancing acidity, and a pleasantly persistent finish. Dosed at 4 g/l."* ****

2 impasse Carnot 51500 Ludes | 03 26 61 11 20
www.champagne-hure-freres.com

Benoît Lahaye

Region: Montagne de Reims | Terroir: Grande Montagne (South)

Benoît Lahaye is one of the leading lights in the organic Champagne movement. He enjoys immense popularity with fans of "natural" and natural-style wines, and his wines certainly stand on their own. He took over his family's 4.8 hectare estate in Bouzy in 1993. Three hectares of the vines are in Bouzy itself, and then there is one hectare in Ambonnay, and 0.6 hectares in Tauxières. Lahaye also has 0.2 hectares of old vine Chardonnay in Voipreux; this is so distant from Bouzy that they are tended by Pierre Larmandier.

By 1996 Lahaye had begun to incorporate organic principles in the vineyards. He officially began conversion in 2003, was certified organic in 2008, and then was certified biodynamic in 2010. The vines are grassed over between the rows, and the soil is tilled by horse. In the winery, the must is not chaptalized, and all of the wines are fermented in cask with native yeasts. The vins clairs are aged ten months on the fine lees and are bottled without fining or filtration. They also receive little or no dosage.

The vintage wine is an assemblage of 70% Pinot from the Bouzy lieu-dit Mont de Tauxières planted in 1966, and 30% Chardonnay from Haut des Argentières in Tauxières, planted in 1960. Lahaye used to block the Malolactic fermentation, but he normally allows it to finish, as he feels that biodynamic processes bring the wines closer to balance with both more ripeness and more acidity. Many biodynamic producers dislike the use of sulphur to block a process that the wine would normally undergo naturally.

The 2004 vintage was stunningly good: *"This shows a forward nose that opens with ripe apples and freshly baked pastry, hazelnut, and fresh and dried flowers. On the palate, it is powerful and vinous, but in no way heavy. There is an intense concentration and plenty of extract, but there is also a firm balancing acidity, great integration, and impressive length. Dosed at 4 g/l"* ***** (Tasted 2020)

In addition to the vintage, there is a Blanc de Noirs that is produced from grapes grown on old vines. This cuvée is not vintage-dated but still comes typically from only one year. From the 2012 harvest: *"Produced from Les Vaux Bétins and Les Hannepés in Bouzy and Les Argentières in Tauxières, this shows aromas of fresh red apple fruit with a hint of flowers. Structured and dense, it avoids heaviness to finish very well indeed."* **** (Tasted 2015)

Although the vintage wine and the Blanc de Noirs are immensely accomplished, several other cuvées have more of an experimental taste. The first is a millésime non-revendiqué called Violaine made entirely without sulfur: *"With its aromas of bruised apple and faded flowers, the Cuvée Violaine, produced entirely without sulfur, struggles to impress. The texture is supple, almost soft, and lacking definition."* (Tasted 2015)

Another millésime non-revendiqué is Le Jardin de la Grosse Pierre: *"This is from a single lieu-dit of the same name. The parcel was initially planted in 1923 by Lahaye's great-grand-father and partially replanted in 1952. It is a field blend of the authorized Champagne varieties: Pinot Noir, Meunier, Chardonnay, Blanc Vrai (or Pinot Blanc), Arbanne, and Petit Meslier as well as some that are not authorized, such as Chasselas, Gros Plant, Teinturier, and others. This shows some similarities with Voilaine, with a nose of bruised apple and bright flowers. There seems to be a bit of volatile acidity, and perhaps the unique grape blend brings a slightly foxy aroma to the blend. The wine is spicy and somewhat marked by the oak. The wine tastes crisp and somewhat lean."* ** (Tasted 2020)

33 rue Jeanne d'Arc 51150 Bouzy | 03 26 57 03 05
[No Website]

Juillet-Lallement

Region: Montagne de Reims | Terroir: Grande Montagne (Northeast)

The first bottles of Juillet-Lallement were produced in 1931 by Paul and Arthur Lallement and their partner René Juillet. Ownership passed in 1963 to Arthur's son Pierre, who turned it over to his son Jean and his wife Virginie in 2003. Juillet-Lallement is based in Verzy, one of the most celebrated villages of the Montagne de Reims. They work 4 hectares, split evenly between the grand crus Verzy and Sillery, and spread over nine parcels. The average age of the vines is 40 years, but the oldest parcels were planted in 1949 by Arthur Lallement. The grape blend in the vineyards is 45% Chardonnay, 50% Pinot Noir, and 5% Pinot Meunier. The vines are sustainably worked: no herbicides are used, and there is grass between all of the rows. The grapes are picked at a maximum of 10° potential alcohol to retain freshness. The two terroirs are very different: the Juillet-Lallement parcels in Verzy have a northeast exposition located almost against the top of the tree line, and the soils are a thin layer of clay over the chalk. Here the morning fog makes the wine firmer and more structured. Sillery has the same chalky soils, but they face almost due north and lack the protection of the trees. Sillery has much more of a gentle slope, and its grapes make a fresher, lighter wine with great finesse. As Jean says, these factors yield Pinot that has the appearance of Chardonnay, "un pinot qui chardonne," as he puts it.

When Jean and Virginie took over the property, they completely renovated the winery, adding a state-of-the-art press and new 50 hl stainless tanks. Fermentation for the classic range of wines at Juillet-Lallement are done on selected yeasts in stainless with rigorous temperature control and a slow settling at cool temperatures (12°C) to preserve the precision of the fruit. These wines all finish their malolactic fermentation. There are two vintage wines in the classic range. The first is called Grand Tradition, produced from a 50/50 blend of Chardonnay and Pinot Noir from the oldest parcels in Verzy and Sillery. From my notes on the 2009: *"...this is the image of a*

vintage from the Montagne de Reims: toasty brioche, walnut, and wood smoke. Despite the rich aroma, there is a fresh balancing acidity and a line that continues seemingly for days. Disgorged in October of 2016, thus six years on the lees. Dosed at 6 g/l." ****
(Tasted 2019)

There also is a marvelous Special Club bottling. Juillet-Lallement has been a member of the Club des Trésors since 1973, and the Special Club bottling[14] is always the best of their production in the best years. This is produced from 70% old vine Chardonnay from Verzy and 30% Pinot Noir from Sillery. The 50-year-old vines are from a high-density planting with a prime exposition and a mid-slope position that allows them to ripen to perfection while still retaining a surprisingly lively structure. Stainless steel ferments yield wines of very pure fruit expression, while the long aging contributes perfectly balanced autolysis. My impressions of the 2006 vintage: *"The aromas combine ripe peach and apricot with buttered toast and a hint of spice and pepper. On the palate, it is supremely rich and dense, yet in no way heavy at all. Six years on the lees, dosed at 6 g/l."* ****
(Tasted 2019)

There is also a second range of wines called "Belle de Juillet". These are all fermented in casks made from oaks harvested from the forest of Verzy. All of the Belle de Juillet wines receive an extra brut dosage. The Blanc de Blancs is produced from old-vine parcels of Chardonnay in Verzy from the lieux-dits La Croix l'Aumonier and Les Champs Saint-Remi with a north-northwest exposition that gives these wines incredible tension and nervous energy. My notes on the 2013 vintage: *"The structure is so massive that the wood and the effects of three bâtonnages in six months hardly ripple the aromatic surface of the wine, which project an intensely tangy citrus burst, a distinctive saline note, and a smoky, spicy hint well hidden in the background. Racy and fresh, this is tightly wound without being too tart, and extremely persistent on the palate. Dosed at 4 g/l."* **** (Tasted 2019)

The Blanc de Noirs is produced from Pinot Noir from Les Cumaines and Les Chemins de Wez in Verzy, and La Vigne

---

14   See Glossary entry for further explanation.

l'Evêque, Le Fossé Blanc, and Les Vins Mousseux in Sillery. Both the alcoholic and the malolactic fermentations were carried out in cask, and the wines underwent aging on the lees in cask for six months before bottling. This was followed by another four years on the lees of the secondary fermentation before disgorging. The 2012 vintage: *"...the result is powerful and vinous, with an intense concentration of aroma and flavor. Although it is wonderful now (especially with food at the table), it will age literally for decades to come."* **** (Tasted 2019)

Finally, there is a very interesting specialty, a 100% Meunier from Grand Cru Sillery. Not yet released, this is a tremendous Champagne produced from 100% Pinot Meunier grown exclusively in the Buissons des Vignes lieu-dit in Sillery, making it very unique and perhaps the only grand cru pure Pinot Meunier in existence. Production is tiny; there are only 16 ares planted in the vineyard, and there will be only 1,600 bottles. The wine should be released by the fall of 2020: *"This shows an intense, fresh nose that leads with violets and continues with red berry fruit before the subtle notes of toast and yeast appear. On the palate, it is exuberantly concentrated but never heavy, and the acidity balances perfectly with the lovely floral expression of the fruit. Substantial but not heavy, this is truly unique wine."* **** (Tasted 2019)

21 rue Irénée Gass 51380 Verzy | 03 26 50 28 43
www.champagnejuilletlallement.com

Laherte Frères

Region: Marne Valley | Terroir: Côteaux Sud d'Epernay

The Coteaux Sud d'Epernay is the subregion formed by the villages that lie directly south of the city of Epernay. These are largely planted to Chardonnay and Meunier, and the only premier cru village in this area is Pierry, which is the most well-known, followed by Moussy. Directly south of Moussy, on the other side of a stream called Le Cubrey is the village of Chavot-Courcourt where Champagne Laherte Frères has its winery. Aurélien Laherte has been working with his father Thierry and his uncle Christian since 2002, and today leads the family estate. He is the seventh generation of his family and is considered one of the bright young stars of the new generation in Champagne.

Laherte Frères are the proprietors of 11 hectares of vines spread over more than 75 parcels lying in the the Coteaux Sud d'Epernay, the Côte des Blancs, and the Marne Valley. They also purchase fruit from another 4 hectares. In their home base of Chavot they have 3.2 hectares of Chardonnay in the chalkiest soils. Nearly two and a half hectares of Meunier are planted in clay soils on largely north-facing sites. There is also just over one-third a hectare each of Pinot Noir and Pinot Meslier, and another parcel planted to a mix of grapes. Other vineyards in the Coteaux Sud d'Epernay include 0.4 hectares in Brugny plant-ed to Chardonnay and Meunier, a half-hectare of Chardonnay in Epernay, and small parcels in Mancy, Moussy, and Vaudancourt. In the Marne Valley they have 0.7 hectares of Meunier planted in Boursault at the top of the slope on chalky soils, and a further parcel of nearly 0.8 hectares planted in Le Breuil in a south-facing, mid-slope parcel. In the Côte des Blancs, there are just over 0.6 hectares planted to Chardonnay between the communes of Vertus and Voipreux. All of the vineyards are replanted slowly using massal selection. Work in the vineyards mostly follows organic principles. The domaine is not certified, but a portion of the vineyards are farmed biodynamically.

Grapes from each of the 75 parcels are fermented separately, mostly in small barriques, but Laherte also employs larger casks and an even larger open-top wood fermenter. There are no hard and fast rules for Aurélien in the cellar – some lots are fermented on native yeasts, while others use selected yeasts; some of the base wines see malolactic fermentation, while others do not. Most of the wines are aged on the fine lees of the fermentation for a time before bottling, and dosage is uniformly low.

Les Empreintes is the top expression of the wines of Chavot. It uses half Chardonnay (including a significant percentage of the Chardonnay Musqué clone) from the terroir called Les Chemins d'Epernay. Chemins d'Epernay is a terroir with a thin layer of clay over chalk, located at the foot of the hill, and planted in 1957. The balance of the wine is Pinot Noir from a lieu-dit called Les Rouges Maisons, located at mid-slope with a clay and flint soil. The 2009 was richly expressive: *"...fermented on indigenous yeasts in large and small barrels has given a lovely expressive wine with aromas of coconut and exotic fruit and a rich, silky texture. Malolactic fermentation blocked, six months on the lees, dosed at 3.5 g/l"* **** (tasted 2015)

Another superb wine from Laherte is the Vignes d'Autrefois. It is produced from very old vine Meunier planted between 1947 and 1953. At least the vineyard is mostly Meunier, but it is co-planted with the odd vines of Chardonnay, Pinot Noir, and Pinot Gris. Vignes d'Autrefois comes from a few select lieux-dits in Chavot (La Potote and Les Rouges Maisons), and in Mancy (Les Hautes Norgeailles). The winemaking is the same as it is for Les Empreintes. The 2004 was exquisite: *"... toasty, exotic, floral nose with nice hints of lemon and passionfruit on the nose. On the palate, the wine is soft and rich without being flabby and shows a fine mousse and lingering finish "* **** (Tasted 2010)

Next in the line-up is another Blanc de Noirs, Les Longues Voyes, which comes from the Laherte holdings Chamery on the Montagne de Reims. In 2013, the base wine spent 24 months in cask on the lees, yet the wood influence did not dominate: *"A voluptuous wine, with forward notes of flowers and spice, yet there are elegance and restraint here that are truly* discreet. *On the palate, there is a bright acidity and plenty of density that lead to a lingering finish. A marvelous success for the vintage."* *** (Tasted 2014)

Laherte also produced a vintage-dated Blanc de Blancs from the Coteaux Sud called Les Grandes Crayères. The 2014 was marvelous: *"Bright and fresh with a forward lemony fruit underscored by a fine minerality. On the palate, the texture was silky and ethereal. Bottled in April 2015 and disgorged in January 2018, this was dosed at 4 g/l."* *** (Tasted 2019)

There is a rosé de saignée to round out the line-up of vintage wines. The wine is called Les Beaudiers and is made with grapes coming from old-vine Meunier from the parcel of the same name. The vines were planted between 1953 and 1965 in this west-facing, mid-slope location. The grapes are destemmed and then macerate for 12 to 14 hours on the skins before a slow fermentation in cask. Malolactic is blocked, and the wine spends six months on the lees with occasional bâtonnage. In the 2013 vintage, the wine was at its exuberant best: *"A lovely wine with an expressive, bright cherry fruit on the initial attack, but there is another dimension as well, with a hint of flowers and a firmly earthy character at the end. On the palate the wine is serious and structured, but never loses its element of fun. This is a great food wine and a delicious rosé."* *** (Tasted 2018)

3 rue des Jardins 51530 Chavot-Courcourt | 03 26 54 32 09
https://www.champagne-laherte.com

Lanson

Location: Reims | Terroir: Blended

The origins of Lanson are intertwined with those of Delamotte, as explained above. The house was owned by the Lanson descendants until 1975 when it was sold to Xavier Gardinier, whose sister had married into the Lanson family. Gardinier (who made his fortune in the fertilizer business), also purchased champagne Pommery from the de Polignac family in 1979, and ultimately also purchased the elegant de Polignac mansion called Château Les Crayères. The Gardinier Group sold both champagne houses to French conglomerate BSN in 1984, who held the properties until 1990 before selling them to LVMH. LVMH sold Lanson to Marne et Champagne in 1994, and in 1996 Bruno Paillard-led BCC (Boizel Chanoine Champagne) engineered the takeover of Lanson and other assets from Marne et Champagne.

Lanson is the proprietor of 57 hectares of vineyard property in Champagne, 16 hectares of which is cultivated using organic principles. However, the parent company BCC-Lanson owns 120 hectares and has contracts for a further 380 hectares. The wines are made by Hervé Dantan, formerly of Mailly Grand Cru, who came to Lanson in 2013 and took over as Chef de Caves in 2015, replacing Jean-Paul Gandon, who had arrived in 1986. Most of the fermentation is done in stainless steel. However, in 2014, Lanson built a cellar for aging reserve wines (and liqueur d'expedition) in cask.

The vintage range was initially called Red Label. In 2020, I tasted the 1969 vintage with Dantan during a visit to the winery: *"The mousse here is rather faint, but the color is still good. The wine is honeyed and mature, with notes of sous bois and soy sauce. It is drinking well, if in decline. Entirely pleasant but time to drink now. The name "quille" ("ten-pin") refers to the bottle shape. This distinctive bottle shape (not unlike the first bottlings of La Grande Dame) was produced only from 1964-1975. the wine is similar to the classic 50/50 blend that is traditional for the vintage bottling from Lanson. 1969 was also the last vintage to be fermented in cask before the advent of stainless-steel tanks."* *** (Tasted 2020)

In 1985, the Red Label vintage range was rebranded as Gold Label. The 2009 was consistent with the house style: *"An expressive, silky wine with an enticing nose of ripe apple, toast, and fresh cream. Not overly autolytic, it has enough biscuity character to round out the fruit. On the palate, the wine is approachable and easy to love, with a rich, creamy texture and a lively mousse. If the acidity is balanced, at best, it makes the wine all the more interesting to drink in its youth. The wine is made from 53% Pinot Noir and 47% Chardonnay – the vintage wine at Lanson is nearly always close to a 50/50 blend of Chardonnay and Pinot Noir from Grand Cru sites. The Pinot comes largely from the north face of the Montagne; the Chardonnay, mostly from Le Mesnil. The wine is made in the classic Lanson style, with malolactic fermentation blocked; dosed at 6 g/l and disgorged one year ago."* **** (Tasted 2020)

Lanson has also released some recently disgorged older vintages called the Lanson Vintage Collection. The 1976 vintage was superb: *"...youthful and fresh. There is still a bit of youthful citrus about this, with notes of confit lemon peel and honey. The wine seems young and fresh compared to the 1990. There is a hint of development here but very well integrated. Surprising youth and vigor from such a hot vintage. This wine is drinking well now, but surprisingly could hold or even improve at this point. Feel free to drink but do not be pressed to do so. Disgorged in the fall of 2018."* ***** (Tasted 2020)

The prestige cuvée of the house is called Noble Cuvée. It is made in regular Brut and Blanc de Blancs versions. The 1979 Lanson Noble Cuvée was particularly delicious: *"This has a complex, smoky nose that starts with toasted brioche and freshly ground coffee and moves on to a Tarte Tatin made from very ripe apples. Smells delicious, tastes delicious. The wine is super-rich on the palate but not soft – there is plenty of structure, lovely depth, and complexity. Although this is made with the 70% Chardonnay / 30% Pinot Noir blend that is the hallmark of this bottling, it was dosed at the level common upon release at 9 g/l. While drinking well now, this will hold for at least another decade."* ***** (Tasted 2020)

66, rue de Courlancy 51100 Reims | 03 26 78 50 50
https://www.lanson.com/index-en.php

Leclerc Briant

Location: Epernay | Terroir: Blended

The house was formed in 1872 in Cumières by Lucien Leclerc. In 1955 Bertrand Leclerc moved to their current premises in Epernay and became a négociant. In 1990 Pascal Leclerc took over from his parents, and in 2012 the Leclerc family sold to Americans Mark Nunnelly and Denise Dupré, who have reinvigorated this pioneering house along with their French partner Frédéric Zeimett and legendary Consultant/Chef de Caves Hervé Jestin. The move towards organic winemaking began as long ago as the 1950s under Bernard Leclerc, and the first official certifications were under Pascal Leclerc in the 1990s. Today Leclerc-Briant buys most of their grapes, but the parcels they own are certified both organic and biodynamic. The house owns 14 hectares of biodynamically-farmed vines located in grands crus Mailly and Le Mesnil and the premier crus Hautvillers, Cumières, Mareuil-sur-Aÿ, Bisseuil, Rilly-la-Montagne, Villers-Allerand, and Trépail. They source from a further 15 hectares of biodynamically-farmed vines, including some from the Côte des Blancs.

The wines are fermented in a combination of stainless steel, wooden casks, and an ovoid-shaped fermentation vessel commonly called a terracotta egg. The eggs are used because the fermentation creates a convection current that keeps the wine in motion while fermenting. The must is not chaptalized, and the wines are fermented on native yeasts. Malolactic fermentation is normally finished, and the wines are bottled unfined and unfiltered. Dosage is low when it is done at all. The majority of the wines from Leclerc Briant are millésimes non-revendiqués. I caught up with Hervé Jestin in the fall of 2019 to taste through a range of the recent bottlings.

The entry-level offerings are referred to as the "Classic Range". The first offering is the Brut Reserve. My notes on the bottling from the 2013 harvest: *This wine is blended from 40% Pinot Noir, 40% Meunier, and 20% Chardonnay from a variety of sources, including growers in Cumières, Verneuil, Sermiers,*

Epernay and Cramant. It is more than three years on the lees and disgorged with 4 g/l dosage. The finished wine opens with fresh floral notes and a bright, ripe apple and pear fruit. The texture is supple, perhaps a bit soft, but the balance is impeccable." *** (Tasted 2018)

The wine labeled Extra Brut Premier Cru is entirely from the 2014 harvest: "The wine is produced from grapes from Hautvillers, Rilly, Cramant, Chouilly, and Avenay. The wine spent ten months on the lees before bottling, during which time it was not racked at all, and then four and one-half years before being disgorged in April 2019 with 2 g/l. The nose shows notes of lemon and toast with great purity of fruit. On the palate, it was extraordinarily silky and with a very lively texture." *** (Tasted 2019)

A Brut Rosé was an undeclared 2014: "95% Chardonnay from Montgueux and 5% Pinot Noir from nearby Les Riceys, done as red wine (and everything done in tank). The wine has a lovely expressive red berry fruit character, silky texture, and impressive length." *** (Tasted 2019)

There is also a blended Millésime. My notes on the 2013 vintage: "40% each Pinot Noir and Meunier with 20% Chardonnay; all the fruit is from Cumières, Verneuil, Sermiers, Epernay, and Cramant. The nose opens with bright aromas of fresh flowers and ripe green apple. The palate demonstrates the delicate elegance that is the hallmark of the house for me. The wine is super-fresh but not excessively racy, and very easy to drink. Extra brut dosage." **** (Tasted 2019)

The next type of wine is the single vineyard wines. La Croisette is one example, from the vineyard next to the winery in Epernay. The wine from the 2014 harvest was marvelous: "Produced from Chardonnay planted in 1960. The base wine is fermented in cask and aged ten months on the lees before bottling. The result is a very ripe, almost tropical fruit character on the nose with a dose of mineral and spice. On the texture, the wine has real weight but also a crisp acidity that balances the creamy texture to perfection." ****

There is another parcellaire Blanc de Blancs called Le Clos des Trois Clochers that comes from a parcel of 30 ares in

Villers Allerand, as well as the Pinot Noir-dominant Les Basses Prières from Hautvillers, but I have not tasted these wines.

Finally there is what Leclerc-Briant refers to as its "Specialty Range". This includes late disgorged vintage blanc and rosé wines, a deeply-colored Rosé de Saignée, a solera, and two mono-varietal wines. The first of these is the Blanc de Meuniers. It is not vintage-dted, but I recently tasted the bottling from the 2015 harvest: *Fruit from Chamery; this shows some very pure floral aromas on the nose with plenty of silky, ripe apricot fruit touched with chalk. On the palate, the wine is fresh but not acerbic despite its lack of dosage. The ripeness of the fruit comes through nicely on the palate and leads to a subtle finish.*" ***

The next wine appeared to be a favorite of Hervé Jestin, who noted that he was trying "...to understand when the oxygen could not be the enemy of the wine." The wine, called Grand Blanc, is a Blanc de Blancs millésime non-revendiqué from the 2013 vintage. *"The fruit is from Cramant and Chouilly, all fermented in cask. The base wines were nine months on the lees before bottling, and it was bottled unfined and unfiltered before being disgorged five years later without dosage. I confess to being somewhat hesitant about the "sans soufre" ("no sulfur") revolution -- I think in the wrong hands it can be problematic. Yet here, it was a bit oxidative but really in a managed, positive way that accented the well-developed tropical fruit notes on the nose while giving a bit of volume on the palate. Very well done."* ****

67 rue Chaude Ruelle 51200 Epernay | 03 26 54 45 33
http://leclercbriant.fr/uk/

Marie-Noëlle Ledru

Region: Montagne de Reims | Terroir: Grande Montagne (South)

My work would not be complete without mention of Marie-Noëlle Ledru, who retired without an heir after the 2016 harvest. She farmed five hectares in Ambonnay and one in Bouzy, planted to 85% Pinot Noir and 15% Chardonnay. She did the alcoholic fermentation in stainless and enameled steel tanks exclusively. She kept only the cuvée for her own wines the sold the tailles. All the base wines completed malolactic fermentation. The wines were lightly sulfured and bottled by hand, unfined and unfiltered. She bottled in April, and the vintage wines were at least five years on the lees before being disgorged. The wines were riddled and disgorged entirely by hand.

Her top wine was called "Cuvée du Goulté" after the local term for the free-run juice. The wine was a parcel selection of her top hillside vineyards in Ambonnay. This has always been a superb wine of great concentration and depth. From my notes on the 2012: *"There is a concentrated aroma of toasted walnuts, ripe apples, fresh pastry, and a hint of flowers. On the palate, the wine is silky, still very youthful, ripe, and rich. However, in spite of the luxuriousness of the cuvée, this is neither too soft nor too hard-edged. A triumph of balance and elegance."* **** (Tasted 2019)

5 place de la Croix 51150 Ambonnay | 03 26 57 09 26
[No Website]

Pierre Legras

Region: Côte des Blancs | Terroir: Côte des Blancs

The original Pierre Legras was born in 1662 in the village of Chouilly. The estate has been passed from father to son for eleven generations; Vincent Legras is the current proprietor. The Legras family has many branches in the Côte des Blancs. Vincent worked until 2003 with the family business of R & L Legras; his uncle owns Legras & Haas. In 2001, the family agreed to go its separate ways, and Vincent branched off on his own after completing his oenology diploma at wine school in Avize.

Today Vincent and his wife Marcelline work a domaine of more than 10 hectares spread over Chouilly, Epernay, Vinay, Moussey, and Boursault, and are actively trying to buy more vines. Currently they have 8 hectares of Chardonnay, and 1 hectare each of Pinot Noir and Meunier. Of particular note are their large parcels in Les Partelaines (3.6 hectares, much of it planted in 1947) and Montaigu, two of the finest lieux-dits in Chouilly. The vineyards are sustainably farmed. They use only organic fertilizer when needed, practice sexual confusion of the insects, and have grassed over every other row in the vineyards.

Vincent and Marcelline renovated the winery when they took over in 2003, bringing in new stainless steel tanks and a new pneumatic press. The wines are fermented in a combination of temperature-controlled stainless and large 400-liter casks. Malolactic fermentation is done for all the wines. Normally the wines are not bottled until May in order to give them additional richness, but if they are already rich (in a year such as 2018), then Vincent will bottle earlier. The tailles are kept separate and are only used if the structure suggests it; otherwise, they are sold off.

There are three types of vintage wine. The first, Monographie, has thus far been vintage-dated, but will develop into a multi-vintage with time. It is produced in both Brut and Brut Nature variations. The cuvée showcases two of the best plots in

Chouilly. The majority is from lieu-dit Partelaines on Mont Bernon. The site at the northern tip of the village of Chouilly has a southeast exposition. Montaigu, at the other end of the village, has northeast-facing vines. My notes of the 2012 Monographie Brut: *"This blend of tank-fermented and cask-fermented wines shows a bit of spice, but the overall impression is one of great purity of fruit, with notes of citrus, apricot, white flowers, chalk, and a mineral/saline edge. Disgorged October 2017 and dosed at 5 g/l."* **** (Tasted 2019)

The same wine but Brut Nature is simply riveting: *"...breathtaking tension and line, this is not lacking the charm of Chouilly, but it also has immense power and a bit more of an emphasis on the saline side, with great purity of fruit. On the palate, there is certainly zingy acidity, but it is not overly tart, and the wine never loses the silky texture of Chouilly. Lovely lingering finish. Disgorged February 2018."* **** (Tasted 2019)

Next is the Brut Vintage, a single vineyard Champagne from Les Partelaines. My impression of the 2006 vintage: *"One-quarter fermented in cask, the wine shows rich, pronounced aromas of brioche, toasted nuts, and freshly ground coffee. On the palate, the wine is powerful and concentrated, with a lush mouthfeel, plenty of structure, and exceptional length. Disgorged October 2016, and dosed at 5 g/l."* **** (Tasted 2019)

Finally, there is the prestige cuvée of the house, Idée de Voyage. The 2008 is marvelous: *"A superb Champagne from a superb vintage. Produced from grapes from Les Partelaines. The wine still has a very youthful appeal, with aromas of bright lemon peel, ripe apricot, and orchard pears. Despite the youthful character, there is already a well-integrated yeasty character that recalls freshly buttered toast. On the palate, the wine is incredibly fresh and lively. The texture is ethereal but not lacking in impact, and the length is impressive. This Champagne is thoroughly pleasant now but will age for decades. Disgorged February 2019, and dosed at 3.3 g/l."* (Tasted 2019)

28 rue de Saint-Chamand 51530 Chouilly | 03 26 56 30 97
https://www.champagne-pierre-legras.com/

Nicolas Maillart

Region: Montagne de Reims | Terroir: Petite Montagne

Nicolas Maillart from Ecueil is among the most interesting producers in the Petite Montage. The Petite Montage lacks official
recognition, yet this area west of the grand crus is among the
liveliest corners of Champagne[15]. Many of the villages here were
promoted to premier cru status just before the echelle des crus
was retired. Of all the villages in the Petite Montagne, Ecueil
is among the best-known. Nicolas is the 9th generation of the
Maillart family to grow grapes here. He joined the estate in 2003
and is now leading it in a direction that is increasingly sensitive to
the environment. They have installed solar panels that produce
enough energy for 90% of their needs, and the estate recently
was certified as an enterprise of Haute Valeur Environnementale
Level 3. The vineyards are spread between Ecueil. Villers-
Allerand, and Bouzy; three-quarters are planted to Pinot Noir
and the balance to Chardonnay. All the work in the vineyard is
done sustainably – essential organic and biodynamic methods are
observed, although the estate is not certified as either.

In the new gravity-flow winery, nothing is set in stone:
some of the base wines are fermented in tank and others in cask;
some undergo malolactic fermentation while others do not, and
some are filtered, yet others are not. I tasted through the entire
range with Nicolas during a visit to the estate in 2018. The first
of the vintage wines is simply called Millésimé, and it is one of my
favorite bottlings from Maillart. Mostly Pinot Noir from Bouzy
blended with Chardonnay from Ecueil. My notes on the 2012:
*"60% from Bouzy and 40% from Ecueil, this is a blend of 55% Pinot
Noir and 45% Chardonnay, 60% of which is fermented in cask. The
wine has forward aromas of ripe pear and apple with a bit of spice,
a suggestion of smoke, and an earthy complexity that is immediately
engaging. On the palate, the wine is dense, creamy, and powerful
with a very long finish. Dosed at 4 g/l."* ****

The Blanc de Blancs called Les Chaillots Gillis features
cask-fermented fruit from several parcels in two lieux-dits in
Ecueil. Les Chaillots is located north of the village, and the vines

---

15   See the glossary entry under Montagne de Reims for more information.

face east and are located at the top of the slope. Les Gillis is situated at the other end of the village on the southern side, more in the middle of the slope, featuring an eastern exposure. The 2012 vintage: *"...lovely richness, with a supple, approachable feel on the palate, this is almost a bit fat, but very luxurious."* ***

The next vintage wine is a Blanc de Noirs called Mont Martin. It is made exclusively from Meunier from west-facing vines in the commune of Villers-Allerand planted in clay soils. The type of soils and the exposition of the vineyard both make this a cooler terroir, lending structure to the Meunier, which as a grape can have the tendency to be a bit soft. From my notes on the 2015: *"Fermented in cask and disgorged without dosage, the 2015 Mont Martin opens with pleasant, youthful aromas of fresh flowers and ripe red apples. On the palate, the wine is silky and soft but not lacking in structure. A lovely example of a 100% Meunier, and very successful even in a warm year."* ***

There is also a second Blanc de Noirs from the lieu-dit Les Jolivettes in Bouzy. This wine is perhaps less aromatic than the Mont Martin, but it is much more powerful. The 2015: *"A bit closed on the initial attack, this opens up on the palate with seductive floral aromas and a sturdy apricot and ripe pear fruit. The toasty autolysis notes arrive only with a bit of time in the glass. On the palate, the wine is vinous and substantial, but even in a hot year, there is enough structure here to balance all of that density and the result should age gracefully for decades."* ****

Finally, Maillart is also noted for his wine called Les Francs de Pied, produced from ungrafted vines planted in a sandy site in the village of Ecueil in 1973. The fruit is cask fermented, the malolactic fermentation is blocked, and the wine is disgorged without dosage. The 2008 was superb: *"Delicious, fascinating wine. Sensitive winemaking here amplifies the unique qualities of this fruit to produce a gentle floral nose with reflections of red fruit, lightly toasted hazelnut, and earth on the nose and delicate toasty yeast aromas. On the palate, there is a fairly vigorous mousse allied with good tension and length on the palate."* ****

5 rue de Villers aux Nœuds 51500 Ecueil | 03 26 49 77 89
www.champagne-maillart.fr/en/

José Michel

Region: Marne Valley | Terroir: Côteaux Sud d'Epernay

A partisan of Meunier before it was fashionable, José Michel is producing marvelously accomplished wines in the village of Moussy just outside of Epernay in the Coteaux Sud d'Epernay. The domaine has owned vineyards in the region since the mid-19th century, and the first domaine-bottled wines were produced before the First World War. The family farms 8 hectares located in Moussy, Brugny-Vaudancourt, Saint-Agnan, and Brasles. The vineyards are planted to 45% Meunier, 45% Chardonnay, and 10% Pinot Noir and are all sustainably farmed. The average vine age is 30 years, and some parcels of up to fifty years of age. In the winery, Michel (who passed away in 2019) adapted his procedures to the wines in question. Some (notably Chardonnay) are fermented in 600-liter demi-muids, while others are fermented in cask. In the same way, malolactic can be permitted or blocked, according to the needs of the year. Dosage usually is moderate at most.

There are several vintage wines, the first of which is called Grand Vintage. 2008 was particularly delicious: *"This is an assemblage of 65% Chardonnay and 35% Meunier. The Chardonnay is fermented in large casks. Disgorged after seven and a half years on the lees and dosed at 8 g/l, this has a lovely density of ripe apricot fruit with a marked minerality and slight saline character. On the palate, it is fresh, concentrated, and quite long."* *** (Tasted 2016)

Not to be overlooked is the Vintage Blanc de Blancs. Recently, the 2012 was impressive: *"Coming from the lieu-dit of Clos St. Jean in the village of St. Agnan, this shows lively citrus aromas, a fair amount of autolytic character, and a hint of spice. On the palate, the wine is fresh and lively, but not lacking in density. The finish is satisfyingly long."* *** Since 2010 this cuvée is entirely fermented in demi-muids with the malolactic blocked. The 2012 vintage was disgorged in January 2019 after six years on the lees and dosed at 5 g/l. (Tasted 2019)

The flagship of the house, however, has always been the Special Club. This is produced from 50% Chardonnay and 50% Meunier, both coming from old vines planted more than seventy years ago. The Chardonnay is fermented in large casks, and the wines are six months on the lees prior to bottling. A bottle of 1983 disgorged in 2016 was still very lively, while the 1998 was rich, honeyed, and seemingly more mature (although it had been disgorged upon initial release). Perhaps the best Special Club I have had from José Michel, however, was the 2008: *"Soft and accessible on the initial attack, this wine seduces with lovely floral notes and a bright, grapey fruit character. On the palate, however, the wine gives a substantial impression with great length, while never losing its elegance."* **** (Tasted 2019)

14 rue Prélot 51530 Moussy | 03 26 54 04 69
www.chamapgne-jose-michel.com

Moët & Chandon

Location: Epernay | Terroir: Blended

Moët & Chandon is the house of superlatives: the largest production, the most extensive vineyard holding, the longest cellars. The bottling line operates at a terrifying speed, and watching it in full swing exerts a hypnotic Rube Goldberg-like fascination. However, despite the enormous size of the operation, it would be a grave error to overlook these wines, as they are made today with consummate care and attention to detail. Perhaps more importantly for the collector, this has been true throughout the 20th century, and older vintages of Moët can be spectacularly good.

The house was founded in 1743 by Claude Moët. The firm continued under his son, Claude-Louis Nicolas Moët, and was greatly expanded by his grandson, Jean-Rémy Moët, a friend of Napoleon Bonaparte. The daughter of Jean-Rémy was married to Pierre-Gabriel Chandon, who ran the company with Jean-Rémy's son Victor, giving the firm its present name.

In general, the house relies on an assemblage weighted towards black grapes, which tends to be 40% Meunier, 40% Pinot Noir, and 20% Chardonnay. Most of the grapes are pressed in the field at several of Moët's own press houses. The wine is fermented in stainless to preserve the purity of the fruit. The key to the Moët style is a reliance on reductive winemaking technique, so everything possible is done to reduce oxygen uptake. The combination of these techniques delivers a fruit character so clear that can initially seem a bit simple, yet the wines manifestly have the potential to develop greatly with age. The Champagne is not crafted for intensity, but balance. My first tasting at the house was with former Chef de Caves Georges Blanck, who described the ideal aromatic profile as "apple-peach-pear-grapefruit." However, with this emphasis on fruit, something more is achieved, as a recent tasting with the current Chef de Caves Benoît Gouez convinced me. Gouez began his career at Moët in 1998 and was appointed Chef de Caves in 2005. Gouez noted in our 2020 interview and tasting that for

Moët, vintage as a category is less than 5% of total production and thus is not a big focus of the house. Recently, however, they have begun to re-release vintage wines as the Moët Grand Vintage Collection (MVC). Moët began to build stocks for this program in 1993, and wines have been aged both under cork and under crown cap. Moving forward, however, Gouez says that all of the wines laid down for re-release will be aged under cork. The production target will ultimately be 40,000 bottles of each vintage, which means a lot of manual disgorging. As of 2020, the 2002 MVC is on the market (along with the current 2012 Grand Vintage).

Gouez can sometimes seem like a contrarian regarding vintages. He said that he felt that the 1996 and 2008 vintages were overrated, and that 1992 and 1993 were underrated. He suggested that '92 and '93 were undervalued because they arrived just after the start of the Gulf War in a period of low sales and high stock levels, and not because they were mediocre vintages. He also professed a fondness for the 2003 vintage that is not universally shared. His thoughts, however, are interesting. He pointed out that 2003 had the second-lowest acidity on record after the 1959 vintage and went on to remind us that all ten of the vintages with the lowest acidity in the past century have been declared. He noted that stylistically "a winemaker, can 'replace' some acidity with bitterness. Freshness is not just about the acidity." He explained that the difficulties of a vintage such as 2003 included wines that were prone to oxidation. The winemaking team realized that one way to combat this is hyper-oxidation of the musts, particularly for the tailles of the black grapes. This the effect of removing vegetal, licorice, and phenolic tastes.

During our interview, we tasted the 2003 vintage, disgorged in May 2017, and dosed at 5 g/l. It was a blend of 28% Chardonnay, 29% Pinot Noir, 43% Meunier: *"The nose opens with aromas of ripe apricot and honey and relatively little of the customary floral notes. On the palate, it is lush and a bit soft, but it retains an elegant balance and lingers lovingly on the finish."* ***

For my part, I thought the 1996 was delicious: *"Aged under cork, this wine is beginning to show very well just now and to open up charmingly. There is still a prominent, primary lemony fruit, with a strong mineral background and a saline note, yet there is a depth of toasty autolytic aromas on top of that to add complexity. On the palate is very fresh and focused, but there is a delicate texture here as well. Delightful. Dosed at 5 g/l."* ****

The Moët vintage wines have shown the ability to age much longer than twenty years, and this is my rationale for including them here. Recently tasted bottles of the 1943 and 1945 vintages were wonderful – notes are included in the section for those relevant years (pages 322 and 324). When these bottles come up, they offer the interested collector a fascinating look at a by-gone era.

20 avenue de Champagne 51200 Epernay | 03 26 51 20 20
www.moet.com

Robert Moncuit

Region: Côte des Blancs | Terroir: Côte des Blancs

Champagne Robert Moncuit is a fresh voice in Le Mesnil. The estate may seem new to American drinkers, but it was established in the 19th century, and there have been domaine-bottled wines under the Robert Moncuit label since 1928. Some Champagne fans still are unfamiliar with this marvelous house because until 2000 their entire production was sold in Europe. Since 2000 the estate has been led by Pierre Amillet, grandson of Robert Moncuit. The family owns 8 hectares of vines in total. There is a very nice holding of 2.2 hectares the well-known vineyard of Les Chétillons (planted in 1956). There is also a 1.5 hectare parcel of old vines in Oger, including 0.66 hectares in the lieu-dit Vozémieux. The vines are cultivated sustainably and propagated using massal selection. Fermentation is done both in stainless steel tank and in cask (for the Chétillons and Vozémieux). The wines are neither chaptalized nor filtered. Moncuit consistently lets his wines finish their malolactic fermentation, and they stay on their fine lees until the summer following the vintage. They receive little if any dosage.

I began tasting these wines a few years ago at the annual Printemps de Champagne tastings. The first wine I encountered (in 2017) was the 2008 Millésime Vieilles Vignes, made from fruit coming from a selection of the oldest estate vines, except Chétillons, which is bottled separately. These vines are 60 to 80 years old, and the wine was immediately impressive: *"There is a bright, pure lemony fruit here with a distinct mineral/saline undercurrent and a hint of buttered toast. On the palate, the wine is fresh, and the aromatic palate continues to expand to include pretty floral notes. There is plenty of tension, but the wine is exquisitely balanced, leading to a lingering finish. Worth seeking out."* ***

At the same time, I tasted the inaugural 2008 vintage of the Chétillons bottling from the large southeast-facing parcel owned by Moncuit. The wine was shockingly good: *"...pointedly aromatic, with a superb lemon/lime/green apple fruit character, and a profound chalky character to the wine with salty, toasty* overtones. *On the palate, it is fresh and super-lively but there is a lush, silky texture in spite of the fact that it was disgorged without dosage. A classic."* ****

In 2018 I tasted the first vintage of another *parcellaire* from Moncuit, the 2010 Vozémieux. This wine is produced from grapes from the north-facing vines in Vozémieux. Despite the northern exposure, it has surprising richness, pointing up the difference between Le Mesnil and Oger. *"Creamy and rich, this opens with a ripe red apple fruit character, a hint of hazelnut, and a subtle toasty character. On the palate, it is rich and ripe but far from flabby. The acidity is balanced and more than sufficient to carry it to a long finish. The Vozémieux is more supple and velvety than the taut, linear Chétillons but compelling nonetheless."* ****

Although I do not have as much experience with these wines as with some others in this group, I feel that this is an estate to watch.

2 place de la Gare 51190 Le Mesnil-sur-Oger | 03 26 57 52 71
[No Website]

G.H. Mumm

Location: Reims | Terroir: Blended

Mumm's history goes back to the 18th century when the family had a wine business in Cologne, founded by Peter Arnold Mumm. In 1827, his sons Gottlieb, Jacobus, and Philipp established a branch in Champagne with local partners G. Heuser and Friedrich Giesler, incorporating as P. A. Mumm, Giesler et C°. In 1852, Georges Hermann Mumm, grandson of Peter Arnold, took over the house and re-christened it with his initials. It was Georges Hermann who created the iconic "Cordon Rouge" during the 1880s and ushered in the first period of popularity for this grande marque. The house eventually received the royal warrant of the Austro-Hungarian empire and of Belgium, the Netherlands, Prussia, Denmark, Sweden, Norway, and England (which they retain today). However, the Mumm property was confiscated during the Great War since the family were still German citizens. It was sold to a group of investors, and from 1935 it was directed by one of them named René Lalou, a Parisian lawyer who had married into the Dubonnet family. Lalou's tenure was the second golden age for Mumm, and under his direction the wines were as famous as his patronage of the arts, including the renowned Foujita chapel. Seagram's purchased a stake in Mumm in 1955.

Succeeding generations were less kind to Mumm. Sam Bronfman passed away in 1971, and his son Edgar took over as chairman. In 1972 Seagram's became the majority shareholder in Mumm; Mumm had also purchased Heidsieck Monopole, and in 1959, Perrier-Jouët, thus Seagrams had a controlling interest in all three. In 1985, Seagram's increased its Mumm stake to 90%. At this time, Seagram's was among the largest wine and spirits companies in the world. By 1994, however, Sam's grandson Edgar Bronfman Jr. had become CEO of Seagram's. Anxious to enter the entertainment business, he sold family holdings and acquired Universal pictures and the MCA movie studio along with record companies Polygram and Deutsche Grammophon. The entertainment assets were taken over by French conglomerate Vivendi in 2000 with Edgar, Jr. as President, and the wine and spirits assets were sold in 1999 to private equity firm Hicks, Muse, Tate & Furst (now HM Capital Partners). Hicks, Muse resold these assets to Allied Domecq in 2000, and Allied Domecq was acquired by Pernod Ricard in 2006.

Today, Pernod Ricard is presiding over a renaissance of Mumm, and the brand is regaining the commercial and qualitative prominence that it had lost at the end of the Seagram's era. Today, the house has nearly 218 hectares of vines. 160 hectares of these are located in grand cru villages, including Aÿ, Bouzy, Ambonnay, Verzy, Verzenay, and Mailly on the Montagne. Overall, 78% of Mumm's vineyards are planted to Pinot Noir but there are also important holdings in Cramant and Avize in the Côte des Blancs. Fermentation is done in stainless steel at cold temperatures, and the wines also undergo malolactic fermentation. The dominance of Pinot Noir generally gives a fairly vinous effect, while the winemaking helps them retain the purity of fruit.

I have long been a fan of the bottling formerly called Mumm de Cramant. It was initially called Crémant de Cramant, and was first produced in 1892. Until 1960, however, it was not sold through regular channels but instead used as a promotional item. After its commercial launch, further changes lay in store. From 1965 the wine lost its vintage date, although some releases were produced from one harvest. In 1990 the EU reserved the use of the word "Crémant" for traditional method sparkling wines produced outside of the Champagne region, and Mumm was obliged to change the name of the wine to Mumm de Cramant. It was rebranded again with the vintage-dated RSRV Blanc de Blancs. According to Pernod-Ricard, "RSRV" ("Reserve") is an private club. The wines have only just been launched in the United States, and the range includes four wines: a Blanc de Blancs, a Blanc de Noirs, a Rosé, and a blended wine called "4+5". From my notes on the RSRV Blanc de Blancs 2013: *"On the initial attack there is a very delicate lemon peel aroma, very typical of Cramant, where the grapes are grown. The citrus is gently complimented by a well-integrated autolytic character. On the palate, the wine has lots of finesse, but it seems to be lacking the edge that Cramant fruit can provide, and the dosage seems somewhat elevated. The texture, however, is creamy and the overall impression is pleasant, if a bit lacking in tension."* ***

The vintage Brut from Mumm is often quite reliable, but in previous years it could be fantastic. In 2015 I was able to taste the 1979 vintage at the winery: *"Lovely, tangy, and rich with aromas of fresh and dried apricot along with a suggestion of saffron and truffle. Exotic, mature, but still lively and very interesting."* ****

I have also enjoyed even older vintages, including the 1928 out of half-bottle, purchased in a Christie's New York sale: *"The wine was over the top, yet still hanging together, showing notes of cream, caramel, and truffle. On the palate the mousse was faint, but the texture still held together, and the fresh acidity carried it through to a respectable finish. Mature, but still very interesting."* ***

The real star for me at Mumm had been the Cuvée René Lalou. This homage to René Lalou was originally produced from 1964 through 1985. Lalou began to work on a prestige cuvée shortly after World War II, and identified seven villages, along with specific lieux-dits, that would compose the blend. I was stunned by the 1969 vintage during a dinner with Champagne collectors in 2009: *"One of the surprises of the evening, a '69 Rene Lalou from Mumm was spectacular. The wine showed notes of fresh black truffle, mineral, smoke, cream, and just a hint of butterscotch. On the palate, the wine was well balanced and crisp but soft, rich, and particularly massive."* ***** I also enjoyed very much the 2002 at the winery in 2015: *"A historic cuvée commemorating the work of Rene Lalou, this 50/50 blend of Chardonnay and Pinot Noir is made from a limited selection of the very best fruit. With a lovely aroma of truffles, vanilla, and brioche, this shows aromatic complexity as well as power and concentration on the palate. Lovely."* **** This was produced from the same 12 parcels identified by Lalou, and dosed at 6 g/l. In total the wine was produced in 1966, 1969, 1971, 1973, 1975, 1976, 1979, 1982, 1985, 1988, 1989, 1999, 2002, and 2006. Now the wine has been rolled into the RSRV program described above.

Mumm has great potential. Older wines amply demonstrate this, and their vineyard holdings are impressive. The winemaking also progressed greatly under Dominique Demarville, Chef de Caves from 1998 until 2006. Demarville left to assume the Chef de Caves role at Veuve Clicquot, and was ably replaced by Didier Mariotti. In 2020, Demarville left Clicquot, and Mariotti has followed him again, taking up the reins as Chef de Caves at Clicquot, and in turn has been replaced at Mumm by Laurent Fresnet, formerly of Henriot. We can only hope that Fresnet's obvious talent will lift Mumm to new heights.

34 rue du Champ de Mars 51053 Reims | 03 26 49 59 70
www.mumm.com

Bruno Paillard

Location: Reims | Terroir: Blended

Bruno Paillard is one of the great personalities of the Champagne region in modern times, as well as the producer of discreet, quality-focused Champagnes. Born in 1953 into an old Champenois family of growers and brokers, he began as a grape broker in 1975. By any measure, his career has been an extraordinary one. He leveraged his deep knowledge of the region and its players to become the chairman of Lanson-BCC, one of the top five largest grossing Champagne producers. The group that he formed is a unique assemblage that includes the remains of the Marne et Champagne empire, founded by Gaston Burtin, whose business until his death was the second-largest in Champagne after LVMH. Upon Burtin's passing, ownership of Marne et Champagne was transferred to his great-niece Marie-Laurence and her husband François-Xavier Maura. When the Maura family took over, the Sales Director Philippe Baijot left and formed a partnership with Paillard. First, they revitalized Champagne Chanoine (among the oldest firms in the region) and formed alliances with the owners of Boizel and Besserat de Bellefon. The group later acquired Philipponnat and Alexandre Bonnet before finally buying the remaining assets of the now-defunct Marne et Champagne group, which included Lanson and Maison Burtin. According to the Union des Maisons de Champagne, Lanson-BCC today generates the fourth largest revenue in the region behind LVMH, Laurent-Perrier, and Vranken-Pommery Monopole.

In addition to this important commercial role, he was chairman of the Appellation and Communication Commission for the CIVC. This committee defends the name of Champagne around the world. He famously resigned this position in 2018 when the cooperative Palmer inked a deal with Constellation Brands. Paillard objected since Constellation produces wine in California and elsewhere labeled "champagne" with blatant disregard for the legal geographic indication of the word Champagne. (To date, only the United States and Russia do not recognize the legally-binding nature of this term).

Quite apart from all of this, he set up his eponymous Champagne house in 1981. This was the first new Champagne négociant founded in more than a century. The story is circulated that he even sold his favorite sportscar -- a 1966 Mark II Jaguar -- to help finance the launch. Initially, all the grapes were purchased. In 1994, however, he began to buy vineyards, starting with a 3 hectare parcel in grand cru Oger. To date, the house has accumulated over 32 hectares over a total of over 100 different parcels. These range over 15 villages throughout the region, including the grand crus Oger, Le Mesnil, Verzenay, and Bouzy (a combined 12 hectares), as well as Cumières, Damery, Festigny, Les Riceys, and elsewhere. These vineyard holdings yield enough fruit for 50 to 60% of their production. Although Paillard is not certified organic, they follow many organic principles in the vineyard, including grassing over between rows and tilling the soil, using no synthetic herbicides or pesticides, and promoting biodiversity in the vineyard.

In the winery, fermentations are done parcel-by-parcel in a combination of stainless steel and cask. Only the cuvée is used, and most wines complete their malolactic fermentation. Aging on the lees is long, and dosage is low.

The Brut Vintage is an assemblage of Chardonnay and Pinot Noir from a selection of villages across the region, customarily aged eight years before disgorging. I have a great memory of the 1999 with several years age on the cork after being disgorged: *"This continues to show well, with mature notes of toasted walnut, truffle, smoke, and mineral on the nose. On the palate, the wine has a lush, soft, round texture with nice length and an indolent mousse."* **** (Tasted 2010)

The Brut Vintage Blanc de Blancs is an assemblage of Chardonnay from a variety of villages, aged nine years before being disgorged. The 2004 Blanc de Blancs was a standout: *"A very sexy wine for drinking now, this is nine years on the lees, and the wine shows mature autolytic character but also retains some lovely primary fruit. On the nose, there is a ripe, lush, tropical fruit character accented by notes of hazelnut, brioche, and a suggestion of ground coffee. On the palate, it still retains a zesty, lemony fruit, and its bright acidity, with a lingering, complex finish."* **** (Tasted 2014)

Finally, in addition to these, Paillard produces a wine called Nec Plus Ultra (Latin for "nothing further beyond") which is his interpretation of the ultimate Champagne. This prestige cuvée is fermented using fruit from only four grands crus: Chardonnay from Oger and Chouilly, and Pinot Noir from Verzenay and Mailly. The must is carefully fermented in cask and aged on the lees for ten months before bottling, and then for a further 12 to 15 years before being disgorged and dosed at 3 g/l.

Avenue de Champagne 51100 Reims | 03 26 36 20 22
http://www.champagnebrunopaillard.com/en

Hubert Paulet

Region: Montagne de Reims | Terroir: Grande Montagne (North)

Olivier Paulet is a thoughtful yet underappreciated vigneron in Rilly on the north face of the Montagne. Paulet took over the family vineyards in 1998 and began to sell wine under the Hubert Paulet label with the 2002 vintage. The family owns 8 hectares, all of it in Rilly-la-Montagne. The vineyards are planted to 51% Meunier, 21% Chardonnay, and 28% Pinot Noir spread over 40 parcels. The vineyards are managed in a sustainable way, with grass between the rows, and yield and canopy are managed to produce fruit with equilibrium and finesse. The vineyards mostly have an east-southeast exposition, and soils that vary from sand to pure chalk.

Except for the top cuvée, the wines are fermented in stainless steel. There is nothing dogmatic about Olivier Paulet, who believes in doing whatever is best for each wine. Sometimes he will block the malolactic fermentation, while other times it is allowed to proceed. In some vintages, the base wines are aged on their lees, while in others, they are not. He continues to experiment and plans to release a small micro-cuvée called Chant-Allots from his best parcel, with fruit from vines planted 45 years ago, fermented in cask. The first vintage will be 2012.

At present there are two vintage wines. The first is Risléus (named for the Roman name of Rilly) is a blend of 47% Chardonnay, 33% Meunier, and 20% Pinot Noir, produced with barrel-fermented base wines with some bâttonage, bottled unfined and unfiltered. Some barrels did their malolactic, while others did not. The result is a wine of winning complexity. My note on the 2004: *"...with subtle notes of tropical fruit and coconut, along with fresh cream and brioche. The texture is silky, but not without density, and the finish is very long. This is a marvelous wine of balance, harmony, and sophistication that deserves to be more well known."* **** (Tasted 2017)

There is also a vintage-dated Rosé. The 2006 vintage proved very seductive: *"...done in the saignée style. Paulet's saignée receives more age than many do, and for this reason, it seems a bit more substantial, although not heavy in any way. Invigoratingly fresh aromas of raspberry, fresh flowers, bread dough, and spice, this is fermented in stainless but aged in cask to give it a roundness and texture that are intriguing."* *** (Tasted 2017)

58 rue de Chigny 51500 Rilly La Montagne | 03 26 03 41 52
[No Website]

Perrier-Jouët

Location: Epernay | Terroir: Blended

Founded in 1811, the auspicious "Year of the Comet," the house of Perrier-Jouët was formed when vine grower (and cork manufacturer) Pierre Nicolas Perrier married Rose Adélaïde Jouët, daughter of a Calvados producer. He began to work with his cousin Eugène Gallice and was succeeded by his son Charles Perrier. The house knew early success in export markets, particularly in England and America, and was the first to market Brut champagne in 1846. Upon his death, Charles Perrier was succeeded by his nephew Henri Gallice. Gallice, along with his brother Octave worked with Emile Gallé to create the world-famous Art Nouveau bottles that served as inspiration for the Belle Epoque bottle. In 1934, the house passed to Louis Budin who had married to the niece of Henri Gallice. His son Michel became commercial director in 1949 and technical director in 1958. In 1959, the house was sold to Mumm, but Michel Budin stayed on in his role until 1983. He was Production Director of Groupe Mumm until 1989 when he retired after 40 years of service. Seagram's had invested in Mumm and eventually took controlling interest, and since that time, the two houses have been under the same management. Seagram's sold them together to the private equity firm Hicks, Muse, Tate & Furst (now HM Capital Partners), who re-sold these assets to Allied Domecq in 2000. Allied Domecq was acquired by Pernod Ricard in 2006.

It was during the tenure of Michel Budin that the bottles designed by Gallé were rediscovered, and the cuvée Belle

Epoque was launched with the 1964 vintage, released in 1969. Belle Epoque is one of the great prestige cuvées of the region. The cuvée is composed of the "emblematic crus" of Perrier-Jouët. The house owns 65 hectares of vines. About half of this is Chardonnay from Cramant and Avize, including the lieux-dits of Bourons Leroi and Bourons du Midi, purchased in the 19th century, and located mid-slope with a south-southeast exposition. There is Pinot Noir from the north face of the Montagne in Mailly, Verzy, and Verzenay, and from the Marne at Aÿ and in Dizy. The wines are fermented in stainless steel and finish their malolactic fermentation. Belle Epoque tends to get dosed at approximately 8 g/l. Former Chef de Cave Hervé Deschamps told me that 22 grams of sugar is added for the prise de mousse instead of the customary 24 grams, yielding a mousse that is just slightly softer than normal. This cuvée was initially called "Fleur de Champagne" in the United States due to trademark issues. These have now been resolved, however, and it is called Belle Epoque throughout the world. Vintages produced include 1964, 1966, 1969, 1971, 1973, 1975, 1976, 1978, 1979, 1982, 1983, 1985, 1988, 1989, 1990, 1994, 1995, 1996, 1998, 1999, 2000, 2002, 2004, 2006, 2007, 2008, 2011, and 2012. In 2018 Séverine Frerson was appointed as Chef de Caves Deschamps, who arrived in 1993. Her appointment surprised the Champagne industry, as it came just five months after she had assumed the role of Chef de Caves at Piper-Heidsieck.

I recently tasted the 2012 Belle Epoque: *"Surprisingly fresh and crisp. This opens with a scent of ripe apricot and fresh white flowers with a slightly smoky character from the lees aging. On the palate, the wine is racy and very fine, the model of delicacy and elegance, with an exuberant mousse, a perfect balance between the fresh fruit and the zippy acidity, and a pleasantly persistent finish. Lovely wine."* **** (Tasted 2020)

Belle Epoque also is produced in a Blanc de Blancs version, produced only from the two parcels in Cramant. 1993 was the first version of this wine, followed by 1999, 2000, 2002, 2004, and 2006. The 2002 vintage was superb: *"Almost Chablis-like in its intensity of green apple and citrus fruit on the initial attack, however with a bit of airy, subtle notes of magnolias and buttered toast appear. On the palate, the wine is crisply refreshing but not acerbic. Production is limited to a few thousand bottles in each vintage. Marvelous."* **** (Tasted 2015)

Although Belle Epoque Blanc de Blancs is relatively recent, the house has long had a close association with Cramant. From the 20s to the 50s, they produced a vintage-dated cuvée called Perrier-Jouët Cramant, and in the 30s, there was also a still white Cramant. Finally, there is also a rosé version of Belle Epoque. In 2009 I had the 1997 vintage with a bit of age: *"...a fairly deep hue, with a pleasantly languid mousse. On the nose, the fruit character showed aromas of raspberry jam and lilacs. On the palate, the red berry fruit and floral aromas came through with a bit of smoky evolution to it, a slightly baked character, and a suggestion of ground coffee. The texture was supple and quite graceful, although the finish was not astonishingly persistent."* **

28 avenue de Champagne 51200 Epernay | 03 26 53 38 00
https://www.perrier-jouet.com/

Suenen

Region: Côte des Blancs | Terroir: Côte des Blancs

Based in Cramant, Aurélien Suenen farms three hectares of Chardonnay in Cramant, Oiry, and Cramant. There is also Meunier planted in Montigny-sur-Vesle in the Massif de Saint-Thierry. Called from his career as a basketball player by the untimely passing of his father, Aurélien completed winemaking school and was mentored by Pascal Agrapart in nearby Avize. Since Suenen took charge of his family's winery in 2009, he has moved steadily towards organic production. He has analyzed the soils of his holdings with Claude Bourgignon and his team, and tills the vines, avoiding all synthetic pesticides and herbicides. Fermentations are done in a combination of tank and cask. Aurélien has also recently added barrels made from acacia wood and a concrete egg for fermentation. Fermentation is done using wild yeast, and the wines are bottled unfined and unfiltered. Sulfur use is kept to a minimum.

There are several vintage wines. The first is produced from the lieu-dit Les Robarts in Cramant. My notes from a tasting of the 2013 vintage in 2018: *"...substantial for a Blanc de Blancs, with a creamy, dense texture. The nose opens with ripe apricot, fresh blossoms, and a hint of spice and progresses on the palate to a firmly structured feel that still does not lack in finesse. Despite the richness, there is a freshness through to the end that is quintessential Cramant."*

In addition to the parcellaire Les Robarts, there is another from lieu-dit La Cocluette in nearby Oiry. Formerly this was nonvintage and blended from several parcels, but beginning with the 2013 vintage, Suenen also produced a vintage parcellaire that I tasted in 2019. *"Marvelous purity of fruit here, with a penetrating lemon peel and wet chalk nose and a refreshing, almost bracing acidity on the palate. The wine is not lacking in substance, however, and lingers enticingly on the palate."* ****

These are substantial, powerful wines with plenty of substance. Finally, there are two small production vintage wines from 2013 that I have not yet tasted. One is from Le Mont

Aigu in Chouilly, and another is from a small parcel of ungrafted vines in Montigny-sur-Vesle called La Grande Vigne, which is aged under cork.

53 rue de la Garenne 51530 Cramant | 03 26 57 54 94
http://www.champagne-suenen.fr/?lang=en

Tarlant

Region: Marne Valley | Terroir: Left Bank

The left (north-facing) bank of the Marne has not always been highly regarded as a terroir for Champagne production, yet this is where you will find an estate that is among the leading lights of the entire region. Not only is Champagne Tarlant among the most creative and inspiring producers today, but it has been working at this very high level for generations. The Tarlant family has been growing grapes in the Marne Valley since the 18th century, and the first domaine-bottled champagnes date to the 1920s. Today the estate is run by Benoît Tarlant, whose father, Jean-Mary, was the president of ITV[16] and legend among vignerons in the region. He and his sister Melanie joined him more than twenty years ago. Benoît makes the wine, while Mélanie works on the commercial side. They represent the twelfth generation to oversee the estate.

The Tarlant family owns 14 hectares of vineyards, spread over more than 40 parcels. The winery is located in Œuilly, and many of the vineyards are found there and in Boursault. There are also holding in St-Agnan and Celles-lès-Condé, both of which are in the Aisne départment. These were formerly were part of the "Terroir de Condé" although now they are classified as "Vallée de la Marne-Ouest" by the Union des Maisons de Champagne. In the vineyard, Tarlant is committed to working sustainably: treatments are used very sparingly and applied through advanced climate modeling. Soil management techniques include crop cover between the rows where appropriate, a practice that dates back to the management of Jean-Mary.

---

16   The Interprofessionnel de la Vigne et du Vin, a technical resource for grape growers.

In the winery, base wines are normally fermented with native yeast. Fermentation is often done in barrel, especially for the vintage and prestige cuvées, and a proportion of these casks are new each year. Malolactic fermentation is not always allowed but each wine is evaluated separately each year. The wines age a minimum of three years sur latte, of which one to eighteen months is *sur pointe* before disgorgement, and then they rest another 6 to 8 months after disgorgement before release.

A bottle of the Brut Prestige 1996 produced on Jean-Mary's watch was exquisitely balanced: *"A blend of 60% Chardonnay and 40% Pinot Noir that aged seven years on the lees, with a dosage of 4 g/l. On the nose, it showed a pleasant minerality and good auto-lytic character, while on the palate, the wine was both crisp and ripe at the same time and impressively long."* **** (Tasted 2004)

The vintage-dated Vigne d'Or 2004 was equally seduct-ive: *"This bottling is 100% Meunier from the lieu-dit of Pierre de Bellevue planted in 1947 in very chalky soils. The fruit has made a wine of compelling depth and concentration, with ripe fruit still showing a fairly primary apricot fruit character with a floral edge. But it has also developed a lovely yeasty autolysis character on the nose while retaining remarkable freshness on the palate."* **** (Tasted 2019)

There is also a vintage-dated expression of the estate vineyards whose name changes each year. The 2002 vintage was called l'Etincelante ("dazzling"): *"A superb vintage, of which Benoît is extremely fond. 57% Chardonnay from 3 vineyards in Œuilly with 29% Pinot Noir and 14% Meunier. The average age of vines in each parcel is more than 40 years. The result opened slowly, with an emphasis on citrus fruit and toasted brioche and a saline undercurrent. With time the wine opened on the palate to reveal a seductive floral note and a nutty, broad texture that became apparent only on the finish. A masterful wine with plenty of potential for improvement in the cellar."* **** (Tasted 2019)

In the hot vintage of 2003, the grapes were picked in the morning, and thus the wine was called "La Matinale". From my tasting note: *"Although marked by its passage in cask, this is fresh and lively with crisp citrus and floral notes barely accented with oak spice on the attack. A classic Marne blend of Pinot Noir (45%) and Meunier (27%) balanced with Chardonnay 28%, it is tender and approachable despite that fact that it is a Brut Nature with the malolactic blocked."* (Tasted 2019)

21 rue de la Cooperative 51480 Œuilly | 03 26 58 30 60
http://www.tarlant.com/

Vazart-Coquart & Fils

Region: Côte des Blancs | Terroir: Côte des Blancs

The Vazart family has been growing grapes since the 19th century, and Jacques Vazart began to bottle Champagne under his own name in the 1950s. His son Jean-Pierre arrived at the estate in 1989 and took over the reins in 2005. The family owns 11 hectares of vines, all of it in Chouilly, with 95% of it planted to Chardonnay and the balance to Pinot Noir. The vines are organically farmed and have recently received certification as such. The estate has additionally been certified Haute Valeur Environnementale Level 3. The fruit is gently pressed and fermented at cool temperatures in stainless steel. The malolactic fermentation is nearly always done.

There are two vintage wines. The Grand Bouquet can be very long-lived. The 1996 vintage tasted almost twenty years on: *"Smashingly good, with a maturing nose showcasing truffle, honey, and ripe, toasty, baked apple fruit. On the palate, the wine is seductive, soft, and supple with plenty of mousse and still enough freshness to balance all of that unctuous fruit and lead it to a surprisingly persistent finish."* **** (Tasted 2016)

There is also a late disgorgement of the 1985 vintage called Le Millésime par Vazart-Coquart. My notes on the 1985 vintage, which is still going strong: *"Aged under cork, this shows lovely lemon curd, brioche, and butter aromas. The wine is still surprisingly fresh; ripe on the palate but balanced, powerful, and long."* **** (Tasted 2015)

There is also the admirable Special Club. The 2012 vintage is representative : *"The nose presents a complex array of ripe apple, citrus, wood smoke, and toast aromas. On the palate, the fruit is almost sweet, but there is plenty of refreshing crisp acidity to balance out the fruit and carry the wine to an elegant finish."* **** (Tasted 2019)

6 rue des Partelaines 51530 Chouilly | 03 26 55 40 04
http://www.champagnevazartcoquart.com/

Veuve Clicquot

Location: Reims | Terroir: Blended

Today Veuve Clicquot is perhaps best known for its ubiquitous "Yellow Label" Brut non-vintage wine, but the house has been producing excellent vintage wines since the 1880s. Older vintages of Clicquot can still bring great pleasure. The house was founded by Philippe Clicquot in 1772. Since its inception, the Champagnes of Veuve Clicquot have been marked by a dominance of Pinot Noir, and the house has been a bit of a specialist in rosé, being the first house to ship rosé Champagne, in 1775. After the untimely death of the founder's son François in 1805, the business was taken over by his widow, Barbe-Nicole Ponsardin, while she was still just 27 years old. The innovative Widow Clicquot won fame with commercial and technical innovation. She was among the first to open the lucrative Russian market with her sales director Louis Bohne in the early years of the 19th century. She also worked with her cellarmaster Anton Mueller to invent the riddling process that removes the yeast sediment from the bottle. In 1841, management shifted to her trusted employee Edouard Werlé, although she took an active role in the management of the house until her death in 1866. The widow's daughter inherited the vineyards, but the business went to Werlé, and his descendants ran the house for generations. Clicquot was taken public in 1963 and purchased by LVMH in 1986.

Work in the vineyard is meticulous. The vineyards of Veuve Clicquot cover 393 hectares, mostly in grand cru and premier cru sites, making it the third-largest vineyard holding in the region. All of these vines are sustainably farmed, and Clicquot has been ISO 14001 certified[17] since 2004. They use no herbicides on their vineyards, and have reduced spraying by 40%, in part by implementing sexual confusion in all of the vineyards. They work with the growers who sell them grapes, and have a staff dedicated to implementing sustainable practices.

The same amount of care is taken in the winery. The modern reputation of the house was built by Chef de Caves Jacques Péters, from 1985 until 2006. In 2006 the talented Dominique Demarville took over. In 2020, however, Demarville departed, and was replaced by Didier Mariotti of Mumm. Throughout these changes, techniques in the winemaking have changed little. Fermentation is carried out at low temperatures in stainless steel, followed by malolactic fermentation. Demarville and his staff lightened the style a bit, moving gradually towards freshness and elegance from a style that was once markedly vinous and slightly oxidative. The house produces vintage-dated Brut and Rosé, as well as late disgorged versions of the same called Cave Privée, These older vintages will delight connoisseurs as well as lovers of the Clicquot brand.

For me, the older vintages of Veuve Clicquot have all held very well. (See the entries for 1928, 1947, and 1955 for notes on some of the more venerable bottles I have enjoyed.) All were in notably good condition for their age; the '47 and the '55 were directly from the cellars, the '28 was sourced at auction and was still in great shape. On the strength of these alone, Clicquot would merit a place in the two-star ratings. Younger vintages have also shown well.

From my notes on the 1976 vintage: *"The '76 Clicquot Reserve was a medium lemon, gold color, showing vibrant crème caramel notes and ripe fruit on the nose. On the palate, it was still very fresh – showing evolution, but no excessive oxidation. Lively acidity carried the wine to a persistent, complex finish, showing ripe fruit, an herbal note, and almost a honeyed character, although it was bone dry."* **** (Tasted 2005)

Similarly, the Veuve Clicquot 1988 vintage was mature, but showing well twenty years later: *"A lush nose of toffee and*

---

17   ISO 14001 is an audit system to ensure a robust Environmental Management System (EMS)

espresso with nutty notes and hints of truffle on the nose. On the palate, the wine shows round and creamy texture and great balance, with all elements being well integrated. The wine is developed but very elegant. Many notes." ****

It has seemed to me that current vintages were exceptionally well made if somewhat anodyne. On the 2012: "Initially the blanc and rosé vintages from Veuve Clicquot were fairly closed and didn't reveal their full potential. Six months on, however, they were more forthcoming: 2012 Veuve Clicquot is done a style that is crisper and fresher and less oxidative than has been the case in recent years. With ripe stone fruit and tropical notes and just a hint of autolysis, the style is fresh and forward. The texture here at first blush is very silky and fine, but with time one sees the true depth and length of the wine." *** (Tasted 2019)

In 1972 Veuve Clicquot introduced a prestige cuvée La Grande Dame. The first vintage was the 1962. The idea behind the cuvée was to create a prestige cuvée using the vineyards purchased by Madame Clicquot during her lifetime. This is normally a consistently top-notch offering in most vintages. The blend is dominated by Pinot Noir, and some vintages such as the 1995 have tended to be a bit heavy and slightly oxidative in style. The best of the older wines can be superb. From my notes on the 1979: "Rich and savory, there is still an elegance and a subtlety to the wine that was very refreshing. Notes of grilled hazelnut, toast and just a hint of soy. Still amazingly fresh, with a lot of mousse, a good firm acidity, and very nice length. This is a wine to drink now, although it will still hold up in the cellar for a few more years." **** (Tasted 2011) A rosé version was also introduced with the 1988 vintage, using a proportion of still red wine from the Clos Colin in Bouzy. A 1961 still red wine from that vineyard (not yet called Coteaux Champenois) was stupendous: "Still showing plenty of ripe cherry fruit with a delicate accent of black truffle, smoke and cedar, this is marvelously vital. On the palate it is holding up superbly well, with plenty of ripe fruit to balance the fresh acidity. Tannins resolved, yet the finish lingers persistently." ***** (Tasted 2007)

1 rue Albert Thomas 51100 Reims | 03 26 89 53 90
www.veuveclicquot.com

Vilmart & Cie.

Region: Montagne de Reims | Terroir: Grande Montagne

Vilmart is located in Rilly-la-Montagne. As elsewhere on the Montagne, black grapes dominate, accounting for 75% of plantings in the village. Vilmart, however, has vineyards planted 60% to Chardonnay and are the proprietors of 11 hectares divided among 13 parcels. The parcels, located in and around Rilly, generally have south and southeast exposures, and the average age of the vines is 30 years. The vineyards are all sustainably farmed. Cover crops are widely used and have been for decades. Sulfur is used to prevent fungal disease, but copper is not employed; sexual confusion has been employed for the control of grape moths by the entire commune for the last five or six years. Laurent is deeply committed to sustainable agriculture, but once remarked that his father had been "more organic than organic," and that his devotion to principle had affected fruit quality and so influenced Laurent in his present path. Since taking over the domaine in 1999, he has charted a resolutely practical course.

The grapes are pressed using a computer-controlled Coquart press, with four retrousses for each lot of grapes. Only the heart of each pressing is used, with the first juice and the tailles sold off. All of the base wines are all fermented in wood. The grapes from the youngest vines are used for the non-vintage wines, and these are fermented in foudres; the grapes from the older vines destined for the vintage cuvées are fermented in smaller casks. Malolactic fermentation is blocked, and after the first fermentation, the base wines spend ten months on the lees.

There are two vintage cuvées at Vilmart. The first is called the Grand Cellier d'Or. This wine is an assemblage of 80% Chardonnay and 20% Pinot Noir, both of them from the lieu-dit called Les Blanches Voies, planted in 1964. Fermentation is in small casks. From my notes on the 2014 vintage: *"A breath of fresh air, the aromas on the attack range from citrus to almond to toast, all with a saline undercurrent. On the palate, there is a great purity of fruit, a lively acidity, and an impressive concentration of flavors, all carried at this point by the spicy, some-what tangy influence of the cask ferment. This wine has the density and structure to age for decades and will richly repay cellaring."* **** (Tasted 2019)

The top wine in the range is known as Cœur de Cuvée (the "heart" of the free-run juice). This wine is made from grapes coming from the same plot of vines in Les Blanches Voies and the same blend as the Grand Cellier d'Or (80% Chardonnay and 20% Pinot Noir), but here it is a selection of the best juice. Cœur de Cuvée refers to the practice of discarding 200 liters at the beginning of the pressing of the cuvée and 700 liters at the end. Only the "heart" of the must is used for the fermentation. The balance of the juice is fermented for the Grande Reserve. This wine is a notch up from the other cuvées, with enormous fruit on the nose, real ripeness, and a candied, ripe, almost tropical fruit on the palate. The 2004 vintage was a tour de force: *"Classic vintage wine from the Montagne de Reims, with notes of apricot, fresh chervil, and roast almond. Impressive Champagne, but quite a mouthful - rich, powerful, dense, and long. Not for the faint of heart, this is produced only with the first press-ing of old vine fruit from their top vineyard, known as Blanches Voies."*

5 rue des Gravières 51500 Rilly-la-Montagne | 03 26 03 40 01
www.champagnevilmart.fr/en/

Yann Alexandre

Region: Montagne de Reims | Terroir: Ardre

Yann Alexandre is an independent winegrower who (for the moment) is flying completely under the radar. He has friends in high places—my first visit was prompted after former Krug Chef de Caves Eric Lebel mentioned his name. Yann and his wife Séverine are based in the Ardre Valley village of Courmas. The village is located on the banks of the Noron, a tributary to the Ardre. He is an eighth-generation vigneron, and the third generation to make Champagne under his own label. Yann and Séverine have 6.3 hectares scattered over 30 parcels in several surrounding villages including Courmas and the neighboring villages of Marfaux, Bouilly, and Chenay in the Ardre valley; in Ville-Dommange, Vrigny, and Coulommes-la-Montagne in the Petite Montagne; in Merfy in the Massif de Saint-Thierry, and in St. Lumier-en-Champagne in the Vitryat. In total, there are 3.45 hectares of Meunier, 1.15 hectares of Pinot Noir, and 1.7 hectares of Chardonnay. The vines are sustainably farmed, and the estate has been certified Haute Valeur Environnementale Level Three since 2015.

The grapes are carefully pressed and fermented plot-by-plot on selected yeasts in a combination of stainless steel and casks. Some lots undergo malolactic fermentation, and some do not since maintaining freshness is an essential consideration for Yann. There are two vintage wines, beginning with a Blanc de Blancs. My notes on the 2010 vintage: *"Very fresh citrus aromas and flavors with a lovely structure and very good length. Crisp and bright, the mineral notes come through on the end. Partially cask fermented."* **** (Tasted 2017)

Next in the range is the parcellaire Blanc de Noirs "Sous les Roses." It has always been produced from a single harvest, but it has not always been vintage dated. The wine from the

2011 harvest was superb: *"60% Pinot Noir and 40% Pinot Meunier from a single parcel in Courmas, this undergoes partial malolactic fermentation before aging five years under cork and then being dosed at 2.5 g/l. On the attack, there are attractive floral notes over a ripe, almost tropical fruit character. On the palate, the texture is creamy and rich with notes of spice, toast, and roasting almonds developing on the finish."* **** (Tasted 2017)

3 rue Saint-Vincent 51390 Courmas | 06 81 03 81 79
https://www.champagneyannalexandre.fr/us/

L. Aubry

Region: Montagne de Reims | Terroir: Petite Montagne

Located in the Petite Montagne, L. Aubry Fils is directed by Pierre and Philippe Aubry. Pierre is the winemaker, with a degree from the prestigious Ecole Nationale Supérieure d'Agronomique in Montpellier. The two brothers work with their brother-in-law Noël Poret to manage 15 hectares of vineyards in the Petite Montagne, including parcels in the villages of Jouy-lès-Reims and Pargny-lès-Reims, Villedommange and Coulommes-la-Montagne. Aubry was among the first producers to emphasize the "heritage varieties" of champagne, expanding the set from the big three grapes of Chardonnay, Pinot Noir, and Meunier to include Arbanne, Petit Meslier, Pinot Gris, and Pinot Blanc. These were planted at the estate in the 1980s, and today the estate counts a half-hectare each of Arbanne, Petit Meslier, and Pinot Gris.

The classic Brut non-vintage is more than 50% Meunier, with Chardonnay and Pinot Noir making up most of the balance and about 5% of the heritage varieties. There is also a traditional vintage wine with a similar profile called Aubry de Humbert. In 2018 I tasted the 2008 vintage: *"This is an assemblage of 5% each Petit Meslier and Arbanne, with 30% each Pinot Noir, Meunier, and Chardonnay. The Chardonnay is fermented in cask, and the other varietals in stainless. All of the wines finish their malolactic fermentation. This bottle was disgorged in June 2017 after more than eight years on the lees. The result is delicious, with notes of marzipan, ripe apples, and a hint of red fruits, colored with toasted brioche and a slightly rustic earthy or savory touch on the nose. On the palate, the wine is crisp and finishes clean with impressive length. The level of complexity adds to the overall high level of quality."* ****

In addition to these, the estate produces an assemblage of old vine Chardonnay and Meunier called "Ivoire et Ebène" drawn from specific parcels. The Chardonnay (which forms the majority) is from a south-facing site in Jouy-lès-Reims called L'Auditeur, and the Meunier is from a vineyard called Les Bonnes Fontaines that faces north. There is also a small amount of Pinot Noir from the same sites in the blend.

The most famous Aubry blend is perhaps Le Nombre d'Or (the golden ratio). This can be done as Campaniae Veteres Vites (with all seven authorized grape varieties), or as a Blanc de Blancs, which includes Pinot Blanc, Pinot Gris, Arbanne and Petite Meslier. The Blanc des Blancs is done in a style called Sablé, which has lower pressure. The blend of the Campaniae Veteres Vites can vary from year to year, but commonly includes 20 – 25% Pinot Blanc and Pinot Gris (planted, picked, and fermented together) along with 15 – 20% each of Petit Meslier, Pinot Noir, Arbanne, and Chardonnay and a trace of Meunier. My notes on the wine made from the fruit of the 2009 harvest (although this is not indicated on the label): *"Disgorged in 2014, this shows a complex nose with hints of fresh and dried flowers and apricot fruit colored by a smoky, toasty note from the yeast. The texture is broad and almost chewy, yet this never loses sight of freshness, and the final wine is a rewarding blend of balance, elegance, and slightly exotic flavors. Dosed at 3 g/l"* **** There is also a Rosé Sablé that also includes a proportion of the heritage varieties. Interesting, well-made, and unique wines from a pioneering property.

4 et 6 Grande Rue 51390 Jouy-lès-Reims | 03 26 49 20 07
http://www.champagne-aubry.com/

Ayala

Region: Marne Valley | Terroir: Blended

Founded in 1860 by Edmond de Ayala, Champagne Ayala was part of the original Syndicat des Grandes Marques. Destroyed during the Champagne Riots of 1911, it was rebuilt, only to be sold in the 1920s to the Lefebvre family. During this time, Ayala reached its initial peak of popularity and sales reached one million bottles per year. Ayala was known at the time for lower-dosage Champagnes, a tradition that the house has resurrected. However, the Great Depression and the Second World War were more difficult times, and Ayala was sold in 1932 to the British bank Guinness. The house changed hands several more times during the century, and in 2000 it was sold to the Frey family, who sold it on in 2005 to Bollinger. Although the Frey family retained the vineyards, Bollinger has invested here to bring vineyard holdings up to 32 hectares, located in the Côte des Blancs and the Grande Vallée. The purchase by Bollinger also meant an influx of investment that financed a new winery in stainless steel, giving Chef de Caves Caroline Latrive (appointed in 2011) the ability to vinify each parcel separately. Malolactic fermentation is normally completed for all base wines. Filtration and the use of sulfur are handled with extreme care. Latrive imbues the winemaking with an appreciation of elegance and delicacy. Although the wines of Aÿ can be quite vinous and masculine at times, those of Ayala are unusually understated.

There are two vintage wines. The first is the Blanc de Blancs. I was particularly taken with the 2007 vintage: *"Produced exclusively from fruit from the Côte des Blancs (Avize, Oger, Vertus, Cuis, and Cramant), this is aged six years on the lees before being disgorged, and is dosed at 6 g/l. The wine opens with a delicate nose of lemon peel and mineral and well-integrated autolysis. The texture on the palate is creamy and very fine, and the wine is the very picture of elegance."* ***

The prestige cuvée from Ayala is called Perle d'Ayala, and the elegance of the other offerings carries over here. My notes from the 2005 vintage, tasted in 2015: "*80% Chardonnay and 20% Pinot Noir, all from grand cru sites, this is fermented and aged under cork for eight years; dosage is 6 g/l. The aromas include spices and brioche on the initial attack, and with time it opens to show ripe apples and a fine mineral underpinning. The texture is creamy and dense, and a great complexity develops on the lingering finish.*" ****

1 rue Edmond de Ayala 51160 Aÿ | 03 26 55 15 44
http://www.champagne-ayala.fr/fr

Paul Bara

Region: Montagne de Reims | Terroir: Grande Montagne (South)

The Bara family of Bouzy traces its roots to the beginning of the 17th century. They have worked in wine since the 19th century, but Paul Bara began to bottle under his own name only in 1950. He was joined by his daughter Chantale in 1986, and she directs the estate today. The family owns a total of 11 hectares, mostly planted with Pinot Noir, all of it in Bouzy. The vineyards are sustainably farmed. There are no synthetic pesticides or herbicides, and the vines are grassed over between the rows.

Fermentation is done in stainless steel, and malolactic fermentation is blocked to maintain freshness. Only the cuvée is used, and the tailles are sold off. The house is known for its delicious rosé, although there are several vintage wines of interest. There is a classic vintage, with 90% Pinot Noir and 10% Chardonnay, but perhaps most elegant of the range is the Special Club bottling. This wine is typically a blend of 70% Pinot Noir and 30% Chardonnay. Chantale feels that it is perhaps "less typical" of the village because of the Chardonnay. Typical or not, I enjoyed the Special Club 2008 very much: "*...opens with notes of toasted hazelnut, white flowers, and ripe red apple. On the palate, it is concentrated but never heavy as the malic acid provides super balance for what might otherwise be very vinous. This is a rich Champagne, but a superbly proportioned example from the south face of the Montagne.*" **** (Tasted 2018)

This bottling can age very well. At a retrospective tasting in Reims I tasted a bottle of the 1982 disgorged in 1993 that retained great freshness: *"Truffled and mature on the nose, it is still holding its own, with buttered toast, a hint of caramel, and a luxurious Tarte Tatin nose. On the palate the wine is rich but not cloying, even in its maturity, and it holds its elegance right to the very end."* **** *(Tasted 2017)*

Bara was also the first to produce a Rosé Special Club. This is the same blend, except that 5% of the Pinot Noir is in the form of Bara's superb Coteaux Champenois. From my note on the current 2013 vintage: *"With well-integrated red fruit aromas and hints of violets and freshly turned earth, this presents a very forward nose. On the palate, the fireworks continue, a powerful wine with concentration, density, but also the freshness to carry it to an impressive finish."* **** (Tasted 2019)

The prestige cuvée of the house is called Comtesse Marie de France, a Blanc de Noirs very typical of Bouzy in its vinosity and heft. My note on the 2006 vintage: *"100% Pinot Noir of great ripeness and concentration. This wine shows pronounced yeasty autolysis with a fruit ripeness that is almost honeyed. On the palate, the wine is full-bodied, almost massive. It is a majestic Champagne, but one that is best taken with food lest it overwhelm you with brute force."* *** (Tasted 2018)

4 rue Yvonnet 51150 Bouzy | 03 26 57 00 50
https://www.champagnepaulbara.com/en/

Francis Boulard et Fille

Region: Montagne de Reims | Terroir: Massif de Saint-Thierry

The history of the Boulard family in Champagne goes back to the 18th century, and they have been making wine for seven generations. In 2009 the family holdings were separated among the children, and Francis created Champagne Francis Boulard et Fille with his daughter Delphine Richard-Boulard. A portion of the vineyards of the original family estate (Raymond Boulard) had been worked organically, and Francis wanted to move further in this direction, but his siblings did not agree. His share of the inheritance, thr hectares, is now certified organic and is farmed using biodynamic methods. Following Francis' retirement in 2017, Delphine is now in charge of the domaine. The vineyards are split between the Massif de Saint-Thierry, the Right Bank of the Marne, and the Grande Montagne. Those of the Massif de Saint-Thierry are planted mainly to Chardonnay in the villages of Cormicy and neighboring Cauroy-lès-Hermonville. Cormicy lies where the Grande Montagne meets the Petite Montagne, and is the northernmost village in Champagne. In the Marne, the vineyards are mostly planted to Meunier, in the charmingly-named hamlet of Paradis. In the Grande Montagne, Boulard has Chardonnay and Pinot Noir planted in grand cru Mailly.

The fruit is carefully pressed in a small press that allows Boulard to work parcel-by-parcel. Fermentation is done on native yeasts in a combination of 2,000-liter foudres, 600-liter demi-muids, and 300-liter casks. The lees are stirred every 10 to 12 days according to the biodynamic calendar. Malolactic fermentation is normally completed, and the wines are bottled unfined and unfiltered. Today, nearly everything is from a single harvest, whether it is labeled with a vintage date or not. Formerly reserve wines were used for the entry-level wines, but this is less true today. The only exception to this is the cuvée called Petraea (after the species of oak used to make barrels). This wine was formerly a blend of cask-aged vins clairs. A new solera was begun in 2012, and this will eventually be a reserve perpetuelle. The 2012 bottling is the only one I have tasted (in 2019), and thus it is a vintage wine here as well: *"From the lieu-dit Le Murtet, planted in 1947, this Blanc de Noirs is slightly reserved on the nose, with time it opens with floral notes followed by marzipan and finally, fresh biscuits. On the palate, the wine is powerfully structured, with an almost trenchant acidity and impressive density and length."* ***

The entry point for the range is called Les Murgiers, a Blanc de Noirs from 100% Meunier from the vines in the Marne Valley. My notes on the wine from the 2012 harvest: *"This bottling shows ripe apple and pear fruit, with a floral overlay on the nose and some toasty autolysis notes. The wine was three years on the lees, and was dosed at 5 g/l. (This has since come down further). On the palate, the wine is silky and supple, approachable and easy to drink."* *** (Tasted 2019)

The next wine is called Les Vieilles Vignes. It is a Blanc de Blancs from the Massif de Saint-Thierry. My notes on the wine from the 2011 harvest: *"Made from grapes from the lieu-dit Le Murtet, this is fermented exclusively in small casks. The wine shows a focused lemon and lime peel nose, with a dash of salt and a hint of flowers. It is structured and fairly tightly wound, but there is plenty of substance here, and it should open nicely with time."* *** (Tasted 2019) There is also a vintage-dated wine exclusively from Mailly called "Grand Cru / Grande Montagne" that I have yet to taste.

The top wine of the estate is the vintage-dated Les Rachais. It is a parcellaire from l'Hurtebise/Les Rachais, planted mostly to Chardonnay in the 1960s. The 2009 vintage was crisp and fresh, despite the warm nature of the vintage: *"Crisp, fresh Champagne with penetrating lemon peel and mineral notes on the nose and a lovely tension on the palate. Expressive, elegant Champagne with verve but also real concentration."* **** (Tasted 2015)

There is also sometimes a Les Rachais Rosé produced with the addition of old vine Pinot Noir planted in the same parcel. The 2005 vintage was a saignée with a 12-hour maceration: *"A fine, elegant rose de saignée, with a restrained red fruit expression and a lovely lemony acidity on the palate. There is a combination of delicacy and depth here that is surprising for a Blanc de Noirs 100% Pinot Noir."* **** (Tasted 2015)

13 rue de la Censé Flancourt 51170 Faverolles-et-Coëmy | 03 26 61 52 77
https ://www.francis-boulard.com/en/

Etienne Calsac

Region: Côte des Blancs | Terroir: Côte des Blancs

The Calsac family has owned vines in the Côte des Blancs for several generations, but they did not bottle wine under their own label. Etienne was the first to do so in 2010 when he took over his grandparent's 2.8 hectares of vines that had been leased out to négociant houses. He works the land very carefully and has received certification both for Haute Valeur Environnementale Level Three and Viticulture Durable en Champagne. Although he is not certified organic, he uses many techniques of organic farming. His holdings are spread over three villages: Avize (where he is based), Grauves, on the back side of the Côte des Blancs, and Bisseuil in the Grande Vallée of the Marne. Base wines are fermented in a combination of stainless steel and cask.

His flagship wine is the Clos des Maladries, a chalky parcel near his grandfather's house (who enclosed his portion of the Maladries within a wall to form the clos). The vineyard is grassed over and worked by horse. The 2014 vintage was fantastic: *"Opens with penetrating aromas of lemon, green apple, and toast with a firm, stony minerality. The wine is dosed at 2 g/l, but on the palate, there is nothing harsh. Malolactic fermentation was completed, giving the wine a silky, creamy texture, and an aroma that continues to develop. The wine is lithe and very fresh, but there is plenty of density here. This wine should age for decades in a proper cellar."* **** (Tasted 2019). All of the wines from Calsac are worth seeking out, but as they use reserve wines they are not included here.

128 allée Augustin Lorite 51190 Avize | 06 11 83 69 49
[No Website]

Vincent Charlot

Region: Marne Valley | Terroir: Left Bank

Vincent Charlot is based in the Marne Valley village of Mardeuil, across the river from Cumières. His family has owned vines here for some time but delivered the fruit to the cooperative. In 2001, Vincent took over the family vines and is now the proprietor of 4.2 hectares around the village, spread over 33 parcels. He produces wine under two labels, although he makes all of the wine and farms the vineyards in the same way. The Charlot-Tanneux label is used for wines blended across the entire property; the Vincent Charlot label is used for parcellaires. These last were always produced from the grapes of a single year, but were not always sold as vintage wines. Today they are increasingly vintage-dated.

Charlot began organic conversion at the domaine in 2010 and has received both his organic and biodynamic certification. The soil is not tilled, since Vincent relies on cover crops exclusively. Much of the vineyard is planted to Meunier, but he has some Chardonnay and Pinot Noir, as well as a bit of Arbanne, Petit Meslier, Pinot Gris and Pinot Blanc. Fermentation is done on native yeasts in used oak casks. Malolactic fermentation is generally discouraged, and the wine is bottled without fining or filtering. The dosage is very low.

The most well-known wine in the line-up is the Fruit de Ma Passion. From the bottling of the 2014 harvest: *"55% Meunier, 25% Pinot Noir, and 20% Chardonnay fermented in cask, from the lieux-dits of La Genette and Les Chapottes, on the lees for four years and then dosed at 4 g/l. The wine has a pure, clean, pronounced aroma of ripe red apple and fresh flowers on the nose. On the palate, it is silky and supple, but the red fruit character gives body and depth to the blend."* **** (Tasted 2019)

There is also a Blanc de Blancs called "l'Or des Basses Ronces," produced from Chardonnay planted in Mardeuil. My note on the 2011: *"This Champagne shows seductively ripe apples fruit with a distinctly buttery edge. The texture is creamy and rich, with a pleasantly plump weight on the palate carrying it through to the lingering finish."* (Tasted 2016)

I tasted the 2014 L'Extravagant at the annual Bulles Bio (the organic Champagne producers' group) tasting in Reims in 2019. Only later did I find that it is a cuvée that changes every year. In 2014, it was an assemblage of 95% Chardonnay and 5% Pinot Noir from Mardeuil and Epernay: *"Produced from the lieux-dits including l'Or des Basses Ronces and the Clos des Futies. In some vintages, it has been a light Rosé or a Blanc de Blancs. Here the wine was produced with no added sulfur. I found it to be a bit nutty on the nose in a way that indicated a bit of oxidation. Dosed 3 g/l."* **

Finally, there is a Meunier Rosé called l'Ecorché de la Genette. From my notes on the 2013: *"A delightful rosé de saignée. This is produced from the lieu-dit La Genette, planted in 1957. The fruit was macerated for 14 hours and resulted in a beautiful yet restrained color, and an exuberant fresh raspberry and violet aroma with a subtle earthy background. The texture is tender and lush, but the wine is dry, with a dosage of 4 g/l in (done with RCGM, rectified, concentrated grape must). Superbly balanced, this coasts to an elegant finish. Delightful."* **** (Tasted 2019)

Charlot makes a number of cuvées, all in tiny quantities. In some vintages the grapes from the Clos des Futies in Epernay (used in l'Extravagant in some years) is vinified on its own. I recently tasted the 2012: *"Rich, almost too much so – seems heavily dosed and lacks the finesse of some other offerings."* ** There is also Les Vossnelles, from a plot of old vine Pinot Noir; an old-vine Rosé de Saignée called "Le Rubis de la Dune" which is Pinot Noir and a bit of Meunier that I have yet to taste.

23 rue des Semons 51530 Mardeuil | 03 26 51 93 92
[No Website]

Chevreux-Bournazel

Region: Marne Valley | Terroir: Marne West (Aisne)

Chevreux-Bournazel redefines the term boutique – Stéphanie Chevreux and Julien Bournazel work just 40 ares of vines in the village of Connigis in the Aisne département in the Surmelin Valley. The steep, south-facing parcel at the further reaches of the western Marne Valley is entirely planted to Meunier and farmed biodynamically. Fermentation is done on native yeasts in cask. Malolactic fermentation is normally blocked, and after an elevage on the lees with bâtonnage, the wines are bottled unfined and unfiltered.

The wine is called La Parcelle, and the 2013 vintage was a delight: *"The wine is a bit closed on the nose but opens with time to show fresh floral notes, a bit of spice, and a firm minerality. The wine is produced as either a brut nature or as an extra brut with 4 g/l dosage. This brut nature was a bit strict but had enough fleshy Meunier fruit to round it out."* **** (Tasted 2019)

31 Hameau de Lauhay 02330 Connigis | 06 21 91 24 34
https://www.facebook.com/champagnechevreuxbournazel

Coessens

Region: Aube | Terroir: Barséquanais

Jérôme Coessens produces a surprising range of Champagnes from a single parcel of the lieu-dit Largillier in the Aube village of Ville-sur-Arce. The Coessens family has owned this parcel, already planted to vines in the 14th century, for five generations. Jérôme began to bottle Champagne from the site under his own label in 2006. The south-exposed site is at the top of the slope on a ridge above the river Arce on Kimmeridgian marl and is planted exclusively to Pinot Noir. Coessens has subdivided the parcel into four sections that he labels Mineral, Fruit, Flower, and Substance. He tills the soil and allows grass to grow between the vine rows. The fruit is fermented either in stainless steel tank or in old wooden casks; malolactic fermentation is normally completed, and the wine is matured on the lees before bottling. The various iterations include a Brut Nature; an Extra Brut called "Les Sens Boisés", a Rosé de Saignée, and two versions of Coteaux Champenois.

My first encounter was with the cask-fermented Sens Boisés in the 2009 vintage: *"Clean, ripe, almost tropical fruit on the nose with a prominent baking spice character, this is marked by the wood but not unpleasantly so. The wine is substantial but well balanced. Even in a warm year such as 2009, there is enough freshness to balance things out here, and the length is good."* *** (Tasted 2016)

The Brut Nature 2010 was substantial wine: *"This wine is what I call strict: slightly closed, at least on the initial attack, and not very expressive aromatically, although notes of marzipan, flowers, and mineral develop with time. On the palate, the wine is substantial, with a creamy texture and a long, vinous finish. This Champagne will doubtless develop well with time."* *** By contrast, the Brut in the same vintage was much more forward: *"Lovely floral fruit with aromas of ripe red apple. On the palate, the wine is elegant and balanced, with a silky texture and charming length. The wine is dosed at 9 g/l, although it does not feel heavy."* *** (Both tasted 2015)

I tasted the Rosé de Saignée in the 2012 vintage: *"10% of the fruit was crushed, and the balance was fermented as whole bunches. The juice was pressed off the skins after five days, and the fermentation was completed without the skins. This treatment gives a deep color and a lovely expression of ripe raspberry fruit. Although the dosage (9 g/l) is a bit generous."* *** (Tasted 2016)

In 2017 I tasted the 2014 vintage of both Coteaux side by side. The difference between the two cuvées is that one is fermented as whole bunches (labeled Vendange Entière), and the other is wholly destemmed (labeled Vendange Egrappée). Both had 21 months in cask. I enjoyed both wines, although I felt that the destemmed version showed the influence from the cask aging more transparently and that the oak was better integrated in the version fermented as whole clusters. The destemmed version was a superb Coteaux, among of the best of the vintage: *"Magnificent, with a gorgeous fruit expression of ripe cherry, violets, and freshly turned earth. The wine is firm and elegant, with plenty of density and the tannic structure to age for years. A delightful wine and certainly a reference for the region."* ****

6 Les Farces 10110 Ville-sur-Arce | 03 51 63 70 48
https://www.champagne-coessens.com/

Ulysse Collin

Region: Côte des Blancs | Terroir: Val du Petit Morin

The Collin family has been growing grapes in the Val du Petit Morin south of the Côte des Blancs since the 19th century. Early in the 20th century, they were among the first wave of growers to domaine-bottle their wines. By the 1980s, however, the vines were leased to Pommery. Olivier Collin, who heads the domaine today, studied law before switching to œnology and training with Anselme Selosse from 2001 until 2003. He took back 8.7 hectares of family vineyards and began production with the 2004 vintage.

Collin owns two vineyards of Chardonnay in Congy, both 0.6 hectares in the lieux-dits of Les Enfers and Les Roices. In neighboring Vert-Toulon, there is another 1.2 hectare parcel called Les Pierrières, also planted to Chardonnay. In the village of Barbonne-Fayel, there is a 2.5 hectare parcel in a site called Les Maillons that was planted to Pinot Noir in 1971. The vines are sustainably farmed, but much like his mentor, Olivier Collin is not certified organic, nor does he wish to be. Vines are grassed over between the rows, and the soil is tilled at the beginning of each season.

All of the fruit is fermented in large and small wooden casks (15% new) on native yeasts and is bottled unfined and unfiltered after maturation on the lees. There are five wines in total: one for each site, including both a Blanc and a Rosé from Les Maillons. The Rosé is the only wine that comes from a single harvest. The bottle says "36 months", but the vintage is not declared. My notes on the wine from the 2015 harvest: *"Deep pink in color, almost a light red. The aromas are very vinous and concentrated, with red cherry fruit and a strong earthy note. The texture is firm, with fresh acidity and good balance, but for me the extraction seems a bit overdone."* *** Nearly all of his Champagnes include some reserve wine, since for Collin, the site is everything, and the vintage is almost a distraction. For this reason the wines are not included here, but they are eminently worth seeking out.

19 Rue des Vignerons 51270 Congy | 03 26 52 46 62
[No Website]

Corbon

Region: Côte des Blancs | Terroir: Côte des Blancs

The Corbon family has farmed in Avize for four generations and today owns 6 hectares of vines in total, with two in Avize and the balance located in the Marne Valley. For many years the family bottled little under their own name. However, this began to change in the '70s under Claude Corbon, and today, Claude's daughter Agnès has taken over the estate and bottles her share of the family's vineyards. These include 1.1 hectares of old vines in Avize in the lieux-dits of Les Maladeries, Le Chemin de Chalon, La Fosse aux Pourceaux, and Les Terres de Maladeries, complemented by another 0.8 hectares of younger vines. The balance of the grapes come from vines in the Marne Valley spread among the villages of Vandières, Verneuil, Vincelles, and Trélou-sur-Marne.

The vintage-dated Grand Cru Avize is fermented in stainless and in concrete. Malolactic fermentation is blocked, and the wine is dosed at 5 g/l. The effect is delicious, if decidedly old-school. The 2004 vintage, tasted in 2015: *"...on the nose the wine is smoky and expressive, with ripe apple and citrus fruit aromas colored heavily with toasty autolytic character. On the palate, the wine is lush and velvety, with notes of smoke and caramel on the finish."* ***

541 avenue Jean-Jaurès 51190 Avize | 09 66 42 34 93
http://www.champagne-corbon.fr/

Vincent Couche

Region: Côte des Bar | Terroir: Barséquanais

Vincent Couche is a certified organic and biodynamic grower working in the Aube at Buxeuil. He is the owner of ten hectares of Pinot Noir in Buxeuil and another three hectares in Montgueux. The vines at Buxeuil are in Kimmeridgian soil with southwest exposure on fairly steep slopes, while those in Montgueux have a full southern exposition in thin clay soils over pure chalk. The wines are fermented in a combination of stainless steel tanks and oak casks on native yeasts. The base wines complete their malolactic fermentation and are bottled without fining or filtration. In addition to his nonvintage cuvées, he produces a Millésime which is a 50/50 blend of Chardonnay and Pinot Noir and a Blanc de Blancs called "ADN Montgueux" from his vines there. This is unique wine – my notes from the 2009 vintage: *"Entirely fermented in cask and vinified without any sulfur. It spent three years on the fine lees in cask before bottling, and a further five years on the lees of the second fermentation. It is disgorged without any dosage. This Blanc de Blancs is truly a superb bottle of "sans soufre" (made without sulfur) with a clean and pure fruit character that tends toward the tropical. There is a pronounced buttery element, and strong smoky, toasty notes from the lees work. On the palate, the texture is creamy and very dense; the finish is superb."* ****
(Tasted 2015)

29 Grande Rue 10110 Buxeuil | 03 25 38 53 96
[No Website]

R. H. Coutier

Region: Montagne de Reims | Terroir: Grande Montagne (South)

The Coutier family traces its roots in Ambonnay to the early 17th century, and they have been growing grapes here since before the French Revolution. By the turn of the 20th century, they were bottling some of their own Champagne as well as selling to négociants. René Coutier worked with his father for a dozen years before taking charge in 1983, and today he is joined by his son Antoine, who takes increasing responsibility for the family business. The family owns a total of nine hectares in Ambonnay. The estate is planted two-thirds Pinot Noir (parcels with southern exposure) and one-third Chardonnay (the east-facing parcels). The vineyards are sustainably farmed, with as few treatments as possible. Coutier uses no systemic herbicides, and wherever possible employs alternatives to chemical pesticides.

Most of the fermentation takes place in temperature-controlled stainless steel, although there are a few parcels vinified in oak, and Antoine is enthusiastically experimenting, including some lots fermented in ceramic amphora. Malolactic fermentation is done on a case-by-case basis, but it is usually blocked for the vintage wine, which is normally dosed at 6 g/l. The estate is known for its non-vintage Rosé, which is among the best in the region. At present, there is a single vintage Champagne, produced only in the best years. The 2005 vintage was particularly good: *"There is a rich tropical fruit character with an edge of floral and lush, toasty, autolytic aromas. On the palate, the wine is silky and rich, with a long, vinous finish. Full-bodied, but utterly delicious in its style."* ***

Coutier also produces one of the best Coteaux on the south face of the Montagne. It is made with grapes from well-exposed parcels with a high clay content. The grapes are sorted bunch by bunch and are 100% destemmed before fermentation. The 2012 Coteaux was particularly delicious: *"A green harvest was done in the vineyard to concentrate the fruit destined for the Coteaux, and after the initial alcoholic fermentation, the wine spent two years in cask. Antoine did his studies in Beaune, and the winemaking for the*

Coteaux is resolutely Burgundian. There is a lovely ripeness here and plenty of rich cherry fruit expression. The vineyard from which this wine comes is planted with 60-year-old vines; they normally ripen to at least 12° natural alcoholic content. This wine is not produced every year, and the next vintage will be 2015." **** (Tasted 2017)

7 rue Henri III 51550 Ambonnay | 03 26 57 02 55
[No Website]

De Sousa

Region: Côte des Blancs | Terroir: Côte des Blancs

The De Sousa family in Avize is the proprietor of 11 hectares of vines spread over 42 parcels, mostly in the grand cru communes of the Côte des Blancs, although they also cultivate some plots of Pinot Noir in the Aube. They have a range of domaine-bottled wines under the De Sousa label, and a négociant label called Zoémie De Sousa. The estate is certified organic and biodynamic. In the winery, the fruit of the younger vines is fermented in enameled steel tanks, and the old vine material is fermented in small oak barrels. Only the cuvée is used, and the wines are fermented on cultured yeasts. All of the cuvées undergo malolactic fermentation each year.

There is only one vintage wine, but it is impressive. The Cuvée des Caudelies is produced from the oldest vines -- more than 60 years of age -- and is fermented in cask. The lees are stirred while it is in barrel, and it is bottled unfined and unfiltered. During the time sur lattes, the wine is shaken to put the lees of the second fermentation back into suspension. The 2008 vintage was produced exclusively from Le Mesnil fruit and dosed at 3 g/l: *"Rich and slightly oxidative in style, this shows an almost coppery color and a pronounced leesy nose, with hints of bruised apple and a firm mineral backing. On the palate, the wine is silky and rich, perhaps lacking a bit of freshness. Still, this is a wine of concentration and length."* *** (Tasted 2015) The Champagne from De Sousa has a particular style that will be appreciated by fans of natural wines.

12 place Léon Bourgeois 51190 Avize | 03 26 57 53 29
www.champagnedesousa.com/en/

Deutz

Region: Marne Valley | Terroir: Blended

Deutz was founded in 1838 in Aÿ as Deutz Geldermann. The brand grew rapidly throughout the 19th century and was one of the original grande marque houses. Although they suffered during the Champagne Riots of 1911 and during the First World War, the house remained in family control through the Lallier branch. The prestige cuvée of the house, William Deutz, was launched in 1959. However, sales had declined slowly over time, and the Lallier family sold to the Rouzaud family of Roederer in 1993. In 1995, Fabrice Rousset was appointed president of Deutz and set out to reinvigorate the house. In 1999 Deutz launched the 1993 vintage of a Blanc de Blancs prestige cuvée called Amour de Deutz. It is composed mainly of fruit from Le Mesnil and Avize in the Côte des Blancs, with 5% from Villers-Marmery in the Perle Blanche section of the Montagne. In 2003, Michel Davesne was named chef de caves. He has maintained the vinous house style, typified by Pinot Noir, especially from Aÿ; this comprises 20 – 25% of the blend (except, of course, for Amour de Deutz), as Davesne is not a fan of Chardonnay from Aÿ. His work has been consistently elegant and discreet.

Because of the dominance of Pinot Noir, the wine can age quite well. I enjoyed a bottle of 1974 Millésimé while visiting the region: *"...45 years on, it is still hanging together well. The nose had rich notes of toffee, ground coffee, and honey, and on the palate, the wine was rich and dense but holding well and retaining enough freshness. A fascinating bottle, as '74 is not a well-noted vintage."* **** (Tasted 2019)

The Cuvée William Deutz also holds up well. My notes on the 1988 : *"Drinking quite well, with notes of rich apple fruit character with a yeasty edge and notes of truffle and cream. On the palate, the mousse was still very vigorous, and the acidity racy and firm. A lovely bottle of wine, probably drinking at its peak just about now."* **** (Tasted 2013)

The 2009 Amour de Deutz was typical of the vintage: *"Consistent with the vintage, the wine shows ripe apple fruit with an almost tropical edge and a good amount of toasty autolysis. On the palate, the wine is clean, round and fairly lush, with a texture that is a bit soft."* *** (Tasted 2019)

Amour de Deutz is also made as a Rosé in the vinous style of the house. The 2008 vintage was a delight: *"Based Ay, Deutz produced the marvelous Rosé Amour for its 170th-anniversary vintage. The blend is 64% Pinot Noir (with 9% done as still red wine) with 36% Chardonnay from Avize and Le Mesnil. On the nose, there is a pronounced cherry and red berry fruit with a floral edge and a suggestion of fresh brioche. On the palate, the wine is rich without being heavy. The mousse is creamy, and the finish is satisfyingly long."* **** (Tasted 2019)

16 rue Jeanson 51160 Aÿ | 03 26 56 94 00
https://www.champagne-deutz.com/en

José Dhondt

Region: Côte des Blancs | Terroir: Côte des Blancs

It seems to me that perhaps the delicate, elegant wines of José Dhondt have been slightly forgotten by the market. I was reminded recently at the trade tasting of their New York importer Pas Mal Selections in the fall of 2019 how much I like them. The Belgian Dhondt family moved to the Côte des Blancs in 1924. José Dhont was the first member of the family to bottle Champagne under the family name. They are the proprietors of six hectares, with most of the vines in Oger, in addition to small holdings in Le Mesnil and the Sézannais. The vines are farmed sustainably. In the winery, fermentation is done in small, temperature-controlled, stainless steel tanks. There are three wines -- a brut non-vintage, a rosé (made with Pinot Noir from the Sézannais) and the cuvée called Mes Vieilles Vignes. This last wine is vintage-dated, and absolutely delicious. My notes on the '13 vintage : *"This Champagne is produced from a single parcel in the lieu-dit of Les Noyérots in Oger, planted in 1949.*

Pronounced aromas open with a bright lemon peel and green apple fruit and an accent of saline minerality. On the palate, the wine is crisp and refreshing, but there are the creamy texture and impressive density to consider, since the old vine material adds plenty of breadth and power. A lovely wine to seek out." ****

1 rue de Flavigny 51190 Oger | 03 26 57 96 86
[No Website]

Doyard

Region: Côte des Blancs | Terroir: Côte des Blancs

The Doyard family traces their presence in the Côtes des Blancs to the 17th century, and Yannick is the 12th generation to grow grapes. The family has been domaine-bottling their production since 1927. The Doyard name is a well-known one since Maurice Doyard was one of the co-founders of the CIVC. Based in Vertus, they are proprietors of 11 hectares of vines scattered throughout Vertus, Le Mesnil, Oger, Avize, and Cramant. There is also one hectare of Pinot Noir, split between Vertus and Aÿ. In total, there are 54 parcels. The vineyards are sustainably farmed, and although they are not certified organic they use many organic principles in their farming.

The winemaking is not dogmatic but instead adapted to each wine. In some instances, only the cuvée is used, while for other blends, both the cuvée and taille are used. For the non-vintage, the base wines are vinified in tank, but much of the vintage wine is fermented in cask. Sometimes the malolactic is done while at other times it is avoided, giving the wines marvelous tension and nervous energy, as in the Blanc de Blancs Grand Cru 2009. *"This is a blend of 70% grapes Avize with additional fruit from Le Mesnil, Oger, and Cramant, entirely fermented in cask. The wine was six years on the lees before being disgorged and dosed with just 0.6 g/l. The use of older casks (at least five years of age) ensures that the wine is not overly marked by the wood. Instead, there is a lovely lemon / chalky mineral nose, with nicely ripe stone fruits and a great purity through and* through. *On the palate, there is a smooth mousse and great fresh-ness, but the wine is not tart or acerbic."* **** (Tasted 2018)

There is also a very delicate rosé sold as Oeil de Perdrix. My notes on the 2011: *"This is entirely from grand cru fruit: 75% of the blend is Pinot Noir from Aÿ, and 25% is Chardonnay from Avize. Only the cuvée is used for the Chardonnay but for the Pinot Noir, both the cuvée and the taille are used. The wine has a very light color, and it is only the color that comes from the Pinot during the pressing that gives it this tint. The Chardonnay is fermented in tank, while the Pinot is fermented in cask. Malolactic fermentation is blocked. The wine is aged 4.5 years in the cellar and dosed at 3 g/l. The finished Champagne has a lively, fresh stone fruit character with a suggestion of fresh flowers, barely touched with red fruit character. On the palate, it is lively, well-balanced, and exuberantly fruity."* *** (Tasted 2015)

The most compelling wine from Doyard is the Clos de l'Abbaye, produced from a half-hectare walled clos in Vertus that was planted in 1956. My notes on the 2011 vintage: *"Only the cuvée is used, and the fermentation is done entirely in cask, with the malolactic fermentation blocked. The wine is 4.5 years on the lees and disgorged with 2 g/l dosage. On the nose, there is a bit of spice from the wood, but soon an exotic coconut/tropical fruit appears with a strong mineral undercurrent. On the palate, the wine is elegant but also quite powerful, with impressive density and length. A superb effort in a fairly modest year."* ****
(Tasted 2015)

39 avenue Général Leclerc 51130 Vertus | 03 26 52 14 74
www.champagnedoyard.fr/en/

Fallet-Dart

Region: Marne Valley | Terroir: Western Marne (Aisne)

The Fallet family have been vignerons since the early 17th century and have bottled Champagne under their own label since the early 20th century. The house is today run by cousins Adrien and Paul, who joined in 2009 and took over from their fathers Daniel and Gérard in 2016. They are based in Charly-sur-Marne in the western Marne Valley, and own 18 hectares of vines spread over five villages. The vineyards are planted to 45% Meunier, 30% Chardonnay, and 25% Pinot Noir. The vineyards are sustainably farmed, with grass grown between the rows. Fermentation is done parcel-by-parcel in a combination of stainless steel tanks and oak barrels.

The vintage Champagne is a blend of 70% Chardonnay with 30% Pinot Noir vinified in a combination of cask and stainless. Chardonnay from the lieu-dit Malivas brings freshness to the blend. It is six years on the lees before disgorging. My notes on the 2008 vintage: *"Bright aromas of lemon peel, fresh apricot, and spice on the attack. Initially, on the palate, the wine is very fresh, but an expressive fruit reveals itself as it opens. Well balanced and elegant."* *** (Tasted 2019)

In the hamlet of Drachy, the Marne makes a 180° turn, providing the site for the winery and the vineyard site known as Les Hautes des Clos du Mont. There is no clos, but the historic property once belonged to the Bishop of Soissons. My notes on the 2004: *"Holding well, with notes of truffle, toast, and oak spice on the nose. On the palate, the wine is rich and creamy but still fresh. There is an enjoyable evolution, but the wine is still youthful at heart."* *** (Tasted 2015)

2 rue des Clos du Mont 02310 Charly-sur-Marne | 03 23 82 01 73
https://www.champagne-fallet-dart.fr/en/home/

Fleury

Region: Aube | Terroir: Barséquanais

Champagne Fleury was one of the pioneers of biodynamic viticulture in Champagne. The house is based in the village of Courteron in the Barséquanais, and dates to the late 19th century. Fleury has been bottling Champagne under its own label since the 1920s. Jean-Pierre Fleury, grandson of the founder, began converting the vineyards to biodynamics in 1989, and by 1992, the entire estate was being farmed biodynamically. The wines have long been a beacon of what is possible with these techniques in the region. The domaine is led today by Jean-Pierre's sons -- Jean-Sébastien in the winery and Benoît in the vineyards -- and his daughter Morgane on the commercial side.

The domaine consists of 15 hectares, planted 85% to Pinot Noir, 10% to Chardonnay, and a small amount of Pinot Gris and Pinot Blanc. The fermentation take place on native yeasts in either enameled stainless steel or in cask. Jean-Sébastien has cultured a strain of biodynamic yeast that he now sells to other growers. There is a vintage bottling that has been for years among the most successful biodynamic wines in the region. The 2002 vintage was typical: *"Entirely convincing. This delicious vintage Champagne is showing delightful mature aromas of brioche and black truffle, along with a supple, nicely silky texture and satisfying weight. 25% Chardonnay and 75% Pinot Noir, fermented 40% in cask, it is now showing a delightful evolution with a supple texture, marvelous complexity on the palate, and good weight on the finish."* **** (Tasted 2015)

There also is an old vine cuvée named for Robert Fleury. From my notes on the 2005: *"35% Pinot Noir, 25% Chardonnay, 28% Pinot Blanc, and 12% Meunier. This shows a bit of evolution on the nose, with ripe apple fruit colored with truffle and smoke on the opening. On the palate, the depth of flavor is even more impressive, and there is a good balance of freshness and weight."* **** (Tasted 2016)

Finally there is a third wine which is not vintage-dated, but comes exclusively from one harvest. It is called Sonate.

The bottling labeled "Opus 10," for example, uses fruit from the 2010 vintage exclusively: *"...75% Pinot Noir and 25% Chardonnay, elaborated without the use of sulfur at all. 30% of the base wines were fermented in cask. On the nose, there are lovely apricot and marzipan aromas with accents of brioche and a subtle, well-integrated, earthy character that is very pleasant. Despite the lack of sulfur, the wine is clean and fresh with a pleasantly lingering finish."* **** (Tasted 2015)

43 Grande Rue 10250 Courteron | 03 25 38 20 28
http://www.champagne-fleury.fr/

Val Frison

Region: Aube | Terroir: Barséquanais

Valérie Frison cultivates 6 hectares of vines in Ville-sur-Arce in the Barséquanias region of the Aube. The vines are sustainably farmed, and the must is fermented in cask on native yeasts with as little intervention as possible. Malolactic fermentation occurs naturally, and the base wines stay on the fine lees until the June following the harvest. The wines are bottled without fining or filtration. Sulfur is kept to an absolute minimum, and all the Champagnes are shipped without dosage, and all come from a single harvest, although they are not vintage-dated.

The Champagne called Goustan from the 2013 harvest was structured and powerful: *"This Blanc de Noirs (100% Pinot Noir) is bone dry, yet showing plenty of fruit, with a marvelous purity of apricot and pear fruit and a suggestion of beeswax and freshly-mown hay on the nose. On the palate, there is substantial vinous power, density, and an impressive length on the finish."* **** (Tasted 2016)

Cuvée Lalore is a Blanc de Blancs from the lieu-dit Les Cotannes. My notes on wine from the 2015 harvest: *"Elegant and charming, this has plenty of citrusy fruit upfront with a clean mineral/saline note underneath, more reminiscent of the Marne than the Aube. On the palate, the wine is clean and crisp, with a silky texture yet no lack of substance."* *** (Tasted 2018)

Portlandia is a blend of 75% Pinot Noir and 25% Chardonnay that are planted together in deep limestone soils, harvested together, and fermented together. My notes on the wine produced from the 2014 harvest: *"Remarkably approachable, this has an easy, ripe, apple fruit with a suggestion of spice and hint of citrus. On the palate, the wine is supple and soft yet there is still breadth and an impressive concentration on the finish. Lovely."* **** (Tasted 2019)

14 rue François Jacquelin 10110 Ville-sur-Arce | 06 11 78 00 53
https://www.champagnevalfrison.com/

Gatinois

Region: Marne Valley | Terroir: Grande Vallée

The Gatinois family has been growing grapes in Aÿ since the late 17th century, and they have been bottling under their own label since the early 20th century. The estate is directed today by youthful Louis Cheval, the 11th generation. Since the earliest days, the vineyard has remained the same – 7.5 hectares in Aÿ, divided into 30 different parcels, planted to 90% Pinot Noir and 10% Chardonnay. Gatinois still sells some of its harvest to négociants, notably Bollinger, but Louis is intent on increasing the proportions that are domaine bottled each year.

The vinification here is carried out in small, enameled steel tanks of 12 to 130 hl with no use of barrique. The wines always undergo their malolactic fermentation and are bottled unfined and unfiltered. Dosage is uniformly low, rarely above 6 g/l. There is one vintage wine, which is not made every year. I was particularly impressed with the 2008: *"On the nose, the wine was elegant, with notes of white flowers, marzipan, beeswax, and toast. But on the palate, the true colors of this wine were revealed, with a lush density, and a powerful, vinous concentration, with a finish that lingered seemingly forever and a mineral note to the end."* *** (Tasted 2015)

7 rue Marcel Mailly 51160 Aÿ | 03 26 55 14 26
https://www.champagnegatinois.com/en/

Philippe Glavier

Region: Côte des Blancs | Terroir: Côte des Blancs

Philippe and Véronique Glaivier are based in Cramant, and farm 4.5 hectares spread over 52 different parcels in the grand cru villages in the Côte des Blancs. The vines are sustainably farmed, and the grapes are pressed in a small press and vinified parcel-by-parcel. The base wines are fermented in a combination of cask and stainless steel, and the malolactic fermentation is completed for all wines. The first of the vintage wines is Emotion. From the 2012 vintage: *"An assemblage of fruit from Cramant, Le Mesnil, Oger, and Avize. The wine shows ripe apple and citrus notes on the nose, with a hint of smoke and a touch of salty minerality. Fermented in stainless steel tank, this Champagne is aged four years on the lees before being disgorged with 4.5 g/l dosage. The wine is crisp and refreshing, but there is also a buttery richness to the wine that balances out lively acidity."* *** (Tasted 2018)

The vintage-dated Folie de Cramant is a parcel selection of the best plots in Cramant. The 2010 vintage was superb: *"The fermentation is done in cask, but the wine is not overly marked by the wood. There is a pleasantly ripe and tangy lemon curd note on the nose of lemons allied with cream and underpinned with a chalky minerality. On the palate, the texture is creamy and denser than many Blanc de Blancs, with a pleasant spice note to the fruit that echoes straight through the finish."* **** (Tasted 2018)

82 rue Nestor Gaunel 51530 Cramant | 03 26 57 58 86
http://www.champagne-philippe-glavier.com/famille-en.html

Gonet-Médeville

Region: Marne Valley | Terroir: Blended

Understanding the history of the two families helps one truly appreciate the range of the wines produced by Champagne Gonet-Médeville. The Gonet heritage is from Xavier, descended from a long line of Champagne producers in Le Mesnil. His sister is Chantale Gonet, who runs the family estate called Philippe Gonet. Julie Médeville comes from the family that owns Château Gilette in Sauternes as well as other property in Champagne. Xavier brings an array of premier and grand cru vineyards to the union - they own 12 hectares in eight different villages. This array includes vines in Le Mesnil, Oger, and Ambonnay, as well as Mareuil-sur-Aÿ, Billy-le-Grand, Trépail, and Vaudemange, and in Bisseuil, where they are based. The lieux-dits in Le Mesnil include Lauvière, Champs d'Alouette, and Boulangère; lieu-dit Tilleuil in Oger; and in Ambonnay they include Grandes Ruelles and Champs Muets (planted to Pinot Noir). The vines are sustainably farmed using organic methods as much as possible, although they are not certified. Vinification is parcel-by-parcel, and the base wines are fermented in a combination of stainless steel and oak. Malolactic fermentation is avoided, and the dosage is very low.

For me, three vintage wines stand out in the range. The first is a parcellaire from Champs d'Alouette in Le Mesnil. This wine is fermented entirely in cask. The 2004 vintage was superb: *"...fantastic richness, complexity, and depth here. This parcel is located in the southern portion of Le Mesnil on the slope. It from the top to the bottom of the hill and is always the first to be picked. The aromas include a complex blend of citrus and ripe peaches, with notes of flowers, chalk, smoke, and spice in the background. On the palate, it is firmly structured but not inaccessible. There is a supple elegance that belies the freshness of the acidity, and the whole combines to lead to a marvelous finish."* **** (Tasted 2018)

The next is a rosé made using Pinot Noir (40%) from the lieu-dit Grande Ruelle in Ambonnay along with Chardonnay from le Mesnil (60%). My notes on the 2009: *"Fermented entirely in old casks and aged five years on the lees, this is expansive and vinous on the nose, with ripe, lush, red apple fruit character and notes of mineral, toast, and hazelnut with a subtle, spicy edge. The wine is rich but exquisitely balanced and very long. Malolactic fermentation is blocked, and the dosage is 2 g/l."* **** (Tasted 2019)

Finally, there is one of the best Coteaux made anywhere in Champagne, the Coteaux Champenois Rouge Cuvée Athenaïs. From my notes on the 2012 vintage: *"An intense and ripe still Pinot Noir from old vines planted in 1905 in the Ambonnay lieu-dit of Champ Muets and pruned to just four bunches per vine. These excruciatingly low yields give the wine an intensely ripe and concentrated black cherry and plum fruit with silky tannins and impressive length. Perhaps a bit marked by the cask upon initial release, this will assuredly repay a bit of cellaring. A wine to seek out."* **** (Tasted 2015)

1 Chemin de la Cavotte 51150 Bisseuil | 03 26 57 75 60
http://gonet-medeville.com/en/

Gosset

Location: Epernay | Terroir: Blended

Gosset was founded in 1584, making it the oldest wine house in Champagne. "Wine house" is the operative term: initially, they produced still red wine and not sparkling Champagne. Aÿ long had a strong reputation for red wine. As tastes shifted in the 18th century, Gosset changed with the times and began to produce sparkling Champagne. The house remained in family hands for more than 400 years, until 1993 when they sold to the Renaud-Cointreau family, who retain ownership today. Vineyard holdings are limited, so Gosset sources almost all of their grapes, from mostly premier cru and grand cru vineyards. Chef de Caves Odilon de Varine ferments the wines in tank and routinely blocks fermentation. There are two vintage wines. The first, called Grand Millésime, is produced from slightly more Chardonnay than Pinot Noir. I loved the 2004 vintage: *"Notes of biscuit, toast, and a bit of lemon on the attack, with a sumptuously creamy texture, and nice richness and density that is balanced by lively acidity. Good concentration and breadth. Love the '04s."* **** (Tasted 2015)

The prestige cuvée called Celebris is made with an extra brut dosage. The 2002 was magnificent: *"Charming wine, with notes of brioche, honey, and truffle on the nose that expands as the wine opens up. Dosed extra brut, the texture is structured and lively, but this wine also has the weight and complexity that maturity brings. Drinking very well just now."* **** (Tasted 2015)

12 rue Godart Roger 51200 Epernay | 03 26 56 99 56
https://www.champagne-gosset.com/

Guiborat

Region: Côte des Blancs | Terroir: Côte des Blancs

Members of the Fouquet family have been vignerons in Cramant since the end of the 19th century. Today the family owns 8 hectares, split between grand cru properties in the Côte des Blancs (Cramant and Chouilly) and premier cru parcels on the Left Bank of the Marne in Mardeuil. Richard Fouquet joined his grandmother in 1993 when he was 18 years old, and assumed management of the estate in 1996. Much of the family's fruit is sold to Laurent-Perrier, but Richard has been vinifying the best and bottling it under the Guiborat label. They have in total four hectares of Chardonnay and two hectares each of Pinot Noir and Pinot Meunier. The vines are sustainably farmed using organic techniques, although the estate is not certified.

The winemaking is adapted to the type of cuvée. Fermentation is done in varying proportions of stainless steel tanks and cask. Sometimes the malolactic fermentation is completed, and sometimes it is avoided. Dosage usually is 4 to 5 g/l. The first of the wines is called Prisme. In 2013 all of the fruit was from that harvest, although other bottlings have used reserve wines and the wine is not vintage-dated. Grapes come from vineyards in Cramant (lieu-dit Les Bergeries) and Chouilly (Mont Aigu and Les Caurés). Only the cuvée is used, and most of it is fermented in stainless, although a small amount was done in large neutral oak barrels. The wine was aged 44 months and dosed at 4.5 g/l—delicious wine: *"...really intense stuff. On the initial attack, there is a veritable assault of lemony fruit with a very pronounced saline character, a hint of white flowers, and a bit of smoke. On the palate, the wine is powerfully concentrated and fresh, with a steely acidity but plenty of fruit to balance it out. Refreshing, a bit angular, but with food, truly marvelous."* *** (Tasted 2018)

In 2008 Fouquet produced a parcellaire from Mont Aigu in Chouilly: *"Made with vines planted in 1970, with 20% of the fruit fermented in cask. All of the base wines were aged on the fine lees for seven months before bottling, and the wines were on the lees of the second fermentation for more than six years. The result has the trademark lemon-peel notes that I associate with Guiborat, but rounded out here with a bit of spice from the cask ferment and given a bit of amplitude from the smoky character that comes from a bit more time on the lees. The wine is dosed at 5.7 g/l, which also helps round it out, but this is still a very concentrated mouthful of wine. Should last a couple of decades in the cellar should you be able to wait. Marvelous."* **** (Tasted 2015)

There is another vintage wine labeled simply Millésime. The grapes come partly from Mont Aigu and partly from Les Caurés (also in Chouilly). The vines in Les Caurés were planted in 1946, although a portion of the vineyard was replanted in 1998. For the 2009 vintage, half of the wine was fermented in cask, and malolactic fermentation was blocked: *"Pronounced aromas of ripe apricot and white flowers with an accent of lime zest. On the palate, the wine is firm yet supple. There is a round-ness that is missing from the somewhat linear offerings in the rest of the range. This is dosed at 4.5 g/l, but there is no evidence of sweetness, only a silky, approachable feel on the palate that bodes well for future aging."* **** (Tasted 2016)

99 allée de la Garenne 51530 Cramant | 03 26 57 54 08
https://champagne-guiborat.fr/

Jeaunaux-Robin

Region: Côte des Blancs | Terroir: Val du Petit Morin

Jeaunaux-Robin is a small producer located in the Val du Petit Morin south of the Côte des Blancs, where they own 5.7 hectares. The vineyards are sustainably managed and in organic conversion. The parcels are planted to a combination of Meunier (60%), Pinot Noir (30%), and Chardonnay (10%). Fermentation takes place in a combination of casks and stainless steel.

Although it is not noted on the label, the cask-fermented "Marnes Blanches" comes from a single harvest, and all the grapes come from the lieu-dit Les Vignes Douces in Talus-Saint-Prix. My notes on the wine from the 2011 harvest: *"Planted on clay over limestone, this gives a pure, clean citrus expression with a slightly salty edge. There is a nice toasty note from the yeast and a hint of fresh flowers to the nose. On the palate, the wine is fresh, silky, and just a bit light. Malolactic is blocked, and the wine is a Brut Nature, although it is extremely well-balanced and not aggressive or tart at all. It is drinking well now but will also hold for several years."* *** (Tasted 2019)

The next wine is a Rosé de Saignée, also from a single harvest, and exclusively from Meunier. I enjoyed the bottling from the 2012 harvest: *"This comes from a specific site with iron-bearing red clay, where the vines are afflicted with court-noué and thus give tiny grapes. The wine is racked after a maceration of 2.5 days and finishes its alcoholic fermentation without the skins. The malolactic fermentation is not done. The length of the maceration gives a deep color and a pronounced red fruit character on the nose. Supple and rich, the wine still retains plenty of crisp acidity to carry the fruit well on the finish. Dosed at 8 g/l"* *** (Tasted 2019)

The top cuvée is called Les Grands Nots. It is an assemblage of one-third of each grape variety from 45-year-old vines. Only the cuvée is used, fermented in cask, and it stays six months on the fine lees before bottling, followed by twelve years on the lees of the second fermentation. It is disgorged without dosage. The 2005 vintage was delicious: *"On the nose, there was a ripe apple fruit, strongly colored with notes of smoke and brioche,* *and the autolysis was a dominant factor on the initial attack. On the palate, the minerality began to show with a bit of time in the glass. Structurally there is still enough freshness to balance the maturity and a density that carries the wine to a very nice finish. Well done and drinking nicely now, but this is a wine at its peak."* *** (Tasted 2019)

1 rue de Bannay 51270 Talus-Saint-Prix | 03 26 52 80 73
https://www.champagne-jr.fr/

Lacourte-Godbillon

Region: Montagne de Reims | Terroir: Petite Montagne

Located in the Petite Montagne, the Lacourte and Godbillon families have been growing grapes for several generations. They traditionally sold much of their fruit to négociant firms, and the co-op vinified the rest since the father of current proprietor Geraldine Lacourte was the co-op president. The first wines produced under the family name date to the 1960s, but there were only a few thousand bottles made. Since Lacourte and her husband Richard Desvignes have moved to Ecueil and taken over, they have changed their status to Recoltant-Manipulant and now work their 8.5 hectares of vines in organic conversion themselves. The vineyards are grassed over between the rows, and the soil is tilled. More than 80% of the vineyards are located in Ecueil; nearly that much is devoted to Pinot Noir.

The winemaking is done parcel-by-parcel in a combination of stainless steel and cask, and the base wines are kept on the fine lees until bottling. The vintage is a blend of 60% Pinot Noir, 40% Chardonnay, one-quarter vinified in cask, with five years on the lees and disgorged with a dosage of 3 g/l. I enjoyed the 2012 vintage: *"Delightful, with a nose that combines exotic notes of ripe tropical fruit with black truffle, butter, and toast. Rich and dense, with a creamy texture and enough acidity to give it a very hedonistic feel on the palate, leading the wine to a lingering, lovely finish."* (Tasted 2018)

There is also a parcellaire called Les Chaillots, produced with old-vine Pinot Noir, fermented in casks made from wood from the forest of Ecueil. It is bottled under cork and sees four years on the lees. The 2012 vintage was disgorged as a without dosage. The wine is impressive: *"A bit closed initially, the Chaillots 2012 began to open with a bit of time in the glass to show notes of marzipan, flowers, and toast. On the palate, the wine is dense and tightly wound, but there is a silky, creamy texture, and an elegance in the midpalate that is striking."* **** (Tasted 2018)

16 rue des Aillys 51500 Ecueil | 03 26 49 74 75
http://www.champagne-lacourte-godbillon.com/en/

Philippe Lancelot

Region: Côte des Blancs | Terroir: Côte des Blancs

Philippe Lancelot is a small organic and biodynamic producer (certified in both) based in Cramant who farms 4.28 hectares of vines spread between Cramant, Chouilly, and Epernay. His parents formed the estate in the 1970s. Philippe studied oenology in Avize and rejoined the family domaine in 2007. He began organic conversion in 2010, and instituted biodynamic practices in 2012. Hervé Jestin of Leclerc Briant has worked with him as consultant winemaker since 2009. The winemaking is as "natural" as possible: the must is not chaptalized, little sulfur is used, and the dosage is Brut Nature or Extra Brut.

I tasted the range across the 2012 vintage at the "Bulles Bio" tasting of organic Champagne in Reims in 2018. The Fine Fleur is an assemblage of Chardonnay from Cramant, Chouilly, and Oiry. *"Lovely and concentrated citrus fruit on the opening, with some biscuity yeast notes that develop with time. This is a wine of elegance and finesse, with a tightly wound texture and plenty of crisp acidity. The wine is Brut Nature, but has enough fruit to balance out the acidity."* ***

The bottling called Les Hauts d'Epernay is a blend of all three grape varieties. *"Opens with floral aromas and notes of almond and beeswax. The texture is fleshy and approachable, surprisingly so since it is Brut Nature. This Champagne is seductively silky, with a less penetrating intensity than the Blanc des Blancs."* ***

The top wine for me was the Brut Vintage Ivresse, entirely fermented in cask. This is made from a selection of vineyards at the foot of the Butte de Saran, including Le Bateau in Cramant and Fond du Bateau in Chouilly. *"The nose is beguiling, with a lovely concentration of lemon peel, chalk, and white flowers, edged with a bit of spice from the cask ferment that will no doubt integrate with time. On the palate, the wine is pure and concentrated, but there is plenty of ripeness and breadth to balance the fresh and lively acidity. I wrote 'remember this wine' – I'm sure that I will."* ****

155 rue de la Garenne 51530 Cramant | 03 26 57 58 95
https://www.philippelancelot.com/fr/

Lancelot-Pienne

Region: Côte des Blancs | Terroir: Côte des Blancs

Gilles Lancelot at Lancelot-Pienne is a marvelous producer mysteriously flying under the radar in Cramant. He makes elegant, focused wines, and given the quality, it is curious that he is not more well-known. The domaine dates to the early 20th century when Jean-Baptiste Lancelot, in charge of vineyards for G.H. Mumm, began to cultivate some vines of his own. These were inherited by his son Jean who began to bottle Champagne under his own label after the Second World War. Jean's son Albert married into the Pienne family, and their holdings were combined in 1967. His son Gilles began working at the estate in 1995 and took over in 2005.

The family works a total of nine hectares spread over 55 parcels. Three hectares are located in the Côte des Blancs in Cramant, Avize, and Chouilly. A further three hectares are located south of Epernay in Montenon, and there are two hectares in Boursault in the Marne Valley. The vineyard is planted to 50% Chardonnay, 40% Pinot Meunier, and 10% Pinot Noir. The top wine is the vintage Blanc de Blancs Marie Lancelot, produced from 100% Cramant fruit coming from five parcels: Les Bourons, Les Buzons, Les Gouttes d'Or, Les Fourches du Midi, and Les Moyens du Couchant. Annual production of this cuvée is tiny, ranging from 1,000 to 1,500 bottles. The wine is a superb expression of the chalky minerality of Cramant. The 2008 vintage was simply spectacular: *"The wine has much more to offer than racy lemon peel and minerality. There is a full range of expression from almonds to flowers, toasted brioche, and butter. This is extraordinarily good, one of the highlights of the trip. Dosed at 4 g/l."* ***** (Tasted 2013)

1 place Pierre Rivière 51530 Cramant | 03 26 59 99 86
http://www.champagne-lancelot-pienne.fr/en/

Joseph Loriot-Pagel

Region: Marne Valley | Terroir: Left Bank

Jean-Philippe Loriot is the sixth generation to grow grapes in Festigny on the Left Bank of the Marne. The family began growing grapes in 1838, and the first champagnes labeled with the family name were produced in the 1920s under Germain Loriot. His son André built new cellars in 1964, and in 1980 his son Joseph married Odile Pagel of Avize and launched his Loriot-Pagel label. They were joined by their son Jean-Philippe in 2006. Today the domaine is nine hectares, spread over Festigny, Mareuil-le-Port, Nesle-le-Repons, and Le Breuil on the Left Bank of the Marne well as in the grand cru Côte des Blancs villages of Avize, Cramant, and Oger. The vineyards are sustainably farmed and are certified Haute Valeur Environnementale Level Three.

The vintage-dated Cuvée de Reserve is a blend, generally one-third of each grape variety, although sometimes it is weighted a bit more towards Meunier. The 2008 vintage was fairly traditional in style: *"Toasty aromas open and expand to include ripe apricot touched with honey and flowers. On the palate, the wine is rich and dense, with a vivacity and a touch of sweetness. Fermented in tank, the base wine does undergo malolactic fermentation. It is four to five years on the lees and then disgorged, and dosed at 9 g/l"* ** (Tasted 2015)

The Special Club (like that of Moussé Fils), is 100% Meunier, fermented in tank. The fruit comes solely from Festigny, a blend of four lieux-dits. The 2009 vintage was typical: *"...lush stone fruit aromas with a suggestion of white flowers. On the palate, it is rich and creamy, just a touch soft."* *** (Tasted 2015)

My favorite wine from Loriot-Pagel is called Cuvée No. 6, produced with 40% Chardonnay from Cramant and Avize, 30% Meunier from Festigny, and 30% Pinot Noir from Labreuil fermented in old casks. The malolactic fermentation is blocked, and the wine is aged on the lees before bottling and then spends ten years on the lees before disgorgement and dosage at 6 g/l. The inaugural 2004 vintage was genuinely delicious: *"The nose opens with a bit of spice from the wood and brioche from the long aging* *on the lees, but it is very well integrated with the ripe red apple and citrus peel fruit. On the palate, the wine is lively and fresh, with a bit of tang to it, and a remarkably persistent finish." **** (Tasted 2015)*

40 rue de la République 51700 Festigny | 03 26 58 33 53
https://www.champagneloriotpagel.com/en/

Mailly Grand Cru

Region: Montagne de Reims | Terroir: Grande Montagne (North Face)

Champagne Mailly Grand Cru is a co-operative whose members own 70 hectares, exclusively in the village of Mailly. The co-op was founded in 1929, and it is still run today by the same 25 families that founded it three generations ago. Sébastien Montcuit took over from Hervé Dantan in 2013 as Chef de Caves when Dantan moved to Lanson. Mailly is located on the north face of the Montagne, and this cooler terroir yields structured wines with lots of finesse as compared to the riper, lush wines from the south-facing slopes such as Bouzy and Ambonnay. The vineyards of the village are divided into 480 parcels planted to Pinot Noir (75%) and Chardonnay (25%). At the time of my visit, Mailly Grand Cru was producing about 700,000 bottles, approximately 500,000 bottles labeled as "Mailly Grand Cru," supplemented by two private label Champagnes, one for Berry Brothers & Rudd, and one for Porsche.

The winery is very modern, with state-of-the-art gravity-flow construction. The vat room has enough tank space to allow parcel-by-parcel winemaking in increments from 40 to 80 hl. The fermentation is done to the greatest extent possible with wild yeasts, at temperatures from 8 to 12°C. Cask fermentation is used for the Brut Reserve, although this represents less than 5% of the volume. The minimum aging on the lees is 30 months, and the wines rest for three months after disgorging before shipment.

The Brut Vintage, recently renamed L'Intemporelle, shows well. I tasted the 2008 vintage in 2018: *"A blend of 60% Pinot Noir from selected parcels (Les Chalois, Les Côtes, Les Godats, Les Bara-quines, and others), and 40% Chardonnay also from key plots (Les*

Crayats, Les Coutures, and Les Roses), dosed at 8 g/l, and disgorged after five years on the lees. This is a rich wine with great definition. There are exotic tropical aromas, a strong sense of minerality, and a bit of spice. The texture is creamy and dense, although it never loses the vibrancy of its fresh acidity. Good length, marvelously elegant."
****

Les Echansons is the prestige cuvée of Mailly. It is a blend of 75% Pinot Noir and 25% Chardonnay, dosed at 6 g/l. In 2018, I tasted a late-disgorged bottle of the 1988 that was lovely: *"Truffled, with notes of honey and tropical fruit on the nose. On the palate, the wine was mature, ripe, and starting to soften around the edges. The texture is lush and showing what it should at this age. On the finish, there was a bit of butterscotch a hint of soy."* ***

28 rue de la Libération 51500 Mailly | 03 26 49 41 10
www.champagne-mailly.com/en

Sadi Malot

Region: Montagne de Reims | Terroir: Grande Montagne

Sadi Malot is based in Villers-Marmery, a premier cru village in the Perle Blanche of the Montagne de Reims, directed today by fifth-generation winemaker Cindy Malot. The Malot family owns ten hectares divided between Villers-Marmery and Verzy, the neighboring grand cru known for its Pinot Noir. The estate has received the Haute Valeur Environnementale Level Three certification and has been in conversion to be certified as organic since 2018, with an expected certification in 2021.

Most of the wines are fermented in tank, but their prestige cuvee Coup de Foudre is fermented in large casks. The 2008 vintage was lovely: *"There is a pleasantly forward fruit that balances between ripe apple and lemon peel, with an edge of toasted brioche and just a hint of well-integrated truffle aromas as it takes on a bit of age. On the palate, the wine is very expressive, with lively acidity (malolactic fermentation is blocked here) but also a silky density that carries the wine to a firm finish."* *** (Tasted 2015)

35 rue Pasteur 51380 Villers-Marmery | 03 26 97 90 48
https://www.champagne-sadi-malot.com/en/

A. Margaine

Region: Montagne de Reims | Terroir: Grande Montagne

Arnaud Margaine is a fourth-generation grower in the premier cru village of Villers-Marmery in the Perle Blanche region of the Montagne. Gaston Margaine founded the estate in 1910, and he began to domaine-bottle a portion of his harvest as early as the 1920s. However, the quantities produced under their own label were tiny, and the expansion was pushed by his son André from the 1950s and by his grandson Bernard. Arnaud joined his father in 1989. The estate is 6.5 hectares, mostly in Villers-Marmery, with a bit of Pinot Noir in Verzy. The vineyards are sustainably farmed, with cover crops between most rows and no synthetic herbicides used. Wines are fermented partly in stainless steel tank and partly in cask. Sometimes malolactic fermentation is done, and sometimes it is blocked.

The first of the wines is the Millésime, a Blanc de Blancs that represents a selection of the best parcels, including Champs d'Enfer, Bayons, and Broccots. The base wine is 30% fermented in cask, with malolactic fermentation avoided. My notes on the 2008: *"A landmark year. This is a rich style of Chardonnay. In French, they say 'un Chardonnay qui Pinote' in other words, one that almost resembles the Pinot Noir grown nearby, with floral and nutty aromas and richness and density on the palate that belies its origin. A lush, lovely wine, it is vinous on the palate but never loses its freshness. Disgorged October 2014, and dosed at 7.5 g/l"* *** (Tasted 2015)

2012 was the second vintage of Margaine's Rosé de Saignée: *"70% Pinot Noir and 30% Chardonnay from Villers-Marmery, this was done with a 24-hour maceration on the skins of the Pinot Noir and Chardonnay. In 2011, the malolactic was blocked, but my notes on the 2012, tasted in Reims, says that ma-lolactic was done for this vintage. Malolactic fermentation gives the wine a lush, exuberant, red berry fruit with floral overtones to complement the fairly deep color. On the palate, the texture is creamy and fairly dense. There is an extra brut dosage at 4.5 g/l that helps the wine to retain enough freshness to balance all of that fruit."* *** (Tasted 2019)

The top wine is the Special Club; a Blanc de Blancs made exclusively from Villers-Mamery fruit of old vines planted in the lieux-dits of Voies des Prêtes, Levoies, and Cugnets. 20% of the fruit was fermented in cask. My notes on the 2012: *"The nose shows ripe golden delicious apple and freshly buttered toast. On the palate, the wine is creamy and dense but balanced by very fine acidity (malolactic fermentation completed). This is substantial yet elegant wine and quite persistent on the finish. This Champagne should age extremely well."* **** (Tasted 2019)

3 avenue de Champagne 51380 Villers-Marmery | 03 26 97 92 13
http://champagnemargaine.com/

Marguet

Region: Montagne de Reims | Terroir: Grande Montagne

Benoît Marguet has become an icon in the natural wine movement and today heads his family estate based in Ambonnay. The path to his present success, however, has not always been an easy one. The family built a domaine of 90 hectares in the 19th century, but then sold their vineyards only to eventually start again. In the 1970s, his parents created a brand called Marguet-Bonnerave (after his mother's side of the family), and then a négociant label called Charles Marguet. Benoît began to make the wines in 1999 and gradually convinced his family to allow him to produce wines in a biodynamic fashion. He has been working with consultant oenologist Hervé Jestin since 2006, and he has been certified biodynamic since 2008.

The vineyards are at the heart of the work at Marguet. There are 8 hectares in total, comprised of old vines (average age 42 years), all biodynamically farmed, and plowed with a horse. There are 7.3 hectares in Ambonnay (in the lieux-dits of Les Saints Remys, Les Beurys, Les Crayères, La Grande Ruelle, Les Bermonts, Le Parc, and others), and a further 0.7 hectares in Bouzy, in the lieux dits of Les loges and Les Hannepés. Winemaking also proceeds according to biodynamic principles. The fruit is not chaptalized and is fermented in cask on native yeasts. An absolute minimum of sulfur is used, and none at all for many of the cuvées. The wines are bottled without fining or filtration, and little if any dosage is added.

The vintage brut was formerly called Amboniacus, and the blend varied each year. However, this label was discontinued and replaced by the Lieux-Dits collection after 2009. The inaugural vintage of Lieux-Dits, called Les Crayères, was superb: *"Impressive wine with a lovely concentration and depth of flavor, it features toasted brioche and roast walnut, ripe pear, smoke, and mineral aromas. With a year and one-half on the cork after disgorging, it is starting to open up now and showing a rich, lingering finish. A wine to seek out."* **** (Tasted 2014) Marguet continues to add new lieux-dits to the collection, and he has released wines from Les Bermonts, Le Parc, and La Grande

Ruelle. These are meant to be produced only in the best years. He has also launched a series of mono-crus, coming from one single village, but a blend across sites. Typical of this is the 2010 vintage from Ambonnay: *"Tender and fresh, this is produced from 42% Chardonnay blended with Pinot Noir. The leitmotif of the wine is elegance – there is nothing heavy here, and the wine is neither overly vinous or oxidative, just pure, clean floral and almond notes with a bit of brioche on the attack. On the palate, it is very delicate, yet there is enough weight to give it astonishing persistence on the palate."* **** (Tasted 2016)

Finally, there is a wine called Sapience. My notes from the inaugural 2006 Vintage: *"Billed as the first prestige cuvée to be certified organic and biodynamic, this is a joint project between Marguet and Hervé Jestin. The pair use old-vine fruit from Vincent Laval and David Léclapart, although blend is meant to change each year. Some love its "natural" appeal, but to me, the nose of fresh and bruised apple is a bit more oxidative than I would hope, although the texture on the palate is sharp and crisp on the palate and it regains its balance here."* *** (Tasted 2016)

1 Place Barancourt 51150 Ambonnay | 03 26 53 78 61
http://www.champagne-marguet.fr/en/

Serge Mathieu

Region: Côte des Bars | Terroir: Barséquanais

Avirey-Lingey is located in Bar-sur-Seine, to the east of Les Riceys, on the little stream called La Sarce. Isabelle Mathieu and her husband Michel Jacob are the proprietors of 11 hectares based in Avirey-Lingey in the Aube. The production is 80% Pinot Noir and 20% Chardonnay, planted in clay over Kimmeridgian marl. The largest parcel, La Bressoire, is 3 ha in size and boasts steep slopes and south-southeast exposition. There also is a series of parcels in the lieu-dit Bagneux and another set in the lieu-dit Les Couins. The average age of the vines is 23 years, although some are as old as 50 years.

Michel Jacob describes his approach to viticulture as "ecolo-pragmatic," and "somewhere between sustainable and organic." The estate uses no systemic herbicides at all. Cover crops are employed on every other row, and only fertilizers approved for organic use are used. The domaine has largely abandoned insecticides and fungicides.

There is one vintage wine. Previously it was assembled from Chardonnay and Pinot Noir, but recent vintages have been 100% Pinot Noir. The 2008 vintage is showing well: *"Ripe, with slightly restrained aromas of marzipan, pear, smoke, and toast on the nose with a distinct mineral note. On the palate, the wine is rich, perhaps slightly soft, but nicely elegant, with balance and enough freshness to carry the finish."* *** (Tasted 2015)

6 rue des Vignes 10340 Avirey-Lingey | 03 25 29 32 58
www.champagne-serge-mathieu.fr

Christophe Mignon

Region: Marne Valley | Terroir: Left Bank

Le Breuil is a village on the Left Bank of the Marne bordering the Aisne department. The sub-region is known as the Terroir de Condé, and it follows a stream known as Le Surmelin. In the Terroir de Condé, Meunier is king, accounting for 82% of plantings, and Christophe Mignon and wife Laurence specialize in Meunier. They are proprietors of 6.5 hectares between Le Breuil and Festigny. Nearly all of the practices in the vineyard are organic or biodynamic, although the domaine is not certified. Plant infusions are dynamized and sprayed on the vines for pests according to lunar cycles, and the vineyards are either grassed over or tilled.

The main vintage wine is called Pur Meunier, produced in both an Extra Brut and a Brut Nature style. The 2010 vintage was remarkably fresh, even in this warm year: *"From mature vines the lieu-dit of Les Varennes in Le Breuil. The fruit is fermented in stainless, and the malolactic fermentation is blocked. The wine is 36 months on the lees, and there is no dosage. The result shows an impressive concentration of floral notes on the nose and a very fresh character on the palate."* *** (Tasted 2016)

There also is a small production of Blanc de Blancs from mature vines produced similarly: ferment in stainless, malolactic blocked. The wine is matured for a year in large oak foudres, aged five years, and disgorged with an Extra Brut dosage.

4 rue de la Boulonnerie 51700 Festigny | 03 26 58 34 24
www.champagne-christophe-mignon.com/en/

Jean Milan

Region: Côte des Blancs | Terroir : Côte des Blancs

The wines of grand cru Oger are very distinctive among those of the Côte des Blancs: pure Oger is powerful and rich, ample and almost broad without being heavy. At the same time, it lacks the minerality of Le Mesnil or the Avize or the floral delicacy of Chouilly or Cramant. Champagne Jean Milan exclusively produces wines from their six hectares of Oger fruit, where it was founded in 1864. The vineyards are sustainably managed, and fermentation is done for the most part in enameled steel tanks, although some are done in cask.

There are three vintage wines. The first, a Brut Nature, is called Transparence. The 2013 vintage was lovely: *"Delicious, with a much more pronounced mineral-saline side and some nice toasty notes. Brut Nature means no added sugar, but here there are about 2 grams residual left in the base wine since they pick very ripe fruit for this bottling. This generosity gives it a softer, rounder feel than many brut natures on the market. Very well done."* **** (Tasted 2017)

The next cuvée is called Symphorine. The 2013 vintage was delicious: *"Symphorine is an assemblage from several sites within Oger, including Zailleux, Baudure, Barbettes, Chenêts, and others. The wine is dosed at 6 g/l, yet there is no sensation of too much sugar. In fact, it has a nose of fresh flowers and ripe orchard fruit, but the key elements are balance, harmony, and a very silky texture."* **** (Tasted 2017)

The highlight for me, however, has long been their parcellaire called Terres de Noël. From my notes on the 2012 vintage: *"Produced with fruit from a single lieu-dit planted with 70-year-old vines. Somewhat similar to Symphorine, but more intense and concentrated, with a nose of cream, ripe pear, a bit of spice, and a lovely dense texture balanced with superb acidity to give it marvelous length and complexity. Dosed at 6 g/l."* **** (Tasted 2017)

4 rue d'Avize 51190 Oger | 03 26 57 50 09
www.champagne-milan.com

Pierre Moncuit

Region: Côte des Blancs | Terroir: Côte des Blancs

The Moncuit family has significant landholdings in Le Mesnil, and the house of Pierre Moncuit owns 15 hectares in the grand crus of the Côte des Blancs and another five in the Sézannais. The house has been directed since the 1970s by Nicole Moncuit and her brother Yves, and they were recently joined by Nicole's daughter Valérie. The house makes wines of great purity and finesse. Only the free-run juice is used, the base wines are fermented in stainless steel, and all of the wines finish their malolactic fermentation.

All wines at Pierre Moncuit are produced from a single harvest, since no reserve wine is used. The first wine used to be called Cuvée Réserve, but it is now labeled Cuvée Pierre Moncuit-Delos. My notes on the wine from the 2000 harvest: *"...disgorged six months ago, this shows bright citrus fruit upfront with a chalky, saline undercurrent and a suggestion of white flowers. On the palate, the wine is lively and admirably fresh, and the minerality seems to grow in amplitude and finally take on an almost honeyed note."* *** (Tasted 2004)

The Vintage Grand Cru is produced in Brut and Brut Nature versions and is even more expressive. From my notes on the 1996 and 1995, tasted side-by-side: *"The 1996 vintage has a lovely aromatic fragrance, with ripe pear and apricot fruit and significant autolysis, showing crème brûlée notes on the attack, but retaining its freshness on the palate, with crisp acidity and impressive length. The vintage 1995 was softer, with more tropical than orchard fruit and a honeyed note with time. On the palate, the acidity is balanced but not nearly as fresh, and the finish falls a bit flat."* *** (Tasted 2004)

The top of the range is called the Cuvée Nicole Vieille Vigne, produced from 90-year-old vines in Les Chétillons. The 2005 vintage was superb: *"This masterful champagne has a densely aromatic nose, with pronounced aromas of brioche and baked apple. The yeasty character is emphatic, but the wine is by no means overly mature – just a small hint of caramel. The texture is rich and creamy, with a lush character that never falls into heaviness."* ****

11 rue Persault Maheu 51190 Le Mesnil-sur-Oger | 03 26 57 52 65
www.pierre-moncuit.fr

Moussé Fils

Region: Marne Valley | Terroir: Right Bank

"Profondément Meunier" ("Deeply Meunier") is the tag line for the Moussé Fils web site, and Meunier is undoubtedly the focus here, as elsewhere in this section of the Marne Valley. At Moussé Fils, however, Meunier is not a default choice but a conscious one, since they love the fit of the grape to their terroir. The Moussé family has been growing grapes since the 17th century and bottling under their own name since the 1920s. The estate is currently directed by youthful, energetic Cédric Moussé, who joined his father Jean-Marc at the estate in 2003. The family farms 5.6 hectares of vines spread over Cuisles and the neighboring villages of Jonquery, Châtillon-sur-Marne, and Vandières. All of the vineyards are sustainably farmed, and although they are not certified organic, they use many organic principles in their farming, including the use of herbal infusions to protect the plants, grassing the vineyard over between rows, and plowing by horse. The wines are fermented in stainless tanks, malolactic fermentation is generally finished, and the dosage is usually very low.

The first vintage wine is named Terre d'Illite after the type of subsoil. The soil is composed of chunks of calcium-rich marl over a deep bed of green clay, called illite by geologists. The wine is a Blanc de Noirs (95% Meunier and 5% Pinot Noir) assembled from 23 different parcels. I was impressed with the 2012 vintage: *"There is an immediacy of bright floral notes on the nose and a silky texture on the palate with a surprisingly persistent finish. Disgorged after four years on the lees and dosed at 5 g/l.* (Tasted 2018)

The other wine of compelling interest from Moussé is the Special Club. They were the first producer to make a 100% Meunier Special Club; it is still a reference. I recently enjoyed the 2013 vintage: *"Produced from four distinct parcels within the lieu-dit Les Fortes Terres in Cuisles. Clay, sand, illite, and calcareous marl. The cuvée is 100% Meunier, Moussé's ultimate expression of the grape. The wine is three years on the lees and disgorged with 1 g/l dosage. On the nose, there is plenty of ripe peachy fruit with a distinctive floral cast. The texture is fresh and lively, with a creamy mousse and an exquisite balance between the freshness, the yeasty character, and the fruit."* ****

5 rue de Jonquery 51700 Cuisles | 03 26 58 10 80
http://champagnemoussefils.com/en/?i=0

Penet-Chardonnet

Region: Montagne de Reims | Terroir: Grande Montagne

The wines of Verzy producer Penet-Chardonnet delight and intrigue. The Penet family has lived on the north face of the Montagne for centuries, but the house dates only to the 1967 marriage of Christian Penet and Marie-Louise Chardonnet. They own six hectares of vines in Verzy and Verzenay, spread among 27 parcels. The grapes are fermented parcel-by-parcel, both in tank and in cask. Malolactic fermentation is usually blocked, and the wines are very low dosage.

There are two vintage wines of great interest. Both are parcellaires from Verzy, but they are completely different. The first is from the lieu-dit Les Fervins, with a south-eastern exposition and a 15% slope. The blend is 70% Pinot Noir and 30% Chardonnay, co-planted by his grandfather together in the vineyard. Today, Penet picks them together and ferments them together in the tank, malolactic blocked. The wine has extended contact with the lees before bottling. My note on the 2009 vintage: *"The wine is initially a bit closed on the nose but opens with time to show a great aromatic complexity that melds notes of toast, fresh flowers, ripe apricot, and hazelnut. On the palate, it is firmly structured, with very fresh acidity, but there is also good breadth across the palate and plenty of length."* **** (Tasted 2019)

The second wine is from the lieu-dit Les Epinettes. This is remarkably distinct, even in the same vintage: *"This parcel is exposed north-west but is almost flat – there is only a 3% slope here. The vineyard is planted to forty-year-old Pinot Noir, which is vinified in the same way as Fervins. Here the nose opens with a strong lemon peel note accented with wood smoke and mineral. On the palate, the acidity is fresh but well balanced by the substantial nature of the wine."* **** (Tasted 2019)

These wines provide a fascinating exploration of the terroir of Verzy. There is another cuvée that I have yet to taste: Les Blanches Voies, another parcellaire from Verzy, but this one is planted to Chardonnay. In addition, the Prestige and the Cuvée Diane Claire, which formerly used some reserve wine, are expected to become vintage wines with future releases.

12 rue Gambetta 51380 Verzy | 03 51 00 28 80
https://www.lamaisonpenet.com/index.php?dir=penet-chardonnet

Laurent-Perrier

Region: Grande Vallée | Terroir: Blended

Laurent-Perrier is one of the iconic houses in Champagne. Owned by the de Nonancourt family, this is the flagship of the Groupe Laurent-Perrier which was second in turnover only to Moët-Hennessy in 2019 with €216 million in revenue according to the Union des Maisons de Champagne. The group owns not only Laurent-Perrier, but also de Castellane, Salon, Delamotte, and the lesser-known Château Malakoff (which produces the Beaumet, Jeanmaire, and Oudinot brands). The company was founded in 1812 and flourished in the 19th century, building more than 500,000 bottles eventually. One early highlight was the development of the first Brut Nature, the "Grand Vin Sans Sucre," launched in 1889. The house fell upon difficult times after the outbreak of the First World War, however, and was sold by Eugenie Hortense Laurent to Mary-Louise Lanson de Nonancourt in 1939. This daughter of the Lanson clan devoted herself to the company with the intention that her eldest son Maurice would run it, but he was killed at the Oranienburg concentration camp during the Second World War for his work with the Resistance. Maurice's younger brother was Bernard de Nonancourt, also active in the Resistance. He was a decorated war hero famous for uncovering Hitler's wine cellar during the taking of Berchtesgaden and the Eagle's Nest which containing hundreds of bottles of Salon 1928 – a firm which de Nonancourt would go on to purchase. He apprenticed after the war at Delamotte and Lanson, the Champagne houses owned by his mother's relatives, and ultimately took Laurent-Perrier to unprecedented heights. One of his early innovations was the cuvée known as Grand Siècle, launched in 1960. This was traditionally a multi-vintage blend, although it was produced for a time in a vintage-dated version. I tasted the 1990 vintage in 2019: "*Wonderful Champagne, lush and ripe. The nose showed baked apples and pastry drizzled with honey. The wine had good autolysis and a bit of evolution. It was mature and softening up, but there was still plenty of mousse and enough acidity to keep it in* *balance. Ready to drink now and probably one should do so soon, but it was delightful with Cantonese food recently in San Francisco's Chinatown."* ***** *(Tasted 2019)* Although it is no longer a vintage wine, this bottling should not be overlooked.

Another of de Nonancourt's innovations was the use of stainless-steel fermentation tanks, which were installed in the 1950s during the reign of the first of de Nonancourt's Chef de Caves, Edouard Leclerc. Leclerc was followed by Alain Terrier, who assumed the role in 1981 and worked alongside Michel Fauconnet, who took over the management of the winemaking in 2004. Fauconnet retired in 2019, and in 2020 Dominique Demarville was named to the post. Demarville, however, departed shortly after his arrival, and for now Fauconnet has retaken his duties. Laurent-Perrier is based in Tours-sur-Marne. The house is well-known for its non-vintage rosé champagne made using the saignée method.

Visitors to the facility are told that vintage is "not a priority," although I found the Millésimé to be a fantastic bottling. My notes on the 2008 vintage: *"The vintage wine from Laurent-Perrier a blend of half Chardonnay, half Pinot Noir, coming only from grand cru sites. The Chardonnay is from Cramant, Chouilly, and Le Mesnil, while the Pinot Noir is from Verzy, Verzenay, Mailly, Tours-sur-Marne, and Bouzy. Like all of the wines at Laurent-Perrier, each parcel is fermented separately in temperature-controlled stainless steel, and the malolactic fermentation is completed. The result is generously structured, opening with aromas of ripe apricots, toast, and honey, but enlivened by an attractive freshness on the palate. There is a pleasant richness to the texture and a luxuriously long finish."* **** (Tasted 2019) It is due to this lack of emphasis on vintage wine that Laurent-Perrier is placed here in this volume, although the overall quality of the range definitely merits consideration.

32 Avenue de Champagne 51150 Tours-sur-Marne | 03 26 58 91 22
https://www.laurent-perrier.com/en/

Piollot Père et Fils

Region: Aube | Terroir: Barséquanais

Roland Piollot is married to Dominique Moreau of Champagne Marie Courtin. While they collaborate on much of the work, each of them makes their own delicious Champagne. The Piollot estate dates to the 19th Century. Athanase Piollot planted the first vines, and his grandson Robert cleared the lieu-dit Colas Robin and planted it to Pinot Blanc in the 1950s. In addition to growing grapes, Robert worked as a *pépiniériste*, producing rootstock for neighboring vignerons. Due to this work, all of the vines were planted using massal selection. Robert's son Roland joined the estate in 1986 and began to bottle the entire production under the Piollot name. Organic conversion began in 2009, and the estate was certified in 2014. Biodynamics are now practiced across the whole estate, and it is also Demeter-certified. Roland farms 8.5 hectares, planted 62% to Pinot Noir, 19% Chardonnay, and 12% Pinot Blanc, with a bit of Meunier and Arbanne. The wines are fermented in a combination of tank and cask on native yeasts. The base wines finish their malolactic fermentation, and all of the cuvées except the Rosé are Brut Nature.

The Colas Robin was the first Piollot Champagne I tasted. I thought the 2014 wonderful: *"100% Pinot Blanc from 65-year-old vines with a south-facing exposition. One-fifth of the must is fermented in tank, and the balance is fermented in cask. There fragrant aromas of ripe melon and apricot, and a silky, supple texture on the palate. The wine is rich without being heavy, and the finish is balanced and elegant. Five years on the lees, this was disgorged July 2018 and shipped Brut Nature."* **** (Tasted 2016)

Mepetit is a Blanc de Noirs from Meunier planted in the lieu-dit of the same name. My notes on the 2015: *"From 45-year-old vines with a south-east exposition, fermented in cask. The nose shows aromas of fresh flowers and ripe, red apple fruit with some smoky yeast notes. The texture is supple if a bit soft. Aged on the lees four years and shipped Brut Nature."* *** (Tasted 2016)

Les Protelles is a Rosé produced exclusively from Pinot Noir. The 2015: *"The fruit is pressed after a three-day maceration in tank. The nose shows beautiful ripe berry fruit aroma and a bright, crisp texture that is elegant if the end is a bit lean. Dosed at 3 g/l."* (Tasted 2016)

13 rue de Tonnerre 10110 Polisot | 03 25 38 57 45
https://www.piollot.com/en/home/

R. Pouillon

Region: Marne Valley | Terroir: Grande Vallée

Founded by Roger Pouillon in 1947 and based in Mareuil, R. Pouillon is directed today by his grandson Fabrice, who farms 6.5 hectares over 36 parcels planted between Mareuil, Aÿ, Mutigny, and Epernay. The estate is not certified organic but farms sustainably, and employs a variety of organic and biodynamic methods in the vineyard. The vines are tilled with a horse, and yields are modest. Winemaking is done parcel-by-parcel with an old Coquard press. Fermentations are done in a combination of vessels: both enameled steel, terracotta, and both large and smaller casks, all on native yeasts. The malolactic fermentation is completed for each wine.

Les Valnons is a Blanc de Blancs from Aÿ from the lieu-dit of the same name. The 2008 vintage was superb: *"Fermented completely in used casks on native yeasts with bâtonnage and aged under cork, this has a pronounced aroma of ripe apricots, marzipan, citrus peel, and toast. On the palate, it is round and rich without being heavy – it brings the vinous nature of Aÿ without any excess. Brut Nature, but the richness perfectly balances the racy acidity. Marvelous wine."* **** (Tasted 2019)

Les Blanchiens is one of the traditional parcels of the estate. The 2008 vintage: *"This is a blend of half Chardonnay, half Pinot Noir, both from the lieu-dit of the same name from a south-facing site at mid-slope in Mareuil. It is fermented in older casks with bâtonnage and aged under cork, malolactic done. The nose opens with rich, smoky yeast aromas, a ripe pear and apple fruit, and a strong mineral underpinning. On the palate, there is a tangy note and a richer, riper, rounder texture with an appealing hazelnut note on the finish. Brut Nature"* **** (Tasted 2016)

The top wine for me is the single-vineyard Pinot Noir from Chemin du Bois in Mareuil. The 2008 vintage: *"The wine is not chaptalized, and is produced using what Fabrice calls the 'Methode Pouillon' -- only very ripe fruit picked at 12% potential alcohol is used. The fruit is fermented on native yeasts in a variety of casks, both new and neutral, and then bottled. To this is added unfermented must from the previous vintage to provoke the secondary fermentation. The results are delicious, with an intense aroma of marzipan, fresh flowers, and brioche with a salty, savory edge. Firmly structured, this has plenty of substance but also a fresh, forward acidity that balances everything to perfection and drives the wine to a satisfyingly persistent finish."* **** (Tasted 2019)

There is also a single vineyard Meunier that I have not tasted called Les Chataigniers from Festigny, vinified in the same way, and shipped with an Extra Brut dosage. As well, Pouillon makes both a red and white Coteaux.

17 rue d'Aÿ 51160 Mareuil-sur-Aÿ | 03 26 52 63 62
https://champagne-pouillon.com/en/

Ruppert-Leroy

Region: Aube | Terroir: Barséquanais

Ruppert-Leroy is a producer in the Côte des Bar who owns four hectares based in the village of Essoyes. They are certified organic and biodynamic. There are three sites: La Fosse, on red clay over chalk, planted to Pinot Noir and Chardonnay; Martin Fontaine on chalky soils, planted to Chardonnay; and Les Cognaux in clay and marl soils, planted to Pinot Noir.

In the winery, the must is moved by gravity and fermented on native yeasts without the addition of sulfur. Fermentations are in large or small oak casks on native yeasts. The base wines all finish their malolactic fermentation and are bottled without fining or filtration after nine months on the fine lees. They are shipped Brut Nature. There is a cuvée called "11, 12, 13..." that comes from a réserve perpetuelle, but everything else is a from a single harvest, whether this is noted or not.

Martin Fontaine is a Blanc de Blancs. My notes on the wine from the 2013 harvest: *"...lovely nose of fresh apricot and lemon peel with hints of white flowers, chamomile, and mineral. On the palate, there is a lively acidity but also a round, supple texture and a pleasantly lingering finish."* *** (Tasted 2016)

The Fosse Grely is a 50/50 blend of Chardonnay and Pinot Noir. The fruit from the 2013 harvest: *"The first aromas are citrus and floral with an element of green apple and hazelnut touched with smoke. On the palate, it is rich if somewhat restrained, with pleasant ripeness, perfect balance, and delightful length."* **** (Tasted 2016)

The top wine for me is Les Cognaux. My notes: *"Planted in deep, grey clay and fermented in large casks, this has a deeply resonant nose with a lovely complexity of toasted almond, violets, and ripe apple, with a savory edge and a slightly earthy note in the background. The wine is vinous and substantial but not lacking balance or elegance. Accomplished and delightful."* **** (Tasted 2016) A Rosé de Saignée from the same vineyard in the same vintage: *"...nice expression of red berry fruit on the nose. This rosé is slightly lean but fresh and clean, with excellent balance and length."* *** (Tasted 2016)

La Bergerie, Chemin Gabrielle Renard 10360 Essoyes | 03 25 29 81 3
http://champagne-ruppert-leroy.com/

Denis Salomon

Region: Marne Valley | Terroir: Right Bank

The Salomon family owns 3.6 hectares on the right bank of the Marne at Vandières. Vineyard holdings include 2.1 hectares of Meunier and 0.75 hectares each of Pinot Noir and Chardonnay. The vineyards are sustainably farmed, and the estate has Haute Valeur Environnementale Level Three certification. Fermentation is done in a combination of stainless steel tank and cask. The bottling called "Elegance" is labeled as nonvintage, although it was produced exclusively from the 2015 harvest: "*Produced from grapes grown on a parcel with a steep slope and sandy soil. The wine has lovely citrus aromas with a hint of smoke on the initial attack. On the palate, the wine is very fresh with a bit of reduction.*" ** (Tasted 2018)

The Saignée de Meunier also comes from a single harvest. My notes on the wine from the grapes of 2012: "*This Champagne is made from Meunier coming from a single lieu-dit called Les Chennevières, planted in 1962. The fruit undergoes a 48-hour maceration, after which the fruit is pressed off skins. The malolactic fermentation is blocked. The result has a fairly deep color and a pronounced cherry fruit note on the nose with a hint of violets. On the palate, there is balanced acidity and substantial texture.*" *** (Tasted 2018)

The Vintage 2011 was fairly traditional in style: "*50% Chardonnay, 20% Meunier, and 30% Pinot Noir. Toasty and rich on the nose with ripe apple fruit. On the palate, the wine is balanced with a very fine mousse and enough acidity to balance the richness.*" ** (Tasted 2018)

The top wine for me was the 2013 Cuvée Vitalie, named for Eric's daughter. "*One-third of each grape variety, vinified in wood, partly new. This marks the flavor of the Champagne, but it retains a compelling freshness and a decided aroma of citrus, and also of ripe pear. Aged under cork, bottled in March 2014 and disgorged in 2018, dosed at 3 g/l.*" *** (Tasted 2018)

5 rue Principale 51700 Vandières | 03 26 58 05 77
http://www.champagne-salomon.com/

Camille Savès

Region: Montagne de Reims | Terroir: Grande Montagne (South)

Hervé and his son Arthur represent the fourth and fifth generation of the Savès family from Bouzy. They farm 10 hectares spread over 25 parcels; nine hectares are located in the grand cru villages of Bouzy, Ambonnay, and Tours-sur-Marne, with an additional hectare in the premier cru village of Tauxières. They take great pride that the vineyards are worked in a "more than sustainable" fashion, with no herbicide for the past fifteen years and no insecticide for the past twenty. All of the soils are tilled. The average age of the vines is more than 35 years, and they are typically renewed using massal selection. The parcels that Hervé singles out in Bouzy as being of exceptional quality include La Poivresse, Les Loges, Hautes Brousses, among others for Pinot Noir, and Hauts Chemins for Chardonnay.

In the winery, the fermentations are done in a combination of enameled steel and cask. The tailles are not used, and the malolactic is generally blocked. All of the vins clairs are bottled unfiltered. The winery is known for its nonvintage Rosé, but the vintage wines are also very much worth a look. From my notes on the 2011: "*A selection of particular parcels in the heart of Bouzy – 80% Pinot Noir (several parcels including Les Loges and Les Pierres Aigües, all mid-slope) along with 20% Chardonnay from Les Hauts Chemins. The wine presents as mature, but not overly; there is a ripe apple fruit up front, with a hint of candied fruit and just a note of caramel and truffle. On the palate, the texture is creamy, and there is an impressive vinous density here.*" *** (Tasted 2019)

The wines can hold very well. During a visit to the domaine in 2008, I was lucky to taste a bottle of the 1969 vintage: "*A deep golden color with very fine bubbles and notes of truffle, honey, sous bois, saddle leather, and ground coffee on the nose. The wine is still very fresh and integrated, with a fantastic, lingering finish. Truly memorable.*" ****

There is another vintage cuvée called Anaïs Jolicœur. From my notes on the 2012 vintage: "*Structured, powerful, dense, and long, this is superb Champagne with notes of ripe pear and marzipan, toasted brioche, and fresh flowers. The blend is 90% Pinot Noir and 10% Chardonnay, completely fermented in cask. The fruit comes from the lieux-dits Les Cercets, Les Pierres, Le Bas de la Haie de la Lue, Les Loges, and La Poivresse. In spite of the obvious concentration and power, this remains well-balanced and supple, demonstrating the 2012 vintage in all its genius."* **** (Tasted 2019)

Finally, there is a Coteaux that has long been among my favorites. Notes on the 2012: *"A truly wonderful still red wine from the best parcels at the middle and top of the slope in Bouzy. There is a marvelously transparent expression of bright cherry fruit, pomegranate, and fresh flowers that is underscored with an earthy character that complements without overwhelming the wine. The emphasis is on the silky texture and the perfume rather than the power of the wine, although there is plenty of structure here, and the wine will not only last but improve with mid-term cellaring."* **** (Tasted 2017)

4 rue de Condé 51150 Bouzy | 03 26 57 00 33
http://www.champagne-saves.com/en/welcome/

J.M. Sélèque

Region: Marne Valley | Terroir: Coteaux Sud d'Epernay

The Sélèque family arrived in Pierry in the Coteaux Sud d'Epernay in the 1920s but did not begin to bottle Champagne under their own label until the 1970s. Jean-Marc, the grandson of the founder, arrived at the domaine in 2008. Today the family is the proprietor of nine hectares across 45 parcels in Pierry, Moussy, and Epernay in the Coteaux Sud d'Epernay along with plots in Dizy, Mardeuil, and Boursault in the Marne Valley and Vertus in the Côte des Blancs. The vines are sustainably farmed, with vineyards either grassed over between the rows or tilled using a horse. After a slow pressing and short settling, the must is fermented in a combination of tank, cask (large and small), concrete eggs, and amphorae. The wines are produced with a minimum of intervention and are bottled unfined and unfiltered.

Soliste is a 100% Meunier Blanc de Noirs. My notes on the 2012 vintage: *"Produced from fruit from the lieu-dit Les Gouttes d'Or in premier cru Pierry, planted in 1951, this was fermented half in cask and half in concrete egg, aged under cork for four years, and disgorged with 2 g/l dosage. The nose shows flashy floral aromas upfront with ripe apricot fruit and a hint of toast. On the palate, the texture is supple and silky, perhaps a bit light, with balanced acidity and a lingering finish."* *** (Tasted 2016). This wine is also produced in a Rosé version with Meunier from the Pierry lieu-dit Les Charmiers, and in a Pinot Noir version with fruit from the Pierry the lieu-dit of Les Gayères.

The top bottling from Sélèque is called Partition. They explain the name: there are seven parcels of old vines fermented in seven casks, meant to resemble seven notes of music resulting in a harmonious composition. The first bottling was 2008, which I did not taste. However, the 2010 vintage was delicious : *"This is a blend of 72% Chardonnay with 14% each Pinot Noir and Meunier. Grapes come from La Justice in Vertus (planted 1950), Moque-Bouteille in Dizy, Les Frileux in Epernay, Les Basses Ronces in Mardeuil, and several sites in Pierry. The must is fermented in cask and aged five years under cork before being disgorged and dosed at 2 g/l. On the opening, the wine presents notes of ripe pear and peaches with a hint of lemon peel and a dose of spice and toast. On the palate, it is fairly rich and structured, with plenty of acidity to balance a fairly significant density, a lively mousse, and a lingering finish."* **** (Tasted 2016)

Jean-Marc has also released a few cuvées this year that I have not yet tasted. There is a late-disgorged version of Partition known as "Partition - 2ème Lecture". The current release is from 2009. There are also two Coteaux Champenois. The first is a white from the village of Dizy (lieu-dit Moque Bouteille), which is fermented in cask, aged 18 months and bottled unfiltered. There is also a red from Pierry. It is fermented in earthenware amphorae using 10% whole clusters. The press wine is added back in, and the blend is aged in cask for 18 months prior to being bottled unfiltered.

9 allée de la Vieille Ferme 51530 Pierry | 03 26 55 27 15
https://www.jmseleque.fr/

Soutiran

Region: Montagne de Reims | Terroir: Grande Montagne (South)

The house of Soutiran was founded in 1950. Valérie Souti-ran, the granddaughter of the founder Gérard, is the third generation to run the estate, along with her husband, Patrick Renaux. They are the owners of six hectares of vines, mostly in Ambonnay, but also in neighboring Trépail, Chigny-lès-Roses, Ludes, and Chamery. About 20% of the vines are more than 45 years of age. The grape blend of the estate vineyards is 70% Pinot Noir and nearly 30% Chardonnay, although some Meunier for the Cuvée Alexandre is obtained from the commune of Chigny. Fermentation is done in a combination of stainless steel tanks and wood casks, and the base wines normally finish their malolactic fermentation. They are aged on the fine lees before bottling.

The Brut Vintage is a selection of the best parcels and made only in top years. As one might expect in Ambonnay, it is full-bodied, concentrated, and vinous. It can occasionally be a bit heavy, but I still have very pleasant memories of the 2002 vintage: *"...a blend of 50% Chardonnay and 50% Pinot Noir, with about 8,000 bottles produced. The wine shows silky aromas of fresh, red apple and toast on the nose, with a creamy, buttery texture on the palate. Despite this silky, creamy texture, the wine is undeniably substantial and finishes long. Normally dosed at 8 g/l."* *** (Tasted 2007)

There is also a vintage Blanc de Blancs. Formerly it was sold as non-vintage even though it was all from one harvest. In recent years, however, it has been labeled with the vintage. It is to my taste a bit heavy. From my notes on the 2006: *"...creamy and round, this is rich, powerful. On the nose, there is a suggestion of coffee and almost caramel, and it lacks the fresh appley fruit one might desire. On the palate, it is round and dense, perhaps a bit heavy."* ** (Tasted 2016)

3 rue de Crilly 51150 Ambonnay | 03 26 57 07 87
www.soutiran.com/en/

Stroebel

Region: Montagne de Reims | Terroir: Grande Montagne

The Stroebel family settled in Champagne from Alsace after the Second World War. The first estate-bottled wines, however, were not produced until 2005. Champagne Stroebel is directed today by Timothée Stroebel. It has been certified organic since 2014 and biodynamic in practice since then. Stroebel farms 3.5 hectares in and around Villers-Allerand: two hectares of Meunier, one hectare Pinot Noir, and 0.5 hectares of Chardonnay. Only the cuvée is used. The must is fermented in cask on native yeasts, and the wines are bottled unfined and unfiltered.

The cuvée called Héraclite Sous Bois is a Blanc de Noirs from 60% Pinot Noir and 40% Meunier. The 2012 vintage was delightful: *"Marked by the wood but not overly so, the nose shows a sweetly ripe pear and apricot fruit with floral notes and a hint of spice. On the palate, there is superb concentration and a plump, satisfying finish."* *** (Tasted 2016)

4 Place des Déportés 51500 Villers-Allerand | 03 26 97 60 63
[No Website]

Jean Velut

Region: Côte des Blancs | Terroir: Montgueux

The Velut family has been growing vines in Montgueux since the 16th century, but they began to bottle at the domaine only in 1976, led at the time by Jean's son Denis. The domaine, led today by Benoît Velut, is the proprietor of 7.7 hectares of vines, planted mainly to Chardonnay. The vines are sustainably farmed, and Benoît is gradually moving towards incorporating more organic techniques in the vineyard. The domaine is certified Haute Valeur Environnementale Level 3. In the winery, the must is fermented in stainless steel tank, and malolactic fermentation is normally completed.

The vintage wine is called Temoinage because it is intended as a testament to the quality of the Montgueux terroir. My notes on the 2008 vintage: *"Impressive concentration of lemon peel and chalky aromas with a substantial dose of toasty autolysis and an almost saline underpinning. On the palate, the wine is structured and fresh, but there is a silky finesse to the wine that is beguiling. Dosed at 4 g/l."* **** (Tasted 2019)

9 Rue du Moulin 10300 Montgueux | 03 25 74 83 31
https://www.champagne-velut.fr/en/

J.L. Vergnon

Region: Côte des Blancs | Terroir: Côte des Blancs

The Vergnon family has lived in Le Mesnil for nearly two centuries, and have been growing grapes since the 1950s. The first domaine-bottled wines were produced in 1985, and today the house is managed by Didier Vergnon working with winemaker Julian Goût. The family owns 5 hectares of vines, mostly in Le Mesnil, with some parcels in Avize, Oger, Vertus, and neighboring premier cru Villeneuve-Renneville-Chevigny. The vines are sustainably managed, and the domaine is certified Haut Valeur Environnementale Level Three. The wines are fermented in a combination of stainless steel tanks and oak barrels. Malolactic is generally blocked, and the dosage is uniformly low – all of the cuvées are either Extra Brut or Brut Nature.

Resonance was formerly an assemblage of five parcels in Le Mesnil. As of 2010 this has been renamed "Msnl", and it comes from two lieux-dits exclusively: Les Chétillons and Les Musettes. My notes on the 2008 vintage: *"Fermented in tank, this has a potently aromatic, green apple fruit with a strong suggestion of lime peel and a hint of salinity. On the palate, the wine has a beautiful tension and concentrated power. Seven years on the lees before being disgorged with a dosage of 3 g/l."* **** (Tasted 2016)

Confidence was produced from the oldest vines of the estate. From 2011, it has been renamed with the name of the lieu-dit, Les Hautes Mottes. The 2009 vintage: *"Lovely! This engaging Champagne from Le Mesnil has a pronounced aroma of green apple and spice with a firm mineral edge. The wine is fermented in cask and bottled without filtration, giving it a soft, tender texture."* **** (Tasted 2015)

Expression[18] was produced with the fruit from Oger. From 2010 it has been renamed "OG": *"From the single lieu-dit Chemin de Flavigny, this Brut Nature is fermented in tank and does not finish malolactic fermentation. However, balance is maintained because the fruit ripens extremely well here. The wine has*

---

18   Different from their current bottling called "Expression de Terroir," which is from Le Mesnil and Avize

an expressive, forward apple and citrus fruit on the attack with a pronounced chalky minerality and plenty of toasty yeast character. On the palate, there is certainly freshness, but there is no suggestion of tartness – the acidity is perfectly balanced. Impressive concentration, impressive ripeness. Five years on the lees." **** (Tasted 2016)

1 Grande Rue 51190 Le Mesnil-sur-Oger | 03 26 57 53 86
https://champagne-jl-vergnon.com/en/

Veuve Fourny

Region: Côte des Blancs | Terroir: Côte des Blancs

Veuve Fourny is a small quality-oriented, family-owned négociant house located in Vertus. The estate is run by brothers Charles-Henry and Emmanuel, fifth-generation proprietors. The vineyard is spread over 40 different parcels in Vertus, most planted by massal selection. The vineyards are sustainably farmed, and are either grassed over or are tilled. Few if any synthetic products are used in the vineyards. The average age of the vines over the entire estate is over 40 years. The house owns just over eight hectares and purchases fruit from approximately half that much to complete their needs.

In the winery, only the cuvée is used, and the fermentation is done in a combination of stainless steel tanks and in cask. The base wines are kept on the lees for six months before bottling. Malolactic fermentation can be either allowed or suppressed, depending upon individual lots and their characteristics; the dosage is normally quite low. There are two vintage cuvées. Monts de Vertus comes from fifty-year-old vines on chalky, hillside slopes north of Vertus drawn from three lieux-dits: Les Barilliés, Monts Ferrés, and Monts Ferrés Bas. Les Barilliés is also one of the sources for Larmandier-Bernier's Terre de Vertus; the vines at this end of the village (near Le Mesnil) are particularly prized. The wine is tank fermented and bottled unfiltered before a five-year élevage on the lees and is normally dosed at 3 g/l. The 2012 vintage was delicious:

"...entirely fermented in stainless, this is concentrated and powerful, yet it does not lack in elegance. The fruit character has a pronounced citrus/green apple cast, and there is plenty of minerality here. Lively but not shrill. Very well done." **** (Tasted 2019)

The Clos Faubourg Notre Dame is the second if Fourny's vintage cuvees, made with 100% estate-grown Chardonnay from the Clos called Faubourg de l'Abbaye Notre Dame. The Clos was purchased by the family in 1930 and is 0.29 hectares in size; the average vine age is 60 years. The base wines are fermented in cask and bottled unfiltered before spending nine years on the lees. Dosage averages 3 g/l. My notes on the 2009 : *"Richly aromatic with a nose of dried apricot, ripe melon and pomelo, this has a profoundly deep yeasty character and a firm mineral underpinning. On the palate the texture is structured and fresh, but the overall feel is still silky and supple – the wine is not overly strict or tense by any measure. While drinking well now, this has plenty of substance, and will definitely age for twenty years or more if properly cellared."* **** (Tasted 2020)

5 rue du Mesnil 51130 Vertus | 03 26 52 16 30
http://www.champagne-veuve-fourny.com/

PART II

The Vintages

The second section of this work is a look at the vintages between 1899 and 2019. It is, of course, a personal, subjective assessment, but I have tried to ground it in the quality of the wines and their ability to age. In general, the five-star years are superb, exceptional years, capable of producing "wine-of-the-century" quality; the best can last for fifty years or more. Four-star years are excellent years that have produced a large number of delicious wines, although the balance of these wines can seem for one reason or another less perfect than the five-star years. Still, the best wines produced in four-star years can last for thirty years or more. Three-star years produced some very good wines, but the success is not as general, and the level of quality not as high in most cases. The best wines from three-star years will improve in a proper cellar for more than a decade. Two-star years produced some good wines but these generally lack the balance, finesse, and substance of the better vintages. The best can age for up to a decade. One-star vintages produced some vintage wine, but few, if any, rise to the level of the very good years – these are wines that should be drunk. Little if any vintage wine is produced in years rated "No Stars".

Five-star vintages: *1906, 1911, 1914, 1921, 1928, 1929, 1945, 1947, 1955, 1959, 1964, 1973, 1979, 1982, 1985, 1988, 1996, 2002, 2008, 2012*

Four-star vintages: *1900, 1904, 1919, 1926, 1934, 1937, 1943, 1949, 1953, 1961, 1966, 1969, 1975, 1976, 1990, 1995, 1998, 2004, 2006, 2009, [2018]*

Three-star vintages: *1901, 1905, 1913, 1915, 1920, 1933, 1938, 1939, 1942, 1952, 1962, 1970, 1981, 1983, 1989, 2000, 2005, 2007, 2014, 2015, 2016, [2019]*

Two-star vintages: *1903, 1907, 1908, 1909, 1932, 1935, 1941, 1948, 1957, 1960, 1965, 1971, 1974, 1977, 1986, 1992, 1993, 1997, 1999, 2010, 2013*

One-star vintages: *1902, 1912, 1923, 1925, 1931, 1950, 1958, 1967, 1978, 1980, 2003*

[No star] vintages: *1910, 1916, 1917, 1918, 1919, 1922, 1924, 1927, 1930, 1936, 1940, 1944, 1946, 1951, 1954, 1956, 1963, 1968, 1972, 1984, 1987, 1991, 1994, 2001, 2011, 2017*

A note on the vintage statistics and methodology:

The foundation of the information at the beginning of the profile of each vintage year comes from *"Plus d'un siècle de vendanges*[19]*".* This useful resource was published as a spreadsheet by Association Viticole Champenoise (AVC) and the Syndicat Professionnel des Courtiers en Vins de Champagne. This same information was expanded by the editor Dominique Fradet to produce the work entitled *"Un Siècle De Vendanges En Champagne".* These two sources include the harvest date, yield, the area under vine, sales, and the price of grapes. In later years the AVC made other information available, including the potential alcohol at harvest, the total acidity[20], and ultimately the level of gluconic acid. This last has been used since 1996 as a marker for the extent of rot in the vineyard at harvest. These figures are approximations at best since they are averages, and will vary by grape variety and by subregion. Still, they can help give us a technical understanding of the ripeness and balance of a particular year. As the understanding of ripeness developed with time, harvest dates were staggered by region and by grape variety. There are other changes as well: the fixed price for grapes became a guideline ("prix indictif"). When the prix indictif was forbidden, the observed price ("prix constaté") is documented. All of this information provided by the CIVC has been combined with personal interviews with winemakers and with the work of other authors (notably André Simon and François Bonal) to form what I hope is a well-grounded opinion of each vintage. I have combined this with my personal experience of tasting to produce the ratings in this section of the work.

---

*   Rankings for 2018 and 2019 are provisional.
19   Originally published online, it has been brought up to date with data kindly provided by the CIVC.
20   Expressed as sulfuric acid, as is the practice in France. To convert to tartaric acid, multiply by 1.5

CHAPTER I

1900 – 1909:
Luxe, Calme, et Volupté?

Luxe, Calme, et Volupté is the title of a 1904 painting executed by Henri Matisse, yet it might well stand in for a working definition of the French Belle Epoque. The period between the Franco-Prussian War of 1870 and the First World War was for some a time of great prosperity; for many, a time of peace; and to judge from the abundance of champagne consumed, a voluptuous moment indeed. In truth, it was also a tumultuous time – the dawn of the industrial revolution, colonial expansion around the globe, and of an epic shift in many countries from a rural existence to an urban one. Above all, it was a time of change. 1901 saw the death of Queen Victoria and the ascent of Edward VIII in England, ushering in the Edwardian Era, while in the U.S., President McKinley was shot by an anarchist and succeeded by Theodore Roosevelt at the height of what is called in the U.S. the Gilded Age.

This period was also called "The Golden Age of Champagne" by André Simon. This exuberance, however, ignores the fact that there were serious issues in the region that needed to be addressed. The most important of these was the phylloxera crisis. This root louse attacked the native French vines, ultimately destroying the quasi-totality of the vineyards in France (and throughout Europe). The scourge was imported to Europe by English botanists who had brought specimens of native American vines (which are resistant to the pest) in the 1850s. It was first seen in France in the Rhône Valley in 1863 and gradually made its way north. Champagne was one of the last regions affected, but the first sightings were in 1891, and the problem proliferated from there. By 1901, phylloxera contaminated the entire *département* of the Marne. By the decade's end, nearly half of the region's vines had succumbed.

Although the Association Viticole Champenoise was organized in 1898 to combat phylloxera, they focused their initial efforts on the use of carbon disulfide in an attempt to kill the root louse. With time it was generally realized that this was not effective, and replanting began with vines grafted onto resistant American rootstock, the only viable solution to the problem. According to Bonal, by 1910 2,000 hectares had been replanted with this method. Initially, there was considerable resistance to this method since winegrowers felt that they were losing the very identity of their wine. However, with time they began to appreciate some of the advantages of the new system, as it reduced work in the vineyards and allowed for the use of horses in the vineyards, which had not been possible with vines planted in the old way.

The other main issue for the Champenois at the dawn of the 20th century was also ultimately tied to phylloxera. As yields declined in Champagne due to phylloxera, some négociants of the region felt obliged to look outside the region for grapes. Growers who owned vines in the Marne were understandably enraged. The conflict also fueled a popular attachment to the "purity" of the wine of Champagne. This drama unfurled in the context of a broader national discussion about counterfeit products, purity, and consumer safety, and in 1905 a general anti-counterfeiting law known as the *Loi du 1er Aout 1905* came into effect. Another law followed in 1908, setting the basis for drawing the borders for certain agricultural products, although the Champagne industry had already been working on defining this. These boundaries were laid out in the *Décret du 17 décembre 1908*, published in early 1909. This delimitation, however, excluded the growers of the Aube department, which set up the conflicts of the following decade. Ultimately, the tenor of the decade depended on one's perspective. The quality of vintages such as 1900, 1904, and especially 1906 was a great boon to négociants, as long as grape prices were kept low. For the growers, however, menaced by phylloxera on one hand and foreign competition on the other, the outlook was different indeed.

1899

****

Prelude: A beautiful end to the 19th century.

I couldn't resist adding in the year 1899 as it has an excellent reputation, although I have not drunk any. It also forms, with 1900, one of the rare "pairs" of excellent back-to-back vintages. The year is known by its reputation among the authorities of the day. Few statistics, however, survive. Instead, I have combed the periodical *Le Vigneron Champenois*, which relates the following:

"The harvest of 1899 was a little above the average in terms of quantity. The Marne Valley produced little, and the vineyards planted to white grapes almost nothing; on the Montagne de Reims, the quantity produced was much more significant.

The quality of the wines of 1899, in general, is recognized as good, in the grands crus as in the petits crus. The wine has finesse and a certain body. The remarkably healthy state of the vines, which retained all their leaves until the harvest, assures the wines of 1899 a perfect solidity.

The prices, in these favorable conditions, were higher than those of 1898. The vines that were spared from the spring frosts have given their owners and excellent yield. There are few or no wines remaining, everything having been purchased at harvest or as vins clairs by négociants,

The hurry of the négociants to purchase at harvest demonstrates their eagerness to use the wines of 1899 to their advantage in their blends. It is probably due to the rarity of wines made from white grapes that these bottlings will be limited to those that are strictly necessary, and will not surpass the quantities that are typically shipped from Champagne."

1900
****

Overview: A solid start to the new century.

There are also few statistics remaining to document the 1900 vintage in Champagne. The renowned wine writer André Simon notes that it was a vintage of both quality and quantity, and one that sold for the reasonable price of one *ancien* French franc per kilo. Bollinger notes: "'A vintage for beginning the century.' A freezing winter, late frosts. A very hot summer saved the situation and allowed for a fine harvest in terms of both quality and quantity. A powerful, generous wine." Simon sums up: "The 1900s were no better than the '99s, but they were very good, rather smoother, softer, and sooner ready do drink."

1901
***

Harvest: September 27th
Yield: 6,700 kg/ha
Area under vine not reported

Total Sales: 28,055,045 btl
France: 7,426,794 btl
Export: 20,628,251 btl
Price of grapes not reported

Overview: Many grapes of moderate quality.

A hot year, almost tropical. Flowering took place under ideal conditions. Rain right up to the harvest exacerbated existing problems with botrytis in the vineyard. On harvest day, however, the weather was beautiful. André Simon comments: "The 1901 vintage was one of the most plentiful on record, but the quality of the wine was not very fine..."

1902

*

Harvest date not reported
Yield: 3,200 kg/ha
Area under vine not reported

Total Sales: 28,205,410 btl
France: 7,894,212 btl
Export: 20,311,228 btl
Price of grapes not reported

Overview: A challenging year.

After a reasonably successful budbreak, there was a hard frost on the 7th and 8th of May.   Flowering was difficult, with incidences of coulure. Mildew and vine moths plagued the vineyards throughout the growing season. Weather at harvest was stormy, and the exact start date of the picking was not recorded.   André Simon comments, "In 1902 the quantity of wine made was below the average, and the quality of most of the wines was only fair to middling; there were, however, a few wines of fine quality made in some of the more favoured vineyards."

1903
**

Harvest: October 3rd	Total Sales: 31,859,158 btl
Yield: 4,300 kg/ha	France: 9,335,412 btl
Area under vine not reported	Export: 22,523,746 btl
	Price of grapes: 1.00 F/kg

Overview: A modest improvement in quality, but growers still struggled.

In 1903, there was hard frost and hailstorm on the 18th and 19th of April, causing localized damage. The flowering took place under favorable conditions, but the growing season was troubled by vine moths. Rain at harvest diluted the musts. The price per kilo for grand cru fruit was one ancien franc[21]. According to André Simon: "In 1903, the quantity was an average one, and there were some good wines made...."

---

21   . The ancien franc is the name used today for the currency of France between 1795 and 1960. Under de Gaulle and his finance minister at the time, Antoine Pinay, the franc suffered several devaluations. After a devaluation in 1960, the currency was renamed the "new franc," which was worth 100 ancien francs. In today's terms, 100,000 *ancien* francs is worth roughly 150 euros. We will abbreviate this henceforth as F, the same abbreviation as after the devaluation in 1960.

1904
****

Harvest: "Under sunny conditions"
Yield: 7,700 kg/ha
Area under vine not reported

Total Sales: 30,893,655 btl
France: 9,808,774 btl
Export: 21,084,881 btl
Price of grapes not reported

Overview: A marvelous year, with both quality and a generous yield.

A precocious year, with early flowering and few problems with pests during the growing season. Sunny weather at harvest brought a healthy yield.

Bollinger notes: "'A golden year.' Exceptional budding and early flowering. Very healthy harvest and extraordinary quality," while André Simon enthuses, "The 1904 vintage ranks as the finest of the twentieth century so far..."

1905
***

Harvest Date: September 20th
Yield: 4,300 kg/ha
Area under vine not reported

Total Sales: 28,710,799 btl
France: 8,864,947 btl
Export: 19,845,852 btl
Price of grapes not reported

Overview: Success despite setbacks.

After a normal to strong budbreak, the vineyards were damaged by several episodes of frost in May, as well as multiple hailstorms in June and July, followed by struggles with mildew in the vineyards during the growing season. Moderate to good quality.

1906
****

Harvest: September 18th
Yield: 4,500 kg/ha
Area under vine: 15,500 ha

Total Sales: 35,591,135 btl
France: 11,714,404 btl
Export: 23,876,731 btl
Price of grapes: 1.33 F/kg

Overview: A great year.

After frost and hail in May, flowering was generally successful, but the growing season was disturbed by vine moths. The harvest began under sunny, warm conditions. Bollinger notes: 'Small year, superb quality...musts above 10°" André Simon explains: "The 1905 vintage was an utter failure, but the 1906s were a very great success, the last of the great Champagne vintages".

My own experience with the only 1906 that I have tasted was not as encouraging as André Simon suggests. A 1906 Pol Roger tasted while I was head of Department at Christie's in New York: *"Interesting, impressive, even, but not what one expects. The wine was nearly brown, with no discernable bubbles. The aromas were ripe and truffley, with lots of earthy notes and a slight hint of sherry and tropical fruit. Finally, on the palate, the wine was round and soft, melting seamlessly at the end."* ** (Tasted 2008)

1907

**

Harvest: September 30th

Yield: 3,200 kg/ha

Area under vine not reported

Total Sales: 33,171,395 btl

France: 10,114,548 btl

Export: 23,056,847 btl

Price of grapes not reported

Overview: A modest year.

After an abundant budbreak, the flowering stalled and took a month to complete, leading to millerandage but not much coulure. Vignerons struggled with botrytis and mildew throughout the growing season, and the harvest began in abysmal weather. Quality was generally modest, although there were some localized successes.

It is perhaps ironic that one of the only vintages from this decade to survive to modern times in any quantity was this relatively modest quality vintage. As described in the introduction, this is the Heidsieck Monopole "Goût Américain" from 1907, with 3,000 bottles salvaged from the wreck of the Jönköping. I have tasted the wine twice. Once it was muddy, brown, and dank – a total loss. A second bottle was much more pleasant, even at the remove of 105 years. From my note from the successful outing: *"A revelation – sweet, with notes of honey and truffle and still very fresh. While there was no perceptible mousse (perhaps since the bottle was opened with a sabre), the wine was holding up very well. It retained an excellent balance and a delightful charm. Fully mature, the wine did not give the impression of decrepitude, but there would seem to be little to gain by additional aging."* **** (Tasted 2009)

1908
**

Harvest: September 15th

Yield: 1,400 kg/ha

Area under vine not reported

Total Sales: 33,734,618 btl

France: 11,522,272 btl

Export: 22,212,346 btl

Price of grapes not reported

Overview: A good year, lacking greatness.

After a solid budbreak, there were several minor episodes of frost in May followed by a flowering that began well only to slow before completion. Mildew started in June and continued to grow in severity and eventually destroyed a large part of the harvest. A late invasion of vine moths added insult to injury.

At this remove of distance, the most reliable information we have about the vintages of the "Golden Age" comes from the Vigneron Champenois in the form of statistics, and the writer André Simon. While the quality of some vintages may seem lackluster to judge from the mere statistics, they were somewhat more highly regarded by Simon. Authorities everywhere agree that 1904 and 1906 were exceptional vintages. Regarding the others, he notes "1905, 1907, and 1908 were all good but not nearly as good,"

1909

**

Harvest date not reported
Yield: 3,100 kg/ha
Area under vine not reported

Total Sales: 32,705,338 btl
France: 12,713,024 btl
Export: 19,992,314 btl
Price of grapes: 0.40 F/kg

Overview: A difficult year.

After a very cold winter, there was a strong budbreak, but severe frosts all but destroyed the potential crop. Losses ranged from 10 – 50% . Early flowering was interrupted at the moment of fruit set by cold weather, leading to coulure. Vine moths posed a problem during the growing season, and botrytis moved in at the harvest. The harvest of 1909 (starting date not recorded) yielded 3,100 kg/ha and was judged "acceptable" quality at the time. Few wines remain.

CHAPTER II

1910 - 1919:
Riots and War

Three events inevitably mark any discussion of the second decade of the century in Champagne. The first of these chrono-logically was known as the "Champagne Riots" of 1911. There were, in fact, two distinct sets of "Champagne Riots," both of which came to a head in 1911. One concerned the growers of the Marne, who were upset that the négociant houses were using grapes from outside the region. These tensions led to outbursts of violence. A partial solution to placate the growers was a legal delimitation of the Champagne region. These limits, however, excluded the growers of the Aube, which set off a different set of riots. The initial force behind the riots was the increasingly frequent practice of négociants to source wines from outside of Champagne to complete their blends in the face of dwindling supply due to the phylloxera epidemic. Oppressed by the houses and egged on by anarchists and colorful figures such as Paul Bolo (Bolo-Pacha), growers were ready for revolt.

Mediocre vintages had exacerbated tension in the region in 1909 and 1910, and following the harvest of 1910 growers became incensed as négociants continued the practice of sourc-ing fruit from outside Champagne. Vignerons began to band together in the waning months of 1910, and on January 17[th,] 1911, a number of them seized a shipment of wines from outside the region they believed destined to be sold as champagne. The growers dumped the wine into the Marne river and destroyed the premises of the négociant. Similar actions were taken by the assembled growers on the following day as well, and the government responded by sending 40,000 troops into the re-gion. Local authorities, chastened by the presence of soldiers in the vineyard, worked to introduce legislation aimed at stemming the problem. On February 10th, the Senate and the House of

Deputies adopted a law requiring négociants to keep wines from Champagne in separate cellars from those used to house wines from any other region. This law was the measure sought by the trade, and everyone believed that this would bring an end to the matter.

The law of February 10th, however, did little to appease the growers of the Aube. They maintained justifiably that their fruit had been bought and sold for centuries as champagne. The deputies of the Aube responded to the law by requesting a reconsideration of the new boundaries. Officials in Paris declined, however, and the municipal council of Bar-sur-Aube resigned, and the town stopped providing civil services. Other villages followed suit to show support, and in April, the wine-growers of the Aube began menacing protests in Troyes, the ancient capital of the duchy of Champagne. Tensions escalated, and on April 11th, the mobs of the Marne Valley destroyed winer-ies in Damery, Dizy, and Aÿ. The central authorities once again sent armed troops.

On June 7th, an attempt at compromise included the Aube, but only as a secondary zone (Deuxième Zone). Although this was enough to quiet the demonstrations in the short term, it was only a stopgap measure. The troops stayed in place, and over the summer, newspapers noted that there were "more troops than winegrowers" in the vineyards. Ultimately, they remained until the harvest of 1911. Fortunately for everyone, 1911 was the best harvest the region had seen since 1906. The rule of the "secondary zone" would remain in force until 1927, as more significant events on the world stage eclipsed the fight between the winegrowers of the Marne and the Aube.

In practical terms, 1911 was also an important year be-cause it was the first time growers and houses sat down together to create the "échelle des crus." This refers to the scale (échelle) or ranking of the villages which enabled the efficient setting of prices throughout the region. The balance of power in Cham-pagne long favored the houses at the expense of the growers. Not only were there the entwined specters of the phylloxera epidemic and competition from foreign grapes but even in the best of times the houses kept the price of grapes as low as possible. Sometimes this was accomplished through collusion between the houses and by the coercion and intimidation of the growers. In 1904 the growers banded together to form the Fédération des Syndicats Viticoles de la Champagne, which would later become the Syndicat Général des Vignerons. This union paralleled the creation in 1882 of the Syndicat du Commerce des vins de Champagne, which later became the Syndicat des Grandes Marques, organizing the négociant houses. In two organizations met in 1911 and agreed to a system of ranking each of the villages. This scale was not created out of thin air. The origins of the classification go back to the documentation of the Church's vineyard holdings in the 12th Century Grande Charte Champenoise issued by Guillaume de Champeaux, bishop of Châlons-en-Champagne. The Grande Charte served as the foundation for the 1752 book by Nicolas Bidet called Dissertation sur les Vins.

The price of grapes was set each year in the annual meeting between the growers and the houses. Fruit from the twelve villages that were classified as 100% (called grand cru) received 100% of this agreed-upon price for their produce. Growers in villages rated at 90% would receive 90% of this price, and this proportional pricing continued down the scale of prestige. Villages ranked between 90% and 99% were considered premier cru; below 90% they were called "other cru." The original échelle classified about three-quarters of the villages in the Marne, and the range went down to 46%. Unclassified villages were paid 25% of the price received by growers in the grand crus. The classification was revised in 1919 and again in 1920, and later revisions included all the communes of the Marne. Later revisions also increased the price paid for fruit from the villages with the lowest classification to 56% of the price of grands crus, and the ranking for the villages rated above 80% also increased by an average of five percentage points. The base price of grapes each year applied to the first press juice (called the cuvée), while the second press juice (called the taille) sold for at 20% less, and the third press juice (second taille) sold for 40% less than this base price.

The more significant global events of the decade also played out in the vineyards of Champagne, including the First World War. After Germany invaded Belgium in August of 1914, their army began to move towards Paris. The French and English allies stopped the advance of the Germans in the Battle of the Marne, 6 – 12 September 1914. Having halted the Germans, the Allied troops pressed their advantage in the Battle of the Aisne (named for another river in Champagne) and pressed on to outflank the German forces. Neither side prevailed, however, and the two armies dug the trenches that formed the Western Front and led to the loss of countless lives. These trenches ran right through the vineyards of Champagne.

The war disrupted everything in Champagne. The town of Epernay fell briefly to the enemy before the Germans were forced to retreat. Most of the grape growers had been conscripted into the army. Despite the lack of manpower, Maurice Pol Roger rallied the wives and daughters to pick the grapes even as the vineyards were being shelled. Bonal relates that the trenches ran only 1.5 kilometers from the center of Reims and that these lines were subject more than 1,000 days of continuous bombing. Air raids were such a common event, particularly in Reims, that life gradually moved into the caves hollowed into the chalk, known as crayères, that dot the landscape. Schools, hospitals, and even concert halls were re-located underground. Given these complications, it is remarkable that Champagne makers produced (and sold) as much champagne as they did during the war years.

The third significant event of the decade in the region was perhaps less immediately apparent to those outside Champagne, but its impact on the champagne industry was just as inevitable: the loss of important export markets. The first of these to go disappeared in 1917. Russia had been one of the earliest countries to embrace Champagne, and throughout the 19th Century, shipments continued to grow. Many négociants, particularly Clicquot and Roederer, had close ties to Russia. Clicquot was among the first to open the Russian market. Louis Bohne, working as a sales agent for Clicquot, became close friends with Tsar Alexander I. Later, Bohne and Clicquot would come up with a plan to evade the Prussian blockade of Napoleonic France and send a shipment to Russia. The house of Roederer first created Cristal champagne as an exclusive cuvee for his Nephew Alexander II in 1876. Under his grandson Nicholas II, Roederer was named the official wine supplier to the Imperial Court. Unfortunately for these champagne houses and others, however, this business evaporated in 1917 with the Russian revolution.

The second vital market to fall at the end of the decade was the United States. Champagne producers had significant success here in the 19th century as well, notably Krug and Heidsieck. The Civil War-era exploits of Charles Camille Heidsieck (founder of firm Charles Heidsieck) are legendary, and Champagne sales flourished in antebellum America. Despite competition from local imitations, authentic Champagne sold well throughout the Gilded Age, often at prices higher than first-growth Bordeaux. Shortly after the loss of the Russian market, however, exports to America came to a halt as well, as America passed first the Wartime Prohibition Act and then the Volstead Act in 1919, ushering in Prohibition. Changes in the tax structure in England also reduced sales there slightly, and for the first time, the French domestic market began to assume the commercial importance that it has enjoyed to this day.

1910
[No Stars]

Harvest date not reported
Yield: 115 kg/ha
Area under vine not reported

Total Sales: 39,294,526 btl
France: 13,120,946 btl
Export: 26,173,580 btl
Price of grapes not reported

Overview: A poor year – among the worst of the century.

After a strong budbreak, there were minor frosts on the 18th of April. However, conditions deteriorated rapidly, with thunderstorms, hailstorms, and floods in every month. Mildew began in May and got worse as the year wore on, and by fruit set, nearly the entire crop was affected. By July, the crop was essentially lost. Growers harvested a paltry 115 kg/ha on average.

1911
*****

Harvest: September 10th
Yield: 1,600 kg/ha
Area under vine not reported

Total Sales: 38 584 402 btl
France: 15,517,879 btl
Export: 23,066,523 btl
Price of grapes not reported

Overview: A very good year and a great relief to many.

After a weak budbreak, the flowering was early and quick. Chlorosis set in after fruit set in a dry season, limiting the weight of the bunches, but the dry weather also limited the damage from pests and disease. The harvest began in lovely conditions, although the yield was reduced both by low bunch weight and by vines that had been poorly treated for mildew in the previous year. A minimal harvest by any measure, but the quality was very high. Bollinger notes: "...magnificent quality - the best in 40 years! Something to console all the Champenois players after the uprisings of the month of April."

1912

*

Harvest date not reported
Yield: 3,400 kg/ha
Area under vine not reported

Total Sales: 29,373,899 btl
France: 9,084,936 btl
Export: 20,288,963 btl
Price of grapes not reported

Overview: A challenging year.

After an uneven budbreak, millerandage disrupted fruit set, and the mildew beset the vines during the growing season. There was frost in May and "deplorable" weather throughout the campaign.

1913

***

Harvest: "Late"
Yield: 1,400 kg/ha
Area under vine not reported

Total Sales: 30,097,644 btl
France: 9,151,110 btl
Export: 20,946,534 btl
Price of grapes: F 3.25/kg

Overview: Good but not great; the wines did not last.

There was an early budbreak with the potential for a large harvest. Frost in April and hail, however, reduced yield by one-third to one-half. A drawn-out flowering led to coulure. There were limited problems with mildew in the vineyards during the growing season and some damage from vine moths. Cold nights in September slowed maturation and delayed the harvest, and the date that it began was not recorded. We do know that growers only gathered a fraction of a normal harvest, but that the average price for grand cru fruit was more than three times what they earned in the preceding years. Opinion at the time was that this harvest provided "good quality."

1914

*****

Harvest: September 28th
Yield: 2,200 kg/ha
Area under vine not reported

Total Sales: 26,544,632 btl
France: 8,134,196 btl
Export: 18,410,436 btl
Price of grapes not reported

Overview: A classic year; the best wines are the stuff of legend.

It is famous as "The Woman's Harvest" due to the general mobili-
zation of troops for the Great War. There was favorable weather
during budbreak, but a drawn-out flowering led to problems
with coulure and thus fruit set. Although there were sporadic
problems with mildew during the growing season, the harvest of
1914 began at the end of September under beautiful conditions.
This places the harvest right after the Battle of the Marne, and
Bonal relates that some of the fruit was picked early due to fears
that German troops would reappear, thus giving the wines a firm
acidity that took many years to resolve. Bonal counts 1914 as one
of the "vintages of the century." Many of the wines held up well,
and the Pol Roger 1914 was particularly renowned.

1915

***

Harvest: September 10th
Yield: 3,600 kg/ha
Area under vine: 6,000 ha

Total Sales: 10,362,010 btl
France: 3,126,833 btl
Export: 7,235,177 btl
Price of grapes: F 1.50/kg

Overview: A war vintage: reputedly "excellent" at the time, none remains today.

With attention focused elsewhere, few details survive of conditions in 1915. Even less information survives about the quality of the wines, but Bonal assures us that 1915, along with 1917, were "excellent" vintages. We do know that the planted area had shrunk to 6,000 ha in total, a reduction of nearly 40%. Flowering took place quickly. After fruit set, however, the vines suffered an invasion of vine moths.

1916
[No Stars]

Harvest: September 30th
Yield: 700 kg/ha
Area under vine not reported

Total Sales: 11,405,557 btl
France: 4,680,398 btl
Export: 6,725,159 btl
Price of grapes not reported

Overview: A war vintage. Quality reputed to be poor, but 1916 saw little vineyard work.

There were still vines, but complications to the growing season only added to the ravages of war. Coulure and millerandage disrupted flowering, and the vineyards were washed by constant rain throughout the growing season. The rain set off an attack of mildew that began in July. Authorities report that vines suffered an onslaught of nearly every type of parasite. Growers could not combat them, however, due to a lack of chemicals. By all accounts, the weather at harvest was disastrous.

1917
[No Stars]

Harvest: September 10th
Yield: 2,500 kg/ha
Area under vine not reported

Total Sales: 16,001,816 btl
France: 7,565,602 btl
Export: 8,436,214 btl
Price of grapes not reported

Overview: A war vintage; none remains.

In 1917 the vignerons (or their wives) were hardly able to work the vines at all: the Syndicat des Courtiers en Vins de Champagne note simply "nonculture." Other than a bit of mildew in the vines, however, it appears that conditions would have been favorable. Those who were able to pick began in early September in warm, dry weather.

1918
[No Stars]

Harvest date not reported
Yield: 2,000 kg/ha
Area under vine not reported

Total Sales: 17,615,734 btl
France: 10,679,116 btl
Export: 6,936,618 btl
Price of grapes not reported

Overview: The final vintage of the First World War. Attention focused elsewhere.

Another year when the vines were not worked; spring frosts reduced yields on what fruit the vines did bear. The date of the beginning of harvest was not recorded. Records do indicate that some fruit of an "honest" quality was harvested, according to the Vigneron Champenois. No wines remain today.

1919

****

Harvest date not reported
Yield: 5,500 kg/ha
Area under vine: 12,010 ha

Total Sales: 15,755,299 btl
France: 10,687,628 btl
Export: 5,067,671 btl
Price of grapes: F 4.00/kg

Overview: A very good vintage.

In the first year of peace, the planted area of the region incre-as-ed to 12,010 ha, more than doubling from the area reported four years earlier. Budbreak and flowering were solid. The vines suffered somewhat from moth damage. Sunburn that affected some areas of Champagne further reduced yields by 10 – 15%. Compensating for this, the vines yielded generously. The growing season was dry throughout, with beautiful weather reported for the harvest. Bollinger notes: "Excellent ripeness of the grapes giving the wines a lovely opulence."

CHAPTER III

1920 - 1929:
Les Années Folles

"The Roaring Twenties," known as the *"Les Années Folles"* in France, was above all a period of rebuilding, particularly in Reims. The war had destroyed over 14,000 buildings in the town, and only a handful were left fully intact. The rebuilding of France was undertaken with the patronage of numerous international donors, led by Americans such as John D. Rockefeller and Andrew Carnegie. Their efforts were coordinated by Myron T. Herrick, U.S. Ambassador to France from 1912 – 1914, and again from 1921 – 1929. This rebuilding was done mainly in the Art Deco style, which reached its apogee with the International Exposition of 1925 in Paris. Many architectural treasures, such as the Carnegie Library in Reims, remain as a testament to this period. If it was necessary to reconstruct the town, it was also essential to rebuild the vineyards. In total, the area planted to vines had diminished by 40%, and in some villages, only 20% of the pre-war vines remained. The lack of funds for replanting in a region depleted by war compounded the challenge of recovering from phylloxera. The cost to replant a hectare of vines was roughly equivalent to the revenue produced by that area of vineyard in a good year at reasonable prices. Faced with such costs, some growers chose to replant ungrafted vines, although these were virtually worthless. Replanting was further hampered by a lack of manpower since many vignerons had perished during the war, while others, discouraged by the costs of replanting, had sold their vineyards to négociants. Even when it was possible to do the work and to afford it, the unexploded ordnance that littered the vineyards made replanting treacherously dangerous. It is in this context that the Association Viticole Champenoise, founded in 1898 to combat phylloxera, began the necessary research to facilitate replanting, aided by the large négociant houses. Little by little, vines were replanted, and yet it would require until 1965 for the planted area of the region to regain the extent of roughly 15,000 ha that it enjoyed in 1906.

These were not the only issues facing the vignerons of the 1920s. Although the law of 10 February 1911 required négociants to keep Champagne separate from the wines of other regions made sparkling here, but it did not forbid this type of production. In 1920 "vins mousseux ordinaires" from outside Champagne accounted for 12.75% of sales, and the commerce in this type of wine continued until 1934. Other pieces of landmark legislation were enacted in the 1920s. Among the most important was the law of 22 July 1927. This law re-integrated the Aube into the appellation of Champagne, and villages that had historically produced Champagne were allowed to continue to do so. Since the villages of the Aube fulfilled this requirement, the category of the "Deuxième Zone" was finally eliminated. The law also fixed the grape varieties that could be used to produce Champagne to include all types of Pinot, including Pinot Noir, Pinot Gris, and Pinot Blanc. Arbanne and Petit Meslier were also allowed, but the use of Gamay was forbidden. At the time Gamay was widely planted in the Aube, and growers with Gamay in the Aube were given 18 years to phase it out of production.

It seemed that what the world wanted most in the Twenties was to forget the horrors of the preceding decade. Steadily rising sales suggest that drinking champagne was one of the best ways to forget. However, despite the rebuilding and reformatting of the vineyards that took place in the Twenties, there were still trying times ahead.

1920
***

Harvest date not reported
Yield: 7,300 kg/ha
Area under vine: 11,043 ha

Total Sales: 23,016,017 btl
France: 9,433,636 btl
Export: 13,582,381 btl
Price of grapes: F 4.50/kg

Overview: Solid quality and reasonable quantity.

Mildew followed a solid budbreak and flowering and reduced the potential harvest by about 20%. Localized hailstorms in July caused substantial damage in the Marne Valley, but in the region overall, the crop size and the price of fruit continued to progress. Beautiful weather at harvest helped the vines to produce a reasonably abundant harvest for the period, although Bonal notes few vintage wines produced.

1921
*****

Harvest date not reported
Yield: 2,000 kg/ha
Area under vine: 10,625 ha

Total Sales: 21,108,379 btl
France: 8,361,571 btl
Export: 12,746,808 btl
Price of grapes: F 2.50/kg

Overview: A superb vintage, providing wines that are still drinking today.

After a solid budbreak, the region suffered severe frost on the 15th and 16th of April, drastically limiting yields – estimates ran as high as 80%. Hot, dry weather during the growing season conspired to accentuate the loss of volume. Despite marvelous weather at harvest, the yield was tiny, but the quality of the wines that were made was exceptional. Those that remain, particularly Dom Pérignon and Pol Roger are legendary.

1922
*

Harvest date not reported
Yield: 12,400 kg/ha
Area under vine: 10,055 ha

Total Sales: 12,543,873 btl
France: 5,884,377 btl
Export: 6,659,496 btl
Price of grapes: F 2.50/kg

Overview: A problematic vintage.

With just over 10,000 ha in production, the vines still managed
to be much more productive. Impressive budbreak was followed
by a flowering that started well and then stalled, leading to
some millerandage. Black rot was present in many areas, and
September rains brought botrytis that spread quickly and necessitated careful sorting in the vineyard. Despite the rot, the
crop averaged a startling 12,400 kg/ha – the first time during
the century that the harvest exceeded 10,000 kg/ha. Abundant
quantity, mediocre quality at best. Bonal states that vintage
wine was not made.

1923
**

Harvest date not reported
Yield: 3,400 kg/ha
Area under vine: 10,426 ha

Total Sales: 18,544,100 btl
France: 9,465,717 btl
Export: 9,078,383 btl
Price of grapes: F 3.50/kg

Overview: A difficult vintage.

Frost in April followed a solid budbreak. It struck again on
the 18th of May, reducing yields by 30 – 50% for the year. The
flowering was affected by coulure and millerandage, further
reducing yields. Black rot invaded the vineyards during the
growing season. Finally, the harvest coincided with rain. Fortunately for the growers, prices inched forward, and sales also
rebounded slightly, helping to lift the region as a whole, even if
it was mainly the négociants who benefitted from the increased
sales. Bonal states again that vintage wine was not made for the
second year in a row.

1924

*

Harvest: September 26th
Yield: 6,400 kg/ha
Area under vine: 10,904 ha

Total Sales: 31,499,474 btl
France: 17,877,017 btl
Export: 14,072,407 btl
Price of grapes: F 4.27/kg

Overview: A problematic vintage.

The vineyard area in Champagne increased to 10,900 ha. Difficulties in the vineyard included black rot, downy mildew from the second half of July, and vine moths. Grey rot appeared in August and continued in September, necessitating careful sorting. In the end, the grapes lacked maturity, and quality was mediocre at best.

1925

**

Harvest date not reported
Yield: 4,500 kg/ha
Area under vine: 11,551 ha

Total Sales: 30,199,640 btl
France: 15,514,036 btl
Export: 14,685,604 btl
Price of grapes: F 4.27/kg

Overview: Another challenging vintage.

Hailstorms followed uneven budbreak in both the Côte des Blancs and the Montagne de Reims. Flowering was interrupted by cold weather, bringing some problems with both coulure and millerandage. Downy mildew and grey rot both made an appearance without significant consequences. Yield per hectare declined significantly from recent years even as sales remained relatively robust. Because of the relatively low yield few if any vintage wines were produced.

1926

****

Harvest: October 10th
Yield: 6,400 kg/ha
Area under vine: 11,946 ha

Total Sales: 36,167,285 btl
France: 20,537,877 btl
Export: 15,629,408 btl
Price of grapes: F 4.27/kg

Overview: A classic vintage saved by the sun.

Providential sun at the end of the season is fortunately frequent in Champagne, and growers call it *"une belle arrière-saison."* It would have had to have been to get a good result in '26, given the progress until that point. A slow flowering followed an abundant budbreak, and coulure and millerandage reduced the yield. Hailstorms rained down in the vineyards throughout the growing season: on the 3rd and 4th of July; again on the 15th of July; then again on the 7th of August. During this time, the vines were also plagued by vine moths and attacked by mildew. Dry, sunny weather followed, however, and the vines finally ripened their fruit. Harvest began nearly into the middle of October, and in the end, the average yield across the entire region was relatively healthy. According to Bollinger, "Fine concentration for a generous wine."

My own experience with 1926 is limited to a single bottle, but it was magnificent. During my tenure as head of the wine department at Christie's in 2010, I had the good fortune to dine with a serious collector of Champagne. He was to bring a bottle, and I was to do the same. I scoured the warehouse for an enticing bottle, and decided on a bottle of 1926 Krug. In "original condition," the foil peeling away (but cage intact), the bottle slightly (but not dramatically) ullaged, and the color seemingly somewhat dark, so I had cause to doubt it was sound. In the end, however, it came through wonderfully, making a slight "pop" as the sommelier eased the cork out of the bottle, and miraculously there was still noticeable mousse remaining. From my note: *"The color was good, a deep Sauternes-like gold without anybrown. On the nose, there was a hint of Madeira. Yet, the wine*

*was very much alive and lovely, with a nose that evolved through-
out dinner from a caramel toffee truffle confection to coconut and
gingerbread, with a slightly gamey, almost savory note at the end.
Sublime."* *****

1927
[No Stars]

Harvest: September 22nd
Yield: 1,700 kg/ha
Area under vine: 12,133 ha

Total Sales: 32,216,289 btl
France: 17,527,436 btl
Export: 14,688,853 btl
Price of grapes: F 8.00/kg

Overview: A poor vintage.

It took until 1927 for the size of Champagne's vineyards in
Champagne to advance past 12,000 ha. Despite this incremental
growth, however, the size of the harvest plummeted due to a
host of factors throughout the year. An uneven budbreak was
followed by a flowering disrupted by cold weather, bringing on
coulure and millerandage. During the growing season, the vines
were again troubled by vine moths, and grey rot moved in with
a vengeance just before harvest, which began once the weather
had cleared. Even this, however, was not enough to save the
crop, which produced a paltry amount of grapes of mediocre
quality at best. Bonal states that vintage wine was not made.

1928

*****

Harvest: September 28th
Yield: 6,000 kg/ha
Area under vine: 12,159 ha

Total Sales: 21,215,938 btl
France: 8,169,248 btl
Export: 13,046,690 btl
Price of grapes not reported

Overview: An exceptional vintage, producing concentrated, structured wines.

A universally renowned Champagne vintage. The potential yield was slightly reduced by frost in May (particularly in the Côte des Blancs) and some difficulties with coulure during the flowering. A series of hailstorms followed the flowering, but the balance of the season provided perfect weather for ripening, and large bunches of grapes ripened well. Harvest began at the end of September in glorious sunshine, but the rain returned with a vengeance shortly after that. Bollinger notes that "1928 is one of the two vintages of the century, along with the 1990... The 1928 has kept remarkably well, preserving its freshness."

Although I have not had the '28 Bollinger, I have enjoyed the 1928 Veuve Clicquot on two occasions. Once was out of a half bottle, and despite its small size, the bottle showed well. However, the regular size bottle that I drank in 2008 must be more representative. From my note: "...*complex, somewhat rustic aromatics, with notes of truffle, toast, soy, and a distinct but not off-putting oxidative character and an almost sauvage animal note. On the palate, the wine was still very fresh with miraculously some sparkle left, a fine balance, and a lingering finish. While mature, the wine still has life and vitality to it – not just interesting, but delicious.*" ****

1929

*****

Harvest: September 26th	Total Sales: 23,821,361 btl
Yield: 10,800 kg/ha	France: 11,307,691 btl
Area under vine: 12,220 ha	Export: 12,513,670 btl
	Price of grapes not reported

Overview: Another exceptional vintage, producing richer, softer wines than 1928

Another exceptional vintage. 1929 marked the next back-to-back successful vintage. "Twins" of this sort had not occurred since 1899/1900, and would not happen again until 1952/1953. Other examples include 1969/1970, 1975/1976; and 1995/1996. Even more rare is the trifecta, which occurred only once in the century: 1988/1989/1990.

The winter that preceded the season was cold, with many hard frosts, driving the sap deep into the roots and killing vine pests. Budbreak was ample, and the flowering was solid, leading to a very large crop being set on the vines. The weather was beautiful throughout the summer, and the harvest began in perfect weather near the end of September. Rain began to pour just after the start of the harvest, however, which brought some problems with rot. However, the season concluded with a bumper crop for the period. Bollinger notes: "The wines are seductive and balanced, less concentrated than in 1928."

My experience of the 1929 vintage is limited to a single bottle of Heidsieck Monopole Dry. Purchased in London from a merchant who sourced it "from an old country house," it was, like my '26 Krug, in original condition. The wine had a deep amber color and no mousse. Despite this, all of the tasters that night at the Ledbury in 2019 agreed that it was very much alive. From my note: *"Toffee and caramel on the nose, with hints of burnt orange peel and exotic spices. The rich sweetness of the fruit is the overwhelming sensation, yet there is also abundant acidity here to carry the wine all night. Impressive freshness and length."* ********

CHAPTER IV

1930 – 1939:
Depression & Innovation

The Great Depression was an enormously trying time in Champagne as it was nearly everywhere. To make matters worse for long-suffering Champagne growers, poor vintages followed each other in rapid succession as the world slid into a deep economic morass. The vintages of 1934 and 1937 were the only relief for grape quality. As the decade wore on, the clouds of war increasingly gathered, culminating in the outbreak of hostilities in September 1939. These were dark times indeed, and yet, the decade was also a time of progress in Champagne.

Following on the heels of the stock market crash in the fall of 1929, the world's economies spiraled downward. According to the Wall Street Journal, the global economy lost 15% of its Gross Domestic Product between 1929 and 1932. Unemployment rose to between 25% - 33% of all eligible workers, and deflation set in. Grape prices collapsed as did those for many other crops and commodities. Growers earned half in 1930 what they had in 1927; by 1932, they earned half of what they had in 1930. In 1934, the best vintage of the decade, some earned less than they had thirty years before. Between 1929 and 1932 in France, unemployment increased more than 200%, foreign trade was cut in half, and wholesale prices fell by a third. Surprisingly, however, champagne sales continued to grow during these difficult times due to increasing sales in the French domestic market. In 1928, the region as a whole sold 21.2 million bottles, just over 38% of the total sold in France. By 1937, sales were over 40 million bottles, and more than 70% of these were sold in France. While sales would slump again before grinding nearly to a halt during the war, the die was cast, and until 2018 the French market would remain as large as all the export markets combined.

The management of the market also became increased sophisticated in the 1930s. The creation in 1935 of "La Commission de Châlons" formalized the ad hoc arrangements begun in 1911 between growers and houses. Membership was equally divided between representatives of the grape growers and the negociant firms. The commission set the price of grapes, which was then ratified in a decree issued by the local government. In return for establishing a base price for the grapes, houses insisted on the regulation of the amount of juice that could be pressed and they also imposed a maximum yield. Both measures regulated the market for grapes and also improved wine quality. Difficult trading conditions hastened reform of this nature during the depression. Before the big harvest of 1934, wine inventories were already sufficient for demand. Even though the grape quality was excellent in 1934, the wines sold with difficulty.

The hard times endured by the growers during the decade produced two significant developments whose influence has only grown in the years since the Depression. The first is that the unsold fruit was a major spur for the growth of the cooperative movement. By the end of the 1930s, there were 26 cooperatively-owned wineries throughout the region. Another result was the growth of the recoltant-manipulant. This term refers to a grower who makes wine from the produce of his own vineyards. This phenomenon had hardly existed before the depression. Vine growers who wanted to vinify their own wine faced enormous challenges. Not least of these challenges was the capital necessary to establish a winery. However, by the end of the decade, growers were selling nearly two million bottles of wine that they had produced themselves. While the winemaking (and commercial) challenges of this approach are numerous, it is a viable long-term solution for talented and passionate growers.

The 1930s were also a time of increasing mastery over the secondary fermentation. One element of this was the use of techniques such as warming the fermentation vats to ensure a complete primary (alcoholic) fermentation, giving a stable base wine. To this stable base a winemaker could carefully the amount of yeast and sugar to add and create a reliable pressure in the bottle. In previous times this was not done, which resulted in inconsistency and accidental explosions in the cellars, causing injuries and loss of revenue. The second aspect of this was the general implementation of carefully cultured yeasts for the fermentation, which assured a clean, rapid, and thorough secondary fermentation. These yeasts also had the advantage of being easier to riddle, thus improving the clarity of the champagne.

The final element perfected in this decade was the production of machine-blown bottles. Until the Great War, the majority were blown individually by hand, which tended to accentuate the inconsistency of the mousse. Given the losses of manpower during the war, it was essential to mechanize this process. The combination of thoroughly fermented base wines, carefully cultured yeast, and sturdier bottles reduced breakage to less than 1% according to Bonal, as the pressure inside the bottles was gradually standardized as 6 atmospheres (for fully sparkling champagne) 2.5 – 3 atmospheres for the style formerly called "crémant". It was also during this period that filtration and fining for color were standardized in the industry. Bottling, disgorging, and corking were all increasingly automated, and Bonal notes that the production of champagne by the end of the 1930s was very similar to the way in which it is done today.

There were also significant evolutions in taste in the '30s. One trend was a decline in the popularity of rosé champagne. This fall from grace would continue until recent times. Rosé had seen several vicissitudes of fashion over the years. As recently as 2003, growers told me that they disapproved of rosé, since "The first duty of champagne is to be elegant." The rosé of the day could be luridly colored and sweet – not what one would today consider "serious" wine at all. Paradoxically, at this same period, it was still possible to find sparkling red champagne produced by the addition of 50 – 65% red base wine to the blend. Another trend was the slow and progressive diminution of the level of dosage. Brut champagnes were not unheard-of, but they still were not common, although more and more consumers preferred demi-sec, sec, and extra-sec champagnes.

1930
[No Stars]

Harvest: September 18th
Yield: 4,000 kg/ha
Area under vine: 12,300 ha

Total Sales: 27,384,216 btl
France: 13,146,057 btl
Export: 14,238,159 btl
Price of grapes: F 4.00/kg

Overview: A challenging vintage.

After a solid budbreak, frosts on the 20th of April and the 9th of May destroyed nearly half of the crop. Continued rain from the end of June until the harvest promoted rot and mildew throughout the growing season. Harvest began in mid-September in rainy conditions and eventually yielded a modest crop, although high levels of rot led to poor quality. Bonal states that vintage wine was not made.

1931
*

Harvest: September 25th
Yield: 5,500 kg/ha
Area under vine: 12,282 ha

Total Sales: 24,626,844 btl
France: 15,207,429 btl
Export: 9,419,415 btl
Price of grapes: F 2.50/kg
(epluché)

Overview: Another problematic vintage.

Good budbreak and successful flowering, but the growing season was beset by rot, mildew, and vine moths. The harvest was allowed to proceed from the end of September, although some growers waited until early October. The results were described as mediocre quality with very high acidity. Bonal states that vintage wine was not made again this year.

1932
**

Harvest: October 4th
Yield: 5,100 kg/ha
Area under vine: 12,020 ha

Total Sales: 22,841,972 btl
France: 16,238,524 btl
Export: 6,603,448 btl
Price of grapes: F 1.50-2/kg
(epluché[22])

Overview: Modest quality .

Frost struck on the 9th of May, followed by millerandage again at flowering. During the growing season grape moths damaged the bunches somewhat, and grapes were slow to ripen. The harvest, however, began in early October under perfect conditions, and the vines ultimately yielded a modestly good crop of healthy fruit. Bonal states that vintage wine was not made in '32 for the third year in a row.

1933
***

Harvest: September 22nd
Yield: 4,400 kg/ha
Area under vine: 11,990 ha

Total Sales: 25,472,836 btl
France: 20,902,169 btl
Export: 4,370,667 btl
Price of grapes: F 2.50/kg

Overview: Good quality, some vintage wines.

There were frosts in April that damaged 10 – 15% of the vineyards. Flowering was irregular, and a grape moth infestation was were severe in some places. The harvest, however, began under beautiful weather, and the yield was moderate.

---

22   Several times in the 1930s, the Syndict de Courtiers noted a distinction in the price between grapes "trié" (sorted) and those that had been epluché (cleaned). The first term refers to sorting individual bunches. It assumes that a picker will use the tip of his pruning shears to remove any bits of the bunch that are rotten or are not ripe, and that completely unripe bunches will be left on the vine. Epluchage was a process traditional in the Montagne de Reims according to Bonal. As he describes it, fruit was sold an entire vineyard at a time, and the purchaser of the fruit had the right to demand that the bunches be cleaned "as if being sold for table grapes." Improvised stations were set up at the ends of the rows, and the wives of the pickers carefully groomed the bunches.

1934

****

Harvest: September 16th
Yield: 10,500 kg/ha
Area under vine: 11,940 ha

TotalSales: 30,427,574 btl
France: 21,961,249 btl
Export: 8,466,325 btl
Price of grapes: F .75-1.50/kg

Overview: Excellent quality

1934 has always enjoyed a strong reputation. There was a solid budbreak, particularly for Chardonnay. There was scattered frost damage in May and some problems with millerandage at flowering, but the growing season of 1934 was a good one, with little damage from disease or insects. Unfortunately for the growers, the price per kilo was depressed both by abundance and by broader economic trends. However, the quality of the fruit was reliable, and the yield was significant: it was the second-largest of the century after 1922. These wines enjoyed an excellent reputation, although fewer and fewer are seen today. I know the '34 vintage through a single example, a half bottle of Pol Roger that I drank in 2019. The color was amber, and there was no perceptible mousse remaining. From my note: *"Mature but still alive. There are hauntingly complex aromas of dried flowers and fruits, with an edge of lemon peel and an exotic spice element that reminded me of saffron. On the palate, the wine was fresh and lively still – drinking like a white Burgundy wine – and paired extremely well with the oysters."* ***

1935

**

Harvest: September 30th
Yield: 9,500 kg/ha
Area under vine: 11,930 ha

Total Sales: 27,679,850 btl
France: 20,302,324 btl
Export: 7,377,526 btl
Price of grapes: F 1.30/kg

Overview: Another large vintage, but little vintage wine was made.

Another abundant harvest for the growers, despite coulure and millerandage at flowering. During the growing season, there was a bit of mildew, but the weather for the harvest was dry. Bonal states that no vintage wine was made, although this may have more to do with economic conditions than with viticultural reasons. Georges Chappaz, writing in Le Vigneron Champenois of January 1936, expressed a desire to limit both the size of the appellation and the allowed yield. "A plentiful harvest realized due to seasonal conditions can go hand in hand with quality. We observed this in Champagne in 1904 and 1934. An abundant harvest pursued by the grower through manipulation by the method of pruning or by fertilizer is generally in opposition to quality, and there is a difficulty to distinguishing through law the difference between an excess due to nature and one due to the grower."

1936
[No Stars]

Harvest: October 1st
Yield: 3,400 kg/ha
Area under vine: 11,630 ha

Total Sales: 33,182,245 btl
France: 25,327,283 btl
Export: 7,854,962 btl
Price of grapes: F 3.45/kg

Overview: A poor vintage, in difficult economic times. Little or no vintage wine

The 13th of April saw both frost and hail, limiting yield by any-where from 20 – 80% according to the region. Millerandage plagued the flowering, and rot and mildew took their toll during the growing season, right up to the harvest. The grapes rip-ened with difficulty, and picking was delayed until October. In the end, the quality of the fruit was mediocre at best, and the wines very acidic. Not a vintage year.

1937

****

Harvest: September 21ˢᵗ
Yield: 4,700 kg/ha
Area under vine: 11,400 ha

Total Sales: 40,032,788 btl
France: 28,297,501 btl
Export: 11,735,287 btl
Price of grapes not reported

Overview: An excellent vintage

After a relatively uneventful spring and healthy flowering, the growing season was troubled by damage from grape moths and episodes of rot. However, the weather improved at harvest as picking commenced. Quality overall was good, with observers at the time reporting ripe fruit and firm acidity. Sales were also brisk: the region shipped a record number of bottles for the decade. These wines have a good reputation. I know the 1937 vintage from a bottle of Mumm Cordon Rouge consumed in 2019. The wine was a rich, golden color with no noticeable mousse. Although this is not completely unacceptable for a wine of this age, the bottle did not conform to my hopes. From my note: *"Rich and slightly soft, with a creamy texture and an enjoyable taste of caramel and honey. However, on the palate, the acidity was a bit flat, and the wine did not have the aromatic depth or vibrancy of other older champagnes of my experience."* **

1938
***

Harvest: September 28th
Yield: 8,400 kg/ha
Area under vine: 11,689 ha

Total Sales: 35,729,847 btl
France: 23,772,427 btl
Export: 11,957,420 btl
Price of grapes: F 5.20/kg

Overview: A "useful" vintage; good volume, acceptable quality

A very strong budbreak was followed by a flowering that was disrupted by coulure and millerandage, and a growing season plagued by rot. However, the fruit ripened in the end, and harvest commenced at the end of September. The rot meant meticulous sorting, but in the end, yields were abundant for the period.

1939
***

Harvest: October 4th
Yield: 7,400 kg/ha
Area under vine: 10,799 ha

Total Sales: 31,820,608 btl
France: 21,610,935 btl
Export: 10,149,673 btl
Price of grapes: F 3/kg (trié)
4/kg (épluché)

Overview: Mixed reviews, but good yield and some potential for vintage wines.

The potential yield in 1939 was reduced by coulure and mille-randage at flowering, and by a growing season troubled with grape moths and rot. Picking could not begin until early October, but in the end, produced a respectable yield for the period, although good results demanded careful sorting. Bollinger reports "Powerful and balanced wines," although this view was not universally shared.

CHAPTER V

1940 – 1949:
War and Postwar

Just as the First World War marked the second decade of the century, the history of the Second World War is forever intertwined with the 40s. The war is commonly said to begin with the German invasion of Poland on September 1st, 1939, but the roots of the conflict stretch back further. The annexation of Austria in 1938 and the invasion of Czechoslovakia in March of 1939 were important preludes. Britain, France, and other nations declared war on Germany after the invasion of Poland, and then on June 10th Germany invaded France arriving in Paris four days later. Contrary to what the region experienced in the First World War, the vineyards of Champagne suffered little physical damage during the Second World War. The region was occupied for the four years of the war, but the buildings and the vineyards suffered relatively little damage. The people, however, were decimated, and work proceeded only with great difficulty since the region lacked material and workers.

There was no commerce in wine recorded at all. During the years from 1941 – 1946, however, the champagne industry continued under the occupation. Representatives of the growers led by Maurice Doyard and of the houses, led by Robert-Jean de Vogüé formed the « Bureau national de répartition des vins de Champagne » in 1940 in response to German requirements for Champagne. Rather than having the occupying troops take Champagne at random, the committee took equitable levies from each producer to supply their demands. One year later, this office became the CIVC (Comité Interprofessionnel du vin de Champagne or Comité Champagne), which continues today[23]. In addition to the requisitions of the Germans, Bonal estimates that there were at least two million bottles unofficially seized in addition to the quantities left by civilians in their

23   The Comité Champagne helps organize the market, and plays an essential role in the generic promotion of the category, media relations, and the defense of the name "Champagne".

cellars as they fled the occupation. The official in charge of the requisitions was Otto Klaebisch, known in the region as the führer du champagne, or merely the weinführer. Each year he requisitioned between 15 – 18 million bottles. The négociants were paid below the market rate, but a sum roughly sufficient to cover their costs. They were free to sell the surplus to neutral countries.

Under these conditions, the trade continued until 1943. However, the Germans gradually became aware that the Resistance was operating in Champagne, with an active cell at Moët & Chandon. They arrested the directors, including Paul Chandon-Moët and Robert-Jean de Vogüé, who narrowly escaped death. Ultimately, they also detained the leaders of the CIVC, the grower's union called the Syndicat Général des Vignerons (SGV), and Veuve Clicquot. The Marquis Suarez d'Aulan, who was the head of Piper-Heidsieck, was killed fighting for the Resistance, and the winery was taken over by the German authorities. Epernay was liberated on August 28th, 1944, and the German surrender took place in Reims on May 7th, 1945, in a building near the train station that still stands today. The year of victory also brought a triumphant vintage, not only in Champagne, but also in other regions. There were three superb vintages in the latter half of the '40s: '45, '47, and '49. Small recompense for the immeasurable troubles visited upon the region in prior decades. Still, the tide was about to turn, and the next thirty years would be a period of expansion and prosperity for Champagne.

1940
[No Stars]

Harvest: None due to war
Yield: 1,100 kg/ha
Area under vine: 7,814 ha

Total Sales: 27,683,910 btl
France: 17,003,788 btl
Export: 10,680,122 btl
Price of grapes: F 8.50/kg

Overview: WWII disrupted an already difficult year

In 1940, Germany invaded France, and there was no organized grape harvest this year in Champagne. The invasion prevented spraying for rot or mildew, devastating the crop.

1941
**

Harvest: October 5th
Yield: 4,000 kg/ha
Area under vine: 8,556 ha

Total Sales: 102,224,090 btl
France: 71,169,802 btl
Export: 31,054,288 btl
Price of grapes: F 15.10/kg

Overview: A war vintage; some good reports.

The Syndicat des Courtiers en Vins de Champagne note "non-culture" for the vintage 1941. Still, Bonal relates that in fact that most of the war years were dry and relatively stable in terms at least of the weather, and he places '41 as one of the years that generally produced vintage wines. In 1941 specifically, the vines suffered a bit from chlorosis. Few, if any, wines remain.

1942

***

Harvest: September 29th
Yield: 4,200 kg/ha
Area under vine: 10,960 ha

Total Sales: 102,224,090 btl
France: 71,169,802 btl
Export: 31,054,288 btl
Price of grapes: F 17.50/kg

Overview: Some vintage wines produced.

The total planted area rebounded in 1942 – it is odd to envision the growers replanting during the war. Still, it is proof that the life of the vineyard can continue even in the most difficult conditions. Frost damaged the vineyards on the 4th and 5th of May, and the vines suffered sporadically from mildew during the growing season. Few wines remain.

1943

****

Harvest: September 15th
Yield: 5,000 kg/ha
Area under vine: 11,004 ha

Sales not reported
Price of grapes: F 18.00/kg

Overview: The best of the war years. Good results where possible.

Modest budbreak followed by coulure and millerandage at flowering due to cool weather and rainy conditions, reducing yields throughout the region, but particularly in the Marne Valley. Significant attacks of mildew during the growing season necessitated treatments, but the weather improved in August, and the harvest began under perfect conditions. Bollinger notes: "A difficult year for an exceptional result... The 1943 wines are very concentrated." 1943 produced some vintage wines, and they are seen in the market from time to time. Their reputation is good, but few remain. My only experience of 1943 was with a bottle of Moët & Chandon Imperial Dry Vintage. I was struck at the time by the relatively youthful character of the wine. From my note: *"Sweet and soft, showing surprisingly little evolution. The nose opens with a hint of cotton candy and only with time shows yeasty, brioche notes and a darker, smoky cast, with a suggestion of toffee at the end. On the palate, the wine was very fresh. It lacked perhaps the depth of the Pol Roger '34 on the same evening, but tasters were recompensed by the youthful vivacity of the bottle. A suggestion of mousse remained."* **** (Tasted 2019)

1944
[No Stars]

Harvest: September 27th

Yield: 4,200 kg/ha

Area under vine: 10,712 ha

Sales not reported

Price of grapes: F 18.00/kg

Overview: A poor year

Significant frosts in May severely limited yield in 1944. Affected vineyards lost anywhere from 20 – 100% of their crop and overall quantity was reduced by 50% across the entire region. The remaining fruit was attacked by rot, which was prevalent throughout the growing season. The harvest began in the pouring rain (which swelled the bunches) on September 27th and yielded 4,200 kg/ha of fruit, but fruit quality was modest at best. I have not seen any vintage wines from 1944.

1945

*****

Harvest: September 8th
Yield: 4,400 kg/ha
Area under vine: 10,728 ha
Average potential alcohol: 10.5%
Average total acidity: 6.5 g/l

Sales not reported
Price of grapes: F 37.50/kg

Overview: A superb vintage and a historic one. Top wines still lively today.

There were localized frosts in April, with most of the damage limited to the Montagne de Reims. Flowering and fruit set suffered a normal amount of coulure and millerandage, reducing yields, and alternating periods of drought and rain brought attacks of grape berry moths and other pests, including a severe outbreak of Rotbrenner, a type of fungal disease. However, the weather cleared in August, ripening the small crop to an exceptional level and ultimately providing one of the century's greatest vintages. Bollinger notes: 'Nature comes to the rescue of the victory despite a difficult year...Solid wines that later proved to be a great vintage, powerful, and able to be kept for a long time." 1945 is a spectacular year, and worth going out of your way to taste. My best experience of 1945 was a bottle of 1945 Moët & Chandon Imperial Dry Vintage. From my note: *"Still a bit of mousse left. The wine is a fairly robust golden color with amber reflects. The nose began with fresh and dried flowers, toasted brioche, and a touch of honey and almost caramel at the bottom. On the palate, the wine retains a lovely freshness that is truly astonishing. The aromas on the palate became a bit more savory at the end, and the finish lingered almost indefinitely. Truly an impressive wine."* *****

1946

*

Harvest: September 29th
Yield: 3,600 kg/ha
Area under vine: 11,071 ha

Sales not reported
Price of grapes: F 70.00/kg

Overview: A modest year at best.

Budbreak in 1946 was decent, if not extravagant. At flowering, however, coulure and millerandage led to losses of 30 – 70% of the crop, depending on region. The growing season was very cool and ripened the grapes with difficulty. Weather at harvest was dry, salvaging the vintage to some extent for a few growers—no vintage wines produced to the best of my knowledge.

1947

*****

Harvest: September 5th
Yield: 4,100 kg/ha
Area under vine: 10,805 ha

Total Sales: 21,665,178 btl
France: 12,380,470 btl
Export: 9,284,708 btl
Price of grapes: F 70.00/kg

Overview: An exceptional vintage.

The winter before the growing season was cold and dry. There was localized hail in April in the Côte des Blancs, and the flowering was disturbed by adverse weather conditions. This limited yield, but the growing season was magnificent, and the small crop ripened to perfection. The only exception to this generally halcyon progression was in the Aube, where summer hail destroyed some of the vineyards. The harvest, which began on September 5th, was the earliest start since 1893.

The 1947 vintage has provided me with a few of my most moving experiences of tasting Champagne. Krug '47: *"Extraordinary wine, with a richly aromatic nose with notes of truffle, honey, caramel, and a super-ripe tropical fruit. Lush and rich, almost heavy, but balanced by lively acidity. This wine walks a fine line between excess and luxury but does so expertly. Exotic, beautiful, rare."* ***** (Tasted 2011)

Veuve Clicquot '47: *"A deep gold color, showing a few bubbles still wandering to the top. The nose showed a wonderful, strong aroma that was surprisingly fresh. There were some notes of caramel and biscuit as well as truffle and morel and a slight sherry character. On the palate, it was still fresh and well balanced, with a long, elegant finish."* **** (Tasted 2006)

1947 is a superb vintage, and the best wines can still show well today. At this remove of time, look for bottles with as good a fill level as possible and as light a color as possible. If late-disgorged bottles come up for sale, snap them up.

1948

**

Harvest: September 20th
Yield: 5,200 kg/ha
Area under vine: 10,957 ha

Total Sales: 27,345,977 btl
France: 17,125,003 btl
Export: 10,220,974 btl
Price of grapes: F 82.50/kg

Overview: A difficult vintage, with frost damage throughout the year.

The flowering was disrupted by poor weather, and there was rot throughout the season. Hail destroyed enough fruit for several thousand barrels of wine. However, Richard Juhlin notes in his book that it was successful in the Côte des Blancs.

1949

****

Harvest: September 19th
Yield: 4,500 kg/ha
Area under vine: 10,774 ha
Average potential alcohol: 10.5%
Average total acidity: 6.5 g/l

Total Sales: 27,225,166 btl
France: 16,184,132 btl
Export: 11,041,034 btl
Price of grapes not reported

Overview: An excellent year, hot and dry.

The year began with a mild winter followed by frosts in February and then colder weather. Remembered as one of the great vintages, it was not, however, without challenges. At the outset, there was hail during budding, and then millerandage during the flowering. During the growing season, hot and dry conditions were punctuated by violent storms that led to difficulties with rot. Fortunately for the vintage, the hot, dry weather dried the fruit for harvest, reducing the risk. Bollinger notes: "A difficult year with a happy ending"

A bottle of the 1949 Krug Collection was quite mature in 2010 but very distinctive. I note *"...a nose of yeast, mineral, truffle, pastry, and soy. Perhaps a bit over the top and past its peak, but very interesting. On the palate, the wine was soft and silky, but with little mousse to enliven it, there was a heaviness that was a bit difficult."* ****

A recently-consumed bottle of Clicquot '49 original disgorgement was perfectly preserved. The bottle bore the legend "English Market," and it was an absolute delight. From my note: *"Still a bit of mousse left. The color is fairly dark, and there are plenty of mature aromas, but the wine is ultimately fresh and very lively. The aromas open with dried fruit and honey and then progress to truffle and toffee. It almost veers into soy sauce, but not quite. There is an almost saline edge to the complexity, but as described, there is an essential freshness that keeps it vital after seventy years in the bottle."* ***** (Tasted 2019)

A classic vintage that produced legendary wines. Unfortunately, many are now showing a very mature character due to the baking hot conditions. Still worthy of trying if one comes across bottles with proper storage and where the color and the fill are still sound. Of course, late-disgorged bottles that have been recently tasted by the chef de caves are often the best bet at this age.

CHAPTER VI

1950 – 1959:
Les Trente Glorieuses Begin

French writer Jean Fourastié referred to the period from 1946 – 1975 as *"Les Trente Glorieuses"* (the glorious thirty [years]) because it was a period of steady growth. This was true in Champagne as elsewhere. During this period, sales steadily increased, and the area devoted to vineyards continued to grow. At the same time, techniques in the vineyard and in the winery continued to improve. This is fortunate for all concerned, as the growth during this period was astonishing. The average planted area of the first five years of this period was 10,944 hectares, while the average of the last five years was 23,433 hectares, an increase of 114%. The growth in sales was even more spectacular: the average from the first five years was 32,175,782 bottles, while that of the last five years was 164,167,289 bottles, thus 410% growth. Continued advancement in every sphere was necessary to sustain such growth. The average productivity growth during the period was also astonishing: the average yield during the first five years was 5,300 kg/ha, and by the last five years it had climbed to 8,587 kg/ha, an increase of 62%

The Fifties began in Champagne with a reasonably sizable harvest. Sales also began to re-start from the low levels in the immediate postwar years, and by 1950 they had passed the milestone of 30 million bottles again. By the end of the decade, however, sales would approach 50 million. Despite this growth, difficulties remained to overcome, at least in the short term. 1955 was a vintage of superb quality and reasonably good quantity. Unfortunately, with the slow sales in the immediate post-war years, the négociant's cellars were well-stocked and it proved maddeningly difficult to sell this vintage despite its undisputed quality.

One of the critical initiatives begun in the 1950s was the modernization of the vineyards. The AVC encouraged compliance with regulations and modernization of the vineyards through a system of incentives to growers. The work in the vineyards was most pointed in the Aube, where the grape mix was different than that of the Marne. Growers in Champagne have relied on a variety of grape varieties over the centuries. In modern times the region has settled on a blend of approximately one-third of Pinot Noir, Meunier, and Chardonnay. There are other authorized varieties, however that date to the 19th century and before, including Pinot Gris (called Fromenteau locally), Pinot Blanc (Blanc Vrai), Petit Meslier, and Arbanne. These "heritage" varieties were much more common in the Aube than in the Marne and Aisne. Part of the work of the 1950s for better or worse was a concerted effort to extinguish them. However, as we write, growers are re-examining these varieties since they may hold part of the key for advancing quality in a time of global warming.

Another certitude of the 1950s was faith in technology, such as it was at the time. This faith helped drive the move towards the use of tractors and away from horses. The invention in 1952 of the "tracteur-enjambeur" that straddles a row of vines (and a later development that straddled two rows simultaneously) was enough to convince the quasi-totality of growers to make the switch. There were other, even less fortunate, "advances" in the vineyard that began in the 1950s, including the widespread use of herbicides to remove the foliage from between the rows. Herbicide, pesticide, and fungicide use were all facilitated by the mechanized tractor, which made it much easier to spray.

The work in the winery was modernized beginning in the 1950s as well. The great revolution was the replacement of wooden casks of various sizes by tanks, either in concrete, enamel, or, later, stainless steel. Bonal relates that in 1939 there were more than 100 barrel-makers in Florent-en-Argonne in the forest near Champagne but that today there is only one. At the same time, the move away from wood facilitated better temperature control. Temperature control brought greater purity of fruit to the wines, changing the style for better or worse. Other innovations were introduced or became widespread during this period, including a more generalized use of cultured yeast for fermentation, centrifuging, filtering, and fining of the base wines. Later in the 1960s, the industry moved towards the use of gyropalettes for riddling and disgorging by machine à la glace, which required the use of crown capsules instead of the old-fashioned agrafe-et-liège that required so much labor. Most of these techniques had a trade-off, however, and the style of the wine was inevitably slowly changing.

The 1950s also saw the elaboration of the system of managing the market for Champagne. From the end of the '50s until the harvest of 1990, the CIVC facilitated contracts. Under these "interprofessional contracts," growers and houses committed to cooperate in exchange for advantageous terms. The terms guaranteed to the growers that would sell all their grapes, assured the houses that they would have enough fruit for their needs, and allowed all parties to avoid price fluctuations. The system relied on signed contract orders called *bons de commande*. There were three types of bon: *bons rouges*, which were the barrels pledged for sale by the growers; *bons blancs*, which were the barrels agreed at a given price that exceeded this amount, and *bons bleus*, which were the barrels produced from the grapes of the vineyards owned by the houses themselves. The number of contracts assigned was estimated a month before the harvest based upon the yield obtained the prior year and the conditions of the growing season. This contract system generally worked very well. A year such as 1959, however, was an exception, since much more fruit was expected than delivered. In 1959, it took all the political savvy of the CIVC to save the day. Until the late 1950s, the buyers of fruit typically had the upper hand in such transactions. With the explosion of demand that began to take place at this time, the growers increasingly were in an advantageous position. The system also established a policy of pegging the price of fruit to the average sale price of a bottle of Champagne. More than two-thirds of the growers signed such contracts, and nearly all of the négociants participated. Any shortfall in the needs of the négociants would be satisfied by the "free agent" growers. This evolved and efficient system stayed in place until the 1990 E.U. decree by Brussels that this amounted to price-fixing and was therefore forbidden.

1950
*

Harvest: September 11th
Yield: 6,800 kg/ha
Area under vine: 10,958 ha

Total Sales: 31,139,333 btl
France: 17,178,971 btl
Export: 13,960,362 btl
Price of grapes: F 100.00/kg

Overview: A challenging vintage.

Vineyards were hit by frost in April and hail in May and again in July. There was rot during the growing season and rain at harvest. Observers report that the fruit that remained after a serious sorting was of acceptable quality. I have not tasted any vintage wines from 1950.

1951
[No Stars]

Harvest: October 1st
Yield: 2,900 kg/ha
Area under vine: 10,716 ha

Total Sales: 36,258,274 btl
France: 20,750,839 btl
Export: 15,507,435 btl
Price of grapes: F 140.00/kg

Overview: Catastrophic frosts, poor flowering, mildew

The frost on April 30th limited yields by up to 70% throughout the region. The remaining fruit was affected by coulure and millerandage at flowering. Severe sorting was also necessitated by mildew during the growing season. The harvest, however, took place under beautiful, dry conditions. Due to the tiny size of the crop, few vintage wines were produced, and fewer remain today.

1952
***

Harvest: September 8th
Yield: 5,500 kg/ha
Area under vine: 11,080 ha

Total Sales: 30,727,512 btl
France: 18,651,060 btl
Export: 12,076,452 btl
Price of grapes: F 140.00/kg

Overview: Modest conditions, but some excellent wines produced

The early months of the growing season took place under ideal conditions, or very nearly so. Later in the season, the vines were damaged by cochylis moths. After veraison, rain straight through from late August through early September set off a round of rot, and the harvest was moved forward to begin on September 8th. Fortunately, by this time, the skins were sufficiently thick that the damage was mitigated to some extent. Bonal counts 1952 as one of the years that "generally produced vintage wines". Despite the poor weather for the harvest, Bollinger reports that powerful, vinous base wines were produced in 1952, and they chose this vintage to create the first vintage of R.D., released in 1961. Another success was the Dom Pérignon. In my notes, many decades on the wine was *"...still vibrant, fresh and crisp, with a nose of truffle, smoke, and ripe green papaya, while on the palate the acidity still kept it admirably together. Mature but still drinking very well."* **** (Tasted 2010)

1953

****

Harvest: September 15th
Yield: 5,400 kg/ha
Area under vine: 11,023 ha

Total Sales: 30,578,008 btl
France: 19,477,929 btl
Export: 11,100,079 btl
Price of grapes: F 145.00/kg

Overview: An excellent year, balancing ripeness and structure.

The year began with frost in May that caused sporadic damage and continued with a flowering that began under good conditions but then stalled as the weather turned cold, leading to coulure and millerandage. From August, however, conditions were ideal, and the beautiful weather continued straight through the harvest, which produced somewhat more than expected due to rain just before picking swelling the grapes. Despite this rain, there was essentially no rot at harvest, and quality was excellent. Bollinger notes that the base wines were "supple and elegant with a fine concentration." A bottle of Krug consumed with friends in 2015 was the greatest of the '53s that I have enjoyed. From my notes: *"...amazingly fresh aromas on the nose of brioche, smoke and lemony fruit along with a hint of truffle. On the palate, the wine was crisp and fine, with impressive extract and a lingering finish. "* *****

1954
[No tars]

Harvest: September 27th
Yield: 5,900 kg/ha
(800,000 barrels; 12,000 kg/ha AC)
Area under vine: 11,345 ha

Total Sales: 32,977,780 btl
France: 22,153,428 btl
Export: 10,824,352 btl
Price of grapes: F 123.00/kg

Overview: A challenging year

April was icy, impeding shoot growth. There was some loss to frost on April 20th, May 4th, and May 7th. Conditions generally through May were cold and dry, with less sun than usual. From June, however, the vines subjected to nearly every possible difficulty during the growing season: coulure and millerandage at flowering; grape berry moths and rot during the growing season. Ripeness at the beginning of September was spotty due to the cold growing season, and then the rain began in September before the harvest, causing rot to spread.

1955

*****

Harvest: September 29th
Yield: 8,500 kg/ha
Area under vine: 11,471 ha

Total Sales: 37,706,826 btl
France: 25,773,214 btl
Export: 11,933,612 btl
Price of grapes: F 129.00/kg

Overview: An exceptional year, with firm acidity and good ripeness.

As in other regions of France, there was severe frost in Champagne in 1955, which happened on May 12th. The weather leading up to the flowering was cool, and thus the vine flowered late. However, the weather from this point on in the summer was magnificent, and the bunches matured to perfection. This ripening was slow, however, and the harvest was delayed until October. In the end, because of this additional time on the vines, the bunches picked up more weight than expected, the yield was high, and yet quality was exceptional, with powerful wines marked by very firm acidity. In 2003 I was working for Veuve Clicquot and had the opportunity to taste a bottle of the '55 hand-carried from the cellars to our offices in New York. I noted it as *"A wonderful smoky, minerally nose with plenty of aged sous bois character and a lovely fruit nose of candied lemon and kumquat. The balance was exquisite, and the finish very long."* ***** If well stored (or late-disgorged), the wines of 1955 are still delicious today. Collectors are advised to seek them out when possible.

1956
[No Stars]

Harvest: October 8th
Yield: 4,600 kg/ha
Area under vine: 11,814 ha

Total Sales: 44,304,197 btl
France: 31,278,718 btl
Export: 13,025,479 btl
Price of grapes: F 132.00/kg

Overview: A short vintage troubled by hail and rot.

As often happens, a year of relative abundance was followed by one with a much smaller harvest. Some vines were lost to hard frosts in the winter of 1955 – 1956. Yields were further reduced by coulure at flowering, and again further diminished by hail in August. There was also an outbreak of grey rot that set in just before harvest. After sorting, there was very little fruit left and even less of a quality appropriate for vintage wine. It is unlikely that any remains.

1957
**

Harvest: September 20th
Yield: 2,600 kg/ha
Area under vine: 11,553 ha

Total Sales: 48,422,119 btl
France: 35,705,008 btl
Export: 12,717,111 btl
Price of grapes: F 195.00/kg

Overview: A frost year with meager yields; good conditions, but few vintage wines made.

Frost in April and May greatly diminished the yield in 1957. Flowering and fruit set, however, happened under perfect conditions. Harvest began on September 20th for what fruit there was. Because of the minimal crop, it is unlikely that any wines survive to this day.

1958

*

Harvest: October 1ˢᵗ
Yield: 4,800 kg/ha
Area under vine: 12,029 ha

Total Sales: 40,702,291 btl
France: 27,587,354 btl
Export: 13,114,937 btl
Price of grapes: F 230.00/kg

Overview: A challenging harvest.

In 1958 the vines saw coulure and millerandage at flowering. This was followed by attacks of mildew throughout the season. There were also episodes of hail between June and August. Spiders, moths, and rot all attacked the vines. Harvest began for the surviving fruit on October 1st. The fruit that did survive was acceptable quality after a serious sorting and selection. Few vintage wines were made, however, and I have tasted none.

1959

*****

Harvest: September 10th
Yield: 7,000 kg/ha
Area under vine: 12,089 ha
Average potential alcohol: 11.5%[24]
Average total acidity: 5.5 g/l[25]

Total Sales: 42,270,073 btl
France: 28,731,117 btl
Export: 13,538,956 btl
Price of grapes: F 245.00/kg

Overview: 1959 is generally counted as a superb year.

The yield in 1959 was reduced somewhat by millerandage at flowering and by drought. Otherwise, the vintage was one of textbook growing conditions. The weather was mild and warm throughout the season, although there was some damage to Chardonnay from powdery mildew. Growers hoping for rain to swell the berries were disappointed, and in the end, there was a shortfall of fruit that had the CIVC working overtime to satisfy everyone. The grapes were very healthy and picked at between 11% and 13% potential alcohol. This ripeness led to what is an issue with the vintage for some: very rich wines that can lack balancing acidity. Overall, the consensus is that it is a top-rated vintage. Bollinger notes: "A dream year," but in my experience, the '59s can be a bit over the top. For me, a bottle of Salon drunk at dinner in 2011 was typical of my experience with the vintage: *"The 1959 Salon was a monument to the wine that it once was. The nose showed a rich caramel/toffee character, but most of the primary fruit was gone. On the palate, the wine had no remaining mousse and consequently, a massive, almost oily feel. Not unpleasant to drink, but not the Champagne that it once undoubtedly was."* **

The same wine, consumed out of magnum in 2019 was better, but still far from perfect: *"The color of the wine was very good, but unfortunately there was no mousse but rather the suggestion that it once had bubbles. On the nose, there was a pointedly smoky aromatic character, and the fruit had been completely transformed....much of the joy has gone out of this wine. It wasn't*

---

24   No average is given, but no finished wines registered < 10%; 61% were 11% - 12%; and 30% were 12 – 13%, with some > 13%; 69% of wines were < than 6 g/l TA; 29% were 6 g/l – 7 g/l. Only 2% were > 7 g/l
25   Expressed as sulfuric acid

faulty or unpleasant, but it was hard to generate much enthusiasm beyond the fact of drinking wine of such rarity. Structurally it was sound, with fresh acidity (surprisingly so given the year) and good density, but a lack of charm that frankly disappointed. ***

However, this is not universally the case. I greatly enjoyed a recently-disgorged bottle of the Grand Cru Blanc de Blancs from A. R. Lenoble: *"Caramel and butterscotch; mature; rich and soft but still holding on. There is not much mousse left but a wine of great density and elegance,"* **** (Tasted 2018) Another recently disgorged bottles from Michel Loriot also showed well: *"Evolved, with notes of honey, roast coffee, and dark chocolate. Little mousse is left, but the wine is impressive, with a softly lingering finish."* **** (Tasted 2016)

By far the best '59 I have had, however, was the Roederer Cristal: *"This was a spectacular bottle of Cristal. The bottle opened with a hiss, and the wine still retained a delicate mousse. The color was commensurate with age, and the nose was rich and sweet. It opened with brioche and baked apple with a hint of spice and evolved to take in a slight hint of truffle and ground coffee. The wine retained an astonishing freshness that balanced the epic density of the wine to perfection. This bottle is drinking supremely well now, but astonishingly will continue to hold. This is among the best bottles of Champagne I've ever had from any vintage."* ***** (Tasted 2019)

1959 is, without a doubt, a legendary year. If a bottle has hasbeen well stored it may still harbor delightful surprises. Late-disgorged wines can also be marvelous from this vintage. However, the collector should be aware that there is a chance that wines from this vintage are today past their prime.

CHAPTER VII

1960 – 1969:
Goodbye to All That

The decade of the 1960s was the start of a revolution for the wines of Champagne. At the beginning of the decade, the wines were still made largely as they had been after the First World War. By the close of the decade, they were on their way to becoming the Champagne of today. Changes both positive and negative happened during the 1960s. One of the less happy changes occurred as the "modernization" of the vineyards continued. Many of the vines planted in the immediate postwar era were replaced, since it was common to replant vines every twenty-five years. This replanting occurs because growers often crop at high levels, a practice which can exhaust the vines. As was common at the time, replanting was often done with clones rather than via massal selection. This had the potential to diminish fruit quality for the next quarter-century, since the clones developed in the 1960s were often selected for their productivity and for their resistance to frost and disease more than for their depth of character.

Since the phylloxera epidemic, the most common way to choose vines was for a grower to select from his existing vineyards the vines that were particularly successful and to take cuttings from these vines. These cuttings are planted in a nursery where they are grown for several years before being grafted onto phylloxera-resistant rootstock and planted in the vineyard. This method preserves the diversity of the individual vineyard site. The more modern approach is to select clones bred in a nursery for specific characteristics. While clonal material has improved today, this was not universally the case in the 1960s.

Other trends in the vineyard also continued to have an insidious effect as growers moved towards greater use of synthetic fertilizers, fungicides, and pesticides. This contributed to the steady evolution in yield, which tracked nicely with the continued development of sales, but less well with the state of the environment. There was also extensive use of synthetic herbicides, which were increasingly adopted. After the herbicides were applied, the soil was "nourished" with urban compost taken from the city dumps of Paris, called "boues de ville".

In the winery trends toward "modernization" also continued as winemakers increasingly used pectolytic enzymes, filtration, and sorbic acid (for its antimicrobial properties) to increase the stability of the musts and to ensure rapid, thorough fermentation of the base wines, sometimes at the expense of character. Research into these techniques was pursued throughout the 1960s and they really took root in the following decade. The 1960s were thus the end of the "old school," and the last time that champagne was still made largely as it had been at least since the 1920s.

Not only were techniques in the vineyard and the winery changing, but the style of the wines themselves continued to evolve. Producers slowly moved towards styles that favored tension and structure as they increasingly fermented in stainless steel and gradually reduced dosage. Because wines from the 1960s are still available on the secondary market, we have a valuable glimpse into the winemaking of a different era. The glorious heights of quality attained in the 1960s were amplified by the fact that there were a number of exceptional vintages in the decade: 1961, 1964, 1966, and 1969 were all standout vintages that still drink well today. One difference with the Champagne of today, however, is that growers lacked the technology to salvage reasonable quality from poor conditions. 1962 was a good quality vintage, if not to the level of the others, but 1963, 1965, 1967 and 1968 all varied from poor to abysmal, and little wine remains.

1960

**

Harvest: September 12th
Yield: 10,100 kg/ha
Area under vine: 12,375 ha
Average potential alcohol: 10.5%[26]
Average total acidity: 5 g/l[27]

Total Sales: 49,265,501 btl
France: 35.356,579 btl
Export: 13,908,922 btl
Price of grapes: F 2.60/kg

Overview: A large harvest, modest quality.

1960 was the biggest harvest of the preceding twenty-five years despite millerandage at flowering and rot during the growing season. The season was cool, which slowed the ripening of the large crop on the vines. At the end of the growing season there was rain at harvest, causing the grapes to take on water weight in the weeks prior to the harvest. For this reason, quality is described as moderate at best. This marked the first year of the "new franc" after de Gaulle's devaluation, but in relative terms, the price of grapes continued to advance. Although this was a large harvest in terms of the times, I have never encountered a wine from this vintage.

---

26   Published date is limited. In 1960 this is the average for the finished wines
(i.e. after chaptalization)
27   Published date is limited. In 1960 19% of the finished wines analysed were < 4 g/l;
40.5% were 4 g/l – 5 g/l, and 31% were between 5 g/l and 7 g/l

1961

****

Harvest: September 20th
Yield: 7,800 kg/ha
Area under vine: 12,494 ha
Average potential alcohol: 9.5%
Average total acidity: 8 g/l

Total Sales: 54,187,849 btl
France: 38,658,873 btl
Export: 15,528,976 btl
Price of grapes: F 2.70/kg

Overview: An excellent vintage.

1961 was marked by a solid bud-break for Chardonnay and Pinot Noir, but somewhat irregular for Meunier. Flowering was slow at first but then completed quickly, and yields were reduced by coulure and millerandage. Weather during the growing season was hot and dry, causing the vines to struggle with chlorosis. This disease reduces the ability of the vines to produce sugar through photosynthesis. August was hot, but rain began in September, fattening the bunches. Although there was some botrytis in the Montagne de Reims, the effects were not widespread or serious. The harvest began under excellent conditions. It was felt at the time that quality was best for Chardonnay, but the yield was higher for Pinot Noir in the Montagne de Reims. The portion in excess of the statutory limit (called in French the *cuidage*) was reclassified to appellation status as it was in 1959, making for three abundant harvests in a row. Bollinger notes: "A fine year for the new wave".

I find that the wines are now often fully mature. Several years ago, a bottle of the original disgorgement of Dom Pérignon left the following impression: "*Sweet caramel, honey, and tropical fruit aromas along with a well-integrated truffle or sous-bois element. The wine is lacking a bit of mousse, however, and lies a bit flat on the palate, although this could be attributable to storage conditions.*" *** (Tasted 2017) This is consistent with a bottle of the '61 Heidsieck Monopole Sec tasted in 2010. I felt that it showed what I took at the time to be the typical character of the vintage "*...all butterscotch and roast nuts with a creamy edge. On the palate the wine retained a lovely firm acidity that was totally unexpected. Mature and quite delicious.*" ***

On balance, these are very good quality wines that fall just short of the top level because many if not most are nearing full maturity. A recent bottle of Taittinger Comtes de Champagne was not appealing: *"No mousse and fairly dark in color. This had a fresh acidity that was bolstered by a fair bit of volatility. Beginning to maderize now, this was in decline, bordering on undrinkable."* *[No stars]* (Tasted 2019)

1962
***

Harvest: October 4th	Total Sales: 57,919,826 btl
Yield: 6,300 kg/ha	France: 42,484,190 btl
Area under vine: 12,915 ha	Export: 15,435,536 btl
Average potential alcohol: 10.8%	Price of grapes: F 2.80/kg
Average total acidity: 9.3 g/l	

Overview: Another year saved by good weather late in the year. Good quality but not top tier.

Yields were reduced by millerandage at the flowering due to cold weather. The vines also suffered a severe mite infestation during the growing season. However, there was beautiful weather at the harvest.

I harbor a great memory of a bottle of 1962 Krug tasted over a decade ago, while I was working for their American importer. I found that it showed *"...a perfectly balanced equilibrium between freshness and maturity, with some crisp, lemony fruit overlaid with aromas of toast, butterscotch and truffle on the nose. On the palate the wine was lively and fresh, yet integrated and round – no hard edges, great staying power."* ***** (Tasted 2007)

1963
[No Stars]

Harvest: October 5th
Yield: 9,100 kg/ha
Area under vine: 13,414 ha
Average potential alcohol: 8.4%
Average total acidity: 10.7 g/l

Total Sales: 64,018,259 btl
France: 46,831,453 btl
Export: 17,186,806 btl
Price of grapes: F 2.85/kg

Overview: A poor year.

A challenging campaign to say the least. The year began with a strong bud-break, but then there was a bit of coulure and more extensive millerandage at flowering due to cold weather. Rot and mildew were particular problems, above all in the Pinot Noir and Meunier throughout the growing season right up to harvest.

During a visit to Charles Ellner the proprietor inquired about the year of my birth, and was kind enough to open a bottle, the first and only time I've had champagne from 1963. My impression: *"Showing its age. The nose is very truffle and forest floor with hints of wild mushroom and black licorice spice. The bubbles have completely disappeared, and on the palate it is slightly sweet. An interesting drink, but not a compelling one. With the right cheese, it would be at its best." [No stars]* (Tasted 2007)

1964

*****

Harvest: September 16th
Yield: 9,100 kg/ha
Area under vine: 14,047 ha
Average potential alcohol: 10.6%
Average total acidity: 7 g/l

Total Sales: 70,204,695 btl
France: 52,050,368 btl
Export: 18,154,327 btl
Price of grapes: F 2.88/kg

Overview: A superb vintage, with good ripeness and firm acidity.

The season began with a solid bud-break for Pinot Noir and Chardonnay, less consistent for Meunier. Some millerandage at flowering and a bit of chlorosis due to the hot weather. The harvest began in the rain, but the rain let up after two days, and afterwards it was particularly hot and dry. Because of the heat, the potential alcohol continued to rise during the harvest, but acid levels did not diminish greatly. Bollinger notes, "'Abundance and quality'...The wine is opulent, generous and fruity."

A bottle of the original disgorgement of the 1964 Dom Pérignon tasted in New York was mature, but not over the top. I noted *"...rich and full bodied, with aromas and flavors of caramel and toasted walnuts. On the palate the wine was soft and silken, definitely mature but holding well."* **** (Tasted 2015)

However, it pays to be cautious, even in '64. A bottle of the original disgorgement of the Dom Ruinart was sound but in decline: *"No mousse and fairly dark in color. The nose was clean, but it was very mature, with a strong note of caramel and wood smoke. On the palate the wine was sweet and didn't show the tension I'd hoped for this vintage. I liked it much less than my fellow tasters I'm afraid, and I felt it was fundamentally sound, but in decline."* * (Tasted 2019)

1965

**

Harvest: October 9th
Yield: 6,900 kg/ha (320,000 barrels)
Area under vine: 15,069 ha
Average potential alcohol: 8.6%
Average total acidity: 10.5 g/l[28]

Total Sales: 78,621,036 btl
France: 58,192,955 btl
Export: 20,428,081 btl
Price of grapes: F 2.91/kg

Overview: Modest quality. Almost, but not quite, saved by good weather at the end.

After slow but steady growth during the postwar period, 1965 marked the first time in the 20th century that more than 15,000 hectares were under vine in Champagne. The year, however, provided a difficult vintage despite a very solid budbreak across all grape varieties. The weather was inconsistent throughout the growing season, beginning with a cold spell during flowering that brought notable millerandage and some coulure, particularly for the Chardonnay. Frequent thunderstorms and hailstorms throughout the growing season led to extensive rot that wiped out hundreds of hectares of production. The season was saved to a certain extent by cool but sunny weather for the harvest, which began very late. In the end, they ripened to just 0.1% more than that the statutory minimum alcohol, with an acidity over 10 g/l. It is notable that this vintage was the culmination of a rather rapid expansion of the statutory limits on yield. These had been 7,500 kg/ha in 1961, and this was raised to 9,000 kg/ha in 1963, and then again to 10,000 kg/ha in 1964, and then finally to 12,000 kg/ha for the first time in 1965. Minimum potential alcohol was fixed at 8.5% by article 26 of the decree of 16 May 1959. I have not had any vintage wines from 1965.

---

28   These are the figures for the must not finished wine in samples taken on the 7th of October

1966

****

Harvest: September 22nd
Yield: 7,000 kg/ha (340,550 barrels)
Area under vine: 15,884 ha
Average potential alcohol: 9.0%
Average total acidity: 9.6 g/l

Total Sales: 86,887,944 btl
France: 64,847,515 btl
Export: 22,040,429 btl
Price of grapes: F 3.10/kg

Overview: An excellent year, but falls just short of '64 and '69.

Yields were reduced at the outset of the 1966 season by winter frosts that followed a rather inconsistent budbreak. Chlorosis set in prior to flowering, limited yields. The flowering itself was quickly and thoroughly completed, although hailstorms during the growing season destroyed approximately 200 hectares of vineyard. The growing season had plenty of rain and little sunshine, but in the end there was a fine September with sunny, dry weather that led to improving conditions and ultimately to a moderate harvest of healthy fruit. Records indicate that there were also 950 barrels of Vin Nature de Champagne[29],

I've had a fortunate number of experiences with the '66 vintage. The first was with a bottle of the original disgorgement of Dom Pérignon. I was shocked at the freshness of the bottle, which was forty years old at that point. From my note: *"The nose shows a softly delicate floral aromas along with a verdant and lush stone fruit and honeydew melon character. Some developed forest floor aromas on the finish are very well integrated into the whole. Wonderful."* ***** (Tasted 2006)

Several years later while working for Christie's in Hong Kong, I had an opportunity to taste the Œnothèque release. I felt that the smoky notes of ground coffee and toast were very typical of of late-disgorged champagne. However, I also noted, *"...a citrusy freshness on the nose that was very impressive. A full complement of mousse, a great acid balance, and a wonderful rich-ness, density and length that is a great validation of the Œnotheque program. Stupendous, and not yet near its peak."* ***** (Tasted 2011)

---

29   This former appellation for still wine from the Champagne region, abbreviated VNC, became Coteaux Champenois in 1974. The appellation can be followed by the names of the following communes for red wine: Bouzy, Aÿ, Sillery, Cumières, Vertus; and by Chouilly or Mesnil-sur-Oger for white wines.

Later that same year I also had a bottle of the original disgorgement of the '66 Krug. As with both bottles of Dom Pérignon, I was struck by the freshness: *"Makes a very fresh impression, with mature aromas of toast, truffle, yeast and mineral and a lively and an impressively youthful finesse on the palate, with a fine and fairly lively mousse, good acid balance, a wonderfully silky texture and great length. Drinking well, still with years to go. Truly wonderful."* ***** (Tasted 2011)

1967

*

Harvest: September 28th
Yield: 8,500 kg/ha
(421,300 barrels+3,600 barrels of VNC)
Area under vine: 16,324 ha
Average potential alcohol: 9.6%
Average total acidity: 9.2 g/l

Total Sales: 93,061,047 btl
France: 68,562,592 btl
Export: 24,498,455 btl
Price of grapes: F 3.75/kg

Overview: A difficult vintage

After an abundant bud-break, there was frost on the 8th of April and the 4th of May that damaged 1,200 hectares of vines. Although the flowering was quick and thorough, there was millerandage across the region. The growing season was afflicted by a severe bout of grey rot. Weather was foul at harvest; the initial date of the 26th had to be postponed, and it eventually began on the 28th. The rain-swollen grapes produced a large total harvest, but the condition of the grapes was not good. Poor quality, and few if any vintage wines remain.

1968
[No Stars]

Harvest: October 3rd
Yield: 7,200kg/ha
(377,500 barrels+1,250 barrels of VNC)
Area under vine: 16,972 ha
Average potential alcohol: 8.6%
Average total acidity: 10.3 g/l

Total Sales: 86,496,902 btl
France: 59,982,335 btl
Export: 26,514,567 btl
Price of grapes: F 3.95/kg

Overview: Even more difficult than the year before.

After another abundant bud-break, Champagne was hit three times by frost in 1968, on the 13th, 18th and 20th of May. The damage was the worst on the Côte des Blancs, although the effects were felt throughout the region, and in total, fruit was lost to over 2,000 hectares of vines. Flowering got off to a slow start but finished quickly, and the vines generally were affected by both coulure and millerandage, decreasing yield by about 10%. Vineyards were further damaged by hailstorms (fortunately limited in damage), and rot, which began in early August and grew in severity through the harvest. The grapes that were picked were in poor condition. By all accounts 1968 was a disastrous vintage. I have never tasted a vintage wine from this vintage and do not expect to see any.

1969
****

Harvest: October 1st	Total Sales: 93,983,820 btl
Yield: 6,100 kg/ha (333,670 barrels)	France: 67,086,841 btl
Area under vine: 17,362 ha	Export: 26,896,979 btl
Average potential alcohol: 9.7%	Price of grapes: F 4.14/kg
Average total acidity: 9.6 g/l	

Overview: An excellent vintage, steadily improving after a poor start.

Budbreak was solid in the vines that had frozen in '68, but less consistent elsewhere, and poor weather in the early spring delayed flowering, which led to coulure and millerandage. Conditions did not improve until mid-July, leading to the worst mildew in a decade and to incidents of several types of rot, all of which reduced yields. Violent thunderstorms and hailstorms occurred throughout the summer, destroying another 900 hectares of vines. Fortunately, it was dry and sunny for the harvest. In addition to the base price for fruit, bonuses were paid to the pickers of 0.25 F/kg for noble grape varieties, 0.10 F/kg for delivery in good and uniform condition, and a signing bonus of 0.50 F/kg, contributing to the steady rise in price for grapes in the region.

I have always loved champagnes from 1969. Although it was not the product of the best growing conditions, the wines have immense charm and continue to please. As with 1966, I have done a comparison of the original disgorgement of Dom Pérignon and the Œnothèque version of the same, this time side-by-side. I note of the original disgorgement *"...a lovely bottle, showing extremely well. On the nose there was a markedly fresh citrus element to the fruit character along with the smoke, mineral and truffle notes that one would expect. On the palate the wine had a weight and power that spoke to the richness of the year without being heavy in any way. A great rival to the '66, with years more time if properly stored,"* ********* while of the Œnothèque, I note *"...pronounced notes of coffee and wood smoke* *that suggest that the influence of the additional time on the lees has transmuted the wine, taking over somewhat the original character of the vintage. Nonetheless, on the palate the wine was effortlessly sophisticated, long and rich, with density, elegance and balance that was truly impressive,"* ***** consistent with my impression of the same wine in the '66 version. (Both tasted 2009)

The wines are marked by a fresh acidity (as they were in '66), which is probably why I love the vintage. Of the late-disgorged Krug Collection I noted *"...very fresh, with tropical fruit aromas, a pronounced mineral side and only a very slightly oxidative note. On the palate the wine was very clean and fresh while not lacking at all in power. Superb."* ***** (Tasted 2011)

Slightly more mature but ravishing was the 1969 "Réné Lalou" from Mumm. I note: *"One of the surprises of the evening, a '69 Réné Lalou was spectacular. The wine showed notes of fresh black truffle, mineral, smoke, cream, and just a hint of butterscotch. On the palate the wine was well balanced and crisp but soft, rich and particularly massive."* ***** (Tasted 2009)

A superb year. The best wines, many tasted fairly recently, are still holding well. This is a year to seek out and to cellar for the future with little reservation.

CHAPTER VIII

1970 – 1979
Dawn of the Modern Era

According to Moët & Chandon Chef de Caves Benoît Gouez, 1969 was the last vintage of the "traditional era" and 1970 was the first vintage of the modern era. Growers and houses were utterly unprepared for the record-breaking abundance of 1970. Some finished wines were even stored on boats lining the Marne. By the end of the decade, the revolution would be essentially complete. Nearly everyone made the transition from fermenting the base wines in cask to fermenting them in stainless steel tanks. Most winemakers also made the transition from doing the second fermentation under cork to doing it under crown cap. Gouez mentioned in a 2019 interview that the liners of the first crown caps were made of cork, which let too much air into the wines. This oxygen uptake means that wines from the early 70s wines are can be lacking freshness or even frankly oxidized. Today crown caps liners are made from PVC combined with a "plasticizer" to make it more flexible. This composition makes it possible to control oxygen uptake very precisely. Beginning in the 1970s, winemakers in Champagne emphasized stability, consistency, and volume. The increasing use of clones in the vineyard, along with the ever-increasing technical mastery of the fermentation process, made the ever-larger harvests possible. This period marked the region's transition from a small, artisanal craft that was barely economically sustainable to a modern, sometimes industrial process that would become the economic engine of the region and one of the most substantial elements of French foreign exchange after aerospace.

    The decade began with great promise, and despite a dip in 1974 following the Arab oil embargo, strong sales generally continued. However, the price of grapes also continued to rise, which more than doubled during the decade. Rising grape prices helped develop the cooperative movement which had begun in the early years of the century. The Centre Vinicole de la Champagne in Chouilly (CVC), formally founded in 1972, is a perfect example. The CVC was initially a group of individual growers, local cooperatives, and regional cooperatives that ultimately included 4,000 growers who worked a combined total of 1,200 ha over 150 villages. It began as a place to vinify and store wines starting with the bountiful harvest of 1970. In time they began to produce their own finished wines, some of which are sold today under the name brand of Nicolas Feuillatte. Feuillatte today is the number three brand globally, selling approximately 11 million bottles each year.

During this period, co-ops strengthened their hand considerably. In general, the négociants didn't own enough land to supply the majority of their grapes, and when interest rates were high (as they were in the '70s), the need to finance purchases of the fruit caused the cost of production to spiral. Many couldn't afford the grapes they needed to supply their demand. Some turned to a seldom-discussed mechanism called *vins sur lattes* to satisfy their needs. In Champagne it is most common to buy unfermented grape juice (must) to produce wine, although sometimes the grapes themselves are purchased directly, and finished base wines may also be purchased. It is also entirely legal to buy bottled wines that have already finished their secondary fermentation, called vins sur lattes. The "lattes" are wooden slats upon which the bottled wines rest while they undergo the aging process. It is generally estimated that sales of vins sur lattes account for 3 − 8% of overall champagne trade. While this may not seem like a large percentage taking the midpoint and multiplying by a total market of 300,000,000 bottles gives 16.5 million bottles produced in this fashion.

Reliance on vins sur lattes means brand owners are ceding control of production to third parties. Furthermore, the wines that they sell as their own are not produced entirely on their premises. Most purchasers of vins sur lattes will give the wines their stylistic stamp through the type and quantity of dosage. However, they usually have little if any input on the initial blend, or how the wine is made. However, the interest for the sellers is evident: finished wine sells at a higher price than base wines, juice, or grapes. Houses often need to source fruit at Champagne's co-ops, and insiders have suggested that some co-ops oblige the négociants—even the most renowned among them—to buy a portion of the total in the form of vins sur lattes. Significantly, in times of oversupply, sales of vins sur lattes can be suspended, as was the case in May of 2020 during the COVID-19 pandemic.

1970

***

Harvest: September 27th
Yield: 13 800 kg/ha
(660,700 barrels+140,600 barrels of VNC)
Area under vine: 17,888 ha
Average potential alcohol: 9.3%
Average total acidity: 8.35 g/l

Total Sales: 102,224,090 btl
France: 71,169,802 btl
Export: 31,054,288 btl
Price of grapes: F 4.27/kg

Overview: A record crop, reliable quality

Solid budbreak followed by good weather at flowering and only minor instances of coulure and millerandage led to a very heavy crop load. There was localized damage from a July hailstorm in the Aube, but in general, growing conditions were exceptional, and bunch weight climbed to very high levels. Because of the size of the crop, harvest was delayed. In the end, however, a very healthy crop was harvested. The INAO granted the growers a derogation, and the authorized limit was increased to 13,800 kg/ha, a record up to this point, giving more than 800,000 barrels, including 660,700 barrels of Champagne and 140,600 barrels of still wine. Growers were also paid record prices for the time, with bonuses of 0.25 F/kg for noble grape varieties and a signing bonus of 0.44 F/kg.

Dom Pérignon Œnothèque drunk in 2014 was marvelous: *"A rich, complex bouquet that marries mineral, smoky, almost saline notes with aromas of butterscotch, truffle, and coffee that develop with time. Silky, subtle, and enchantingly long on the plate."* *****

1970 was a year of quantity as well as quality. The best wines are still vivacious today, and although the renown of the vintage has fallen a bit compared to other stars of the '70s such as 1973 and 1979, it remains a reliable vintage and one to seek out.

1971
***

Harvest: September 18th	Total Sales: 117,342,447 btl
Yield: 5,100 kg/ha (310,400 barrels)	France: 66,012,349 btl
Area under vine: 18,782 ha	Export: 51,330,098 btl
Average potential alcohol: 9.9%	Price of grapes: F 4.66/kg
Average total acidity: 9.6 g/l	

Overview: A challenging year, but some good wines made despite the problems

As is often the case, a bountiful year was followed by a meager one. Following a solid budbreak, frost struck on the 27th and 29th of April, damaging 1,000 hectares of vineyards. Hailstorms on the 27th of April destroyed a further 650 hectares. During the flowering, cold weather led to coulure and millerandage, and during the growing season, chlorosis reduced the vine's efficiency. Most of July was sunny and mild. On the 27th of July and again on the 18th of August, however, hail struck again, destroying a further 2,650 hectares. At the end of the season, both rot and mildew necessitated more than ten treatments with fungicides. In the end, fair weather in September helped dry out the grapes and slow the rot, and the growers were able to bring in a modest harvest.

With the 1971 vintage, I have been able to compare the original disgorgement and the Œnothèque version of Dom Pérignon. Of the original disgorgement, I noted: *"At or just past its peak, with a butterscotch and pineapple fruit along with mineral notes, smoke and truffle: soft mousse, fresh, tangy acidity, creamy texture, and impressive length. The wine is delicious now, although it seems that there is little reason to continue to hold at this point,"* ***

The late-disgorged version, however, I found much fresher: *"Seductive wine, with great aromatic complexity, showing hints of coconut, passionfruit, lime leaf, truffle and smoke on the nose. Very rich – round, lush and slightly fat, with an almost oily texture that was compelling. Drinking well and still intriguing."* ****

A recent bottle of 1971 Lanson was pleasant but had lost its mousse. From my notes: *"The color here was surprisingly bright, but unfortunately no mousse at all. Aromatically the wine was beyond reproach: fresh for its age with a ripe apple and pear fruit, brioche, honey, and a suggestion of ground coffee. On the palate, the wine was surprisingly crisp and holding well except for the unfortunate lack of mousse."* ** (Tasted 2019)

1972
[No Stars]

Harvest: October 12th
Yield: 9,000 kg/ha (557,350 barrels)
Area under vine: 19,384 ha
Average potential alcohol: 8.0%
Average total acidity: 11.9 g/l

Total Sales: 122,065,653 btl
France: 71,245,063 btl
Export: 50,820,590 btl
Price of grapes: F 5.33/kg

Overview: A miserable year. Cold rain prevented rining and rot plagued the vineyards.

Severe frosts and hailstorms conspired to reduce yield in 1972. There was coulure at flowering and rot during the growing season. The harvest could not begin before the 12th of October. Despite this delay, the grapes struggled to ripen. Minimum potential alcohol was set at 8.5%, but in many instances, this was not reached. 1972 is a poor year that produced few vintage wines. Fewer, if any, remain.

1973

*****

Harvest: September 28th
Yield: 11,750 kg/ha (768,000 barrels)
Area under vine: 20,108 ha
Average potential alcohol: 9.1%
Average total acidity: 7.8 g/l

Total Sales: 123,921,586 btl
France: 76,352,157 btl
Export: 47,569,429 btl
Price of grapes: F 6.37/kg

Overview: A superb year, the best of the decade, just edging out 1979 in my view.

Moderate budbreak, followed by very good weather. Hail on the 3rd of May was an exception, but the damage was relatively limited. Quick and thorough flowering with little or no coulure or millerandage, followed by a hot, dry summer, which led to sunburn of the bunches in some instances, particularly in the heatwave of the 10th and 11th of August. Growers thought yield would be low, but this was not to be the case. Rain began to fall on the 18th of September, leading some rot in the Chardonnay. However, it also helped swell the bunches. Given the heat of the summer, acidity was balanced at best, but quality overall was superb.

I am fortunate to have many notes from the '73 vintage. It is interesting to note that most of the Champagnes disgorged at the time of the original release are still showing well, but the developed, mature character is as notable as the character of the vintage itself. In contrast, late-disgorged champagnes can still be very fresh. My very top note is for Dom Pérignon Œnothèque, although the original disgorgement provided similar pleasure. From my note: *"Extraordinary! Amazing definition of fruit flavors, with a great yeasty, toasty, developed side and a lush apple pie fruit. The wine is rich, powerful and complex on the palate, but it still fresh enough to impart a fine sense of balance and length."* ***** (Tasted 2011).

I have fewer notes on 1973 Krug, but this was a great era for Krug. A typical note: *"From the original disgorgement, this bottle of '73 Krug was holding up magnificently well. Despite an almost alarmingly dark color, the wine is still a great pleasure to drink, with notes of honey, almond, toasted brioche, and tropical fruit on the nose. Great power and great finesse."* **** (Tasted 2011)

1973 is a fantastic year for Champagne. The wines are still holding very well today, and you will find many more notes in the first section of this work. The only problem is that many collectors are aware of this, and purchasers will pay a premium for wine from this vintage. If you are interested in mature Champagne, however, this is a vintage to seek out.

1974

**

Harvest: September 28th
Yield: 9,250 kg/ha (608,200 barrels)
Area under vine: 20,773 ha
Average potential alcohol: 8.9%
Average total acidity: 9.3 g/l

Total Sales: 103,025,402 btl
France: 59,336,954 btl
Export: 43,688,448 btl
Price of grapes: F 7.37/kg

Overview: Potential greatness spoiled by rain.

1974 began with a warm winter and early budbreak, followed by almost two weeks of killing frosts throughout the region in April, with the Aube the most affected. There was a slow flowering marked by coulure and millerandage throughout the region. After this somewhat reduced potential, the summer was dry, sunny, and cool, and hopes were high for excellent quality. However, rain set in a month before harvest and continued right up to the picking, bringing with it increasingly severe rot. Quality was decent in the early-maturing sectors but struggled in the others. The minimum potential alcohol was set at 8.5% for the grands crus and premiers crus, but at 8% in the other crus. The harvest produced a total of 608,200 barrels for AOC Champagne and 12,800 barrels in the new appellation of Coteaux Champenois. The price of fruit was handled slightly differently, and the bonus for delivery in "good and uniform condition" was included in the base price. Additional bonuses of 0.45 F/kg were paid for noble varieties and a signing bonus of 78 F/kg.

A '74 vintage Deutz tasted in the spring of 2017 was surprisingly fresh: *"Rich notes of toffee and freshly ground coffee; there is a honeyed note as well—this is mature, but holding well. Better than "interesting," it is still fresh and lively for its age."* ***

1974 is not a vintage like 1973 to search for high and low, but it was certainly a better year in Champagne than it was in Burgundy or Bordeaux, so do not shy away from this year if it is your birth year and you should come across a bottle.

1975

****

Harvest: September 29th
Yield: 9,082 kg/ha
(640,000 barrels total, 7 500 kg/ha in AC)
Area under vine: 21,708 ha
Average potential alcohol: 9.3%
Average total acidity: 9.1 g/l[30]

Total Sales: 126,538,916 btl
France: 71,692,317 btl
Export: 54,846.599 btl
Price of grapes: F 5.33/kg

Overview: A late harvest brought surprisingly strong results.

Spring was cold, leading to a late budbreak and a late flowering. Full flower was not reached on the 26th of June, and milleran-dage was a general problem throughout the region. Following the flowering, however, summer was hot, sunny, and dry. Because of the late start, the harvest began between the 29th of September in the Aube and Haut-Marne. Begun in fine weather, it began to rain during the picking, necessitating careful sorting. Since the favorable conditions of the summer, however, had swollen the bunches, they could be sorted carefully without reducing yields. Bollinger notes: "'Continental climate, but a great wine"

With the '75s in my experience, there is a similar dichotomy to what one finds with the '73s: still holding very well, but those disgorged on release are now often fully mature. From my notes on a well-stored Comtes de Champagne during an extended vertical: *"...dark golden color and a mature, truffley nose with hints of honeycomb, roast walnut, butterscotch, and caramel. On the palate, the wine has a faint mousse, creamy texture, and balanced acidity. This wine is a bit past its prime, yet it is still a delightful accompaniment to food."* *** (Tasted 2009)

A recently consumed jeroboam of Bollinger, however, was sublime: *"The color was extraordinary. The aromas were very fresh, given its age and the vintage. Certainly, there was a predictable maturity and a pronounced yeasty-toasty character that gave the impression of a bit of truffle around the edges. Still, there is a firm emphasis on classic mature champagne flavors here, and*

---

30   Figures for ABV and TA from the last sampling from the vineyard (not finished wine) were taken four days before the harvest. Assuredly, the average ABV went up and TA went down in those four days.

nothing is exaggerated. On the palate, the wine was rich, with a creamy texture, but there was certainly enough acidity to balance the wine, which combined with an impressive depth of flavor to carry it to a lingering finish. Very good indeed." ***** (Tasted 2019)

A recently disgorged Dom Pérignon Œnothèque from the same year also showed well: *"Amazingly fresh, with plenty of fruit, from ripe apples to a more tropical note, all colored with hints of caramel, honey, and freshly ground coffee. Still vigorously bubbly, with crisp acidity, good extract, and impressive length. An exquisite wine with years ahead of it."* **** (Tasted 2012)

A Bollinger RD disgorged several years ago but tasted recently was superb. *From my notes: "The color is just beginning to show some age, but the nose is still very fresh. There are notes of confit lemon peel, ripe apricot, toasted walnuts, and brioche. On the palate, there is a soft and gentle mousse. The acidity is still firm, and the wine is holding extremely well."* **** (Tasted 2019) 1975 is a very good year, and the best wines can still be trusted to be in good condition if properly stored. The character of the year is lush and dense; they are hedonistic and pleasurable wine. It misses the top level by dint of its relative softness of structure.

1976

****

Harvest: September 1ˢᵗ
Yield: 10,359 kg/ha
(774,419 barrels, 9,000 kg/ha in AC)
Area under vine: 22,988 ha
Average potential alcohol: 10.45%
Average total acidity: 7.2 g/l

Total Sales: 152,260,854 btl
France: 81,839,363 btl
Export: 70,421,491 btl
Price of grapes: F 6.78/kg

Overview: A hot, dry year giving wines with balanced acidity at best, but top wines have held well.

The budbreak was generous but drawn out throughout April. Flowering was early, but there was some coulure. After the budbreak, the summer was scorching hot and very dry, shortening the season to just 84 days. Because the year's results were fairly uneven, the region received a derogation to chaptalize and acidify in the same year (normally forbidden). Bollinger, however, was pleased with their results, noting: "Dryness and power."

I have a plethora of notes from the 1976 vintage. I note an interesting difference from the earlier years of the '70s, in that some of the original disgorgements are still very fresh despite the heat of 1976. My note on the '76 Comtes de Champagne: "*...well-preserved elements of candied lemon peel, smoke, and fresh-baked apple tart. On the palate, the wine is holding well, with lively acidity, nice extract, wonderful balance, and good length.*" *********

As one might expect, the late-disgorged bottles also show well. One example, from the '76 Dom Pérignon Œnothèque: "*...a spectacular success, with a nose that hinted of fresh black truffle, a bit of caramel, and a hint of smoke and buttered toast. On the palate, there was a creamy texture enlivened by a still-vibrant fresh acidity. Mature, but not overly so - fantastic fizz.*" ********* (Tasted 2013)

I was also fortunate to drink a late-disgorged magnum of the Clos des Goisses from this vintage: "*Stunningly fresh. Recently disgorged and released bottle with a poignant aroma of* *fresh flowers, lightly toasted almond, a bit of toast and butter, with mineral and saline notes on the nose. On the palate, the wine was very fresh as well, with lively acidity, a graceful balance, and a sumptuous, lingering finish."* ***** (Tasted 2018)

Another pleasant late-disgorged surprise from '76 was the Lanson Red Label: *"Superb - youthful and fresh. There is still a bit of primary citrus about this, with notes of confit lemon peel and honey. The wine paradoxically seems younger than the 1990 vintage tasted alongside. There is a hint of development here but very well integrated. These are impressive results from such a hot vintage. This wine is drinking well now but could hold or even improve with more cellaring. Free to drink, but do not be pressed to do so. Disgorged one year ago".* ***** (Tasted 2019)

Like '75 a very successful vintage, but utterly different in character. Where '75 was balanced and structured, '76 was a hot year with really lush wines, soft acidities, and lots of substance. These can still be holding well if they have been very carefully stored, and late-disgorged bottles are often sumptuous.

1977
**

Harvest: October 6th
Yield: 8,757 kg/ha
(683,000 barrels, 8,500 kg/ha in AC)
Area under vine: 23,980 ha
Average potential alcohol: 8.9%
Average total acidity: 10.0 g/l

Total Sales: 171,099,352 btl
France: 97,552,430 btl
Export: 73,546,922 btl
Price of grapes: F 7.53/kg

Overview: A problematic vintage, plagued by rot and hail, and the sun came too late to help.

A budbreak that dragged on from early March through late April produced mediocre results in 1977. Budbreak was followed by frosts, which damaged about 10% of the vineyards in the Côte des Blancs. Black rot was common, as was downy mildew and grey rot. Several hailstorms occurred throughout the growing season. Poor conditions overall, through the end of August. However, fine weather began in September, and after a bit more than a month of drying out, the harvest began. Despite the terrible growing season, reasonable quality was salvaged. Not generally declared as a vintage year. I have no notes from this vintage.

1978

*

Harvest: October 9th
Yield: 3,678 kg/ha (290,113 barrels)
Area under vine: 24,256 ha
Average potential alcohol: 9.6%
Average total acidity: 11.5 g/l

Total Sales: 187,824,672 btl
France: 112,199,925 btl
Export: 75,624,747 btl
Price of grapes: F 8.86/kg

Overview: A challenging year, with generally disappointing results.

1978 saw poor weather and a short harvest. Not many vintage wines were produced. Budbreak was late and very drawn out, as was the flowering, which continued until the 20th of July, leading to generalized coulure and millerandage. A severe attack of botrytis began at the beginning of the flowering and grew in severity, while hailstorms caused severe if localized damage. The weather remained cold until the very end. The sun finally came out at the end of the season, but it was too late to improve the fruit.

Relatively few notes from '78; I recall several that I did not even write up because of their disappointing nature. From a somewhat mixed review of the '78 Cristal: *"...a bit evolved on the nose, with notes of soy, truffle, and smoke along with a hint of fig and cherry. On the palate, however, the wine was still fresh, with lots of lively mousse, good, firm acidity, and nice length. This wine is decidedly mature, but drinking well now."* *** (Tasted 2012)

Don't confuse 1978 in Champagne with Burgundy! Although they can be similar in some years (such as '76), in others, they are quite distinct. I would be very cautious about exploring any wines from this challenging vintage.

1979

*****

Harvest: October 8th
Yield: 11,061 kg/ha (835,755 barrels)
Area under vine: 24,234 ha
Average potential alcohol: 9.25%
Average total acidity: 8.75 g/l

Total Sales: 183,122,653 btl
France: 114,971,960 btl
Export: 68,150,693 btl
Price of grapes: F 10.91/kg

Overview: A fantastic year, close to 1973 in quality. Wine to seek out.

A cold winter and cool spring delayed budbreak. All sources comment on the relatively severe damage to the vineyards by rabbits. However, the weather beginning in June was very fine, and flowering was successful. August was sweltering, and a few thunderstorms rolled through, creating a bit of pressure from grey rot. There were also localized problems with vine moths and black rot. However, a lovely period of sunny weather in the first half of September eliminated most worries. Because of the slow start, the harvest did not begin until early October.

I have many notes on 1979 Champagne, including the single greatest Champagne I have ever drunk, which is the 1979 Krug Clos du Mesnil. I have had the good fortune to drink four bottles, and all were exceptional. From a representative note: *"Transcendent. Notes of ripe pineapple and coconut, honey, caramel, toffee, truffle, smoke, and spice. Well balanced, with a mousse that was still lively, a velvet, mouth-filling texture, firm acidity, and wonderful length."* *****! (Tasted 2011)

It was a superb year generally for Blanc de Blancs. A bottle of '79 Salon also seduced me: *"...drinking near its peak, with exotic notes of ripe mango, truffle, mineral, smoke and brioche on the nose. On the palate, the wine was lively and vital, and despite its maturity, the wine was showing supremely well, with a lingering finish that was very impressive."* ***** (Tasted 2010)

However, from my tasting, it appears that Pinot Noir was as successful as Chardonnay in 1979. From my note on the Cristal Rosé: *"The '79 Cristal Rose had an unbelievable nose with smoky, ripe black cherry fruit character, hints of baking bread, and a ripe, vinous edge that distinguishes it here. On the palate, all is soft elegance and finesse – the wine isn't lacking power, but the ripeness has given everything a subtle glow. Lovely."* **** (Tasted 2009)

"Regular" Krug disgorged upon release was also quite satisfying: *"Rich, fragrant aromas of tropical fruit led by coconut along with an almost litchi-like sweet fruit character and a pleasant floral note. Well-integrated yeast, along with white truffle and porcini. Elegant and graceful, this is still buoyed by fresh acidity and light body but with an astonishing length."* **** (Tasted 2007)

It does seem in retrospect, however, that I have noted the Krug Collection slightly higher, both in bottle and in magnum. From a representative note: *"Smoky, truffley, and rapier fine, this wine is concentrated and long, both on the nose and on the palate. It has all of the typical Krug signifiers but transcends the idiom with a warmth and generosity seldom seen in the region. Really special."* ***** (Tasted 2011)

I have many happy memories of Champagne from the 1979 vintage. This is a superb year, and the wines are still showing well, both the original disgorgements and late-disgorged versions. In my view, this is a vintage to seek out. Also notable in the 1979 vintage: Lanson Noble Cuvée and Mumm Vintage.

CHAPTER IX

1980 – 1989:
Mergers, Acquisitions, and Growth

At the end of the Trente Glorieuses came another period of expansion that is nearly comparable in scope. Following short harvests in 1980 and 1981, the CIVC decided to augment the planted surface by 500 hectares annually. In 1980 there were just over 24,000 hectares of vines in the region, and by 1989 there were more than 27,000. At the same time, the yield per hectare also continued to increase due to the changes in viticulture that had begun in the 1970s. Commercial expansion continued along with the increases in production, and the 1980s almost seems like the decade when big business invented big Champagne. Some industry leaders had already foreshadowed the trend towards ever-larger firms. Moët & Chandon had been listed on the stock exchange since 1962 and had merged with Hennessy Cognac to form Moët-Hennessy in 1971. The marriage of big business and big Champagne, however, began in earnest in the '80s. The prelude was the acquisition in 1979 of Lanson and Pommery by Belgian fertilizer magnate Thierry Gardinier. By 1984, however, Gardinier had sold both houses to dairy giant Danone. At around the same time, another powerful force in Champagne was coming to the fore: Bernard Arnault. In 1984, Arnault leveraged his family's real-estate business to purchase the holding company Agache-Willot-Boussac which owned the fashion house Christian Dior and the department store Le Bon Marché. As Arnault was building his empire, others were steadily doing the same. In 1985, Joseph Henriot sold Charles Heidsieck to Rémy-Cointreau and Champagne Henriot to Veuve Clicquot. Clicquot was in turn acquired by luggage maker Louis Vuitton the following year, and in 1987 Vuitton merged with Moët-Hennessy to form LVMH. This was at the time the sixth-largest company in France. Alain Cheva¬lier of Moët-Hennessy ran the combined company with Henri Recamier of Louis

Vuitton as vice-chairman. Joseph Henriot was appointed president of Veuve Clicquot.

At the time of the merger, Recamier reportedly distrusted the representatives of the wine and spirits side of the alliance, and invited Arnault to invest in LVMH. Arnault, however, was also close to Alain Chevalier of Moët-Hennessy. It has been said that Chevalier convinced Arnault to form a holding company with Guinness and purchase a 24% stake in LVMH. The follow¬ing year the investment was increased twice more. By January of 1989, the stake was increased to 43.5%. By June of that year, both Recamier and Chevalier were ousted, and Arnault was named chairman. Eventually, the two threads meet: Danone decided to get out of the wine business, and sold Lanson and Pommery to LVMH. Arnault stripped the brands of their valu¬able vineyard holdings and eventually sold them off. Marne et Champagne acquired Lanson in 1991, and Belgian business-man Paul-François Vranken purchased Pommery in 2002.

1980

*

Harvest: October 9th
Yield: 5,289 kg/ha (413,789 barrels)
Area under vine: 24,057 ha
Average potential alcohol: 9.5%
Average total acidity: 10.1 g/l

Total Sales: 180,298,726 btl
France: 116,721,579 btl
Export: 63,577,147 btl
Price of grapes: F 12.75/kg

Overview: A good start, an unfortunate end.

Solid budbreak and vigorous early growth were spoiled by rain and low temperatures that disrupted flowering. The cold and rain continued well into July, delaying the growing season and the harvest. There was a brief spell of perfect weather in September, but the rain started with a vengeance as soon as the harvest was declared. Despite the severe weather, some vintage wines were made. The opinion of quality was somewhat more positive than it is today. Grapes were sold for a base price of 12.75 F/kg, with a bonus of 0.65 F/kg for noble varieties, a 0.10 F/kg "additional payment" to the grape vendors, and a signing bonus of 1,600 F/ha paid after the harvest.

The only note I have from 1980 is for Dom Pérignon: *"...definitely mature, with notes of caramel and truffle on the nose and a mineral, earthy note with time. On the palate, the mousse was a bit soft, as was the acid balance. A pleasant drink to be sure, but this bottle had seen better days."* * (Tasted 2012)

Few wines remain today, and those that do can be uninspiring. Avoid wines from 1980 if you come across them, at least if you are paying.

1981

***

Harvest: September 28th
Yield: 4,353 kg/ha (337,277 barrels)
Area under vine: 23,823 ha
Average potential alcohol: 9.7%
Average total acidity: 9.15 g/l

Total Sales: 156,059,293 btl
France: 98,731,809 btl
Export: 57,327,484 btl
Price of grapes: F 16.00/kg

Overview: Challenging for winegrowers, but some delicious wines were produced.

Budbreak was reduced due to the prior year's problematic conditions, and spring frost further limited yields by nearly 25%. These losses were compounded by coulure and mille-randage during flowering. This combination led to deficient bunch weight, and the harvest began in poor weather. Despite challenging conditions, some excellent wines were made, although because quantities were so low, they are seldom seen today. Grapes sold for a base price of 16 F/kg., with a bonus of 1 F/kg for noble varieties, a 3 F/kg "additional payment" to the grape vendors, and a signing bonus of 1,600 F/ha paid after the harvest.

I have had the good fortune to drink the '81 Krug a number of times, both the original disgorgement and the late-disgorged version. Of the original disgorgement, I note: *"...shows exotic fruits alongside an important component of rich coffee notes, cream, honey, and toasted hazelnut.... None of the fat of the '79 or the '82 here – very elegant and stylish."* **** (Tasted 2007) Predictably, Krug Collection was even fresher: *"An '81 Collection was fresh and young, with a yeasty, mineral bouquet with a pronounced coconut tang. On the palate, the wine had very active mousse, firm acidity, an exquisite balance, and an utterly addictive creamy texture."* **** (Tasted 2011)

Overall, '81 was a good year, but not up to the standard for very good. The top wines should still be in condition if properly stored.

1982

*****

Harvest: September 20th
Yield: 14,054 kg/ha (1,079,453 barrels)
Area under vine: 23,618 ha
Average potential alcohol: 9.2%
Average total acidity: 7.95 g/l

Total Sales: 147,642,304 btl
France: 95,070,384 btl
Export: 52,571,920 btl
Price of grapes: F 17.51/kg

Overview: Sunny and warm temperatures gave both quantity and quality.

After a slow start to the season, nature rewarded the growers with a plentiful harvest in 1982. Despite scattered problems with downy mildew and red spider mites during the growing season, the weather overall was beautiful. Some rain just before harvest helped plump up the bunches, and harvest began under perfect conditions. The total yield surpassed the previous record set in 1970, and yet despite this volume, the fruit ripened well. Chardonnay is generally considered the most successful variety in 1982. The wines are ripe and lush but can surprisingly fresh. 1982 is a vintage that is ready to drink but also one that will continue to hold well.

Given the success of the Chardonnay, the Blancs de Blancs from '82 are predictably attractive. In first place for me, Krug's Clos du Mesnil: *"... mature, but this wine should continue to improve in the bottle: the nose shows a background of chalk and struck flint behind a ripe, very exotic fruit character on the nose and a lush, velvety and decadent feel on the palate. A very regal wine."* **** (Tasted 2010)

Salon from the same vintage was also superb: *"...An exotic bouquet of ground coffee, licorice, and black truffle. A glowing and burnished richness on the palate that is somewhat reminiscent of the wines from '61. In the register of wines from warm years, this is aging very nicely."* **** (Tasted 2011)

Finally, the Taittinger Comtes de Champagne: *"...holding well, rich with tropical, honeyed fruit on the nose and lush, waxy texture with an earthy element on the finish. Impressive concentration and length. One of the greats."* **** (Tasted 2009)

The '82 that I have had most often, however, is the very Pinot Noir-based Krug, and each bottle has ranged from good to absolutely stunning. Of the notes, this is perhaps the most representative: *"The 1982 Krug had a regal richness, with ripe yet restrained aromas of tropical fruit, fresh cream, and brioche. On the palate, the mouthfeel was massive, and the finish was incredibly long. Still youthful."* ***** (Tasted 2010)

Cristal was also lovely, but seemed more advanced: *"...mellow and soft, with a lovely toasty nose with rich notes of black truffle and freshly baked pastry on the nose. On the palate, the wine was waxy and broad, almost slightly fat, but showing a great presence and mouth-filling, velvety texture, and great length."* **** (Tasted 2013)

Finally, a rosé. The '82 Dom Pérignon Rosé was vinous and lush but still delightful: *"...mature but lovely, with a nose of caramel, ripe fig, and plum, along with a suggestion of sous-bois. On the palate, the wine was soft and lush, with a slightly restrained mousse, balanced acidity, and a lovely richness that went on at the end. Ready to drink."* **** (Tasted 2013)

Overall, a superb year. The best of the wines are still vital, and although most are fully mature, they will continue to hold and provide pleasure for years to come. It is a year in Champagne that provided wines that were ripe and rich yet still showing the structure and freshness to provide balance. Also notable in the 1982 vintage: Billecart-Salmon Cuvée Nicolas-Francois, Philipponnat Blanc de Blancs, and the Special Club bottlings from Pierre Gimonnet, Gaston Chiquet, and Paul Bara.

1983

***

Harvest: September 26th
Yield: 15,012 kg/ha (1,094,000 barrels)
Area under vine: 23,903 ha
Average potential alcohol: 8.9%
Average total acidity: 8.65 g/l

Total Sales: 161,047,359 btl
France: 101,950,525 btl
Export: 59,096,834 btl
Price of grapes: F 14.20/kg

Overview: A second year of abundant harvests. Reliable quality, but not the level of 1982.

The year started cold and rainy—growers at the time qualified it as "particularly detestable weather"— delaying budbreak. Flowering proceeded well, however, and a huge crop was set. The weather following the flowering was warm and dry, although there were some issues with downy mildew in the vineyard during the growing season. Early September saw poor conditions, but they improved in the last week of the month. The large size of the 1983 harvest is because there was a der-ogation in the pressing regulations. Growers were allowed to press a hectoliter of juice from 150 kg of fruit, instead of taking that same amount from 160 kilograms of fruit, loosening the requirements by 6.25%.

Despite the abundant harvest, I have few notes from the 1983 vintage. Typical of my experience was a recent magnum of Dom Pérignon: *"More fat and substance than expected, with a rich, lush nose that featured yeast, butterscotch and mineral. The mousse was velvety but still very lively, and the wine was rich and round with extract, surprisingly long."* **** (Tasted 2017)

1984
[No Stars]

Harvest: October 10th
Yield: 9,048 kg/ha (11,000 kg/ha AC)
Area under vine: 24,638 ha
Average potential alcohol: 8.0%
Average total acidity: 10.8 g/l

Total Sales: 188,193,014 btl
France: 116,723,599 btl
Export: 71,469,415 btl
Price of grapes: F 16.10/kg

Overview: Misery after abundance.

Poor weather at flowering led to coulure and rot. Rains continued throughout the growing season and led to grey rot throughout the vineyards. Adverse conditions delayed the growing season, and the harvest did not begin until the 10th of October. It was an instance of "taking the grapes the least affected by rot" in this case. Fruit ripened with difficulty. I have not tasted any vintage wines from 1984, and I can only imagine that very few were produced.

1985

*****

Harvest: September 30th
Yield: 6,827 kg/ha (550,000 barrels)
Area under vine: 25,039 ha
Average potential alcohol: 9.7%
Average total acidity: 8.6 g/l

Total Sales: 194,951,521 btl
France: 125,099,323 btl
Export: 69,852,198 btl
Price of grapes: F 20.60/kg

Overview: A small yield giving wines that are concentrated and fresh.

1985 is a superb year that produced many wines that are still on their way up. A frigid winter saw temperatures as low as -25° C for three days in January, and the cold weather continued through the spring. The winter frosts caused extensive damage to the vineyards, and more than 2,000 hectares had to be re-planted. Vines on the Montagne de Reims were most severely affected. Another hard frost struck at the end of April. Cool weather continued up to the flowering, leading to millerandage, but good weather appeared on the 1st of July. Favorable conditions helped the small crop to ripen well, and bunches gained in weight throughout September. Due to the cold weather and frost, the yield was restricted, but a small second crop of clusters that formed later in the season matured and was picked in late October. Although the yield was more modest than average, it was more than what was predicted earlier in the season.

Blanc de Blancs seem to be aging well, and the best still have plenty of time. A Krug Clos du Mesnil 1985 tasted a couple of years ago was still youthful and very fresh. From my note: *"...a bit closed on the nose, but beginning to reveal its trademark tropical notes along with freshly floral, citrusy and leesy elements behind the mineral and smoke of the initial impression."* **** (Tasted 2009)

1985 Salon seems to be near its peak: *"Opens with an exotic, tropical note, hints of coconut and butterscotch. Great presence and body, yet it lacks the structure and vivacity of the '88. None the worse for this, the wine shows marvelous texture and great nobility. Drinking perfectly now, yet there is plenty of life left here."* **** (Tasted 2014)

My top notes for the '85 vintage, though, come from Krug. I've had the original disgorgement in bottles and magnums, and it has been superb each time. However, the very best note consistently has been from the late-disgorged Krug Collection. From a representative note: *"The '85 Krug Collection at a recent dinner was amazingly rich, with a pronounced and concentrated nose of ripe pear, toast, and smoke. On the palate, the wine was soft and luxurious but still very tightly wound, with bright acidity, great depth of flavor and a wonderful lingering finish. Still youthful, but magnificent!"* ***** (Tasted 2014)

Roederer Cristal from 1985 is also superb: *"Marvelously aromatic. On the initial attack there are lovely, concentrated notes of mineral and smoke that open up with some time in the glass to reveal rich nuanced of tropical fruit and a pleasantly yeasty character. A very fine mousse, balanced acidity, an impressive level of extract, and great length. Wonderful!"* ***** (Tasted 2015)

1985 is indeed a fantastic year. The best wines are still improving, and should continue to age for years to come. A vintage to seek out.

1986

**

Harvest: October 2nd
Yield: 11,582 kg/ha (11,000 kg/ha AC)
Area under vine: 25,427 ha
Average potential alcohol: 9.0%
Average total acidity: 10.0 g/l

Total Sales: 204,920,108 btl
France: 133,126,140 btl
Export: 72,033,143 btl
Price of grapes: F 19.80/kg

Overview: A challenging year, and yet there were some delicious wines made.

Budbreak was late after a cold winter, although without the extremes of the prior year. There were coulure and millerandage at flowering, without grave consequences at his point, but then the vines were beset by vine moths and rot during the growing season. Hail damaged the crop in August. Harvest was late, and although it began with warm temperatures, rain soon began to fall, and strict sorting was necessary, both for rot and ripeness. Given the weather in 1986, it is surprising that any wines have survived, yet there are some delicious examples. The finest in my view is the Krug Clos du Mesnil: *"A spectacular way to begin a recent tasting: intensely exotic, tropical notes on the nose with a well-integrated oxidative note, the wine was very crisp on the palate but never sharp, lovely, and long. One of the top wines of the tasting."* ***** (Tasted 2009)

There was also a lovely Dom Ruinart, made in the old style: *"An enormously seductive complexity, with notes of toasted walnuts, marzipan, orange peel, brioche, and black truffle. Surprisingly lively acidity and a fairly soft mousse, but certainly sufficient. Light in body, yet remarkably persistent on the palate, the wine was wholly satisfying."* **** (Tasted 2006)

Finally, there was the rare Selosse vintage, Anselme's first. The wine was from a private cellar, but the provenance was excellent. Fun to taste, but less compelling on the palate: *"The 1986 Selosse was a rare treat that I had never tasted before. The wine was very complex, mature, and truffley, but unfortunately lacking mousse. More of a history piece than a lively wine, it was more interesting than compelling."* ** (Tasted 2013)

1986 is a vintage to taste for the sake of curiosity unless you have the chance to try the Clos du Mesnil, which has always been superb.

1987
[No Stars]

Harvest: October 10th
Yield: 11,647 kg/ha
Area under vine: 25,646 ha
Average potential alcohol: 8.3%
Average total acidity: 8.6 g/l

Total Sales: 205,159,283 btl
France: 136,349,116 btl
Export: 81,449,242 btl
Price of grapes: F 19.50/kg

Overview: Another difficult vintage.

The springtime saw hail and rain, and there was a hard frost on the 23rd of May. Cold weather and rain disrupted flowering, leading to coulure and millerandage. There was 70% more rain than an average year. During the growing season, growers struggled with grey rot and downy mildew. Due to poor conditions, picking was delayed until the 8th of October, but circumstances did not improve, and growers describing the weather at harvest as "apocalyptic". The harvest dragged on longer than any other year in the decade.

I have few notes from 1987. From Henri Goutorbe: *"Truffles, smoke, and sous-bois; mature with a sweet edge. Not unpleasant, but not much upside to keeping it."* ** (Tasted 2016) A late-disgorged bottle from Mailly Grand Cru was better: *"A complex nose with smoke, earth, and truffle, but holding well in maturity. On the palate, there is freshness and balance. Harvested on the 8th 8.7° potential at picking."* *** (Tasted 2017)

Not a vintage to seek out.

1988

*****

Harvest: September 19th
Yield: 9,650 kg/ha (820,000 barrels)
Area under vine: 26,221 ha
Average potential alcohol: 9.2%
Average total acidity: 9.4 g/l

Total Sales: 239,319,423 btl
France: 149,352,381 btl
Export: 89,967,042 btl
Price of grapes: F 21.45/kg

Overview: A cool year and a short harvest but superb wines showing both acidity and ripeness.

These wines have lasted well, although opinion at the time of harvest was mixed. The winter was warm but wet, and budbreak in late April set the stage for a good season. Hail struck twice in May. The first instance was on the 7th and 8th of May, which caused widespread damage. Hail struck again in the Aube on the 26th. Flowering was quick and thorough, setting a good crop. The vineyards suffered somewhat from chlorosis, grey rot, and downy mildew during the growing season, but these difficulties did not delay the harvest. Picking began under sunny but cool conditions. Luckily, those vines destroyed by hail had time to bud out a second crop of grapes and ripen it to maturity, and thus the total yield was average for the time. It is generally considered most successful for Chardonnay.

My tasting notes for the Blancs de Blancs brim with excitement. The highest praise was reserved for Krug Clos du Mesnil, one of my favorite vintages after 1979. From a representative note: *"Almost a unique experience in the world of wine, the nose is extremely pronounced and complex, showing several layers of aroma, from the yeasty, biscuity, smokiness to the very ripe fruit character with tropical fruit and a distinct coconut edge. On the palate, the wine is full-bodied, luscious with extract, well balanced by crisp acidity, and extremely long."* ***** (Tasted 2006)

The Salon from 1988 is also exquisite: *"A rich mix of smoke, truffle, lime peel, and buttered toast – overall, still very fresh and primary. The acidity is still resolving, and the wine is nervy and fresh, but beginning to open up and show more richness.*

Great finish. This wine will age for literally decades to come – a true classic." ***** (Tasted 2009)

I have also had the Dom Ruinart many times. It is mature now, but still consistently good: *"The 1988 Dom Ruinart Blanc de Blancs showed a wonderful maturity on the nose, with notes of confit lemon, fig, and smoke as well as black truffle, ground coffee, and soy. On the palate, the wine was well integrated but still showing crisp acidity and great length."* **** (Tasted 2017)

The original disgorgement of vintage Krug is also delicious. A typical note: *"The 1988 Krug was very lemony, minerally and fresh on the nose, showing fairly embryonic development. On the palate, the wine was dense and highly structured. With time in the glass, the bouquet developed: first smoky aromas, then tropical fruit notes such as guava and passion fruit, and finally ground coffee. Astonishingly good."* **** (Tasted 2013)

The '88 Cristal is also superb. A recent note is that *"A bit mature for its age, this is showing a rich, mature sweet fruit bouquet of candied pineapple, coconut, toast, and vanilla. The apparent acidity has softened, the mousse was gentle, and the wine had taken on a luxuriously fat feel, with nice length. A brilliant opening to a great meal."* **** (Tasted 2018)

I favor 1988 because of its racy acidity and concentration of flavor. Some, I know, will prefer the richness of warmer years, but based on the pleasure the wines have brought me over the years, I feel 1988 deserves to be ranked as one of the great years. Also notable in the 1988 vintage: Cuvée William Deutz, Veuve Clicquot Brut Vintage, and Dom Pérignon Rosé.

1989

***

Harvest: September 4th
Yield: 11,619 kg/ha (1,023,000 barrels)
Area under vine: 27,088 ha
Average potential alcohol: 10.2%
Average total acidity: 7.3 g/l

Total Sales: 252,314,759 btl
France: 157,999,199 btl
Export: 94,315,560 btl
Price of grapes: F 24.50/kg

Overview: A hot year with an early harvest and a higher yield than 1988.

Some delicious wines were produced in 1989, but others lack the freshness to sustain them. The year began early with summer-like weather in March, and budbreak on the 1st of April. As many growers feared, frost struck on the 26th of April, damaging 6,000 hectares. The frost was most severe in the Marne Valley and on the eastern edges of the Montagne, but it did not affect the Côte des Blancs. Warm weather quickly returned, and flowering began early on the 25th of May. Adverse conditions at the beginning of June slowed flowering, and coulure and millerandage resulted in limited yields. The growing season was very hot, and maturity was advanced. As in 1985, there was a second harvest of bunches that appeared after the April frost.

The Champagnes of 1989 seem to have matured quickly due to the heat of the growing season. One exception to this has been the Clos du Mesnil. While not up to the level of the '88 or the '79, it is among my favorite wines from this year and should continue to age well: *"...a spectacular lemony freshness on the nose and a stunning deep, almost charcoal mineral depth to it, with none of the caramel notes that can afflict the '89 vintage. Still a fine and lively mousse, wonderful density, and great length."* **** (Tasted 2010)

I was working at Moët-Hennessy when the '89 Krug vintage was released. It has always seemed just slightly over the top: *"...rich tropical fruit aromas, a developed toasty note, plenty of cream and butter notes and a hint of caramel. Approaching maturity but gloriously complex. On the palate, the acidity is*

balanced, the weight is significant, but the finish is endless." ***
(Tasted 2005)

The Clos des Goisses provides a similar sensation: *"Rich and ready to drink, with honeyed caramel notes of minerals, toffee, and smoke. On the palate, it is full and round, almost chewy, with fairly soft acidity but impressive length."* *** (Tasted 2007)

In my view, the '89s today are walking a fine line, but the best can be delicious. The vintage is (or was) well-regarded, but many of the wines have not aged well.

CHAPTER X

1990 – 1999:
Pricing and Pressing

The decade of the 1990s was a tumultuous one for the champagne industry. It began with tension between the growers and the houses but ended on a happy note for all concerned as volumes reached record levels in advance of millennium celebrations. 1990 was the first year that the CIVC did not set a fixed price for the sale of grapes by the growers to the houses. This meant the end of the interprofessional contract that had served the industry well since it was adopted in 1959. Among the reasons for this change is the fact that fewer growers were entering into the contract as more of them sold more wine on their own. Another reason is that the négociant houses disliked the principle of indexing of the price of grapes to the average price of a bottle. For ten years beginning in 1990, the CIVC set an indicative price and contracts were of a synchronized duration.

From this point on, however, the price would not be fixed, but freely negotiated, using the indicative price as a guide. In parallel to the abandonment of the interprofessional contract, many customary bonuses were eliminated. Accordingly, the CIVC set the indicative price at a level of nearly 20% above the price fixed for 1989. As one might expect, prices rose dramatically during the first year of the new system. The increase in the price of grapes caused producers to raise prices, which cut into volumes. This slowing in volume was intensified as the first Gulf War brought on an economic slowdown. 1990 represented a decline in sales volume of slightly more than 6%, and 1991 represented a further decline of more than 10%.

Two developments in the 1990s led to an improvement in the quality of the wine. The first was an adjustment in the pressing regulations[31]. The amount that winemakers could

---

31   See Glossary for more information about presses and pressing.

press from a given quantity of grapes (called the pressing fractions) was always regulated. The quantity allowed related to the number of 205-liter barrels that could be filled (a barrel size unique to Champagne). The first pressing, known as the cuvée, was ten of these barrels, or 2050 liters. Before 1990, there were two barrels of juice from pressing the grapes again, called *première taille* (410 liters), and one barrel of *deuxième taille* for an additional 205, giving a total of 2,665 liters. From 1990, however, the amount of juice that winemakers could press was reduced. The deuxième taille was forbidden, although the première taille was increased slightly from 410 liters to 500 liters. This meant that today there are 2050 liters of cuvée and 500 liters of taille for 2550 liters (102 liters per 160 kg of fruit). This reduction in the final yield improved wine quality since the must pressed at the end of the process has less structure and body than that pressed at the beginning.

A second development of the '90s that allowed for improved quality was the creation of the qualitative reserve. This was a refinement of a system called *"blocage"* that had existed in theory since 1938. 1938 was the first year that supply drastically exceeded demand, and the growers and the houses worked together to store some of this wine and reestablish equilibrium in the market for grapes. During the years of the interprofessional contract, this surplus was purchased by a specially-constituted *Société d'Intervention de la Champagne Viticole.* This was a limited liability company owned and operated equally by representatives of the growers and the négociants. The company then re-sold the wine when supplies were low. Beginning with 1982, the CIVC decreed that a portion would be set aside and not used for AOC Champagne wines. This policy became officially known as the qualitative reserve with the 1998 vintage. From 2007, it became known as the individual reserve (Volume Complémentaire Indivduel in French, or VCI). The VCI allows each producer to manage his reserve and to further push quality by "trading" higher-quality wines into the reserve and sending lower-quality wines for distillation. The amount of the reserve is determined each year by the CIVC and then confirmed by legislation. The base wines in the reserve are not entitled to the appellation "Champagne" while they are in the quality reserve. They become AOC Champagne only when they have been made into finished Champagne. Along with the creation of the VCI, the total permissible ceiling was increased to 15,500 kg/ha.

These two tools gave the champagne producers the ability to manage the Champagne market better and to improve quality at the same time. In 2000, Brussels removed the ability to set even an "indicative" price, however, and since this time, the market has been free—and grape prices have continued to rise.

1990

****

Harvest: September 11th
Yield: 11,963 kg/ha (11,000 kg/ha AC)
Area under vine: 27,542 ha
Average potential alcohol: 11.0%
Average total acidity: 8.0 g/l

Total Sales: 237,105,809 btl
France: 152,318,711 btl
Export: 84,787,098 btl
Prix Indicatif: F 32.00/kg

Overview: Nearly universally acclaimed, the year produced very ripe wines that are maturing now.

After a warm, wet winter, there was early budbreak, followed by frost on the 5th and 19th of April, affecting 45% of the vines throughout the region. However, since the budbreak was copious, the final impact on yields was negligible. Flowering took place in mid-June, with vines somewhat affected by coulure and millerandage. Although temperatures and rainfall were average, 1990 was the sunniest year in a quarter-century. Because of the frost, maturity was uneven, and picking began first for Chardonnay and almost a week later for black grapes. However, late-August rain August caused some difficulty with rot, and some villages were allowed to pick early. As often with a frost year, a second generation of grapes appeared and ripened later.

1990 is often seen as one of the great years for Champagne. Bollinger notes: "A replica of the '28," and the best wines are indeed superb, and retain their vigor. However, several wines seemed to peaked early and have begun to decline. One example of this is the Krug 1990. Some bottles of this have been fresh and youthful, but the wine (released only in 2004) has always seemed decadently lush. Typical of my notes for this wine: *"...perfumed on the nose, with ripe tropical fruit, almost pineapple in character, hints of smoke, and a developed hint of white truffle. On the palate, the wine impresses with its ripeness, showing delicate mousse, enormous extract, and a very long finish,"* ****. However, on more than one occasion, I have noticed maturity more consistent with the following: *"Roasted aromas of caramel and butterscotch, it is soft and rich, with a decadently silky texture and a lingering finish. More* *mature than the '88, and probably at its peak. Drink rather than cellar."* *** (Tasted 2014)

Results have also been mixed for Taittinger Blanc de Blancs Comtes de Champagne. Some have seemed mature: *"...showing its age, with straw yellow color, fairly mature creamy oxidative notes on the nose and a silken softness on the palate."* (Tasted 2013) However, Salon has kept its freshness: *"Thrilling, with a crazy profusion of aromas that ranged from coconut and pineapple to toast, smoke, flint, freshly roast coffee beans and a hint of caramel. Impeccably fresh, with a lively yet silken-textured mousse, crisp acidity, and a substantive finish. Drinking well now, this Champagne has the stuffing to age for the long haul."* ***** (Tasted 2011)

1990 is seen as a classic vintage in Champagne, and I imagine many observers would automatically ascribe five-star status to this vintage. For me, the wines from 1990 have often seemed over-the-top rich to me, and many strike me now as fully mature, and this is the reason that I have come down on the side of four-star as opposed to five-star.

Also notable in the 1990 vintage: Clos des Goisses, Dom Pérignon (the original disgorgement, and the Œnothèque, and the Rosé), Pol Roger Cuvée Sir Winston Churchill, Dom Ruinart Blanc de Blancs, Larmandier-Bernier Cramant Grand Cru.

1991
[No Stars]

Harvest: September 11th
Yield: 11,228 kg/ha
Area under vine: 27,943 ha
Average potential alcohol: 9.2%
Average total acidity: 7.9 g/l

Total Sales: 213,239,497 btl
France: 136,225,162 btl
Export: 77,014,335 btl
Prix Indicatif: F 30.00/kg

Overview: A challenging year, devastated by frost.

Hard frosts on the 17th, 21st, and 24th of April wreaked havoc in the vineyards. More than half the total vineyard area was affected, and more than one third destroyed. Sunshine was scarce after the frost, and conditions were wet and cold. This poor weather delayed the flowering into July, and the vines were behind schedule. There was coulure due to spotty weather, but after July, conditions improved and it was sunny, mild and dry. From the third week in September, however, the difficulties began anew, with rain that diluted the fruit and caused issues with grey rot, above all in the Chardonnay. In the end, dilute and lacking character, this was a very challenging vintage. To make matters worse, the second crop that comes after a frost did not mature because of the season's delay and could not be used.

The only '91 I remember tasting was a Clos des Goisses disgorged à la volée by Charles Philipponnat at the winery in 2004, thus a dozen years after the harvest. He wanted to show that some good wine was made in 1991, and he demonstrated his point conclusively. From my note: *"On the nose, it showed a deep autolytic character with attractive notes of smoke, petrol and ripe tropical fruits. On the palate, it was round in texture with a rich, almost viscous character and impressive length.."* ****

A vintage you will probably never see, and it's just as well.

1992

**

Harvest: September 17th
Yield: 11,844 kg/ha (9,000 kg/ha AC)
Area under vine: 28,516 ha
Average potential alcohol: 10.00%
Average total acidity: 7.8 g/l

Total Sales: 219,412,918 btl
France: 142,648,795 btl
Export: 76,764,123 btl
Prix Indicatif : F 24.00/kg

Overview: A hot, soupy year. Modest quality, with a few stand-outs.

Despite a warm winter, budbreak was delayed, and then struck by hailstorms, although damage was minimal. After the flowering, the weather was hot and wet, leading to rot and mildew in the vineyards, with Pinot Noir particularly affected. The poor weather carried right through the year, and the vintage is considered better for Chardonnay. Bollinger notes: "A hot year for a Meursault."

Indeed a modest year. However, since it is the year of my marriage, I have drunk many of the Champagnes from this vintage. My standby for the last several years has been magnums of late-disgorged Clos des Goisses. From my notes: *"Mature on the nose, but not over the top, with notes of toasted brioche and walnuts gently shaded with truffle and ground coffee. On the palate, the mousse is holding well, and the acidity is balanced but sufficient to carry the wine."* **** (Tasted 2014)

My favorite '92, however, will always be the Krug Clos du Mesnil. When I passed the Master of Wine exam in 2004, I was given a bottle of the 1992 vintage by my employer, so there is a sentimental as well as hedonistic attachment to this vintage of this wine. From my note: *"Primary notes of lemon zest, green apple, freshly buttered toast, and fresh white flowers – complex, without discernable development yet: a wine for the long term. Clean, crisp, and light in body while at the same time coating the palate in a seductively silky fashion. Ethereal, yet not lacking in power."* ***** (Tasted 2004)

Unless you were married or born in 1992, you might not seek out these wines. However, I can assure you that well-stored examples are still in excellent shape, and I would certainly be a buyer of the Clos du Mesnil any time it came up.

Also notable in the 1992 vintage: Dom Pérignon and the Vilmart Cœur de Cuvée.

1993

**

Harvest: September 8th
Yield: 10,379 kg/ha (8,400 kg/ha AC)
Area under vine: 29,183 ha
Average potential alcohol: 9.2%
Average total acidity: 8.1 g/l

Total Sales: 229,089,728 btl
France: 152,669,094 btl
Export: 76,420,634 btl
Prix Indicatif: F 20.50/kg

Overview: A promising year spoiled.

A warm, wet winter and a normal budbreak were followed by a period of rapid growth. Due to the winter conditions, mildew was present early in the year, necessitating frequent treatments. There was a hail storm on the 11th of May, but fortunately, little damage. Flowering and fruit set were both early, and a good harvest was predicted. Weather was warm and dry, and there were some instances of chlorosis. However, the steady, heavy rain that began to fall in September led to a dilution of the fruit and, eventually, rot. Because of the swollen grape bunches, many growers had to leave fruit in the vineyard without harvesting it to respect the limits on yield. In 1993, a law was passed fixing the limit for the yield at 10,400 kg/ha.

Most of the '93s I have had were already mature ten years ago. The original disgorgement of Dom Pérignon struck me ten years after the vintage as already fairly tired: *"Rich, soft aromas of roasted hazelnut, fresh butter, and exotic fruits. Softer and richer than the late-disgorged version, and shows lower apparent acidity. Not unpleasant, but past its peak and ready to drink,"* *** (Tasted 2003)

Dom Ruinart was also showing its age reasonably early on: *"...beginning to mature, with ripe and dried apricot fruit character and hints of marzipan and dulce de leche on the nose. On the palate, the wine shows a balanced acidity and moderate length."* *** (Tasted 2007)

Not a year to seek out or to lay down.

1994
[No Stars]

Harvest: September 15th
Yield: 9,577 kg/ha (9,000 kg/ha AC)
Area under vine: 30,045 ha
Average potential alcohol: 9.1%
Average total acidity: 8.4 g/l

Total Sales: 246,924,948 btl
France: 157,085,789 btl
Export: 89,839,159 btl
Prix Indicatif: F 21.25/kg

Overview: A difficult year.

For the first time in the post-phylloxera era, there were more than 30,000 hectares under vine in Champagne. A rainy spring followed a wet winter. There was frost on the 15th and 19th of April and hail on the 21st of May. The first part of the growing season was dry and sunny, but mildew was set in the bunches. When the rains started up again in September, it led to a high incidence of rot and mildew in the vineyards, and conditions did not significantly improve throughout the harvest. Grey rot of at least moderate intensity was noted over 14% of the vineyard as a whole, the most widespread incidence in recent years. Harvest began under poor conditions. I have no record of tasting any vintage 1994 wines.

In all likelihood, you will see few vintage wines from 1994.

1995

****

Harvest: September 18ᵗʰ
Yield: 10,986 kg/ha
Area under vine: 30,7097 ha
Average potential alcohol: 9.4%
Average total acidity: 9.0 g/l

Total Sales: 249,294,188 btl
France: 157,908,136 btl
Export: 91,386,052 btl
Prix Indicatif: F 22.25/kg

Overview: A very good year, widely vintaged.

Another warm, wet winter was followed by a fairly early budbreak. There was frost on the 20ᵗʰ and 21ˢᵗ of May, with approximately 570 hectares of vines damaged. Weather in June was warm and sunny, and flowering was early and thorough. The early growing season was warm and wet, and rot and mildew set in. Professionals in the field said that the struggle against mildew was the most severe in almost 50 years. The key to producing quality wine in 1995 was an early and vigorous fight against these dangers, and sorting effectively at harvest. Bollinger notes, "To the devil with the malo," and none of their wines did malolactic fermentation.

Overall '95 was better for Chardonnay than for Pinot Noir, in part because the thicker skins were more resistant to the mildew pressure. In my experience, the Blancs de Blancs from 1995 have held up well. I have been consistently impressed with the Clos du Mesnil from this year: *"The wine shows an almost impossibly exotic passion fruit character, with notes of ripe mango and coconut, but light, crisp body, silky mouthfeel, and great length."* ***** (Tasted 2011) I have been hardly less enthusiastic about the '95 Salon: *"A pronounced and elegant lemony fruit is beginning to develop complexity, with a hint of truffle and smoke. Remarkably full and round for a blanc de Blancs champagne, and showed both finesse and power along with very good length,"* ***** (Tasted 2013)

Of the Pinot-based wines, Krug has always impressed me. From many, many notes: *"...notes of citrus and lemon giving way to brioche, toasted hazelnut, and mineral only with time in the glass.*

Rich and powerful, with a lot of structure and loads of extract in reserve. This wine should be one for the ages – a magnificent effort." **** (Tasted 2014) Bollinger RD has also been easy to love: *"Great aromatic complexity, with notes of smoke, minerals, and chalk, followed by truffle and earth and finally by ripe tropical fruit character. Full-bodied and rich, balanced by fresh acidity and lively texture, with a complex and generous finish."* **** (Tasted 2012)

In my view, 1995 has always stood in the shadow of the racy, controversial 1996. However, this is a pity since 1995 is a lovely vintage and worthy of laying down for decades to come.

Also notable in the 1995 vintage: Dom Pérignon (both the original disgorgement and the Œnothèque), Charles Heidsieck Blanc des Millénaires, Pol Roger Winston Churchill, Taittinger Comtes de Champagne Rosé.

1996

*****

Harvest: September 16th
Yield: 10,356 kg/ha
Area under vine: 30,711 ha
Average potential alcohol: 10.3%
Average total acidity: 10.0 g/l
Average gluconic acid: 0.02 g/l

Total Sales: 255,871,575 btl
France: 160,677,346 btl
Export: 95,194,229 btl
Prix Indicatif : F 24.00/kg

Overview: A great year, if somewhat controversial.

Universally acclaimed early on as great both in the region and in the press, it produced some truly spectacular wines. However, some observers believe some wines have either not lived up to their promise or have peaked. I do think, however, that the best of these wines are truly exceptional, and some must be counted among the most exceptional efforts of the century.

After a cold snap with temperatures descending as low as -20° C in some areas during February, winter was cool but not cold. Budbreak occurred from the 20th of April in most villages. There were hard frost and hail on the 17th of May. The weather was fine in June, except for the period of flowering, and Chardonnay especially suffered a bit of millerandage. The early growing season was not uniform, with alternating periods of warm and cold, dry and wet. However, the weather was more cool than warm at the critical moments in the vine's life: budbreak, flowering, and harvest. The weather stabilized in September, with sunny days and cool nights, allowing the grapes to continue to ripen while conserving their acidity. Harvest began in relatively cool weather. Although there was some rain before the harvest, a strong wind from the north kept the fruit healthy and preserved acidity. Grey rot of moderate intensity affected approximately 9% of the vineyard on average, although it was only 3% for Chardonnay.

1996 was also the first year that the level of gluconic acid was widely measured. This compound is produced by the oxidation of the aldehydes found in glucose. It usually is present in only trace amounts in wine made from healthy grapes.

However, it is much more prevalent in grapes affected by botrytis, and it can also form through the action of acetic acid bacteria. For this reason, it was proposed as a marker for the health of the grapes (referred to somewhat technically as their "sanitary condition").

I have had the good fortune to taste the '96 vintage widely. In my view, some wines stand above the rest. The first among these is Krug Clos du Mesnil. The best bottles of '96 Clos du Mesnil are truly profound. I think that initially, the wine was slow to open, but that now it is at its seductive best. From my notes: *"...notes of tropical fruit and lime peel on the nose along with a fresh, primary floral element along with an under-current of mineral notes and a toasty brioche character with time. Fresh, clean, round, rich texture, and firm acidity. Supremely light and seductively persistent."* ***** (Tasted 2008) Like Clos du Mesnil, the '96 Salon was slow to open. However, once it did, the fireworks started: *"Intense citrus, almost herbal nose with notes of mineral, smoke, and a truffle hint. Tense and focused, with a rapier-like acidity, there is an expressive fruit opening up on the palate, incredible finesse, and a great lemony length. Stupendous potential."* ***** (Tasted 2008)

Nearly at the same level is the vintage from Selosse: *"Ripe apricot fruit with a hint of smoke and a suggestion of flaky pastry on the nose. It is substantial and solid, yet still very fine, with great length and a creamy, dense texture. This wine must be drinking near its peak, yet I can certainly see it improving for at least another decade."* *****. (Tasted 2009) Another wine to mention in almost the same breath is the less well-known Diebolt-Vallois Fleur de Passion: *"...an exotic nose, with notes of ripe tropical fruits, white flowers, and candied citrus on the nose and a ripe, honeyed minerality on the palate. This is marvelous wine that will age for decades to come."* ***** (Tasted 2007)

Among the Pinot-based wines, there were also a lot of marvelous wines. Perhaps the greatest of these is the Bollinger Brut Vieilles Vignes Francaises: *"...toasty and super-rich on the nose, with notes of almonds and a hint of red berry fruit. On the palate, the wine was creamy, dense, very vinous, and astonishingly* *long. More about power than finesse, this is undeniably one of the great champagne experiences out there."* ***** (Tasted 2009)

Finally, the rosés. As noted above, perhaps the best of them is the Dom Pérignon rosé. However, there are several other delicious wines. I was impressed on several occasions with the precision and finesse of the Dom Ruinart Rose *"...[made from] 18% pinot noir from north-facing vineyards in Verzy and Verzenay, and the rest is Chardonnay from around the region. The wine shows delicate notes of dried roses, biscuits, and marzipan on the nose and a silky generosity on the palate, with a firm acidity without being overly tart."* **** (Tasted 2013)

One wine that I think typifies the doubts about the '96 vintage is the Veuve Clicquot La Grande Dame. This wine was delicious on release (particularly in large format), but very quickly began to show a ripe, oxidative tendency and a lack of freshness. Noted many times, as I worked for them during the time of its release, and this is perhaps the best note: *"Initially floral and forward on the nose, with a lot of primary fruit. Subsequent notes remark on richer, creamier characters in the nose and on the palate, lending richness. Later notes remark already on butterscotch and caramel. Softer than some years, this is very attractive—complete and round—but softer than one would expect from this year. Drink now"* *** (Tasted 2005)

Connoisseurs are still arguing about 1996, but I refuse to come down on the side of the haters. Frankly, I have had too much pleasure from too many wines to rank this as anything but five-star status. While I recognize the truth in what some commentators say about 1996, I am always willing to roll the dice for this vintage because when it is good, it is very, very good.

Also notable in the 1996 vintage: Krug, Louis Roederer Cristal (the regular and the Rosé), Pol Roger Winston Churchill, Dom Pérignon (original disgorgement and Œnothèque), Philipponnat Clos des Goisses, Dom Ruinart Blanc de Blancs, Taittinger Comtes de Champagne (Blanc de Blancs and Rosé), Gimonnet Cuvée Millésime de Collection, Bollinger Grande Année, Perrier-Jouët Belle Epoque, and the Billecart-Salmon Clos St.-Hilaire.

1997
**

Harvest: September 12th
Yield: 9,402 kg/ha
Area under vine: 30,547 ha
Average potential alcohol: 10.2%
Average total acidity: 8.5 g/l
Average gluconic acid: 0.05 g/l

Total Sales: 269,039,611 btl
France: 165,154,959 btl
Export: 103,884,679 btl
Prix Indicatif : F 24.00/kg

Overview: Somewhat dilute and lacking in concentration.

The year began with winter as cold as -20°C. Temperatures warmed up quickly after that, predictably leading to frost, which hit on the 7th of April and again on the 8th of May. The warm weather advanced ripening, and this trend continued right up to an early flowering that began on the 10th of June. Cooler weather and rain set in during flowering, bringing with it coulure, millerandage, and mildew. July was dry, but August brought stormy weather, particularly on the 7th, and again at the end of the month. September generally was dry and sunny with cool nights, and harvest began under clear skies. Grey rot of moderate intensity affected approximately 5% of the vineyard on average, more or less evenly across the main grape varieties.

'97 was not widely vintaged. There were a few notable wines, however. Salon is perhaps the most successful of the Blanc de Blancs: "...*great balance between cream and lemon notes on the nose – pleasant, friendly, soft yet very interesting. The wine shows a discreet mousse and a vibrant yet crisp and elegant feel on the palate.*" **** (Tasted 2015)

One pleasant surprise of the vintage was the Lanson Noble Cuvée: "...*more impressive than previous outings. It opens with a lemon peel nose accented with smoke, toast, and cream. The mature toasty character is never overdone but very well integrated. Silky but still firm. Should continue to age quite well.*" **** (Tasted 2016)

1998

****

Harvest: September 10th
Yield: 12,926 kg/ha (10,400 kg/ha AC)
Area under vine: 30,370 ha
Average potential alcohol: 9.8%
Average total acidity: 8.1 g/l
Average gluconic acid: 0.07 g/l

Total Sales: 292,419,930 btl
France: 178,965,956 btl
Export: 113,453,974 btl
Prix Indicatif : F 25.00/kg

Overview: An abundant harvest with good quality, giving soft and pleasant wines.

Winter was generally mild, although there were periods of hard frost throughout the spring. Budbreak occurred in early April. Two weeks later, frost hit on the 13th and 14th, destroying 600 hectares of vines and 2,000 hectares damaged in all, with the Côte des Blancs affected the most. The rest of the month and the beginning of May were cool, and after a brief respite, cool weather returned in June, although this did not disrupt flowering. July was overcast, and August was intensely hot, causing the grapes to sunburn. Somewhere from 5 – 10% of the crop was lost when grapes dried by the heat dropped in the vineyard. However, this deficit was compensated by heavy rains in early September that swelled the grapes, lowering acidity. Harvest was interrupted by heavy rain. The growers who picked late did well, as clement weather returned later in September, raising the harvest's potential alcohol. Grey rot of moderate intensity affected approximately 7% of the vineyard on average, more or less evenly across the main grape varieties. It is generally considered that the Pinot Noir was the most successful varietal in 1998.

Among the Pinot Noir-dominant wines, the Krug showed well early on, with potential to age: *"A triumph, with a tremendous concentration on the nose of ripe tropical fruits, mineral, smoke, toast, and some slightly oxidative notes that make the wine very appealing. On the palate, it is firmly structured, but not as mouth-puckeringly acidic as 1996. Great balance and an elegant, persistent finish make this a great champagne."* ***** (Tasted 2014)

However, despite the success of Pinot Noir in '98, Clos du Mesnil figures among the wines of the vintage, surprisingly approachable and open even in its youth: *"...notes of smoke, yeast, mineral and tropical fruit. A very lively mousse and a fine texture along with a nice density and impressive length. This wine makes an immediate impression as a serious contender – less acid and less backward than the '96; it still warrants decades of aging."* ***** (Tasted 2013)

For me, '98 is a year on the cusp between *** and ****. It is only really thinking about the wines themselves that I chose in retrospect to err on the side of enthusiasm. Initially, I had perhaps followed the received opinion about a big vintage, lacking concentration. However, the more '98s I drank, the better I liked them. There is still potential for further improvement for the top wines over twenty years, and for me, this is the hallmark of an outstanding vintage.

Also notable in the 1998 vintage: Roederer Cristal Rosé, Taittinger Comtes de Champagne Blanc de Blancs, Dom Ruinart Blanc de Blancs, Billecart-Salmon Cuvée Nicolas Francois, Pierre Peters Brut Cuvée Spéciale Les Chétillons, Pierre Gimonnet Special Club.

1999

**

Harvest: September 15ᵗʰ
Yield: 12,989 kg/ha (12,000 kg/ha AC)
Area under vine: 30,255 ha
Average potential alcohol: 9.9%
Average total acidity: 6.4 g/l
Average gluconic acid: 0.05 g/l

Total Sales: 327,039,063 btl
France: 190,449,776 btl
Export: 136,589,287 btl
Prix Indicatif : F 25.50/kg

Overview: Potential greatness spoiled by rain at harvest.

Another big harvest, but this time grapes swelled with water. Even the ordinarily sanguine "Vigneron Champenois" refers to 1999 as "The Year of Storms and Tempests." A mild winter led to budbreak early in April. May saw hailstorms, but fortunately, they were localized in nature; about 500 hectares were affected. Luckily, there was no frost at all despite the early budbreak. The early growing season saw reasonably mild temperatures and some rain (although no excess). After veraison, the weather was very dry, but not quite to the point of drought conditions. Rains in September caused the bunches to swell and acidity to drop. The harvest began in the rain. Grey rot of moderate intensity affected approximately 7% of the vineyard on average, but more so among both Chardonnay and Meunier than Pinot Noir.

Bollinger Vieilles Vignes Francaises gets my vote for the wine of the vintage: *"...surprisingly accessible, with a ripe, toasty nose of apples, hazelnut and fresh cream with a mineral undercurrent. On the palate the acidity was lively, yet the wine seemed round and soft, with a luxuriant mousse and great length."* **** (Tasted 2012) Another lovely grande marque success was the 1999 Pol Roger Winston Churchill: *"Showing well, with a nose of ripe apple, cream, toast, and hints of coconut milk and fresh flowers at the end. On the palate, the wine had a balanced acidity, a fine, persistent, gentle mousse, and a pleasantly silky finish. Very elegant, will hold for another decade at least."* **** (Tasted 2014)

Among the Blanc de Blancs from 1999, Salon is undoubtedly the finest. *"Rich and vibrant with a pronounced minerality and a piercing, lemony fruit. Super-concentrated, there is crisp acidity, full body, lots of extract, and great length. 1999 looks to be a fairly early-maturing vintage."* **** (Tasted 2014)

After having prepared the wine, Krug decided not to release the 1999 Clos du Mesnil. However, there were some lovely grower Blanc de Blancs released from the 1999 vintage. Chief among these is the Vieilles Vignes de Cramant from Larmandier-Bernier. *"...shows a toasty nose full of minerally lemon peel notes with a savory edge. On the palate, the wine was crisp, yet rich. Firm acidity carried the wine to a long, lingering finish."* **** (Tasted 2016) I was also impressed with the Cuvée l'Apôtre from David Leclapart: *"This barrel-fermented wine is produced without dosage, and shows on the nose very rich autolysis and a crisp verve on the palate and impressive length. Richer developed aromas are well-integrated and there is no overt oxidative character."* **** (Tasted 2016)

In sum, not a year to seek out, but not one to despise out of hand, and wines from top growers should still be showing well.

CHAPTER XI

2000 – 2009
The Green Revolution

After the high-water mark for shipments at the millennium, the inevitable dip. This was to be expected, but it was still painful since orders were down more than 22% in 2000 compared to 1999. This decline in shipments was due to distributors loading up on inventory in advance of the millennium celebrations in response to fears of a shortage that never materialized. After this momentary pause, however, shipments began to rebound almost immediately. By 2004, the region had recrossed the threshold of 300 million bottles sold, and by 2007, shipments exceeded those of 1999 by 3.6%. Ultimately sales reached 338.8 million bottles. This was a new high-water mark that has not been exceeded since this time.

  As alarming as this is to producers, there are other developments that are cause to celebrate. Chief among these are the strong and continued efforts to make the Champagne region a model of environmental protection. As documented in previous chapters, Champagne's winegrowers had gradually come to rely on heavy regular doses of synthetic fertilizers, fungicides, insecticides, and herbicides. The climate in Champagne is cold and wet, and growers face many climate-induced challenges, including rot, mildew, and similar diseases. It had become the habit over many years to treat for these in advance of problems, and to use broad-spectrum pre-emergent herbicides to remove cover crops. Purified urban compost from Paris, known as *"boues de ville,"* was also used to enrich the soil.

  Boues de ville were used from the 1950s through the 1990s. For many years, they were seen as preferable to manure, largely because of the lack of smell. The process, however, left bits of trash and plastic bags on the surface of the vineyards. These majestic sites, denuded of grass, began to look like a bleak moonscape. There was also speculation that the boues de ville left traces of cadmium, mercury, and toxic metals resulting from contamination from batteries, thermometers, and other types of waste. In 1999 their use was prohibited and the region began a series of initiatives to increase respect for the environment. The first initiative, called *viticulture raisonée,* was a specific program promoted by the CIVC. This program included five actions, each of which would be measured and independently verified.

The first action was the implementation of biological pest control (using bugs to fight bugs). This was accompanied by a steady, measured reduction in the number of synthetic pesticides and fertilizers used following a set of goals that were independently tracked. At the same time, the grower needed to work for the preservation of biodiversity and the natural land-scape of the region. Finally, the system mandates a reduction in the carbon footprint and the treatment of wastewater footprint as well as a reduction in waste produced and packing materials. Since the year 2000, considerable progress has been made using this voluntary system. The carbon footprint of the region as a whole has been reduced by 20%. 25% of the production is now ISO 14001 certified[32]. The use of synthetic compounds of all types in the vineyard has been reduced by 50%, 90% of the industrial waste, and all of the wastewater are now treated and recycled.

In 2014, an official certification of sustainable viticul-ture practices was adopted called "Viticulture Durable en Cham¬pagne". This sometimes works in place of and other times in tandem with different types of certification, including "Haute Valeur Environnementale" (being certified as an enter-prise of "high environmental value"), launched in 2010, as well as sepa¬rate organic and biodynamic certifications, which have become gradually more common. Outside these official certi-fications, there has been an increasing tendency among young growers to use these techniques and to produce Champagne in a "natural" way. This ill-defined category shares some aspects of organic and biodynamic viticulture while imposing additional

---

32   See Glossary

strictures on the producers, notably the elimination or extreme reduction in the use of sulfur. Some define "natural" as "nothing is added, nothing is taken away," which means no dosage, but also means no cultured yeast for the prise de mousse, which is much more challenging to achieve. Other conscientious producers are eschewing certification of any type but still implementing many of the policies. This is amounting to a wholesale reformation of viticulture in the region and a return to cover crops and tilling the soil manually, which reduce vigor, lower yield, increase vinosity, and help keep pH low. Regardless of the semantics of any one movement, however, it is incontestably true that the Champagne region has made enormous progress in respect of the environment.

2000

***

Harvest: September 11th
Yield: 12,577 kg/ha (11,000 kg/ha AC)
Area under vine: 30,407 ha
Average potential alcohol: 9.9%
Average total acidity: 7.6 g/l
Average gluconic acid: 0.12 g/l

Total Sales: 253,209,546 btl
France: 149,626,415 btl
Export: 103,583,131 btl
Prix Indicatif : €4.00/kg

Overview: Disaster averted.

After a summer filled with rain and hail, conditions improved to provide another sizeable harvest of reasonable quality. The winter following the harvest of 1999 was mild, yet budbreak was later than usual. The spring saw scattered showers and hailstorms throughout the region. Flowering was a bit earlier than usual, and the early growing season was hot. However, there was hail on the 2nd of July. Rain and hail throughout the following months led to problems with mildew. From the last half of August, the weather was sunny but not too hot, and harvest began in good conditions. Grey rot of moderate intensity affected approximately 12% of the vineyard on average, but much more so for black grapes (Pinot Noir 12%, Meunier 16%) than for Chardonnay (6%), making this a "Chardonnay" year. Among the grande marque Blanc de Blancs, I was impressed with Comtes de Champagne: *"Marvelous. There is more of a ripe apple than lemon fruit on the nose, along with a distinct note of butter and brioche. On the palate, the texture of the wine was very fine, with crisp acidity and a lingering finish."* **** (Tasted 2011)

Even the Pinot-dominant Dom Pérignon seems almost a lighter style: *"Supremely elegant; the nose is dominated by fresh pear and apple fruit and white floral blossoms. The texture is youthful and tender with little if any evolution – far too young to drink, but pleasant indeed. This wine should hold and improve for decades."* **** (Tasted 2009), although the Bollinger Grande Année was done in a much more vinous style: *"A rich, nuanced nose with ripe, tropical fruit and notes of mineral, smoke and buttered toast. On the palate the wine is refreshing, yet dense, structured and long, with a fine mousse and wonderful length,"* **** (Tasted 2010)

2001
[No Stars]

Harvest: September 20th
Yield: 10,980 kg/ha
Area under vine: 30,504 ha
Average potential alcohol: 8.5%
Average total acidity: 8.6 g/l
Average gluconic acid: 0.13 g/l

Total Sales: 262,695,314 btl
France: 164,522,817 btl
Export: 98,172,497 btl
Prix Indicatif: €4.13/kg

Overview: A poor year.

A rainy season with frequent frosts, leading to rot and mildew. Grey rot of moderate intensity affected approximately 20% of the vineyard on average, most seriously the Meunier, but the other varieties also suffered. The only note I have is not that encouraging. From Mailly Grand Cru: *"A bit of smoke and a bit of botrytis. Concentrated, but not necessarily in a good way. 8.5° potential alcohol at harvest."* *

A poor year with very few vintage wines. The less said, the better.

2002

*****

Harvest: September 14th
Yield: 11,930 kg/ha (11,400 kg/ha AC)
Area under vine: 30,892 ha
Average potential alcohol: 10.3%
Average total acidity: 7.0 g/l
Average gluconic acid: 0.07 g/l

Total Sales: 287,672,421 btl
France: 175,000,710 btl
Export: 112,671,711 btl
Prix Indicatif: €4.22/kg

Overview: A classic warm vintage with excellent aging potential.

After a cold snap in December, the early months of 2002 were fairly mild. Although there was frost on the 14th and 15th of April, the damage was not widespread. Flowering was rapid and thorough, although occasional showers provided some impetus for rot. On balance, however, the pressure was not severe, and there was less rain than the norm. The end of August and early September were warm and dry, concentrating the fruit, but lowering the acidity (and the bunch weight). Nights were reasonably fresh, however, so the effect of the weather was limited. Grey rot of moderate intensity affected approximately 9% of the vineyard on average, more or less evenly across the main grape varieties.

For me, the wine of the vintage was Krug Clos du Mesnil: *"Supremely concentrated aromas that touch on tropical fruit (especially coconut), citrus fruit and mineral, with a saline undercurrent and a bit of spice from the cask, this is a positively bewitching nose. On the palate, the wine is tightly wound with lots of structure and freshness, but there is also a rich, almost unctuous character here and a fine, velvety caress that seemingly goes on forever. A superb wine that will age for decades."* ***** (Tasted 2017)

Because they are both from Le Mesnil and because of the historical ties between the vineyards, one often thinks of Krug Clos du Mesnil and Salon together. Indeed, the 2002 Salon also provides much pleasure: *"A superb magnum of 2002 Salon enormously fresh and youthful but starting to loosen a bit the tension of youth. The nose was forward and lush with ripe apple and toasted* *brioche. The wine was still youthful and showed little development, but neither did it show the steely minerality and saline character that the wine often has when young. It was in a great place and drinking very well."* ***** (Tasted 2019)

Bollinger Brut Vieilles Vignes Francaises was also among the greatest wines of this vintage: *"Bewitching, complex aromas that begin with ripe pears and floral notes, continue to brioche, wood smoke, and cream, and end up with a hint of mineral and the suggestion of truffle. This wine is rich, very dense, and almost fat, but there is enough acidity to give it a sleek finesse and penetrating finish. It should last for decades to come."* ***** (Tasted 2014)

To compare 2002 with two other great years, the level of alcohol is on a par with 1996 and is a half-degree more than 2008, but the level of acidity is markedly lower than either of these two vintages. The net effect is to make the wines more accessible at an earlier age overall. It seems to me that some wines are now starting to mature. The best wines from 2002, however, are still very youthful and should not be drunk yet.

2003

*

Harvest: August 21ˢᵗ
Yield: 8,100 kg/ha
Area under vine: 31,233 ha
Average potential alcohol: 10.6%
Average total acidity: 5.8 g/l
Average gluconic acid: 0.04 g/l

Total Sales: 293,504,960 btl
France: 174,231,485 btl
Export: 119,273,475 btl
Prix Indicatif: €4.39/kg

Overview: The year of the heatwave—and more.

2003 will be remembered for the remarkable heat, but there were other extraordinary aspects to this unusual vintage. The first was a series of severe frosts from the 7ᵗʰ through the 11ᵗʰ of April, which affected 43% of the vines. After this destructive frost came a sweltering heat, as record temperatures began in May and lasted through the harvest. In addition to the soaring temperature, there were no fewer than eight incidents of hail between mid-May and early July, destroying 650 hectares of vines (about 2% of production). 2003 was the earliest harvest on record. Some communes in the Aube even began to pick on the unheard-of date of August 18ᵗʰ. The harvest took place under beautiful conditions. Because of the hot and dry conditions, however, bunch weight was down, and the skins of the grapes were thicker than usual (particularly the Chardonnay), making pressing more difficult. The difficulty in pressing was exacerbated by growers who brought the second and third generation bunches that came out after the frost. Wines were deeply-colored because of the well-developed anthocyanins in the skins of the grapes, and the phenolic content of the must was very high. As one might expect in such a hot, dry year, there was effectively no rot at all in 2003. However, conditions were difficult for other reasons. The ever-sensitive Vigneron Champenois concluded their analysis thus: *"Certain establishments had the curiosity to create vintage cuvées [in 2003]. The information of what will become of these wines will be precious in the future since 2003 remains a completely atypical year without possible comparison to preceding vintages.*" Because of these factors, it was relatively uncommon to produce vintage wines. To bring the wine back into balance it was often necessary to blend the wines with a high percentage of reserve wines.

I have relatively few notes from the 2003 vintage. I was quite surprised to see that the one with the highest rating while I was reviewing my notes was the Brut Inflorescence La Parcelle Blanc de Noirs from Roses de Jeanne, produced in the Côte de Bars by winemaker Cédric Bouchard. *"Racy and fine even in '03, the Inflorescence has pleasant toasty aromas on the nose and a bit of butter and cream, yet on the palate, the wine is still very crisp – an achievement in '03."* **** (Tasted 2013)

The Tarlant vintage '03 La Matinale was holding up well in 2015: *"Although marked by its passage in cask, this is fresh and lively with crisp citrus and floral notes barely accented with oak spice on the attack. A classic Marne blend of Pinot Noir and Meunier balanced with 28% Chardonnay, the wine is tender and approachable despite its lack of dosage."* (Tasted 2015)

I was also quite impressed with the vintage wine from Pierre Peters in 2003: *"Very successful. The wine shows ripe apple fruit character on the nose with a hint of toast. On the palate, it is a bit fat, but essentially well structured, with a nice depth of flavor on the palate and good balance."* **** (Tasted 2014)

A difficult year because of the extreme weather. Some wines from scorching years such as '59 have quite a following, although they are not to everyone's taste. For my part, I will not be laying down any wine from the '03 vintage.

2004
****

Harvest: September 18th
Yield: 13,990 kg/ha (12,000 kg/ha AC)
Area under vine: 31,570 ha
Average potential alcohol: 9.8%
Average total acidity: 7.3 g/l
Average gluconic acid: 0.04 g/l

Total Sales: 301 414 973 btl
France: 178 358 541 btl
Export: 123 056 432 btl
Prix Constaté : €4.62/kg

Overview: A big harvest, with excellent ripeness and balance. Another age-worthy vintage.

2004 was an outstanding year that produced wines suitable for long aging in abundant quantity. The winter before the 2004 campaign was warm, with no periods of intense cold. After rain in January, the early springtime was sunny and dry. Budburst occurred between the 12th and the 20th of April. Flowering took place without incident in mid-June, and an enormous crop was set, necessitating some bud thinning. The latter half of June and July were sunny and relatively mild, but August was quite wet, with 50% more rain than an average year. This rain brought with it swelling of the bunches and an increased risk of rot and mildew. The health of the grapes remained stable for the most part. It took the vines until the end of the month to ripen such an abundant crop. Grey rot of moderate intensity affected approximately 7% of the vineyard on average, more or less evenly across the main grape varieties. In commercial terms, 2004 marked the end of the "prix indicative" at Brussels' demand. The industry now tracks the "prix constaté" – the "observed price" of the executed contracts.

Among the Blanc de Blancs, the Diebolt-Vallois Fleur de Passion was notable: "...*delicate floral hints and a pleasant apple and pear fruit character on the nose, with a typical soft, creamy Cramant elegance on the palate. The wine is very fresh and fine yet not assertively acidic or jarring in any way—creamy goodness,*" **** consistent with the nature of the vintage.

The Krug was impressive and very showy on release and has stayed so, and must be judged among the great successes of 2004: *"Lovely, citrusy and fresh with a very tender texture. However, it seemed slightly closed, and at this stage, it was almost too easy to love and lacking perhaps a bit of tension. With time, this should be spectacular."* **** Also in the Pinot-driven grande marque style, Dom Pérignon '04 has consistently shown very well: *"Very impressive even at an early stage. A recent bottle drank well, with a forward lemon fruit with notes of almond and cream. On the palate it was soft, rich and lingering. This should be another success on the order of the 2002 with an equally long life ahead of it."* ****

A wonderful year producing wines for laying down and generalized success throughout the region. '04 misses out just narrowly from the top category because of slightly soft acidity, yet this still certainly qualifies as a vintage to seek out and lay down the best wines.

2005

***

Harvest: September 9th

Harvest: September 9th
Yield: 12,991 kg/ha (11,500 kg/ha AC)
Area under vine: 31,918 ha
Average potential alcohol: 9.9%
Average total acidity: 7.0 g/l
Average gluconic acid: 0.13 g/l

Total Sales: 307,665,132 btl
France: 178,360,253 btl
Export: 129,304,879 btl
Prix Constaté : €4.65/kg

Overview: Another generous harvest, similar balance to 2004.

A dry winter with little frost was followed by a hot, damp period at the end of June and beginning of July, giving rise to the danger of rot and mildew. Overall, the growing season was the warmest since 2003. Grey rot of moderate intensity affected approximately 12% of the vineyard on average, but it was much more pronounced in the Meunier (15%) than for Chardonnay (7%). As with 2004, 2005 is a vintage that looks mediocre "on paper", although picking was finished in wonderful weather.

I have enjoyed the Bollinger Grande Année on many occasions. From my notes: *"..biscuity, rich, concentrated; a hint of walnuts and smoke"* **** (Tasted 2013) Among other grande marque expressions, the Dom Pérignon was also successful, if somewhat lacking in tension: *"Lovely, with a very creamy mousse and aromas of apricot and stone fruit with a hint of almonds and a mineral underpinning. The 50-50 balance between Chardonnay and Pinot Noir gives an understated elegance on the palate."* *** In general, my feeling is that the wines are rich and a bit soft.

Many of the most successful wines in '05 came from growers. I was impressed with the "Vertus Cœur de Terroir" from Pascal Doquet: *"Concentrated and lemony fruit; saline and fresh; ripe but not flabby"* *** And from the Marne comes Jérôme Dehours' marvelous wine Les Genevraux: *"Complex notes of hazelnut, fresh and dried white flowers, mineral and cream with a smoky note at the end. Crisp but not tart, with a supple texture, nice extract, and a creamy mousse carrying through to a lovely finish."* ****

From the Grande Montage comes the superb "Empreinte de Terroir" from Eric Rodez: *"This is an assemblage of the Rodez holdings throughout the village of Ambonnay across vintage 2005. The fruit is fermented in cask and lightly dosed at 2.5 g/l. The wine ages for ten years on the lees, giving it structure and density, with a vinous texture and lots of yeasty bread dough aromas. This wine will doubtlessly age well over the next two decades. Fabulous quality."* ****

In sum, '05 is a good, solid year with plenty of delicious vintage wines produced. With slightly less acidity and a bit more rot than 2004, however, '05 misses "very good," although one would certainly qualify it as better than "useful." As always, wines from top producers can be marvelous.

2006

****

Harvest: September 9th
Yield: 12,997 kg/ha (13,000 kg/ha AC)
Area under vine: 32,378 ha
Average potential alcohol: 10.2%
Average total acidity: 7.0 g/l
Average gluconic acid: 0.04 g/l

Total Sales: 321,789,798 btl
France: 181,129,602 btl
Export: 140,660,196 btl
Prix Constaté : €4.81/kg

Overview: The third abundant year in a row, with quality edging out 2005.

The wines produced in this vintage tended to have high sugar levels and slightly soft acidity. These conditions are similar to 2005, and it is again another year that was very good but not quite great. The coldest winter in a decade preceded the campaign, and there were scattered incidents of frost that fortunately did little damage. Flowering and fruit set took place in mid-June under good conditions. After an early July hailstorm, the rest of the month was hot and dry. Rain began in August, but fortunately, September was dry and warm. Harvest began under beautiful conditions (with some communes starting as early as the 7th) and continued through the 25th. Low levels of gluconic acid point to less rot than 2005, and on a par with 2004, although the acidity is a bit softer than 2004.

Of the wines released so far, the top wine of the vintage has been Salon: *"Coffee and cream on the nose. The wine is accessible and shows a pronounced toasty note that is wonderful, as well as greater substance and concentration on the palate. The wine is drinking now, but also shows great potential to age."* *****
(Tasted 2019)

Not strictly a Chardonnay year, the top growers on the Montagne also turned in exemplary performances. From Pierre Paillard the "La Grande Récolte" almost seemed delicate: *"A fifty-fifty blend of Chardonnay and Pinot Noir from the oldest vines on the Pierre Paillard estate, this is always a wine of both concentration and elegance. The 2006 today is approachable with a delicate, silky texture. Still, there is also a density of toasted, nutty aromas, ripe orchard fruit and a subtle minerality that testify to its ability to age."* **** (Tasted 2017)

The vintage produced a host of rich, accessible wines that must be qualified as "very good" (or better) because of their depth of flavor and overall balance. The best of these will age for decades, yet as a whole, the vintage misses the top category because the slightly soft acidity means, in most cases, the wines are loveable rather than thrilling.

2007

***

Harvest: August 20th
Yield: 14,242 kg/ha (12,400 kg/ha AC)
Area under vine: 32,722 ha
Average potential alcohol: 9.4%
Average total acidity: 8.6 g/l
Average gluconic acid: 0.17 g/l

Total Sales: 338,796,703 btl
France: 187,950,736 btl
Export: 150,845,967 btl
Prix Constaté : €5.11/kg

Overview: Another large crop. Issues with ripeness and rot.

After a warm winter, the budbreak was exceptionally early. From this point, the vines continued ahead of the pace of an average year. There were warmer-than-usual temperatures throughout the spring, but poor weather from mid-May disturbed the flowering, which had started at the end of May. However, after the and muggy weather in June, temperatures cooled off in July. August turned wet and cold, which delayed picking somewhat but led inevitably to rot and mildew. The average level of gluconic acid in the must was the highest in the past twenty years. Harvest began from the 24th of August, although this varied greatly by village.

2007 is an odd vintage for me in that I have always had a notion of it as a poor vintage, but I realized as I was reviewing my notes over the years (and in light of recent releases) that there were some truly delicious wines produced. Generally, the most successful wines were based on Chardonnay, which is logical given that the skins are thicker and thus better able to resist the rot that was the issue in 2007. One delightful (if not perfect) example was the Fleur de Passion from Diebolt-Vallois: *"All Cramant fruit from the oldest vines spread over seven parcels in the village, completely fermented in cask. Malolactic fermentation is blocked, and the wine is bottled without filtration or stabilization after six months of aging. The 2007 vintage was disgorged in December of 2016 and dosed at 6 g/l. Isabelle describes it as 'The little black Chanel dress.' For me, there is elegance and finesse with a delicate lemony freshness. I can see the dress, but the '07 lacks a bit of the richness that other vintages have had."* **** (Tasted 2017)

Among the most recent releases from this vintage was the Taittinger Comtes de Champagne, perhaps the wine of the vintage. From my notes: *"The nose is elegant but very discreet, with pleasant aromas of citrus and white flowers with a hint of toast but nothing overwhelming considering it was on the lees for a decade before disgorgement. On the palate, the texture is silky and very fine, with fresh acidity and yet impressive extract and length."* **** (Tasted 2018)

While there is no question that it is not among the best vintages of the decade, neither is there reason to reject an '07 out of hand, as there were some notable successes. Ultimately not too many vintage wines were produced, but it is worth trying those by top producers.

2008

*****

Harvest: September 15th
Yield: 14,231 kg/ha (12,400 kg/ha AC)
Area under vine: 32,946 ha
Average potential alcohol: 9.8%
Average total acidity: 8.6 g/l
Average gluconic acid: 0.05 g/l

Total Sales: 322,637,259 btl
France: 181,387,615 btl
Export: 141,249,644 btl
Prix Constaté : €5.40/kg

Overview: Top Quality. This vintage has it all: power, freshness & balance.

A classic year with a big harvest producing balanced wines with good ripeness and acidity. 2008 saw a return to a more "classic" type of weather in the region. After a somewhat disappointing budbreak and a crisp, rainy spring, winemakers were not too enthusiastic about the prospects for 2008. Initial estimates of bunch weight and the prognosis for flowering were pessimistic. The rain continued through much of the summer, leading to problems with rot and mildew. The rain also helped swell the bunches, however, without compromising maturity. Fortunately, the weather cleared at the end of August as it often does. The grapes finished ripening at an average time for the region, and the harvest began under beautiful conditions.

There were many superb wines produced in 2008, and some important ones, such as Krug, have yet to be released. Those that have been so far are of impeccable quality. The Dom Pérignon is marvelous: *"...still young but already showing and expressive stone and orchard fruit character with well-integrated brioche-like autolysis. The wine is elegant and balanced on the palate with a silky, tender texture, but there is still a lot of substance, and this wine is one for the ages."* ***** (Tasted 2018) Cristal was equally delicious: *"Forward, lush notes of ripe pear and apple touched with a marked toasty character from the lees aging. Still, however, the wine is fresh and very tightly wound and should live for decades. Absolutely superb."* ***** (Tasted 2019) Tasting the Philipponnat "Clos des Goisses" on several occasions, it strikes me as perhaps more vinous than these but every bit as concentrated and with just as great a potential to age: *"On the attack, there is a superb balance between the citrus and floral. There are hints of lightly toasted walnut and suggestions of coconut and toasted brioche. There is impressive density on the palate, but there is also a very fresh acidity that delivers a shimmering texture through the long, lingering finish. 55% Chardonnay, 45% Pinot Noir, disgorged in April and dosed at 4.5 g/l."* ***** (Tasted 2017)

In the village of Le Mesnil, Robert Moncuit has turned in a riveting performance with his extremely elegant wine from the lieu-dit Les Chétillons. From my notes: *"Citrus and green apple on the initial attack with well-developed toasty autolysis that blossoms with time, complemented by mineral and saline notes. On the palate, the wine is ethereally light but still long."* **** (Tasted 2016) Results on the Montagne were also encouraging. For example, in Ambonnay the wines from Eric Rodez were spellbinding. From my notes on Les Beurys et les Secs: *"Produced from vineyards with an east exposition and 35 cm of soil over the chalk comes this extraordinary wine, with an exotic aroma that combines tropical fruit, mineral, and floral notes and a suggestion of marzipan on the attack. On the palate, the texture is very creamy and very rich, with admirable length and finesse produced by the balance between crisp acidity and plenty of extract. Fermented in cask, malolactic blocked."* **** (Tasted 2018)

The evidence from 2008 testifies that this is one of the rare years with both quantity and quality. There were many wines of very high quality, and without a doubt, 2008 is a year to buy and lay down for future generations to drink.

2009
****

Harvest: September 8th
Yield: 12,280 kg/ha (9,700 kg/ha AC)
Area under vine: 33,106 ha
Average potential alcohol: 10.3%
Average total acidity: 7.5 g/l
Average gluconic acid: 0.04 g/l

Total Sales: 293,330,613 btl
France: 180,770,128 btl
Export: 112,560,485 btl
Prix Constaté : €5.25/kg

Overview: A warm year producing ripe wines rich in alcohol but somewhat soft.

The year started with rain during the spring and a reasonably cool June, drawing out the flowering and producing milleran-dage in the Côte des Blancs. The cool, rainy weather also led to the beginning of mildew. Fortunately, conditions turned hot and dry and stayed that way until the middle of August. Rain arrived right at the beginning of September to help the grapes finish ripening. There was an episode of hail in the Marne Valley on the 4th of September that caused localized damage. Otherwise, the harvest took place under impeccable conditions.

Releases of the top wines continue as of this writing. There have been enough top wines that one can begin a full as-sessment of the vintage. Among the wines from the negociants, Roederer Cristal is the best that I have had so far: *"Fresh and primary, the nose here is still somewhat closed, but on the palate, delicious bright stone and orchard fruit begin to emerge with hints of flowers and fresh almonds. The wine is lush and vibrant but has enough structure to carry the finish with great elegance.* **** (Tasted 2016)

In a warm year, Blanc de Blancs can often provide a refreshing balance. A perfect example of this is the Vénus from Pascal Agrapart: *"Fresh citrus peel touched with spice, mineral, and toast on the nose as one would expect, but this is dense, rich, and more creamy than is common for this wine in its youth."* **** (Tasted 2015) The tank-fermented Chétillons from Pierre Péters showed good freshness for the vintage: *"Rich, mineral, and silky,* *this is a truly extraordinary wine with a mineral cast to the ripe apple and citrus fruit on the nose and lush texture and deep complexity of flavors."* **** (Tasted 2015)

Because of their cool north-facing slopes, wines produced from vineyards on the north face of the Montagne were also very successful. Penet-Chardonnet from Verzy furnishes a great example: *"Les Epinettes is tank-fermented and aged on the lees without malolactic fermentation. A Blanc de Noirs, it shows strong smoky/mineral character on the nose, yet because of the north-facing slopes, it has almost a lemon peel fruit character. On the palate, the wine is crisp and fresh, but there is still a lovely density and length – a wine to seek out. Impressive results in a warm vintage."* **** (Tasted 2019)

The profusion of vintage wines from 2009 and the quality of those from top producers demonstrates that even in warm years, Champagne can produce top quality.

CHAPTER XII
2010 – 2019:
Limits to Growth

The second decade of the new century was a tumultuous one in Champagne, even if some of the turmoil stayed below the surface. One of the main struggles has been simultaneously managing success and the limits to growth, since sales volume has dropped even as the value of shipments has continued to climb. Champagne sales rebounded fairly quickly following the drop during the economic crisis of 2008 – 2009, and continued to grow until 2011. Since this time, however, total shipments slowly declined to just under 300 million bottles. Even as the number of bottles has declined, the total value of the shipments has risen each year since 2009 to reach a record of nearly €5 billion, During this time, the négociants are in the most influential position of the last 20 years, with a 72.7% share, while the growers are at their nadir at 18.2%. The cause of this trend is that low-value types of Champagne are declining while higher-value wines continue to thrive. Specifically, supermarket brands and lower cost champagnes have slowed, while more expensive grande marque brands have continued to rise. This is most evident in the French domestic market and in the U.K., which are the two largest-volume Champagne markets.

Partially in response to this, the steady expansion of the vineyard area has nearly stopped after years of slow but steady growth. The region added 6,200 hectares in the '70s, 3,400 hectares in the 80s, 2,900 in the 90s, 3,000 from 2000 – 2010, but only 400 hectares since 2010. This virtual halt to plantings came despite an aggressive plan for future growth that was announced in 2008 when the INAO approved a redrawn map of the appellation that increased the number of villages allowed to produce Champagne. In all, forty more villages were authorized to enjoy this right. At the same time, however, the INAO removed some land from production at the same time, revoking the rights of Germaine and Orbais l'Abbaye. In the end, the total number went from 319 to 357, at least in theory. The roots of the proposed expansion go back to the zonage project begun in 1990. During this study, researchers divided the land into 50-meter square parcels and evaluated every aspect of the terroir in each plot. With this knowledge in hand, the Syndicat Général des Vignerons formally requested an expansion in the region from the INAO in 2003. Experts studied the matter from 2004 – 2007, and in 2008 the INAO announced the extension, creating a tremendous general uproar on all counts.

And then – nothing happened. The next step should have been defining the parcels in each of the new villages where grapes could be grown (known as the *délimitation parcellaire*). Mysteriously, this was never finalized. More than a decade after the announcement, we have the possibility that the region may increase substantially, but no vineyards have yet been planted. Even after the *délimitation parcellaire*, individual growers would have to apply for the right to plant a specific parcel. The new vines would not be able to produce wine until its third year, so any increase is still years in the future. The decision regarding the délimitation parcellaire was never announced. The noise surrounding the expansion was gradually allowed to die down, and today the matter is seldom discussed.

Another "stealth" decision was the phasing out of the échelle des crus. The end of the échelle des crus effectively occurred with the banning of the "indicative price" by Brussels in 2000. In 2010, however, a new definition of the rules for making Champagne (known as the *"cahier des charges,"* translated in Appendix I) was issued. The new law stipulates that the name of the appellation can be modified with the mention of "grand cru" and "premier cru" for a specified list of villages. This effectively meant that although the échelle had no further purpose as a price-setting mechanism, the tradition of certain grand cru and premier cru villages was codified in law. With one wrinkle: formerly, Chouilly had been grand cru for Chardonnay only, and Tours-sur-Marne for Pinot Noir alone. With this change, those subtle distinctions were now erased. Welcome to the new classification of Champagne.

These are the substantive changes in this decade. Many aficionados, however, would probably highlight other trends. High-profile growers vinifying their own grapes (known as récoltant-manipulants in French) are much more prominent. Many of these producers are returning to the cask fermentation and heritage grape varieties of previous decades. Some are even going back to using horses for tilling the soil, forgoing herbicides and other chemicals to return to an earlier style of cultivation, and producing small-volume cuvées from specific plots of land. At the same time, many lower dosage levels or avoid malolactic fermentation to combat global warming. These are often-discussed trends, and they are very evident in high-end restaurants and on the shelves of top merchants. However, the truth is that no matter how much attention these trends receive, the rise of the superstar grower has yet to make a dent in the sales of the grandes marques in the broader market. On the contrary, sales by growers overall have been steadily declining.

Even these figures, however, obscure the reality of the situation. The term "grower" (the standard translation of the word "vignerons" used by the CIVC) is somewhat misleading. "Growers" include not only the récoltant-manipulants described above (who number approximately 2,000), but also about 3,000 "récoltant-cooperateurs" who grow grapes that are vinified by co-ops but sold under their own label. These wines bear little resemblance to those of the superstar récoltant-manipulants. The category of "vigneron" also includes what is known as a société de récoltants or "company of growers," a group of growers, often a family, who work together, either by themselves or through a co-op. Sales are not broken out by the CIVC by the different professional registrations, so what people think of as "grower champagne" can be something entirely different. In truth, these distinctions matter little. There are great wines made by producers in every category. What does matter is the quality of the wine in the bottle, and in my view, it has never been better. With all due respect to André Simon, I believe that today, and not the first decade of the 20th century, is the true "Golden Age of Champagne". There has never been more Champagne of better quality produced, in a dizzying array of styles. There is truly something for everyone, so drink up!

2010

**

Harvest: September 13th
Yield: 10,901 kg/ha (10,500 kg/ha AC)
Area under vine: 33,564 ha
Average potential alcohol: 10.0%
Average total acidity: 7.4 g/l
Average gluconic acid: 0.14 g/l

Total Sales: 319,496,853 btl
France: 185,131,973 btl
Export: 134,364,880 btl
Prix Constaté: €5.36/kg

Overview: A year of rain and rot almost redeemed by a beautiful September.

The initial progress of 2010 was dry and warm, although it had been preceded by a hard winter with numerous frosts and a spring with several instances of hail. Flowering took place under cool conditions and required almost a week longer than average, leading to some millerandage. July and early August were again dry and warm, except for some rain in the Aisne and the western Marne Valley in mid-July. Rain began to fall from the 15th of August, however, and rot started to progress in the vineyards. Luckily the weather turned sunny and dry in September, and the harvest took place under beautiful conditions, although strict sorting was necessary. The year is considered best for Chardonnay, and losses to rot for Meunier were up to 40% in some villages. Grey rot of moderate intensity was noted over 10% of the vineyard. In addition to the classic incidence of rot, there was a particularly virulent outbreak of "tourne" in the Chardonnay vineyards. This disease is characterized by grapes whose skin becomes fragile due to botrytis that subsequently turn brown and sometimes burst. The grapes are rotten through and through. Among those who avoided these pitfalls, however, there were some notable successes. Typical of the success in the Côte des Blancs is the Vénus bottling from Agrapart: *"There is a compelling smoky complexity on the nose with notes of ripe lime and tropical fruit and a bit of spice from the cask ferment underscored by a firm mineral underpinning. On the palate the mousse is creamy, but the texture of the wine is racy but not bracing. Lovely and long. pH 3.0 - 3.10."* **** (Tasted 2019)

Other regions were also successful with their Chardonnay. From the lieu-dit Le Mont Benoit in the Vesle et Ardre, Emmanuel Brochet has done impressive work with the Blanc de Blancs called Les Hauts Chardonnays: *"With lovely, bright, lemony fruit, this is more structured than most. After the expressive aromas upfront, the wine shows great tension on the palate, with crisp acidity and impressive length. Dosed at 2 g/l."* **** (Tasted 2018) Talented growers could even make a success of their Meunier. One example is the admirable tension in the Meunier Brut Nature from Christophe Mignon on the left bank of the Marne. From my notes: *"...a nice mix of fresh flowers and citrus fruit on the nose; on the palate, the wine is bright and refreshing, yet there is still concentration here, and the wine sacrifices nothing in length."* **** (Tasted 2016)

It would be remiss not to mention the Côte des Bar, where many winning wines were produced in 2010. Typical of the success stories there was Olivier Horiot, whose "Sève" both in Blanc de Noirs and Rosé de Saignée was lovely: *"The Blanc de Noirs shows pleasant floral and apricot notes on the nose and balanced acidity on the palate, while the Rosé de Saignée has a lovely, expressive red fruit character and a fresh and delicate feel on the palate,"* **** (Tasted 2015)

2011
[No Stars]

Harvest: August 19th
Yield: 13,268 kg/ha (12,500 kg/ha AC)
Area under vine: 33,564 ha
Average potential alcohol: 9.4%
Average total acidity: 7.4 g/l
Average gluconic acid: 0.05 g/l

Total Sales: 322,951,807 btl
France: 181,623,158 btl
Export: 141,328,649 btl
Prix Constaté : €5.60/kg

Overview: A challenging year.

2011 offered "Summer in the springtime, springtime in the summer, and then a return to summer in the autumn," according to many in the region. A cold winter preceded the season, delivering plenty of frost and some incidence of hail. The period from March to May was dry and warm, and budbreak began in the first ten days of April. Flowering was also early and finished by the end of May. Because of this weather pattern, there was very little danger from downy mildew, although powdery mildew was a potential problem. The warm weather put the vines on track to harvest very early, with some predicting that the picking would start mid-August. However, rainy and cool conditions set in near the end of June. Wet, cool temperatures continued for most of July and August, interrupted by several short heatwaves. This type of weather slowed the growth of the vines, caused the berries to swell with water, and increased rot and mildew. Veraison began at the end of July. By mid-August, the incidence of botrytis in the thin-skinned Pinot Noir and Meunier was close to 20% in some regions, although there was far less difficulty with the Chardonnay.

There were relatively few vintage wines produced in 2011, even fewer that stood out. Some of the best examples were from growers who produce a vintage each year, such as Bérèche. Their Le Cran 2011 was among the most successful: *"Fantastic concentration of apricot and peach aromas on the nose are followed by a balanced, accessible elegance on the palate and surprising length."* ****   (Tasted 2019)

2012

★★★★★

Harvest: September 10th
Yield: 9,210 kg/ha
Area under vine: 33,578 ha
Average potential alcohol: 10.6%
Average total acidity: 7.8 g/l
Average gluconic acid: 0.01 g/l

Total Sales: 308,599,509 btl
France: 171,250,077 btl
Export: 137,349,432 btl
Prix Constaté : €5.73/kg

Overview: From the worst to the best.

2012 provided difficult conditions at the beginning of the year, but the growers' fortunes changed completely after flowering, producing marvelous results. After a mild January, temperatures in February reached -10°C several times, and got as cold as -20° C, although there was little permanent damage to the vines. March was warm, and budbreak was early. April was rainy, and May brought frost, damaging between 10% - 17% of the vineyard in different subregions. The rain continued right up to flowering, setting a twenty-year record and bringing mildew. Fortunately for the growers, the rain stopped mid-July, and there was almost no more until the harvest was complete. From this period, sunny and warm conditions set in, with temperatures rising to heatwave levels in mid-August, thoroughly drying out the grapes. As of this writing in 2019, top négociant houses are just releasing their 2012 vintage wines. The 2012 Brut Vintage released by Taittinger is typical of the successes of this vintage. From my notes: *"With ripe apricot and pear fruit touched with a bit of smoke and yeast on the nose, this cuvée makes a lovely impression on the initial attack. There is marvelous concentration and an attractively lush texture on the palate, but there is enough freshness here to balance."* **★★★★** (Tasted 2019)

Gimonnet's Special Club Pure Chouilly shows the marvelous results on the Côte des Blancs; *"Created from their magnificent 3 hectare parcel on Mont Aigu, the grapes ripened to 11% potential alcohol without chaptalization. The wine is simply marvelous. Despite the ripeness, there is plenty of concentration,* and a focused lemon peel and apricot character to the aroma rather than floral notes one often gets from Chouilly. The acidity is lively, and there are impressive depth and complexity on the finish." **** (Tasted 2019)

Results on the south face of the Montagne were also spectacular in 2012. At Pierre Paillard in Bouzy, I loved their Blanc de Noirs. From my notes: "Les Maillerettes is the name of the parcel with the oldest vines and the best mid-slope exposure. The vines originally planted in 1970 now produce an intensely vinous result, with a powerful structure and an almost copper color—a wine of intense ripeness and concentration, with ripe apple aroma marzipan, and toast. The acidity is vivacious, yet there is plenty of density and a powerful, complex finish. This wine will age for decades." ***** (Tasted 2018)

In the Côte des Bar, newcomer Nathalie Falmet showed the potential of the vintage here. From my note on Le Val Cornet: "This wine, produced from the lieu-dit of the same name, was half Pinot Noir and half Meunier in 2012. Half of the fruit was fermented in tank and half in cask. The wine shows ripe apple, toast, and butter on the nose, with just a hint of spice – it is not dominated by the wood. The texture is silky, creamy, and long; well-structured and fresh, with a pleasant hint of bitterness on the finish to give a superb balance." **** (Tasted 2018)

Despite the frost damage and pressure from mildew, 2012 is a particularly successful year and one whose top wines can be laid down for decades of cellaring.

2013
**

Harvest: September 24th
Yield: 12,008 kg/ha (10,500 kg/ha AC)
Area under vine: 33,573 ha
Average potential alcohol: 9.8%
Average total acidity: 8.4 g/l
Average gluconic acid: 0.05 g/l

Total Sales: 304,994,034 btl
France: 167,354,694 btl
Export: 137,639,340 btl
Prix Constaté : €5.80/kg

Overview: A late harvest of uneven quality.

The winter preceding the season was cold, although not as cold as February of 2012. Bud-break was relatively late, and the weather remained cool and rainy through the early spring. Despite this, neither frost, downy mildew, nor powdery mildew posed a severe problem in 2013. However, there were two fairly serious hail incidents, one in June that struck the Côte des Bars and part of the Marne Valley. Flowering was also late, and once completed, the vineyards were hit by another hailstorm in the area around Epernay and the Côte des Blancs. Weather was hot, sunny, and dry from mid-July through early September. However, the rains returned on the 10th of September, and it rained until nearly the end of the month. This rain brought on a virulent attack of grey rot, which hadn't been a problem up to this point. In the end, about 12% of the Chardonnay, 14% of the Pinot Noir, and 15% of the Meunier were affected by rot. The harvest was very drawn out and carried out under warm and wet conditions, and up to 4,000 kg/ha in some regions were lost to rot. Pickers were still working in some parts of Champagne on the 19th of October.

One of the best wines of the vintage (from any subregion) is undoubtedly l'Esprit from Pierre Péters: *"Crafted from selected parcels in Le Mesnil, Oger, Avise, and Cramant, this has done partial malo and saw in 2013 a dosage of 5 g/l. The result shows notes of lemon and white flowers with a chalky underpinning. The texture is silky and very fine, yet there is a rewarding density and length as well – deftly balanced yet powerful."* **** (Tasted 2018)

On the south face of the Montagne, Paul Bara has created a very interesting Special Club Rosé: *"Pure, expressive red berry fruit on the nose prepares one for the powerful impression this makes on the palate, with plenty of concentration, density, and a pleasantly lingering finish."* **** (Tasted 2018)

In the furthest reaches of Château Thierry, the Rue des Noyers from Benoît Déhu had a somewhat similar character: *"Lovely, lively saline and mineral notes. There is a richly lemony fruit but also a beguiling floral note. On the palate, the wine is very crisp and refreshing. Brut nature with malo blocked, completely fermented in cask. The wine was 11 months on the lees in cask before bottled without being racked."* **** (Tasted 2016)

In the Aube, Dominique Moreau from Marie Courtin has given us a trio of marvelous wines, but the Blanc de Noirs « Concordance » was the stand-out for me: *"Completely done in tank, without any addition of sulfur. There is a superb purity of fruit for a wine done even without sulfur. Malolactic fermentation is done here to ensure the stability of the wine. The wine is rich and expressive, yet not heavy at all, with a suggestion of marzipan and fresh white flowers that linger on the delightful finish. A tour de force of winemaking technique as well as of terroir."* **** This is my highest-rated wine produced in 2013 (Tasted 2017).

The relative abundance of exciting, delicious wines in 2013 shows that even when harvest conditions are not promising that one should not rule out any given vintage until the region's most talented winemakers have had their say.

2014

***

Harvest: September 8th
Yield: 11,553 kg/ha (11,000 kg/ha AC)
Area under vine: 33,705 ha
Average potential alcohol: 10.0%
Average total acidity: 8.3 g/l
Average gluconic acid: 0.11 g/l

Total Sales: 307,166,142 btl
France: 162,253,234 btl
Export: 144,912,908 btl
Prix Constaté : €5.89/kg

Overview: An up-and-down year that ended well.

A warm, wet autumn and winter preceding the campaign – the second warmest in twenty years, with only seven days of hard frost throughout the winter. March and April were dry and very pleasant, and budbreak was early. Rain returned in May, and although June was dry, precipitation returned in July. August continued rainy and cool, increasing the risk of rot and mildew in the vineyard. However, botrytis was not as prevalent as it might have been in 2014. Instead, the vines were troubled by sour rot caused by a combination of acetic acid bacteria and yeast that infect grapes damaged by drosophila flies. The sour rot affected Meunier most of all and Pinot Noir to a lesser extent. Chardonnay was mostly spared, as the problem most commonly afflicts thin-skinned varieties. It is chiefly because of this issue that the vintage ranks in the three-star category rather than four-star. Meunier was also most affected by downy mildew. Fortunately, September saw a return to warm, sunny, dry weather, allowing those who had skirted these dangers to make some very successful wines.

One delicious Blanc des Blancs is the vintage Brut Nature from Vauversin in Oger: *"Produced from old vines at the foot of the hill in Oger fermented in cask, this shows a wonderful concentration of lemon and chalk aromas up front, and a silky, seamless texture on the palate. Very good length."* **** (Tasted 2019)

Even Meunier could succeed in the right hands. From my notes on Laherte Frères in Chavot (Coteaux Sud d'Epernay): *"Les Vignes d'Autrefois is a 100% Meunier wine from old vines located at the base of the slope in Chavot and Mancy. The fruit is fermented in neutral casks, and the result has a lovely floral fruit on the attack and a silky texture that hides surprising depth on the finish."* **** (Tasted 2019)

One notable aspect of 2014 is that there were some interesting Coteaux produced throughout the region in 2014. A blanc from Robert Moncuit in Le Mesnil was classic, almost Burgundian: *"Lemons, cream and spice on the nose, with plenty of structure and an ample, round texture on the palate, this is 18 months in 300-litre casks, although the wood influence is very well integrated and melts into the lingering finish."* **** (Tasted 2016)

Tasted quite recently, the 2014 Coteaux Champenois La Côte aux Enfants from Bollinger was riveting: *"Rich, vinous, eminently Burgundian, this opens with a deep cherry fruit character with hints of violets and freshly turned earth. On the palate, there is density and concentration and an elegant lightness and a lingering, limpid finish. Marvelous."* **** (Tasted 2019)

Overall, a very good vintage that misses being top rank because of pressure from disease. 2014 has produced a large number of vintage wines and some of lasting quality.

2015
***

Harvest: August 29th
Yield: 10,602 kg/ha
Area under vine: 33,762 ha
Average potential alcohol: 10.5%
Average total acidity: 6.9 g/l
Average gluconic acid: 0.2 g/l

Total Sales: 312,566,858 btl
France: 161,860,463 btl
Export: 150,706,395 btl
Prix Constaté : €5.89/kg

Overview: A hot, dry year without the excess of 2003

2015 was hot and dry, but it was not quite a replay of 2003. The crucial difference was a fortnight of rain at the end of August. Nonetheless, in the end the wines ended up with a generous level of richness that was not necessarily balanced their acidity. A winter even warmer and wetter than the prior year preceded the campaign. The early spring finished with some storms in April, but then drought conditions set in from mid-May and lasted until mid-August. From mid-August almost up to the harvest there was rain, bringing worries about rot. Luckily, weather that turned clear, sunny, and cool in September, mostly contained the rot.

The principle issue in 2015 was very ripe fruit and a relative lack of acidity. Most of the top vintage wines from 2015 have not yet been released, and my impressions are based on tastings of the vins clairs the following spring, or on Coteaux Champenois. Given the conditions in 2015, a number of the Coteaux Champenois have been excellent. From the north face of the Montagne, Bérèche has produced a wonderful Coteaux Blanc called Les Monts Fournois. *From my notes: "Produced from grapes grown between Ludes & Rilly, where the fruit ripened to 12.2° natural with a pH of 2.84. The wine has a lovely Burgundian freshness but there is also a density here and a creamy texture that makes you want more as the wine lingers seductively on the palate."* ***** (Tasted 2017)

Another winning Coteaux came from Olivier Horiot: *"The Coteaux Champenois En Barmont was produced using semi-carbonic maceration – i.e., the clusters are loaded into the tank and fermented with the just the juice that naturally comes out from the grapes during loading. The fermentation is done with wild yeast, and the wine is aged on its lees in cask for a year, and for another six months in concrete. In 2015 this vineyard produced a Coteaux that shows an exquisite ripe cherry fruit but also plenty of earthy complexity. The texture is silky and fine, and there is an impressive length to the finish. A true delight."* **** (Tasted 2017)

There were undoubtedly some gratifying successes in 2015 despite the heat. The vins clairs from Agrapart showed concentration and balance: *"The Avizoise opened with sweet citrusy fruit underpinned by a strong minerality; Minéral had impressive freshness and elegance, while the vin clair for Vénus showed impressive concentration and depth of flavor while not sacrificing structure."* **** (Tasted 2016)

Perhaps surprisingly in a warm, dry vintage, Meunier seemed to do very well. The new wine from Juillet-Lallement was intense and strikingly original: *"The Belle de Juillet Pinot Meunier Grand Cru is from a 0.16 ha plot in Les Buissons des Vignes in Sillery. The wine shows the typical floral and fresh fruit character of Meunier, but there is an unusual concentration. On the palate, the wine is tightly wound, structured and very long, with plenty of acidity and plenty of substance to carry it to a beautiful, lingering finish."* ***** (Finished wine, tasted 2019)

There have also been some superb Pinot Noir-based wines. In the Grande Vallée, the Noces de Craie from Hébrart was particularly striking: *"100% Pinot Noir from Aÿ from the lieux-dits Cheuzelles, Longchamp, Pierre Robert, Pruche, and Chauffour. Only the cuvee is used, dosed at 5g/l. The result opens with a nose redolent of ripe apple, toast, and grilled almonds; on the palate, the wine is creamy and rich with a satisfying persistence on the finish."* **** (Finished wine, tasted 2019)

2015 is overall a vintage of good quality. Doubtless, there will ultimately be many vintage wines, and one imagines there will be some outstanding ones, although the bulk will lack the riveting attributes of freshness and verve that mark a truly great year.

2016

***

Harvest: September 10th
Yield: 9,163 kg/ha
Area under vine: 33,805 ha
Average potential alcohol: 9.9%
Average total acidity: 7.4 g/l
Average gluconic acid: 0.1 g/l

Total Sales: 306,074,837 btl
France: 157,713,428 btl
Export: 148,361,409 btl
Prix Constaté : €5.90/kg

Overview: A problematic season that ended reasonably well.

Another warm, wet winter preceded the 2016 campaign. Ultimately, however, it was a vintage of floods and drought, frosts, and sunburn, with downy mildew everywhere. By the end of March, there was 50% more rain than in an average year, by the end of June, 71% more, representing by far the most rain in the last twenty years. Springtime temperatures were cooler than usual, culminating in frosts during the last fortnight of April. Damage from the frost was the most significant in the Côte des Bars. The effect of these conditions was the worst outbreak of downy mildew in twenty years, resulting in the loss of approximately 15% of the crop. The rain stopped at the beginning of July for the most part, and the summer was hot and dry, culminating in severe sunburn at the end of August. Ultimately, the ripening was not consistent at harvest, and the Pinot Noir and Meunier were picked well before the Chardonnay, which was not brought in until the end of the month. It was generally considered a better year for black grapes. Fortunately, the warm weather and sunshine at the end of the season reduced the incidence of botrytis. The rate of botrytis overall was about 5% of the surface area of the vineyard. Fortunately, it did not increase even as rain began to fall in the second half of September.

There have been very few finished wines released, and my reaction to the vins clairs that I tasted in the spring of 2017 was mixed. There were relatively few to which I assigned four or five stars. My note for the vin clair for Emmanuel Brochet's Le Mont Benoit was typical of my impression of the year: *"This lacks the structure normally found in a vin clair. It is supple, silky, and remarkably drinkable already at this stage, which does not auger well for the finished Champagne.*" (Tasted 2017) I had a similar reaction to the vin clair Pascal Doquet made from grapes grown in Le Mesnil: *"Sweet and fresh; drinking well now..."* (Tasted 2017). Producers who blocked the malolactic fermentation were on the right track. From my note on a Meunier vin clair from A.R. Lenoble: *"Fermented in stainless steel with malo blocked (as with all wines this year), the fruit had 10° potential alcohol at harvest and lovely fruit expression with notes of fresh flowers and citrus. On the palate, it was surprisingly structured, but certainly not tart. pH 3.04, no botrytis."* (Tasted 2017)

Ultimately, many vintages in Champagne are saved by good weather at the end of the season, as was 2016. There is no reason to dismiss the year altogether, although even the best talents will have to work hard (and have a bit of luck) to produce top-quality results in 2016.

2017
[No Stars]

Harvest: September 26th
Yield: 10,057 kg/ha
Area under vine: 33,868 ha
Average potential alcohol: 10.2%
Average total acidity: 7.9 g/l
Average gluconic acid: 0.3 g/l

Total Sales: 307,379,350 btl
France: 153,512,913 btl
Export: 153,866,437 btl
Prix Constaté : €6.10/kg

Overview: A poor year, with rain and rot at harvest.

An unusually dry winter preceded the campaign of 2017, with 30% less precipitation than average. There were several weeks right after budbreak from the end of March through mid-April that saw a series of severe spring frosts, with twelve nights of hard frost that affected nearly the entire region. From mid-April, however, conditions improved, and fine weather returned. May and June were slightly hotter than average, but rain returned in July. The balance of the month was hot and very wet, ultimately rainier than any other year since 2001. The rain continued into August, but the temperature dropped. The main difficulty in 2017 was grey rot in the vineyard, which began in July and intensified in August. In some areas, the grey rot developed into sour rot. Overall, Chardonnay was least damaged by this problem because of its thicker skin. Approximately 20% of the region was affected by rot in 2017. As with many years with grey rot and sour rot, Drosophila flies were an issue in 2017. The fruit ripened only with difficulty, and the harvest was very late. The quantity of gluconic acid was the highest of the decade thus far. Given the health of the grapes, an exceptionally intense sorting took place during the harvest. Few of the vins clairs that I tasted in the Spring of 2018 were truly exciting. I always hold out hope of some interesting wines, but in general, it seems likely that few if any vintage wines will be made and the best one can hope for from this year is to provide suitable base wines for the non-vintage blends.

2018

****

Harvest: August 20th
Yield: 12,361 kg/ha (10,800 kg/ha AC)
Area under vine: 33,843 ha
Average potential alcohol: 10.2%
Average total acidity: 5.9 g/l
Average gluconic acid: 0.03 g/l

Total Sales: 301,856,265 btl
France: 147,023,258 btl
Export: 154,833,007 btl
Prix Constaté: €6.20/kg

Overview: A new record for heat and sun

2018 was a year of generous yields, lots of alcohol, and unfortunately little acidity. The vintage is popularly considered a success, and doubtless, some excellent vintage wines will be produced. At this early juncture, however, it is impossible to judge well, since exposure to the vins clairs has been brief, and there are no finished wines yet. However, it may well prove the case for the connoisseur that wines from 2018 may lack tension and structure. The winter of 2017 – 2018 was uncommonly warm and wet, becoming both cooler and drier in February and March. Budbreak was in April, followed by rapidly advancing vegetation due to warm weather and a full complement of water in the soil from the prior winter. Although there were some localized storms in the late spring, little damage was done. Flowering was early and thorough. By mid-July, the weather was scorching hot and dry. 2018 is the hottest summer on record since measurements began, breaking the record set by 2003. Fortunately, it lacked the severe heatwave of 2003, and the vines never shut down due to water stress. Harvest began in beautiful if hot, conditions. Eric Rodez delivered a surprisingly elegant Chardonnay vin clair from Les Jeunettes: *"Ripe – loads of tropical fruit here, but there is still enough acidity to balance it."* **** and his Pinot Noir from Les Beurrys was also ravishing: *"Lovely expression of red fruits; exquisite, full-bodied but not heavy at all."* **** (Tasted 2019)

On the north face of the Montagne, the Bérèche brothers have conserved the liveliness of the fruit from Le Cran: *"Lovely freshness and concentration, with floral notes and a well-developed fruit character but enough structure to balance the richness."* ****

Equally enticing was Pinot Noir from Mailly: *"This has an accessible, forward red berry fruit on the attack, but there is plenty of freshness and structure on the palate to deliver a lively wine."* **** (Tasted 2019)

Given these encouraging results, I hope that there will be other surprising successes when the 2018 vintage begins to reach the market.

2019
***

Harvest: September 2nd
Yield: 10,256 kg/ha
Area under vine: 33,829 ha
Average potential alcohol: 10.6 %
Average total acidity: 6.8 g/l
Average gluconic acid: 0.02 g/l

Total Sales: 297,561.896 btl
France: 141,594,046 btl
Export: 155,967,850 btl
Prix Constaté : €6.30/kg

A warm winter with record high temperatures preceded the 2019 campaign, continuing through February. Temperatures returned to normal in March, and bud break occurred began on the 8th of April, in line with the ten-year averages. Unfortunately, there was frost at the time of the bud break, affecting 5,000 hectares in total, with 1,000 completely destroyed. The weather from budbreak to flowering was uneven, with storms and cool weather in early June. Although there were some issues with powdery mildew, fine weather returned around the 15th of June, and flowering began just a few days behind the ten-year average. The end of June was very hot, and the balance of the summer was dry. There was a second heatwave as well, and temperatures reached 42° C (over 107° F), leading to sunburn in the grapes and shriveled bunches. In all yields were down about 17% between the frost, mildew, and sunburn. I was able to taste a very few vins clairs in a January 2020 visit to the region, but due to the Covid pandemic the traditional vin clair tastings were cancelled, and the verdict on this year will have to wait. To judge from anecdotal reports and from the statistics reported by the CIVC, however, we can hope that with slightly more acidity at harvest than 2018, we will have some good results.

Glossary

Agrafe et Liège:

Literally "clip and cork", referring to the system of closing the bottle during the prise de mousse. For many years, the bottle was closed with cork and secured with a metal clip that attached to a squared "ring" of glass at the end of the neck called the bague carrée. Crown caps by contrast, attach to a rounded "bague couronne" and facilitate the automation of the disgorging process which needs to be done by hand for bottles under cork. Some winemakers, however, believe the older system to be superior and there is now a return to this system by some.

Association Viticole Champenoise:

The Association Viticole Champenoise (AVC) is a grape growing and wine-making research institute. It was originally established in 1898 to combat phylloxera but now conducts research on a number of topics relevant to the industry. It was moved in 1941 to the umbrella of the CVIC, and is now part of the Institut Technique du Champagne (ITC), which aggregates all relevant research for parties interested in the industry.

Arm: The part of a vine which extends from the trunk.

Arrière-saison:

The end of the growing season in autumn; the period leading up to the harvest. Good weather during this time of year is known as *une belle arrière-saison* and it can make the difference between a good vintage and a poor one in Champagne.

Autolysis:

Autolysis refers to the breaking down of cells by the enzymes they produce themselves, literally self-destruction. In Champagne production, it refers to the decomposition of yeast cells after the second fermentation. Once the yeast of the second fermentation has consumed all of the sugar in the liqueur de tirage, it has nothing to eat, and it dies. Its decomposition enriches the wine, enhancing texture and adding depth of flavor.

Belon:

A belon is a particular type of tank specific to the production of champagne. It consists of a holding tank, usually stainless steel, which is divided into either two or three sections. The tanks are placed underneath the presses and are used to separate the different sections of must – the cuvée and the taille.

Biodynamic:

Biodynamic wine production refers to the system originally established by Rudolph Steiner. It begins with organic viticulture, including the use of organic compost, cover crops, and "companion planting" to increase biodiversity, but it also employs special soil amendments and vine treatments devised by Steiner. Work is done according to lunar cycles and also according to the biodynamic calendar that characterizes each day as a "root" day, "leaf" day, "fruit" day, or "flower" day. The calendar was developed by Maria Thun building on the ideas of Steiner. According to this calendar, wine tastes better on fruit and flower days. Biodynamics attempts to treat vine diseases and pests with preparations based on other plants. This concept is one of the tenets of biodynamics that is most widely adopted, even by those who do not subscribe to all of Steiner's ideas.

Blanc:

Refers to champagnes that are not pink. These may be made from white grapes (see Blanc de Blancs), but may also be made from black grapes pressed gently and fermented in the absence of their skins (see Blanc de Noirs).

Blanc de Blancs:

Refers to champagne produced from white grapes. This is most commonly Chardonnay, but can also be Pinot Blanc, Pinot Meslier, or Arbanne.

Blanc de Noirs:

A blanc champagne produced exclusively from black grapes. This may be Pinot Noir, Pinot Meunier, or a blend of the two.

Blocage:

The French word blocage refers to a system of managing stocks of wine in the region. In 1938, when producer's stocks exceeded requirements due to the Great Depression, the newly-convened Commission de Châlons instituted the first measures to withdraw (or block) a portion of the stocks from the market. This enabled the industry to maintain prices and equilibrium of sup¬ply and demand. This evolved in the 1950s to the contrat interprofessionnel that made provisions for a limited liability company called the "Société d'Intervention de la Champagne Viticole" that would buy up excess stocks and re-sell them later. The system of managing stocks was codified after the abundant 1982 vintage, and from that time forward maximum yields were agreed (nature permitting) with a buffer amount that could be harvested but had to be kept in reserve. The wines in blocage do not have the appellation "Champagne" until they are "unblocked" for use by the CIVC. In 1996, this was transformed into the Qualitative Reserve, which was transformed again in 2007 into an Individual Reserve, allowing producers to "swap" wines in and out, thus theoretically improving the quality of the wines in the reserve. The amount of wine at present is equivalent to what can be produced from 8,000 kg/ha.

Botrytis:

Also known as grey rot, botrytis is a fungal disease that can cause significant losses in damp conditions. It is important to note that grey rot and the noble rot that produce Sauternes are different phenomenon, the latter being produced by the same organism but in very specific conditions.

Brut:

In the context of Champagne, the word brut refers to the amount of sugar the wine has received prior to shipping. Champagne, to which no sugar is added in the form of dosage is called "Brut Nature." Extra Brut Champagne receives 0 – 6 g/l of sugar. Champagne labeled "Brut" may have anywhere from 0 – 12 g/l of added sugar. Extra Dry (or Extra Sec) Champagne has between 12 – 17 g/l of added sugar; Dry (or Sec) champagne has between 17 – 35 g/l of added sugar. Demi-sec champagne has between 35 – 50 g/l of added sugar, and champagne labeled Doux has 50 g/l or more of added sugar. To a majority of today's tasters, Brut Nature champagnes taste exceptionally dry, while Extra Brut tastes less dry. The upper end of the Brut range can taste sweet to modern palates, and anything more than that tastes decidedly sweet. Many Champagnes produced prior to the 20th century had as much sugar (or more) than Sauternes or Ports.

Budbreak:

Budbreak marks the start of the growth cycle of the vine and occurs when the buds swell, and green shoots begin to grow.

Cage:

Cage is the most common English translation for *muselet* (literally muzzle) which is the wire device that binds the cork to a bottle of Champagne. It was invented in 1844 by Adolphe Jacquesson. Prior to this time the cork was *ficelé*, tied by string to the bottle.

Chalk:

Chalk is a calcium-rich sedimentary rock. It is formed through the accumulation from five to fifty million of years ago of micro-or¬ganisms known as coccolithophore, a single-cell plankton. Chalky soils are one of the fundamental reasons for the quality of the Champagne terroir. The chalk in Champagne is part of the Paris Basin, a vast geological formation that stretches from the Massif Central to the Vosges and northwest into England. In some places the chalk can reach a depths of 300 meters or more. The hills of Marne and nearby départements are formed on a vast expanse of chalk capped by a ridge of Brie limestone. The scarp or slope that descend from this ridge is composed in many places of belemnite chalk laid down in the Campanian Stage of the Upper Cretaceous period. The Campanian Stage lasted from 83.6 to 72.1 million years ago, and the chalk formed in this period is characterized by fossils of belemnoids, an extinct relative of the modern cuttlefish and squid. There is also an older layer of chalk called micraster, characterized by a relative of the sea urchin and starfish of the same name. Many have believed over time that belemnite chalk was innately superior to micraster, but geologist James Wilson in his book suggests that it is not. Because it is an older layer, it is found further out into the flat land, an area less auspicious for vineyards.

Chaptalization:

Chaptalization is the addition of sugar to grape must to enable it to ferment to a higher level of alcohol by volume. In a cool region such as champagne it is quite common, almost reflexive, but some winemakers who oppose adding anything to the must that nature has given them avoid this addition. Producing champagne without chaptalizing is increasingly possible today given the effects of global warming.

Chef de Caves/Chef de Culture:

The Chef de Caves (can also be singular, Chef de Cave) is the head winemaker or cellarmaster of a champagne producer. He is responsible for making, blending, and maturing the wines as well as preparing them for sale. Chef de culture is the French term for the person responsible for growing the grapes, another important role; a slightly old-fashioned term for chef de culture is Chef vigneron.

Chlorosis:

Chlorosis is a disease that impedes the vine from producing chlorophyll which is essential to the production of sugar in the grapes. It occurs in many regions but is exacerbated by the high levels of calcium in the chalk-rich soils of Champagne.

CIVC Comité Interprofessionnel du Vin de Champagne:

The CIVC, known today simply as the Comité Champagne, is the ruling body of the Champagne industry, composed of representatives of both the négociant houses and the grape growers. It has its roots in the Commission de Châlons, set up in 1935 to help regulate the price of grapes in an equitable fashion. During the German occupation in 1940, an organization called the Bureau National de Répartition des Vins de Champagne supervised shipments of Champagne to the occupying German forces. The following year, the name of this organization was changed to Comité Interprofessionnel du Vin de Champagne. The first two co-presidents were Maurice Doyard and Robert-Jean de Vogüé.

The initial remit of the CIVC was the allocation of grapes to the producers and finished wine to the purchasers (the occupying forces). By the end of the war they were also funding co-operatives and pressing centers, and in 1946 the Commission Technique Viticole et Œnologique was established to advise on grape growing and winemaking, while 1947 saw the creating of the Commission de Propagande et d'Information, which was charged with the protection of the intellectual property of the Champagne brand and with the generic promotion of the category as a whole, which is now called the Commission Appellation et Communication Champagne.

Since 1986, the CIVC is given the force of government by the fact that it is overseen by an official of the ruling government. Since 1986 this has been the Prefect of the Champagne-Ardenne region. There are two co-presidents, one from the growers and one from the négociants, who report to the executive board, consisting of an equal number of growers and négociants. The executive board is the decision-making arm of the CIVC. In addition, there are six standing committees.

Vineyard installation (manages vineyards, roads, wastewater and winemaking by-product disposal, etc); Post-production quality control (QA/QC); Technical and Environmental; "Amont" (Lit. "Upstream": adding value, monitoring sales, authenticity, and traceability); "Aval" (Lit. "Downstream": increasing demand, primarily through communication); Appellation Protection (protecting Champagne's intellectual property)

Club Trésors de Champagne: (see Special Club)

Coopérative de manipulation: (see Professional Declaration)

Cork: (see Agrafe et Liège)

Côte des Bar:

The Côte des Bar is one of the four main subregions of Champagne, located mostly in the département of the Aube, the southernmost region where Champagne is produced. There are two main subregions of the Côte des Bar: the Barséquanais and the Bar-sur-Aubois. The first surrounds the Seine and its tributaries, the second the Aube river. The two are separated by the A5 autoroute, which runs southwest from Paris to the Langres region, with the Barséquanais located to the south and the Bar-sur-Aubois to the north. There are 33 villages in the Barséquanais, grouped around the Seine and four of its tributaries: the Arce, the Ource, the Sarce, and the Laignes, each of them offering slightly different expositions. There are 5,474 ha planted in the Barséquanais, 86% of it consisting of Pinot Noir planted in Kimmeridgian marls. This is very similar to the terroir of Chablis, which is much closer to the Barséquanais than the vineyards of the Marne. The distinctness of this geological formation is clearly seen in the maps included in the CIVC booklet *Les Clés des Vins de Champagn*e.

The Bar-sur-Aubois stretches over 31 villages, but there are only 2,423 planted hectares, again dominated by Pinot Noir, which accounts for 80% of plantings. One anomaly is that there are two villages of the Bar-sur-Aubois that extend out of the Aube and into the département of the Haute-Marne: Colombey-les-Deux-Églises and Rizaucourt-Buchey. Colombey-les-Deux-Églises is the easternmost village in Champagne. It is notable as the country home of French President Charles de Gaulle.

Côte des Blancs:

Côte des Blancs is a term with several meanings. The most general meaning is one of the four main subregions of the Champagne appellation. In this sense it is defined by the Union des Maisons de Champagne (UMC) as being further subdivided into the Côte des Blancs proper, the Val du Petit Morin, the Sézannais, the Vitriat, and Montgueux. The subregion as a whole is comprised of 58 villages, with just over 4,100 producers and 6,300 ha of vines. It is planted 84.7% to Chardonnay (hence the name Côte des Blancs, "slope of the whites"), 8% to Meunier (mostly in the Val du Petit Morin), and 7.2% to Pinot Noir (mostly in the Val du Petit Morin and the Sézannais).

What we have referred to as "the Côte des Blancs proper" above is defined by the UMC to include ten communes: the grands crus Chouilly and Oiry to the north; grand cru Cramant due south of the village of Chouilly, and then the grand crus Avize, Oger, and Le Mesnil-sur-Oger in a line to the south. Prolonging the southern trajectory brings one to the premier crus Vertus and Bergères-lès-Vertus. Also included are premier cru Cuis, slightly west of Cramant, along the D10 road, where the vineyards face north/north-east. Premier cru Grauves is also included, which is on the "back" of the Côte itself, with vineyards facing southwest located on the Côte, and facing northeast on the other side of a small stream called Le Darcy.

What is called "the Côte itself" above is a distinction made by some that is mostly local in nature. Within the area included officially in "the Côte des Blancs proper" as defined above, there are four geological formations: Mount Bernon, the Butte de Saran, the "Côte des Blancs itself", and Mont Aimé in the south. Mount Bernon and the Butte de Saran are outliers to the north, and Mont Aimé is an outlier to the south – that is, they are free-standing hills carved away from the main part of the Côte by erosion, and thus have different exposures. This main part of the Côte is what some call "the real Côte des Blancs." In geological terms, this is a cuesta of the Paris Basin (as are most of the champagne vineyards in the Marne, Aisne, and Seine-et-Marne départements). A cuesta (côte in French) is a hill with one side that has a long, slow ascent and another that is a steep drop.

The other sections, or terroirs, within the larger Côte des Blancs subregion are further removed from the Côte itself. The Val du Petit Morin is named for the Petit Morin river, and includes twenty villages south and west of Bergères-lès-Vertus. The Sézannais (also known as the Côte de Sézanne) stretches from the Val du Petit Morin to Montgenost, which borders the Côtes des Bar. The Vitryat is located east of Sézanne along the N40 road on the banks of the Marne. The region includes 15 communes in the hills around the town of Vitry-le-François. Montgueux is typically included here as well, although it is located in the Aube. The village features chalky soils of a type (Turonian) not found elsewhere.

Coulure:

Coulure, sometimes called "shatter" in English is a disruption in flowering caused by insufficient sugar development. This can be caused by cloudy, cold, or rainy conditions around flowering, although an excess of heat at this time can trigger the same phenomenon. This is sometimes referred to as "flower abortion;" the flowers do not turn into berries, reducing yield.

Crayères:

Crayères are chalk quarries used for storing wine since they maintain high humidity and a cold, constant temperature all year. The chalk was excavated and used for building, and there are numerous crayères in Reims, the earliest of which are believed to date to the 4th century. They were re-purposed for the production of champagne beginning in the late 18th century.

Crown Cap:

The crown cap is a bottle closure invented in 1892. In the 1970s many champagne makers began shifted to the use of this closure for aging champagne as it allowed them to automate the disgorgement process. This practice allowed the industry to increase production, but it was not without risks. Early crown caps had cork liners, which allowed too much oxygen into the wine as it aged. Gradually champagne producers moved from cork liners to synthetic liners used today with better results.

Cru:

As a noun in French, "cru" means growth. Use of the term dates back to pre-phylloxera times when vines were all connected below ground and the vines of each village were each their own distinct organism with their own characteristics and reputation. Over time a systematic ranking of the quality of the wines from each village became current. In Champagne, this was codified into a system called the Echelle des crus. This system, devised during a 1911 meeting between growers and négociants, was used to set prices for growers. Each village received a ranking expressed as a percentage: villages rated 100% were designated grand cru villages, those rated 90% or above were known as premier cru villages, and those that were rated less than 90% were termed autres crus (other growths). Each year, a given price per kilogram of fruit was declared by general consensus, and growers in each village received a pro-rata share of the declared price.

Originally there were twelve grands crus. Eight of these were on the Montagne de Reims: Ambonnay, Bouzy, and Louvois, on the south face, and Beaumont-sur-Vesle, Mailly Champagne, Puisieulx, Sillery, and Verzenay on the north face. There were originally two grands crus in the Côte des Blancs: Avize and Cramant, and two in the Marne, Aÿ and Tours-sur-Marne. In 1985, five villages were promoted. Four of them were in the Côte des Blancs: Le Mesnil-sur-Oger, Oger, Oiry and Chouilly. Verzy, located on the north face of the Montagne de Reims, was also promoted.

One particularity of this system was that Chouilly was grand cru for Chardonnay only, and Pinot Noir grown there was classified as premier cru. In Tours-sur-Marne the Pinot Noir was grand cru and the Chardonnay was premier cru. When the European government banned the setting of an indicative price in 2000, this system effectively came to an end. In 2010, however changes were made to the official specifications for making Champagne, called the cahier des charges, that allowed the use of grand cru by the 17 villages noted above, and the use of the term premier cru by the 42 villages that were traditionally designated as such. At the time of this change, the distinction between the grapes in Chouilly and Tours-sur-Marne disappeared.

Cuvée:

The French word cuvée has two meanings. The first is that it refers to the first 2050 liters of grape juice or must to be pressed from the *marc* of 4,000 kg of grapes. This number is derived because the traditional barrel size in Champagne was 205 liters, so the cuvée represents the first ten barrels. This represents approximately 80% of the potential must of this quantity of fruit. The balance, obtained by further pressing, is called the taille, and it is limited to 500 liters. Many producers sell the tailles and do not use them as a point of pride. In general, they have lower acidity and higher tannin, and the quality of the wine obtained is not as fine. Some producers do use the tailles, as they feel it is part of what nature provided and should thus be included in an authentic expression of a vintage or vineyard.

The second meaning is more general, and not limited to Champagne. When the word "Cuvée" appears on the label, it does not have that technical sense, but instead it means a type of wine, one specific blend, or bottling.

Dosage: (see Liqueur d'Expédition)

Département:

A département is an administrative division of France. The country is divided into 18 regions (13 in mainland France and five overseas), and these 18 regions are divided into 101 départements. Two-thirds of Champagne's vineyards are located in the Marne. Twenty-three % are located to the south, in the Aube, while 10% are located in the Aisne, and the final 1% is composed of a few vineyards in the départements of the Haute-Marne and Seine-et-Marne. All of these, save the last, are located in the region now known as *Grand Est*, which includes Champagne-Ardenne as well as Alsace and Lorraine. Seine-et-Marne (like Paris) is included in the Ile-de-France. The only villages located here that are authorized to produce champagne are Saâcy-sur-Marne, Nanteuil-sur-Marne, and Citry.

Derogation:

A derogation is an exemption from a rule or requirement. In France (as is common in old world countries), winemaking is highly regulated. In Champagne this is approved by the CIVC, and it can be an exemption from the limit of the harvest as happened in 1970, an exemption from the prohibition of acidifying and chaptalizing in the same year (1976), or an exemption from the pressing limits, as happened in 1983.

Deuxième Zone:

A secondary zone created in Champagne in 1911 in response to the Champagne riots. The original definition of the geographic borders of Champagne took place in 1908, and it included only villages in the départements of the Marne and the Aisne. The villages of the Aube, which had traditionally sold their grapes to Champagne negociants, were excluded. This led to widespread discontent and ultimately to riots, as described beginning on page 288. The solution was a redefinition of the boundaries that occurred in June of 1911, which included the Aube, but only as a secondary zone. This definition stayed in place until 1927.

Disgorge, Dégorger:

Literally means "to cause to pour out." In the production of Champagne this means to remove the sediment from a bottle, which is done after the riddling process, where all of the sediment gathers in the neck of the bottle. In most instances, the neck of the bottle is lightly frozen, the crown cap is removed, and the pressure inside the bottle causes the frozen plug of sediment to be ejected. The Liqueur d'Expédition is added, and the bottle is corked. Prior to corking, some houses also perform what is known as "jetting," which is when a small stream of wine is injected into the bottle, causing it to foam and thus expel the oxygen introduced during the disgorging process. This allows a reduction in the amount of sulfur used to prevent oxidation.

Today this process is highly mechanized and very efficient. Not all wineries, however, are equally advanced, and the equipment required for the processes is expensive. For this reason, some small wineries do the process by hand, which is known as *dégorgement à la volée* (flying disgorgement). This is done without freezing the neck of the bottle and requires practice to avoid unnecessary loss of wine. When wine is aged under cork (see Agrafe et Liège), it is also necessary to disgorge *à la volée*, since the mechanized version requires the use of a crown cap.

Domaine:

In French, word "domaine" is used in many instances. It can refer to a particular piece of land, or to the totality of a land-holding, or to a general area. The word is closely associated with Burgundy, where it is used in the same way that "Château" is used in Bordeaux. In Champagne, the word "House" is often used, but it has the connotation of a négociant house that is buying fruit in addition to the fruit of whatever vines it might own. However, "grower" champagnes, produced by récoltant-manipulants (see glossary) are more akin to the Burgundian model, and thus are often referred to as a "domaine" by both French and English speakers. The term "Estate," which is more traditionally English usage, may also be used. It has a broad meaning that indicates "everything comprising the net worth of an individual," but also has a more specific meaning as "the collected lands of a single owner for his use (wherever they may be located)." Regardless to how they may be referred to, the legal name of a champagne producer is almost always "Champagne XYZ"

Epluchage:

Epluchage is the dressing of wine grapes as if they were table grapes, in other words bunch-by-bunch grooming and removing less-desirable fruit or sections of bunches, as explained in the footnote on page 312.

En foule: (see Provinage)

Estate: (see Domaine)

Fermentation vessel:

A variety of fermentation vessels are used in Champagne, and these can influence the way the wines taste. This glossary entry gives an overview of the different types of vessels in use.

   Oak casks: Until the 1960s, the overwhelming majority of wine was fermented in oak casks. The traditional size in the region is technically called the pièce champenoise, which holds 205 liters. Pièce is a general term: those from Burgundy, for example, contain 228 liters. The barrels used in Bordeaux are called barriques and hold 225 liters. All are currently in use, but the majority of producers using cask ferments in Champagne employ Burgundian barrels.

   There are also larger barrels in common use – 300 liters is a common size. The word Tonneau used to mean four Bordeaux barrels or 900 liters, but this size is no longer produced, and the word is commonly used to simply barrel, as in un tonneau de 350 litres, a common size. Six hundred-liter barrels are called demi-muids. Very large barrels are called foudres. These are normally custom built and can contain anywhere from 10 hl – 60 hl (1,000 – 6,000 liters). Typically, in champagne they are used for storing reserve wines.

Fermentation in cask will impart more or less flavor from the oak depending on the age of the barrels. Most champagne producers prefer older oak barrels that no longer impart the sweet vanilla aromas produced by fermentation in new casks. This influence is further decreased by the use of larger barrels since there is a greater volume to surface ratio. Part of the interest in larger sizes of oak casks is due to the fact that the wines that are fermented in them show less overt oak influence – less of the spicy character – while still having the benefits of a tiny, controlled addition of oxygen with the fermenting wine. During the fermentation of the wine itself, the fermenting must produces carbon dioxide, effectively isolating it from oxygen, but once the process has finished there is a slight uptake in oxygen which changes both the flavor of the wine and the way that it ages. It is most common to age the wines anywhere from two to ten months with the lees (yeast solids left from fermentation), since the lees react with oxygen, neutralizing it, and act as a buffer to prevent the aromas and flavors of the wine from being overly influenced by the cask.

Concrete Tanks and Eggs: Concrete tanks have been used since the 19th century for wine production, most commonly lined with epoxy to facilitate cleaning. This type of fermentation vessel is neutral and limits contact with oxygen. It also offers the advantage of thermal inertia, which means it heats up gradually and maintains a fairly even temperature. Wine or must can be heated or cooled by the use of immersion heaters or through glycol systems built into the tanks. Despite these advantages, concrete was gradually replaced by stainless steel in the 60s and 70s, although it is now enjoying a resurgence among winemakers. New facilities using concrete are being constructed along classic lines, while some producers are opting for concrete tanks in the shape of an egg. This type of shape causes the fermenting wine to flow through the vessel with a current, essentially stirring itself through the motion generated by the fermentation. Other producers have fashioned tanks for fermentation in this egg shape from wood or ceramic.

Stainless Steel Tanks: From the 1960s, producers began to shift to stainless steel tanks. Like concrete they allow for the exclusion of oxygen, and they present the advantages that they are even easier to clean, and it is easier to control the temperature of the fermentation. By maintaining stable, low temperatures during fermentation and giving winemakers the possibility to exclude oxygen from the fermentation, these tanks helped bring about a revolution in reductive winemaking. This ushered in an era of wines with an exquisite purity and concentration of fruit aromas. In skillful hands, this style of Champagne can be magnificent. But like any tool, it can be misused as well. If too much oxygen is excluded, the wines can take on the struck-match reductive aromas that some find unpleasant.

Filtration:

Wines are often filtered prior to bottling in order to improve their clarity and stability. There are different types of filtration that remove particles from ranging from 1.5 microns down to those as small as 0.45 microns or less. Most yeast cells are 5 – 10 microns, and many bacteria range from 0.5 to 3 microns and are thus removed during filtration. The disadvantage of filtration in the eyes of some winemakers is that this process can remove some flavors and textures in the wine that they find desirable.

Fining:

Fining is a process carried out to improve clarity and stability in wine. A fining agent is added to the wine that binds with particles in the wine. It then settles out, to be removed later by racking or filtration. The most common fining agents in champagne are gelatin and bentonite. Base wines, particularly the taille which is pressed more firmly, have phenolic compounds and sometimes color, that a winemaker may find undesirable. Fining gives winemakers a way to address these issues, but the excessive use of fining agents can create problems during the prise de mousse by depriving yeasts of nutrients.

Foudre: (see Fermentation Vessel)

Grande Marque:

Grande Marque means literally « Big Brand ». The use of this term in Champagne cab refer to large négociant houses generally, to a specific organization of these houses called the Syndicat de Grandes Marques, or to the particular style of champagne they produce. The Syndicat de Grandes Marques defined the term for themselves as meaning "A house known for its eminent and constant quality, [which] justifies an elevated price in the market, but whose production is not necessarily very large." According to Bonal, however, internal rules of membership, however, specified that "A house must annually ship at least 0.5% of the total négociant production; [and must] promote this brand as their principal activity, be traditional and continuous exporters, present wines of a consistent and high quality nature created through blending, practice a traditional grande marque philosophy [sic], and enjoy a certain renown."

The term dates to the late 19th century. In 1882 the large négociant firms organized what was originally known as the Syndicat du Commerce des Vins de Champagne, which soon changed its name to the Syndicat de Grandes Marques. The Reims Chamber of Commerce had set itself in opposition to the main Champagne exporters, and the principal houses organized to defend their interests. The Syndicat de Grandes Marques was always a very select group. By 1983 the members included Ayala, Billecart-Salmon, J. Boffinger, Canard-Duchêne, Veuve Clicquot-Ponsardin, Deutz & Geldermann,

Heidsieck et Cie Monopole, Charles Heidsieck, Henriot, Krug, Lanson Père et Fils, Laurent-Perrier, Massé, Mercier, Moët et Chandon, De Montebello, G.H. Mumm, Joseph Perrier, Perrier-Jouët, Piper-Heidsieck, Pol Roger et Cie, Pommery, Ch. et A. Prieur, Louis Roederer, Ruinart, Salon et Cie, and Taittinger. The Grandes Marques, however, were not the only group of négociants. In 1911 the Syndicat des Négociants en Vin de Champagne (known as the Syndicat d'Epernay) was formed with 62 members. In 1994, these groups of négociants were united in the Union des Maisons de Champagne (UMC) under Yves Bénard, president of Moët & Chandon.

However, more than a specific group, the term "grande marque" now indicates a style of Champagne. There are two factors essential to understanding grande marque style. The first is the stated criterion of the grandes marques that they make wines through blending. Blending is one of the chief factors that separates them from the récoltants-manipulants, who are required to produce wine from their own vines. Many of these grande marque producers also age their wines on the lees much longer than the law mandates. This is because of the additional flavor, depth, and texture such aging can bring. In economic terms, however, it is their size (and thus cash flow) that enables them to age wines for this length of time, since a small family firm vinifying four or five hectares can lack the ability to age wines this length of time. The scale of the large firms thus gives rise to a style that is rich and luxurious, while the smaller scale of many growers nurtures a style that is crisp and refreshing, although one is not necessarily better than the other.

Grey rot: (see Botrytis)

Haute Valeur Environnementale:

Haute Valeur Environnementale (HVE) is a certification for agricultural producers of all types. It was established by the law Grenelle II, known officially as Loi No. 2010-788 du 12 juillet 2010. This law established three levels of certification, Only Level 3, the highest, is entitled to the designation HVE. To achieve this certification a producer must meet certain specific goals and undergo an inspection by an outside agency. These goals must be established for the entire estate, and include the following factors: biodiversity, phytosanitary strategy (i.e. the use of pesticides and fungicides), fertilizer management and waste-water management. HVE is a form of sustainable agriculture that is codified at a national level and verified by outside auditors.

Hectare (ha):

A unit of area measure equivalent to 1,000 square meters or 2.47 acres.

House: (see Domaine)

Kimmeridgian:

In the context of wine, Kimmeridgian refers to a soil type. The name comes from a geological age or stage of the Late Jurassic from 157.3 to 152.1 million years ago, and the term modifies soil types formed during this stage. One can speak of Kimmeridgian clay, Kimmeridgian marl, or Kimmeridgian limestone according to the degree of compaction. The name Kimmeridge comes from a village in Dorset, but these soil formations stretch far to the south. It undergirds the Paris Basin, forming a deeper layer underneath. When erosion from rivers such as the Seine and the Aube, these Kimmeridgian soils are exposed. They form the basis of the terroir of the Côte des Bar (as well as Chablis and Sancerre). They are characterized by the inclusion of a type of fossilized oyster known as exogyra virgula.

Late-disgorged, Recently-disgorged:

These are general terms for champagnes that have been aged longer than usual and released after extended aging. Examples include Bollinger RD, Dom Pérignon P2/P3, and Krug Collection. An increasing number of producers are releasing late-disgorged bottlings, typically at much higher prices than the original disgorgement.

Lees:

Lees are the residue from fermentation. Technically speaking, there are two types: the gross lees are remains of grape skins, seeds, or stems that may remain in the wine post-fermentation. Usually the wine is racked off these lees almost immediately (i.e. pumped away or drained by gravity). The fine lees are a silky-textured sediment that takes longer to precipitate. These are the yeast solids that remain after the fermentation of grape juice into wine, and it is most common to age the wine in cask with the fine lees prior to the secondary fermentation.

Lieu-dit:

The term lieu-dit (plural: lieux-dits) means a named place in French. In geographic terms it is the smallest area known by one particular name with local and traditional meaning. In the context of wine, it refers to a specific vineyard site.

Liqueur d'Expédition (Dosage):

Literally "shipping liqueur", also known as Dosage. This term refers to a sweetening agent added to finished champagne to regulate the sweetness of the finished wine. Either cane sugar or Rectified Concentrated Grape Must (RCGM) can be used for sweetening. This liqueur is made by blending wine (often special or old reserve wines) with the sweetening agent. In earlier times, it was not uncommon to add other elements as well including Cognac or other spirit, although this is now illegal. Also see *Brut*

Liqueur de tirage:

Literally "bottling liqueur". This term refers to the combination of yeast and sugar that is used to create the secondary fermentation in bottle.

Lutte Raisonnée:

Literally "reasoned struggle". This is a general term used for sustainable agricultural practices for which there is no established certification. In practice, it is most commonly used by producers who use synthetic inputs (most commonly chemical pesticides and fungicides), but use the minimum amount possible, only when necessary, and in continuously smaller amounts. Lutte Raisonnée also implies the implementation of measures to encourage biodiversity in the vineyard and responsible waste water management and solid waste management. In Champagne there is a specific application of Lutte Raisonnée called Viticulture Durable en Champagne that is verified by outside auditors.

Marc:

A word with two meanings in French. The meaning specific to champagne is a unit of measure that equals 4,000 kg of grapes. This is the basic unit of pressing in champagne, and it can legally produce only 2050 liters of "first run" juice called cuvée and 500 liters of press juice called tailles. Marc also refers to a spirit distilled from the stems, skins, and seeds of grapes that remain after wine is pressed.

Marl:

Marl is a soil type that includes a high percentage of calcium carbonate along with a proportion of clay. It is normally two-thirds calcium carbonate and one-third clay.

Marne Valley:

The Marne Valley is one of the main subdivisions of Champagne. It includes 103 villages and comprises the largest area of vineyards of any subregion at 12,115 hectares. There are six further subdivision within the Marne Valley: The Grande Vallée, the Coteaux Sud d'Epernay, the Right Bank and the Left Bank of the Marne, the Western Marne Valley, and the Terroir de Condé. The Marne Valley begins to the east with the subregion called the Grande Vallée. The region follows the Marne river beginning at Tours-sur-Marne, one of two grand cru villages in the region (the other is Aÿ), although it should be pointed out that some authorities place Tours-sur-Marne in the Montagne de Reims. However, in the nearby grand crus Ambonnay and Bouzy, the vineyards are up against the slopes of the Montagne; at Tours-sur-Marne, they line the river, so here we follow the consensus of authorities and assign Tours-sur-Marne to the Grande Vallée. Most of the other villages in the Grande Vallée are classed as premier crus, although there are two that do not hold up to this standard: Germaine and Fontaine-sur-Aÿ. Both are classed as "other crus", and in the defunct échelle des crus were assigned the lowest ranking of 80%. In the new list of villages currently being studied, Germaine is one of two (along with Orbais l'Abbaye) that is slated to be removed from the list of villages where Champagne can be produced.

The Grande Vallée continues as far west as Cumières. For the next subregion, we switch sides of the Marne, and consider the Côteaux Sud d'Epernay ("slopes south of Epernay"), which begin in Epernay itself and extend to a series of 11 villages that stretch west and south (away from the Côte des Blancs). The only premier cru among them is Pierry. Proceeding west from Epernay after this detour to the south, the region stretches out along the right and left banks of the Marne. The Right Bank is considered superior, since the vineyards face south and thus ripen fruit better, but none of the villages here are rated more than "other cru."

The next subregion to the west is the Terroir de Condé. This is named for the town in the Aisne département of Condé-en-Brie, a town of Gallo-Roman origins with ties to the French royal line, although this village itself does not possess any vineyards. The region is centered around the valley of the Surmelin, one of the tributaries of the Marne. In recent years this has been trimmed to refer to only four villages, although it used to contain 11 villages. Those villages that used to be considered part of Condé are now included in the Western Marne Valley. Most of the communes of the Western Marne are part of the Aisne Département, although there are three that fall into Seine-et-Marne. Today there are 38 villages in the Western Marne, along both the right and left banks. The district continues until the river reaches Montreuil-aux-Lions, the westernmost village in Champagne.

Marque d'Acheteur: (see Professional Declaration)

Mildew:

There are two types downy mildew (mildiou) caused by Plasmopara viticola, and powdery mildew (oïdium) caused by Erysiphe necator. Both are examples of cryptogamic diseases caused by parasites that reproduce by spores. Powdery mildew develops in dry conditions, and downy mildew in damp ones. They are treated with different compounds, although growers following organic or biodynamic processes are limited and most often treat with copper. Grey rot (botrytis) and black rot (rougeot) are other examples of cryptogamic disease.

Millerandage:

Millerandage is the condition that is (incorrectly) referred to as "shot berries" or "hens and chicks," where in a single bunch there is a mixture of normal berries with seeds that ripen in the customary way (the "hens") and small, seedless berries (technically "live green ovaries") that do not grow or ripen. This is caused by poor weather at flowering.

Millésime, Millésimé:

Millésime in French means vintage year. "Millésime 2012" simply means "vintage 2012". When Millésime appears with an accent on the final "é", it literally means "vintaged," and in this sense it is being used as a noun, the name for a particular wine to distinguish it from other wines in the range.

Millésime non-revendiqué (Millésime non-reclamé):

Both terms refer to a wine produced from grapes grown in one vintage year that is not marketed as a vintage wine. Typically (but not always), this is done because these wines do not qualify as vintage wines since they were not aged for 36 months between bottling and release.

Montagne de Reims:

The Montagne de Reims is one of the main subregions of the Champagne appellation. It comprises 93 villages with over 7,900 planted hectares. It is composed in geological terms broadly speaking of a large outcropping of Campanian limestone between the Vesle and Marne rivers, approximately 30 km long, between six and ten kilometers wide and 200 meters high. The Montagne de Reims (or simply "The Montagne") is a broad subdivision, subdivided in eight parts. The first portion is known traditionally as the Grande Montagne, further subdivided in three portions. The first area is the "North Face", which actually lumps together the premier cru villages that face more or less due north, as well as the mostly grand cru villages that face north east. Proceeding around the Montagne in a clockwise rotation, the next subdivision is referred to as the Perle Blanche because the vineyards are largely dominated by Chardonnay, whereas the Montagne is most well-known for Pinot Noir. Vineyards here are classed as premier cru. Continuing our clockwise circle, the next subdivision is the "South Face" with the grands crus Ambonnay, Bouzy and Louvois and the premier cru Tauxières-Mutry. These last two were merged for administrative purposes in 2016 and are now referred to as Val-de-Livre, although in wine circles they retain their original names.

The next subdivisions of the Montagne are on the western side of the north face, on the far side of the D951 road (the Voie de la Liberté made famous after WWII). The first series of 14 villages is referred to as the "Petite Montagne." All of these villages save two have been classed as premier cru since they were promoted in 1985. The Petite Montagne includes twelve premier cru villages: Sermiers, Villers aux Nœuds, Chaméry, Ecueil, Sacy, Villedommange, Jouy-lès-Reims, Pargny-lès-Reims, Coulommes-la-Montagne, Vrigny, Bezannes, and Les Mesneux ; Ormes and Gueux ranked as "other growths." This term is not used by the CIVC or by the Union des Maisons de Champagne, but it is commonly heard in the region. In most official subdivisions, the Petite Montagne is lumped in with the vineyards of the Ardre and the Vesle rivers. The Vesle is essentially a western continuation of the Petite Montage, while the Ardre lies on the other side of the north-east facing slopes of the Petite Montagne. Meunier is much more commonly planted here than elsewhere in the Montagne.

There are two more subdivisions traditionally included with the Montagne, although they are located at a certain remove. The first of these is the Massif de Saint-Thierry, located north-west of the city of Reims. There are sixteen villages here, and Meunier has a strong presence in the vineyards, dominant in several of them. Grapes have been grown here since medieval times. The Vesle river separates the Massif de Saint-Thierry from those of the Vesle Valley. On the other side of the city of Reims is a free-standing hill called the Mont de Berru. Grouped with another local slope near the village of Selles, the region takes the plural name as "Monts de Berru." This is very close to the border of the Ardennes département; the vineyards are largely planted to Chardonnay.

Mousse: Foam or bubbles.

Moth:

Tordeuse is one type of pest in the vineyards of Champagne, a general term in French for moths of the family Tortricidae, of which there are more than 10,000 species. The general term in English is Leafroller Moth. One specific type of tordeuse is known as Cochylis, which signifies one genus of Tortricidae. Another pest belonging to the same family is referred to in French as Eudémis, (English: the European grapevine moth, Latin: Lobesia botrana). Yet another species, more common in the U.S., is distinct from this European variety is confusingly known in English simply as the grape berry moth, whose Latin name is Paralobesia viteana. Another type of moth is called in French Pyrale after their Latin name Pyralinae, which in English is the Snout Moth. Yet other types of moths attack the buds in their early stages of development, which are collectively known in French as mange-bourgeons (bud-eaters) of which there are numerous species of moths as well as beetles, including those insects known as noctuelle, boarmie, and charançon in French.

Must: Unfermented grape juice or fermenting grape juice before it is wine.

Négociant distributeur: (see Professional Declaration)

Négociant, Négociant-Manipulant:

A négociant is one who buys and sells. For the phrase négociant-manipulant and a description of all of the professional declarations, see the glossary note under Professional Declaration.

Oak: (see Fermentation Vessel)

Organic viticulture:

Organic production is that which conforms to the norms approved by the International Federation of Organic Agriculture Movements (IFOAM) and has been certified as such by an approved body. Certified organic Champagnes will display the EU organic logo (called the Eurofeuille) and the French "AB" organic label regulated by the Agence Française pour le Dévelopement et la Promotion de l'Agriculture Biologique. It has been regulated by the EU since 1991. In order to display these labels a producer must undergo a period of conversion and then submit to an audit by an outside auditing agency. These auditing agencies are certified by the INAO, and include organizations such as Ecocert, Certipaq Bio, Bureau Veritas, and others.

 At its base it is a system that struggles to protect the environment, promote biodiversity and ensure the well-being of local flora and fauna. It does this by forbidding the use of synthetic pesticides, herbicides, chemical fertilizers, and genetically modified organisms. In place of these products, copper, sulfur and clay are used, and an important emphasis is placed on tilling the soil, the use of cover crops, and the use of organic compost.

 Organic production offers several advantages as an environmental management system (EMS) in that it clearly and strictly defines the acceptable OPI (Operational Performance Indicators) and refer to the specific operational steps that impact the environment and establishes a verifiable protocol for auditing progress.

 Some producers criticize organic (and biodynamic) certification because of its reliance on copper sulfate, a heavy metal toxic to humans and animals. This is of particular concern in Champagne where the climate is cold and wet, which gives rise to cryptogamic disease, obliging frequent treatment that can cause a buildup of these molecules in the soil and in plants.

Parcellaire:

A parcellaire in Champagne parlance is a Champagne produced from one single lieu-dit or portion thereof.

Phylloxera:

Phylloxera (Daktulosphaira vitifoliae) is a root louse that feeds on the sap of grapevines, causing deformations of the roots that eventually lead to the death of the grapevine. This insect is native to North America, but vines there have evolved natural defenses against this pest, while traditional European grape varieties of the species vitis vinifera have not. The pest was introduced into France in the mid-19th century. The exact method of introduction is not known, but vines were regularly imported into Europe for various reasons that included experimentation and grafting trials. It is believed that the faster crossings permitted by steamships in the mid-19th century allowed the insects to survive the journey.

 Phylloxera eventually led to the death of nearly all vitis vinifera worldwide. The pest cannot survive in very sandy soils, and has not yet been able to penetrate Chile, as it is protected by the Andes, the Pacific Ocean, and the Atacama Desert. The only way to overcome the pest was to replant and graft vitis vinifera onto resistant rootstocks. However, there are small pockets of ungrafted vines that survive; one of these is in Champagne. Wine from these vines is produced by Bollinger, and it is called Vieilles Vignes Françaises

Phytosanitary:

Relating to the health of plants. Phytosanitary treatments in the vineyard are those treatments performed to ensure the health of the vine, which most often applies to the use of pesticides and fungicides.

Press, pressing:

The process of pressing the grapes in Champagne is strictly regulated, unlike many other winemaking regions, even in France. The size, nature, and action of the pressing centers are regulated as described in the appendix (the cahier de charges), as is the amount of juice that can be extracted from a given amount of fruit. This is fixed at 2,550 liters per 4,000 kg of grapes (or 102 lit/160 kg as written in the legislation). This includes 2,050 liters of first press juice, called cuvée, and 500 liters of second press juice, called taille.

The traditional press used in the region is called the Coquard press after one of the manufacturers. It is horizontal basket press. Many producers favor this type of press as it is easy to load whole bunches of grapes (mandatory in Champagne) and to control the flow of juice. Once the grape bunches are loaded into the press, the plate is lowered and gradually tightened until the juice slows (referred to as a serre, or tightening). The plate is then lifted and using a pitchfork the grapes are heaped up or "forked over" onto each other. This is called a retrousse, a term which means "to roll up," as in roll up one's sleeves. Normally three retrousses are needed to obtain the cuvée, which is kept separate from the tailles to follow. The second press is called taille because the grapes' needs to be chiseled out of the press for the retrousse. Some producers prefer only to work with the cuvée and will sell off their tailles, while others will produce their Champagne from the entire pressing.

Among the disadvantage of the Coquard presses are that they are fairly slow, require a lot of manpower for the retrousses, and expose the fruit to a fairly significant amount of oxidation. Horizontal presses (called Vaslin presses) were introduced in the middle of the 20th century. These are faster and required less manpower, but they treat the grapes rather harshly and tend to deliver juice with a higher phenolic content. Other producers prefer to use horizontal pneumatic bladder presses which are very gentle, require less labor, and can be flushed with nitrogen if desired. The newest type of press is called the PAI press, also manufactured by Coquard. PAI is an acronym for Pressoir Automatique à Plateau Incliné, and the press functions as follows: grapes are loaded in the top and then compressed between two fixed, tilted horizontal plates by the hydraulic action of the press. Once the press is retracted, the grapes fall to bottom of the press and the action is repeated, again eliminating the requirement for a manual retrousse.

Prise de mousse:

The process of making a wine sparkle. This is done provoking an additional fermentation of sugar by yeast after bottling. The process enriches the wine, imparting additional alcohol, and enhances the aromas, flavors, and texture of the wine. The process is carried out by adding yeast and sugar to the wine at the time of bottling.

In English the term second or secondary fermentation is often used, although this term is rather imprecise. The first fermentation (also called the primary or alcoholic fermentation) is the conversion of grape sugars into alcohol under the action of yeast. The next process to occur in the production of sparkling wine is normally referred to as "malolactic fermentation". This term is also somewhat imprecise, since it refers to the conversion of malic acid into lactic acid under the action of bacteria. For this reason, the term "malolactic conversion" is more correct. The next process to occur is commonly referred to as the secondary fermentation, but to clarify the meaning and order of these processes it may be simpler to adopt the more precise French term of "prise de mousse".

Professional declaration:

By law Champagne producers must print the registration and code number issued by the CIVC on the bottle. This begins with two initials that indicate what type of activity they undertake, which include the following possibilities:

NM (Négociant-Manipulant): A company that buys grapes, must or finished wine (including either vins clairs or vins sur lattes), to sell under their own label.

RM (Récoltant-Manipulant): A grower who produces Champagnes from grapes that they have grown in their own vineyards and produced on their own premises. An RM is not allowed to purchase more than 5% of the fruit that they process.

CM (Coopérative de Manipulation): A cooperative is a collectively-owned structure that produces wine from grapes grown by its members.

RC (Récoltant-Coopérateur): A producer who grows grapes, delivers them to a co-op, and markets the wine produced by the co-op under a label of his own.

SR (Société de Récoltants): An association (usually one family) that produces Champagne from vineyards sourced from family vineyards.

ND (Négociant-Distributeur): A distributor that sells finished Champagne produced by others under their own label.

MA (Marque d'Acheteur): "Buyer's Own Brand," or private label, is a Champagne label produced exclusively for one purchaser.

Provinage:

Prior to the Phylloxera epidemic in the 19th century, grapevines were not planted individually as they are today, but instead were propagated via layering. At this time, vineyards constituted what is referred to as a clonal grove – all the vines in one place shared the same root system. New vines were established by forming what is referred to as adventitious roots: roots formed from the shoots when they were placed in contact with the ground. The vines were buried in a trench about six inches deep. The process is described at length in Vizetelly's work A History of Champagne cited in the bibliography. This practice led to vineyards that were in a large single mass or en foule. The phylloxera root louse, however, eventually led to the death of the quasi-totality of vines planted in this way, and today wine grapes (vitis vinifera) are grafted on to resistant rootstocks, usually hybrids created from native North American varieties including Vitis berlandieri, Vitis riparia, and Vitis rupestris.

Rebêches:

The amount of juice pressed from the grapes that is in excess of the legally authorized limit. This juice must be sent for distillation.

Récoltant-coopérateur: (see Professional Declaration)

Récoltant-manipulant: (see Professional Declaration)

Reductive winemaking:

Reductive winemaking is a style of winemaking that strives to reduce contact with oxygen to a minimum in order to preserve bright, fresh fruit aromas. This is a process that is emphasized throughout the winemaking process from harvest until bottling. The use of a pneumatic press, sulfur dioxide, fermentation in stainless steel tanks, temperature control, and the avoidance whenever possible of pumping wine are some of the techniques employed. Traditional methods in Champagne that employed a vertical basket press and fermentation in cask without external temperature control were all fairly oxidative in nature. While these traditional methods did not allow the preservation of bright, forward fruit, there are those who argue that the wines had more complexity to compensate for the relative lack of freshness, and that they aged more gracefully since the exposure to oxygen in their fabrication inured them in a sense to oxidation during bottle aging.

Réserve perpetuelle:

Sometimes (incorrectly) called a solera, reserve wines in Champagne are sometimes kept in one tank or foudre. A portion of the reserve was drawn out each year and used in the blend of the Champagne and the tank or foudre was topped up with the wine of the year. This is what is known as a fractional blend, being composed a certain proportion of wine from previous vintages, and the complexity of the blend increases as the years progress.

Riddle, Remuage:

The French verb remuer means to stir. In the Champagne winemaking process, it refers to the process that gathers the remains of the yeast from the second fermentation (called the lees) in the neck of the bottle. This is done by gradually turning the bottle while inclined until it is positioned with the neck of the bottle upside down. Beginning in the early 19th century this was done by hand in wooden racks known as pupitres (pulpits), starting with the bottles horizontal and gradually rotating them and tilting them until they were vertical. This process, carried out by hand, requires four to six weeks. By the middle of the 20th century the process had become mechanized: a machine known as a gyropalette holds 500 bottles at a time and turns them slowly 24 hours a day. In this way the process is completed in one week, with no manual effort. Some special bottle sizes and shapes that do not fit easily into a gyropalette are still riddled by hand. The yeast produces two types of sediments, one rather coarse, the other much finer. The difficulty is to gather both types of sediment in the neck of the bottle at the same time. They are collected in a small plastic cap that is added at bottling called the bidule and removed at disgorging.

Rosé:

Pink. This type of Champagne is colored with the coloring agents, known as anthocyanins, found in the skins of black grapes. This may be accomplished either by making a white base wine and by making a red base wine and blending the two. This is called a rosé d'assemblage. It can also be made by fermenting all of the must with the skins for a brief period and then running the juice off and finishing the fermentation without the skins, which is called rosé de saignée.

Rougeot (black rot):

Black rot is a disease caused by the fungus Guignardia bidwellii that is particularly dangerous in warm, wet weather and can lead to significant crop loss.

Saignée: (see Rosé)

Second (Secondary) Fermentation: (see Prise de Mousse)

Sanitary condition:

The term refers to the amount of fungal disease (rot and mildew) present in the grapes at harvest.

Saute-bouchon:

Literally, cork-popper; an 18th century synonym for Champagne.

Sauvage: A tasting term that evokes savory or "animal" notes in a wine.

Sexual confusion:

The term sexual confusion refers to the use of pheromones to disrupt the mating of several species of moths. Pheromones are chemicals that trigger a response from members of the same species. Traps that are saturated with these pheromones are hung in the vines, rendering the males unable to find female moths. This is a way to treat a vineyard for a moth infestation without using pesticides.

Solera: (see Reserve Perpetuelle)

Sous bois:

There are two meanings for the term sous bois. In winemaking terms, it means fermented and/or aged in cask (bois = wood). As a tasting term (with a hyphen) sous-bois translates best as forest floor and indicates an autumnal aroma reminiscent of fallen leaves and mushrooms.

Société de Récoltants: (see Professional Declaration)

Special Club (Club Trésors de Champagne):

Special Club is a term that designates a wine selected for and approved by the Club Trésors de Champagne. This club was the first formal association to promote independent grower/producers and their champagne, founded in 1971 as the Club de Viticulteurs Champenois. In 1985 they adopted a distinctive bottle shape (now updated), and changed their name to Club Trésors de Champagne in 1999. In vintage years, these members choose a champagne blend that is typical of their terroir for submission to a jury composed of oenologists and winemakers. The sample is tasted blind by this jury as a vin clair and again as a finished champagne (with a minimum of three years on the lees) and it must be approved both times.

Subregions of Champagne:

Champagne is normally subdivided into four main subregions: Montagne de Reims, Marne Valley, Côte des Blancs, and the Côte des Bar. Each of these has its own entry in the glossary. For the purposes of this book, these four main regions are subdivided into smaller units called terroirs, as follows: the Montagne de Reims is subdivided into the terroirs of the Grande Montagne (North Face, South Face, and the Perle Blanche), the Petite Montagne, the Ardre Valley, the Vesle Valley, the Monts de Berru and the Massif de Saint-Thierry. The Marne Valley is subdivided into the Grande Vallée, the Côteaux Sud d'Epernay, the Right Bank, Left Bank, Western terroirs of the Marne Valley in the Aisne

département, and the terroir of Condé. The Côte des Blancs is subdivided
into the terroirs of the Côte des Blancs proper, the Sézannais, the Vitryat, the
Val du Petit Morin, and Montgueux. The Côte des Bar is subdivided into the
terroirs of the Bar-sur-Aubois and the Barséquanais.

Sur pointes:

After a wine is riddled, it is stored upside down so that the sediment stays
in the bidule (see entry for riddle). This is called "Stockage sur pointes".
All champagnes are stored in this way prior to being disgorged, but for top
vintage wines they may be stored like this for up to five years or even longer.

Sustainable viticulture: (see Lutte Raisonnée)

Syndicat Général des Vignerons de la Champagne (SGV):

Formed in 1904, the union of Champagne grape growers serves as the representative of growers in the region with nearly 20,000 members. The representative of the SGV serves along with the representative of the négociants
(elected from the Union des Maisons de Champagne) to lead the decisions
of the CIVC. They also represent Champagne growers at a national level,
provide technical advice to members, and help to promote Champagnes
produced by récoltants-manipulants and récoltants-cooperateurs under the
umbrella Champagnes de Vignerons.

Syndicat Professionnel des Courtiers en Vins de Champagne:

Courtiers are brokers who arrange contracts between growers and négociants. The Professional Union of Champagne Brokers works with more than
90% of the growers in the Champagne region. The profession has existed
since the 11th century, when it was named by the Provost and the Echevins
(city council) of the city of Reims.

Taille: The juice obtained through a second pressing of the fruit. (See Press)

Terroir:

The French word terroir has two meanings. The general meaning in the
world of wine is the land, considered with respect to the crops that are
produced there. It is most easily expressed as the nexus of climate, soil,
and topography. Some definitions also include the human element as far as
cultural practices, traditions, and regulatory structure. This broader definition is close to what is meant by the term paysage in wine terms. In this
book, terroir is also used in a specific sense to mean a small subregion with
relatively homogeneous growing conditions. For a fuller explanation, see the
glossary entry under Subregion.

Ullage:

Ullage is headspace – the amount of space between the level of liquid in a container (a bottle or a barrel of wine) and the top of the container. This increases over time in older wines.

Veraison:

Veraison is the onset of the ripening of the grapes, marked by the time when the berries turn color.

Vigneron: A French term meaning grape-grower.

Vin clair: Base wine used in the production of Champagne.

Vineux (vinous):

Sometimes translated as wine-like or winey, it is sometimes taken simply to mean "strong in alcohol," but also implies structure and density. It is a characteristic imparted above all by the Pinot Noir grape.

Vintage:

For a Champagne to include a vintage year on the label, it must conform to all of the regulations in the Cahier des Charges (which follows as an appendix). Chief among these regulations is that the base wine must all come from that year, and that the wine must be aged for a period of three years from the time of bottling before it is released. The specific portions of the Cahier de Charges that are relevant include the following:

> *Section IX, Paragraph F Section 7:* "The disgorgement cannot be carried out before a period of twelve months from the date of bottling during which time the wines must remain in bottle without interruption."

> *Section IX, Paragraph F Section 11:* "The wines may be bottled with the vintage date [millésimé in French; "vintaged"] if the grapes used for the development of the base wines are grapes of the vintage concerned, with the exception of the volumes of wines or musts grapes used in the context of authorized oenological practices and processes and products contained in the bottling liqueur or shipping liqueur."

> *Section IX, Paragraph I Section 1:* "a) The wines shall be marketed to the consumer only after a maturation period of at least fifteen months from the date of bottling. b) The wines with a vintage date shall be put on the market only at the end of a maturation period of thirty-six months minimum from the date of the bottling." *See also Millésime and Millésime non-reclamé.*

> Further rules regarding the production of vintage Champagne are found in Appendix V: Decree of 17 October 1952 Concerning the Indication of vintage of AOC "Champagne" Wines.

Viticulture Durable en Champagne:

Viticulture Durable en Champagne (VDC, lit. Sustainable Winegrowing in Champagne) is the name for the sustainable agriculture initiative being spearheaded by the CIVC. It began as Viticulture Raisonnée in 2001 as a voluntary initiative. The name was changed to Viticulture Durable en Champagne, and in 2014 they implemented a process for certification. The process was updated in 2016. According to the CIVC, 20% of the region is certified today, and their goal is to have 100% certified by 2030. VDC includes specific, verifiable goals in six areas: the use of phytosanitary agents, the use of fertilizer, the preservation of biodiversity, the protection of the overall region, the recycling of solid waste and waste water, and the reduction of the carbon footprint.

Appendix I

SPECIFICATIONS OF THE APPELLATION "CHAMPAGNE"[1]

Consolidated Version of May 8, 2019

This text has modified the following provisions:
Law of May 6, 1919: Art. 17

And has repealed the following provisions:
Law of May 6, 1919: Art. 16, Art. 18, Art. 19, Art. 20, Art. 21
Decree of June 29, 1936: Art. 1, Art. 2, Art. 3, Art. 4, Art. 4 bis, Art. 5, Art. 7, Art. 8, Art. 9, Art. 10, Art. 11, Art. 12, Art. 13, the preamble to the Report to the President of the French Republic.
Decree of 17 October 1952: Art. 1, Art. 2, Art. 3, Art. 4, Art. 5

Repealed: the decree of 17 January 1978 on the density of plantations, the methods of conduct and the methods of size of the vines intended for the production of wines with Champagne and Coteaux champenois appellations of origin.

Chapter I

I. Name of the appellation:

Only the wines conforming to these provisions and those of the law of May 6th, 1919 relative to the protection of appellations of origin can claim to be of AOC Champagne[2].

II. Geographical names, indication of the vintage, additional mentions:

A) Wines that respect of the conditions of production fixed for the vintage wines in the present specifications may be labeled with the vintage date.

B) In accordance with local, loyal and consistent practices, the name of the appellation may be supplemented by the terms "grand cru" for wines made from grapes harvested on the territory of the following communes of the Department of Marne: Ambonnay, Avize, Ay, Beaumont-sur-Vesle, Bouzy,

---

1   Cahier des charges de l'appellation d'origine contrôlée Champagne. B.O. n°38 du 15 septembre 2016, JORF n°0273 du 25 novembre 2010 page 21013 texte n° 8 : Décret n° 2010-1441 du 22 novembre 2010 relatif à l'appellation d'origine contrôlée « Champagne ». Online. Available : https://www.legifrance.gouv.fr/affichTexte.do?cidTexte=JORFTEXT000023126020&date-Texte=20190311

2   Appellation d'Origine Côntrolée (controlled appellation of origin), abbreviated throughout as AOC. Most recent EU documents refer to Appellation d'Origine Protegée" but both terms refer to the same concept, known legally in English as Geographic Indication. The present "Cahier des Charges" or Specifications in total serves to define AOC Champagne.

Chouilly, Cramant, Louvois, Mailly-Champagne, Le Mesnil-sur-Oger, Oger, Oiry, Puisieulx, Sillery, Tours-sur-Marne, Verzenay and Verzy.

C) In accordance with local, loyal and consistent practices, the name of the appellation may be supplemented by the word "premier cru" for wines made from grapes harvested in the following communes: Avenay-Val-d'Or, Bergères-lès-Vertus, Bezannes, Billy-le-Grand, Bisseuil, Chamery, Champillon, Chigny-les-Roses, Coligny (Val-des-Marais), Cormontreuil, Coulommes-la-Montagne, Cuis, Cumières, Dizy, Ecueil , Etrechy, Grauves, Hautvillers, Jouy-lès-Reims, Ludes, Mareuil-sur-Ay, The Mesneux, Montbré, Mutigny, Pargny-lès-Reims, Pierry, Rilly-la-Montagne, Sacy, Sermiers, Taissy, Tauxières, Trépail, Trois-Puits, Vaudemanges, Vertus, Villedom-mange, Villeneuve-Renneville, Villers-Allerand, Villers-aux-Nœuds, Villers-Marmery, Voipreux and Vrigny.

III. Color and types of wine:

The AOC Champagne is reserved for sparkling white or rosé wines.

IV. Areas and areas in which different operations are performed:

A) The harvesting of the grapes, the vinification, the elaboration of the wines, including the maturation and bottling are limited to the territories indicated by article 17 of the law of May 6th, 1919, subject to the following provisions[3]:

B) In the district of Vitry-le-François (Marne department), the area that can be planted is defined as that approved by the committee of the INAO at the meeting of the 7 and 8 November 1990, a map of which is filed in the town halls concerned.

C) In the following communes of the Department of Aube: Arsonval, Cunfin, Dolancourt, Jaucourt, the area that can be planted is defined as that approved by the committee of the INAO at the meetings of June 23, 1994, September 8, 1994 and May 19, 1995, a map of which is filed in the town halls concerned.

D) In the following communes of the Aube department: Brienne-le-Château, Epagne, Précy-Saint-Martin and Saint-Léger-sous-Brienne and in the following communes of the Marne department: Esclavolle-Lurey, Potangis, Saint-Quentin-le-Verger and Villiers-aux-Corneilles, no plot was selected in accordance with the decisions of the relevant committee of the INAO in the sessions of 23-24 June 1994, September 7-8, 1994, May 18-19, 1995 and September 6-7, 1995.

---

3   Article 17 refers to the decret of December 17th, 1908, but the exact list is not printed in the law itself. It can be found in the Journel Officiel as cited in the bibliography.

E) In the following communes of the department of Aube: Marcilly-le-Hayer and La Villeneuve-au-Châtelot, no plot was selected in accordance with the decision of the relevant committee of the INAO in session of September 10, 1997.

F) In the municipality of the Marne department of Fontaine-sur-Ay, the plantable area is that approved by the relevant committee of the INAO in session the 9-10 September 1999 and whose map is deposited in the town hall of the municipality concerned.

G) In the following communes of the Marne department: Corfélix, Corrobert, Le Thoult-Trosnay, Verdon, Reuves and Broussy-le-Petit, no plot was selected in accordance with the decision of the relevant committee of the INAO at the meeting of 5-6 September 2001.

V. Grape varieties:

A) Wines come exclusively from Arbane (B)[4], Chardonnay (B), Meunier (N)[5], Petit Meslier (B), Pinot Blanc (B), Pinot Gris (G)[6] and Pinot Noir (N).
B) There is no special provision governing the proportion of varietals within the exploitation.

VI. Vineyard management:

A) Vineyard management norms:
1. Density of plantation:
General provisions: The vines are planted with a spacing between rows that cannot be greater than 1.50 meters. The distance between each vine on the same row is between 0.90 meter and 1.50 meter. The sum of the spacing between the rows and the distance between the feet on the same row may not be greater than 2.50 meters.
2. Particular dispositions:
In order to allow the passage of suitable equipment, parcels presenting either a slope greater than 35%, or a slope greater than 25% associated with a superelevation of more than 10%, may have aisles, with a width of between 1, 50 meters and 3 meters, with a maximum frequency of one rank out of six. In this case, the sum of the spacing between the other rows and the distance between feet on the same row may not be greater than 2.30 meters.

B) Pruning rules:
We understand by the term "œil franc" [free bud] a bud separated from the base of the arm or the head, regardless of the space between the buds. Any overlapping between vines and any overlapping of fruiting canes is prohibited. The number of buds must be less than or equal to 18 per square meter.

---

4   Blanc, a white grape
5   Noir, a black grape
6   Gris, a pink berry. Not mentioned in the Cahier de Charges is the synonym found in the region, Fromenteau

Pruning is carried out at the latest before the phenological stage (F) (12 of Lorentz), the emergence of four leaves.

The vines are pruned according to the following techniques:

1. Taille Chablis

Description:
a) "Taille Chablis" includes arms of at most 0.30 meter.
b) Each arm has a fruit-bearing extension cane at its end.
c) Either a replacement spur called a "rachet" or a "crochet", trimmed to 2 buds maximum is left at the base of the stump, or a renewal spur, called "rentrure", pruned to 2 buds maximum, is left on one of the arms.

Particular Requirements
a) The fruiting cane is pruned with a maximum of four buds for Pinot Blanc, Pinot Gris, and Pinot Noir; and with a maximum of five buds for Arbane, Chardonnay, Meunier, and Petit Meslier.
b) The vine trunks must be planted such that the bud at the end of the fruiting cane is at a maximum height of 0.60 meters above ground level.

Special Provisions
a) In the case of a missing arm, a renewal spur with two buds maximum may be left on one of the arms in additional to the renewal spur at the base of the stump.
b) Meunier vines with a space of more than 1.20 meters between vines can be trained with three arms each carrying a fruit cane, laid down on a wire and pruned with a maximum of six buds.

2. Cordon de Royat

Description:
A single permanent horizontal cordon is established, without length limitation, at a maximum height of 0.60 meters above ground level.

Particular Requirements:
a) The spurs are at least 0.15 meters apart and pruned to:
2 buds for Pinot Blanc, Pinot Gris, Pinot Noir and Meunier grape varieties;
3 buds for Arbane, Chardonnay and Petit Meslier.
b) The replacement spur called "rachet", at the base of the cordon, is pruned to 2 buds.
c) The fruiting cane is pruned to: four buds for Pinot Blanc, Pinot Gris, Pinot Noir; five buds for Arbanne, Chardonnay, Meunier, and Petit Meslier.
Special Provisions:
a) The cordon can be connected to the trunk in one or several places

b) In the case of the progressive renewal using a new cordon but without removing the old arm, this new cordon is trellised along it. The arm requiring this is removed on the old arm so that there is no overlaps or juxtaposition between the shoots of the two arms, and provided that this renewal is not done each year on the same vine.
c) The establishment of a cordon in the opposite direction to that originally existing (called "a return"), and intended to fill an accidental void, is possible under the condition of not giving rise to a growth of new wood each year.
iv) The annual percentage of renewal must not surpass 20% of the vines in a given parcel.

3. Vallée de la Marne

Description:
a) The vines are pruned with:
i) A spur with three buds maximum per vine
ii) A cane from last year's spur with a maximum of nine buds
iii) A fruiting cane established at the end of last year's cane with six buds maximum
b) The fruiting cane is tied down at a maximum height of 0.5 meters above the soil.

Particular Requirements:
This technique is only authorized for Meunier

Special Provisions:
a) When a new fruiting cane is not started every year, one of the two arms may carry a renewal spur, called a "rentrure", pruned to a maximum of two buds. The spur at the base of the vine is then pruned to three buds
b) When one of the two arms is completely renewed, the fruiting cane on the spur is pruned to a maximum of eight buds. The fruiting canes are tied down at a maximum height of 0.5 meters above the soil.

4. Guyot Simple and Guyot Double

Description:
a) the vines are pruned in Guyot Simple with a spur the three buds maximum and a long cane with a maximum of ten buds. In Guyot Double with at most two spurs with two buds maximum and at most two long canes with a maximum of eight buds of which six maximum are tied to the wire in a horizontal position.
b) The long canes are tied down at a maximum height of 0.5 meters above the level of the soil.

5. Guyot Asymmetric

Description:
a) The vines are pruned with a spur of two buds maximum, a cane with a maximum of six buds, a fruiting cane at the end of last years cane, or an additional arm of more than two years carrying a maximum of six buds
b) The vine must be trained so that the last buds are at a maximum height of 0.6 meters.

C) **Trellising Rules:** The trellising system is in place no latter then the year in which the vineyard enters into AOC production.
1. **Tying down:** The canes are tied down before the phenological stage (I) (23 of Lorentz) called "flowering" and is made consistent with the pruning system adopted.
2. **Tying up:** The lifting of the shoots on wires is obligatory. It is carried out at the latest at the phenological stage (L) (stage 33 of Lorentz) called "bunch closure".
3. **Height of foliage:** The height of the trellised foliage, after trimming, is at least 0.6 times the spacing between the rows. It is measured between the wire used for tying down and the upper trimming limit.
4. **Average maximum load for each parcel:** The average maximum load per plot is 19,700 kilograms of grapes per hectare. The number of clusters per square meter of vine area in production is less than or equal to 17.
5. **Threshold of missing vines:** The percentage of dead or missing vines referred to in Article D. 645-4 of the Rural Code fixed at 20%.
6. **Growing condition of the vine:** Viticulture is conducted to ensure a good overall cultural condition of the vine, including its health and maintenance of its soil.

D. Other cultural practices:

A) In order to preserve the characteristics of soils which constitute a fundamental element of the terroir:
1. Permanent grassing of the area around the vineyard is mandatory.
2. The use of household organic compost and waste, sewage sludge other than those of wine-growing facilities, alone or in combination, is prohibited.
3. Any substantial change in the terrain or the subsoil or of the elements that ensure the integrity and durability of the soil of a parcel intended for the production of AOC wine is prohibited, with the exception of classic tilling of the soil.

E. **Irrigation:** Irrigation is forbidden

VII. Harvest, Grape Transport and Grape Ripeness

A) **Harvesting:** The wines come from grapes harvested with good maturity. The date of the beginning of the harvest is fixed according to the provisions of Article D. 645-6 of the Rural Code. An end-of-harvest date is set by prefectural decree proposed by the INAO after consultation with the CIVC.
1. **Special provisions for harvesting:**
Any means that do not allow the harvesting of whole bunches of grapes is prohibited.

B) **Special provisions for the transport of the vintage:**
1. The grapes are transported whole all the way to the pressing facilities.
2. The baskets, cases and crates used to transport the grapes from the picking place to the pressing facility shall have holes in the bottom and on all sides for the rapid and complete flow of the juice while waiting for pressing.

C) **Maturity of the grapes/Sugar content of the grapes:**
The grapes cannot be considered to have good maturity with a sugar content of less than 143 grams per liter of must.

D) **Minimum natural alcoholic strength by volume:**
The wines have a minimum natural alcoholic strength by volume of 9%.

VIII. Yield and the entry into production

A) **Yield:** The yield referred to in Article D. 645-7 of the Rural Code is fixed at 12,400 kilograms of grapes per hectare.[7]
1. **Maximum Yield ("Rendement Butoir"):** The maximum yield referred to in Article D. 645-7 of the Rural Code is fixed at 15,500 kilograms of grapes per hectare.[8]

B) **Storage of part of the harvest (the Reserve):**
1. When a reserve is established pursuant to Article 167 of Regulation (EU) No 1308/2013 of 17 December 2013 on the organization of the common markets for agricultural products, the maximum volume of base wines which may be subject to storage by an operator may not exceed 8,000 kilograms of grapes per hectare of area under production.[9]
2. When grubbing up vineyards for renewal is carried out, the area to be taken into account in determining the maximum volume of base wine that an operator may hold in reserve is the sum of the area under production and the area replanted or removed provided that replanting takes place at the latest during the second season following uprooting.

---

7   Equivalent to 79.05 hl/ha at the statutory pressing fractions. This is given below as 102 liters of settled must per 160 kg of grapes, which is the same ratio as obtaining 2,550 liters of must from 4,000 kg [a quantity known in the region as a "marc"] of fruit.
8   Equivalent to 98.81 hl/ha at the statutory pressing fractions.
9   Equivalent to 51 hl/ha at the statutory pressing fractions.

3. Any operator wishing to supply this reserve may request, for this purpose, to benefit individually from an increase in yield in relation to the annual yield of the appellation fixed in application of paragraph 1 or 3 of Article D. 645 -7 of the Rural Code within the limit of the maximum yield (Rendement Butoir) mentioned above, and when he can demonstrate a qualitative control of his yields.
4. The increase in yield granted individually to the operator shall, depending on the case, fall within the second or the fourth paragraph of Article D. 645-7 of the Rural Code. The increase in yield to supply the reserve, fixed annually, shall not exceed 25% of the yield provided for in these specifications and fixed pursuant to Article D. 645-7 I of the Rural Code[10]. This rate is set at 37.9% for the 2018 harvest. This increase in individual yield cannot surpass the maximum quantity that can be set aside by the operator.
5. The basic wines put in reserve can claim to be AOC "Champagne" only at the moment taking them out of the reserve and after having been the object of a statement of bottling declaration.[11]
6. Base wines that have been placed in a compulsory reserve cannot be used with an indication of a specific vintage. Base wines placed in reserve are subject to qualitative monitoring.

C) Entry into production of the vines:
The benefit of the AOC can only be granted to wines coming parcels of young vines from the second year following the one in which planting was carried out before July 31st.
1. Special provisions:
a) White wines and rosé wines obtained by direct pressing, without maceration or bleeding the tank.
b) Base wines intended for the production of AOC wines must obtained within the limit of a volume of 102 liters of settled musts for 160 kilograms of grapes used. This may be reduced by government decree for a given harvest once its characteristics have been taken into account.
c) The gross lees resulting from pressing will be between 1% and 4% of the amount of settled must. They are disposed of in accordance with the provisions governing the disposal of by-products before 15 December of the year of harvest.
d) The musts intended for the elaboration of AOC wine must be settled before leaving the pressing facility.

D) Red wines and rosé wines of maceration or bleeding:
1. Base wines intended for the production of AOC wines must obtained within the limit of a volume of 102 liters of settled musts for 160 kilograms of grapes used. This may be reduced by government decree for a given harvest once its characteristics have been taken into account.

---

10   Translated separately in Appendix II
11   This means that the reserve wines while they are held in reserve are not considered to be champagne, and only become officially AOC Champagne one the proper paperwork has been filed with the CIVC.

2. Press wines in excess of the maximum allowed yield which are obtained at the end of pressing are added to the "rebêches"[12]

E) Applicability of the AOC label:
The wines are covered by the AOC label from the time of the subscription of the official declaration of harvest at the rate of 98.5% of their volume.

F) Percentage of Rebêches:
1. The percentage of Rebêches referred to in Article D. 645-16 of the rural code[13] is a minimum extraction between 0% and 10% of the amount of settled musts that can be used to produce AOC wine.
2. These rebêches must be sent to a distillery before December 15th of the year following that of the harvest. However, they may be used to obtain a liqueur within the geographical area of AOC Champagne.

IX. Processing, production, maturation, bottling, and storage

A) General provisions: The wines are vinified in accordance with local, loyal and consistent practices.
1. All operators ensure a qualitative selection among all the wines they hold and which were elaborated according to the provisions fixed for AOC Champagne.
2. The growers or producers having the right to give to their sparkling wines the AOC Champagne will have to store, manipulate and completely handle their grape harvests and their wines, including the volumes produced in excess of the authorized annual yield and, for the growers, the wines made from rebêches, in separate premises without any access other than by the public road, with any premises containing grape harvests or wines to which will not apply the rules relating to the appellations of controlled origin "Champagne", "Coteaux champenois" or "Rosé des Riceys".
3. Reception: The grapes must be weighed in the pressing facility and vat room.
4. Pressing of white wines and rosé wines obtained by direct pressing, without maceration or bleeding the tank. Whole clusters of grapes are poured into the press.
5. The pressing facilities will permit the separation of musts in accordance with the practice in Champagne. Any pressing facility must have a basic approval or qualitative approval, according to the rules relating to each of these approvals as listed in the tables below.

---

12   These are the wines produced from musts resulting from extraction of juice in excess of the statutory pressing fractions as described above. It is mandatory to send these wines for distillation.

13   "Must for sparkling or sparkling wines obtained at the end of pressing beyond the volume that can be produced within the limit of the statutory pressing limit, called "rebêches", must be separated from the musts which can be used to produce AOC wine. The percentage of "rebêches" fixed in the specifications of each AOC is expressed as a percentage of the amount of settled musts that can be used to produce AOC wine. The "rebêches" and the wines coming from "rebêches" may not be used to produce AOC wine. The registration of wines from "rebêches" on the harvest declaration, the records of the pressing facility, and, if applicable, on the stock declaration, is mandatory."

6. All new pressing facilities must seek approval at the "qualitative" level. Any modification, extension or transfer entails a new approval of the installation, at the latest before the harvest following the change, in order to verify its conformity with the rules of simple or qualitative approval.

7. Any newly installed press must meet the rules for "qualitative" approval. However, the use of presses meeting the rules for simple approval is allowed for four successive crops when changing the location of an existing pressing center equipped with said presses. Beyond this period, the pressing center must be equipped with presses listed in the list of presses meeting the rules relating to the qualitative approval.

8. All prototype pressing equipment (presses, consoles, sulphiting systems, pumping systems ...) are subject to a probationary period to ensure that they meet the requirements of the approval.

9. The level of approval is obtained by respecting the rules relating to:
a) The presses (Table 1)
b) The loading of the presses (Table 2)
c) Separation of the must into cuvée and taille and settling (Tables 3, 3.1 and 3.2)
d) Hygiene (Table 4)
e) Winemaking effluents (Table 5).

In these tables, the elements quoted in italics and in parentheses are recommendations.

Table 1

Rules Governing Presses

Criteria	Regulations for Basic Approval	Regulations for Qualitative Approval
Location of the press(es)	Covered area	Covered area
Capacity of the press(es) in relation to the annual quantity of fruit pressed (based on actual number of days claimed in the press records)	5 rounds per day per press on average (6 if running 24 hours a day)	4 rounds per day per press on average (6 if running 24 hours a day)
Number of marcs must not exceed	6 per day if operating 24 hr/day	6 per day if operating 24 hr/day
Size of each press(es)	2,000 kg – 12,000 kg (with 2,000 kg = 3.5 cubic meters minimum) No press of 12,000 kg in operation alone	2,000 kg – 12,000 kg (with 2,000 kg = 3.5 cubic meters minimum) No press of 12,000 kg in operation alone
Type of press(es)	All types authorized for basic approval	All types authorized for qualitative approval
Operation of the press(es)	No special provisions	Automated console (except for traditional presses)
Visualization of the level of pressed must from the pressing station	Mandatory	Mandatory

Table 2

Rules Governing the Loading of Presses

Criteria	Regulations for Basic Approval	Regulations for Qualitative Approval
Suitable scale	Mandatory (with maintenance contract)	Mandatory (with maintenance contract)
Storage area	Must be covered No stacking of pallets Surface equivalent to half of the average daily production	Must be covered No stacking of pallets Surface equivalent to half of the average daily production
Drop height of the grapes	2 meters maximum above the press (the lowest possible)	1 meter maximum above the press, except for loading under the plate of presses in place before January 1st 2013 within the limit of 2 meters (the lowest possible)
Conveyor belt for grapes	Forbidden	Forbidden
Quantity of grapes	A press is loaded at one time with the quantity of grapes that corresponds to its capacity. Loading with a lesser quantity may be done only rarely	A press is loaded at one time with the quantity of grapes that corresponds to its capacity. Loading with a lesser quantity may be done only rarely

Table 3

Rules Governing the Separation of the Must and Settling

Criteria	Regulations for Basic Approval	Regulations for Qualitative Approval
Separation and sulfiting of must (see Tables 3.1 and 3.2)	Every press has its own device of separation and sulfiting of must adapted to the approved capacity of the press. (3 measuring containers under each press)	Every press has its own device of separation and sulfiting of must adapted to the approved capacity of the press. (3 measuring containers under each press)
Device for locating the volume of juices in the separation	Mandatory	Mandatory
Number of settling tanks per fraction and in relation to the average daily pressing capacity	At least the average number of rounds per day + 1	At least the average number of rounds per day + 1 (and higher)
Individual capacity per vat and relative to the total pressing capacity in hectoliters of cuvée	2 times maximum (200 hl maximum)	1 time (200 hl maximum)
Nature of the tanks	Except bare iron and non-food plastic Minimum racking device (racking arm)	Except bare iron and non-food plastic (Except bare cement and plastic) (Closed tanks) Minimum racking device (racking arm)
Identification of the volume of each tank	Mandatory	Mandatory (Tracking levels)
Transfer of musts (from the press to the tank or to the fermentation tank)	No special provision	Pumped twice at most (Three times if settled musts are blended)
Accessibility of the settling tanks for the musts transport tanks	No special provision	(4 marcs minimum)
Average distance between the settling tank and the transport tank	No special provision	(25 meters minimum)

Table 3.1

Definition of the approval level of the separation-sulfiting operation in the case of must delivery of musts to holding tanks or into the settling tanks by gravity

Number and volume of holding tanks	Nature of the sulfiting	Must transfer into the settling tank	Evaluation of the separation
Delivery into holding tanks			
3 belon tanks: Cuvée Taille or portion Taille or portion	Manual sulfiting, continuously adjusted or not to the juice flow rate	Either by gravity or by pumping after filling the holding tanks	Qualitative approval
2 belon tanks: Cuvée Taille or portion			
2 belon tanks: ½ Cuvée ½ Cuvée			
2 belon tanks of equal size for taille	Manual sulfiting, continuously adjusted or not to the juice flow rate	Either by gravity or by pumping after filling the holding tanks	Basic approval
Delivery directly into settling tanks			
Delivery directly into settling tanks	Open tank with mixing possible: manual sulfiting, continuously adjusted or not to the juice flow rate	By gravity	Qualitative approval
	Closed tank: sulfiting continuously adjusted or not to the juice flow rate		
	Manual sulfiting	By gravity into a closed settling tank	Basic approval (for all installations before January 1st 2013)
Delivery directly into settling tanks for a portion and delivery into one or two holding tanks for the balance	Refer to preceding guide		Decision according to the least favorable instance

Table 3.2

Definition of the approval level of the separation – sulfiting operation in the case of must delivery into settling tanks via automatic pumping

Measured volume of the holding tank	Positioning of the sufite additions	Nature of the sulfiting	Must transfer to the settling tank	Appreciation of the separation
For a press equipped with an automatic pump				
Usable volume less than 50 liters. The usable volume of the holding tank corresponds to the maximum volume collected between two starts of the pump. It is reported at a pressing of 4000 kg: approx. 50 liters.	At the output of the press or in the holding tank	Continuous sulfiting adapted to the juice flow rate	Quality-certified automatic pump	Qualitative approval reserved for cases where gravity flow is impossible
		Continuous sulfiting not adapted to the juice flow rate	Automatic pump	Basic approval
For two presses, each equipped with an automatic pumping and sending in the same settling tank				
Usable volume less than 50 liters. The usable volume of the holding tank corresponds to the maximum volume collected between two starts of the pump. It is reported at a pressing of 4000 kg: approx. 50 liters.	At the output of the press or in the holding tank	Continuous sulfiting adapted to the juice flow rate	Quality-certified automatic pump	Basic approval

Table 4

Rules Governing Hygiene

Criteria	Regulations for Basic Approval	Regulations for Qualitative Approval
Storage and pressing area	Waterproof coating; bare soil prohibited	Waterproof coating; bare soil prohibited
Cleaning possible (access to water at a minimum)		
Press	Mandatory	Mandatory
Floors	Mandatory	Mandatory
Separation tanks	Mandatory	Mandatory
Settling tanks	Mandatory	Mandatory
Picking bins	Mandatory	Washing machine for bins mandatory
Good condition and cleanliness of premises and equipment	Mandatory	Mandatory

Table 5

Rules Governing Winemaking Effluents

Criteria	Regulations for Basic Approval	Regulations for Qualitative Approval
The operator demonstrates the management of winemaking effluents	Mandatory	Mandatory

B)Analytical standards:

The wines have, after the secondary fermentation in bottle, a content of fermentable sugars (glucose and fructose) less than or equal to 10 grams per liter.

C) Oenological practices and physical treatments:

1. The use of wood staves is prohibited.
2. After enrichment[14], the wines do not exceed, after the secondary fermentation in bottle, a total alcoholic strength by volume of 13%.
3. The increase in the volume of fermenting must may not be greater than 1.12%, for a 1% increase in the alcoholic strength by volume, during the enrichment operation.
4. Excess volumes are destroyed by shipment for distillation for industrial uses before December 15 of the year following that of the harvest in accordance with the provisions of Article D. 645-14 of the Rural Code.

D) Cellar and equipment maintenance:

The winery (floor and walls) and winemaking equipment are in good general condition.

E) Volumes resulting from special technical requirements[15]

1. The volumes resulting from special technical requirements, possibly generated before bottling, are reported on the cellar register, within the limit of 1% of the working volume, this at the end of the winemaking operations of the whole of the winery and no later than 31 July of the year following that of the harvest. These volumes are destroyed by shipment for distillation for industrial uses before December 15 of the year following that of the harvest.
2. In case of inspection before the end of the winemaking operations, these volumes are justified by any means.

F) Provisions by type of product:

1. Rosé wines shall be made from base wines made by direct pressing, maceration or bleeding the tanks, or by the blending of white and red wines.
2. The wines shall be exclusively elaborated by second fermentation in glass bottles.
3. The bottling for the secondary fermentation may only take place beginning 1 January of the year following that of the harvest.
4. The blend is prepared from grape must, wine or the mixture of grape must and / or wines of different characteristics.
5. The increase in the volume of wine and, where appropriate, must may not exceed 1.12%, for 1% increase in the alcoholic strength by volume, after the addition of the bottling liqueur.
6. Volumes resulting from specific technical requirements at the bottling stage may not exceed 1% of the volumes used.

---

14   i.e. chaptalization or the addition of sugar to increase the level of alcohol of the finished wine.
15   This refers to the amount of wine used for the liqueur de tirage and the liqueur d'expédition

7. The elimination of by-products from the second fermentation are removed by disgorging. The disgorgement cannot be carried out before a period of twelve months from the date of bottling during which time the wines must remain in bottle without interruption.

8. The addition of shipping liqueur may not lead to an increase in the volume of wine by more than the sum of the increase in the alcoholic strength by volume expressed as a percentage (A) multiplied by the coefficient of 1.266 and the increase in the sugar content expressed in grams per liter (S) multiplied by the coefficient of 0.0666: $V (\%) = (1.266 \times A) + (0.0666 \times S)$

9. Excess volumes are destroyed by shipment for distillation for industrial uses before December 15 of the year following the disgorgement of the corresponding lots.

10. The elaboration of wines shall be subject to the elimination, within the provisions for the disposal of by-products, before 31 July of the year following that of the harvest, of the by-products of the winemaking process, at the rate of 1.5% of the settled musts, and the by-products resulting from disgorging, at the rate of 0.50% of the volume of wine in bottles to be disgorged. These shall be disposed of in accordance with the provisions governing the elimination of by-products before July 31 of the year following that of the disgorging.

11. The wines may be bottled with the vintage date (*millésimé* in French; "vintaged") if the grapes used for the development of the base wines are grapes of the vintage concerned, with the exception of the volumes of wines or musts grapes used in the context of authorized oenological practices and processes and products contained in the bottling liqueur or shipping liqueur.

12. In order to ensure the qualitative selection among the volumes resulting from a given vintage while maintaining a sufficient volume of wines to ensure the blend and the constitution of reserve wines, essential to the quality of the Champagne wines, the volumes of wines bottled with a vintage date will be less than or equal to 80% of the volumes of wine of the year considered, bought or produced by the operator.

G) Packaging provisions:

1. The wines must be produced and sold in the bottle in which the second fermentation in bottle was done, with the exception of the wines sold in bottles of a volume lower than 37,5 centilitres or greater than 300 centilitres.

2. However, except for vintage wines, the transfer into half-bottles (37.5 centilitres) of wine after the second fermentation in bottle is authorized within the annual limit of 20% of the quantity produced in half-bottles during the calendar year former.

3. As of January 1, 2015, the wines must be produced in newly-purchased bottles.

4. Other elements of the closures or must be newly-purchased as well.

5. For any packaged lot, the operator shall make available to the approved inspection body:

a) the information contained in the handling register referred to in Article D. 645-18 of the Rural Code

b) an analysis carried out after bottling and the second fermentation in bottle. The test reports shall be kept for a period of sixty months from the date of bottling.

H) Storage provisions:
The operator will designate a specific place for the storage of finished wine.

I) Provisions relating to the movement of products and to marketing for the consumer:
1. Date of marketing to the consumer:
a) The wines shall be marketed to the consumer only after a maturation period of at least fifteen months from the date of bottling.
b) The wines with a vintage date shall be put on the market only at the end of a maturation period of thirty-six months minimum from the date of the bottling.
c) In the event of a circular return, in other words the return to bulk storage of previously bottled wines, the minimum maturation period is determined from the date of the new bottling.

J) Circulation with an accompanying document:
Grapes and all products intended for the production of AOC wine may only circulate with a document accompanying bearing the name of the AOC when they originate in a commune belonging to the geographical area defined in section IV of these specifications and are destined for another commune belonging to this same area pursuant to Article 466 of the General Tax Code.

X. Link to the geographical area

A) Information about the geographical area:
1. Description of the natural factors contributing to the link:
a) The geographical area is located in the north-east of the French territory and extends over municipalities spread over the departments of Aisne, Aube, Haute-Marne, Marne and Seine-et-Marne.
2. The parcels, precisely delimited for the grape harvest, are part of a landscape characterized by hillside vineyards resting on the cuestas of the eastern Paris Basin, that features these imposing geological structures:
a) The Côte de l'Ile-de-France in the Marne département, as well as the slopes of the associated valleys, gathering from north to south the Montagne de Reims, the Marne valley (which extends into the southern part of the Aisne département and up to the Seine-et-Marne département), the Côte des Blancs and the Côte du Sézannais to name the most notable sectors;
b) The Côte de Champagne with the Vitryat of the Marne (the area around the village of Vitry-le-François) and the sector of Montgueux in the Aube

c) The Côte des Bar cut through by multiple valleys and uniting the Bar-sur-Aube district in the east and the Bar-sur-Seine district in the west, in the départements of the Aube and Haute-Marne.

3. This geology typical of the cuesta (a hill with a gradual slope on one side and a much steeper one on the other side), with its adjacent valleys, presents slopes exposed to the east and south and sometimes to the north as in the northern Montagne de Reims and on the left bank of the Marne River).

4. The slopes lie on hard layers of limestone or chalk. The steeper slopes have soils that are chalky, marly or sandy; the softer ones have been eroded over time and recovered with colluvial elements from overlying layers.

5. The Champagne vineyard is located in the northern zone. It is subject to a double climatic influence:

a) The oceanic influence, which brings water in regular quantity with temperature swings that are less marked from one season to another;

b) The continental influence, which is responsible for the sometimes-destructive frost and for the sunshine in the summer.

B) Description of human factors contributing to the link:

1. Dating back to antiquity, the vine was well established in Champagne by the ninth century, following the development of monastic viticulture. The phenomenon of naturally sparkling white wine and experiments involving its deliberate production date to the late seventeenth century. At the end of the 19th century, Weinmann, a renowned oenologist, noted that Champagne wine is eminently fermentable and that the wine of Champagne accomplish the second fermentation in bottle more regularly and better than any other type. The first references of this wine, called *"saute-bouchon"*, appear in the poems of the abbot Chaulieu in 1700. The method, however, was first described in 1718 by Canon Godinot, alleged author of *Manière de cultivtiver la vigne and to make the wine of Champagne* (...), specifying that these white wines which must be "clear as tears of eye (...) are made with black grapes. When the grapes are cut, the earlier they are pressed, the wine is white ". In this way, the winemakers strive to preserve the grapes' integrity during the harvest, to take great care in their transport and storage and to take them to the press. The pressing must be smooth and progressive, with fractionation of the juices (wine and size) which are vinified separately. The pressing centers therefore meet strict rules and are subject to rigorously controlled authorization.

2. Precise know-how developed in the abbeys; In 1866, Jules Guyot noted the importance of blending grapes from different grape varieties or different parcels. Since the beginning of the 20th century, three grape varieties have been selected for their sugar / acidity balance qualities and superior second fermentation in bottle: Pinot Noir, Chardonnay and Meunier. The composes his blends by tasting the different basic wines obtained. The blended base wines are bottled for the second fermentation and aging on the lees which is necessarily long, especially for vintage wines.

3. The chalky champagne cellars, combining the ideal natural conditions of temperature and humidity, have favored the development of the second fermentation.

4. After the aging on the lees is completed comes the riddling process, to slowly gather the lees into the neck of the bottle, then the disgorgement, to remove the lees from the bottle. The shipping liqueur is added after the disgorgement is added in order to differentiate several types of Champagne wines.

5. Once the development of bubbles through the second fermentation in bottle was mastered, the "Champagne method" was exported, and very quickly the name "Champagne" was used outside the limits of the region of production. As early as 1882, legal action was taken by the Champagne houses, who united to form the Union des Maisons de Champagne (UMC), on the eve of the law of August 1, 1905 against frauds and counterfeits, jurisprudence recognized that the name "Champagne" is reserved for wines made from grapes harvested in Champagne, and thus inaugurates, for the first time, the protection of a designated region of origin. The work of delimitation of the geographical zone then began in 1908.

6. The people of Champagne stand together, as can be seen through their professional organizations. The houses and the vine growers joined their efforts very early to fight against the phylloxera at the origin of the foundation of the Association Viticole Champenoise (AVC) in 1898. The Syndicat Général des Vignerons de la Champagne (SGV, created in 1904) and the Union of Champagne Houses (UMC, created in 1882) came together to found the CIVC (Comité Interprofessionnel du Vin de Champagne) created by the law of April 12, 1941.

C) Information on the quality and characteristics of the product:

1. The wines can be white (from the blend of white grapes and black grapes, only from white grapes [blanc de blancs], or only black grapes [blanc de noirs]) or rosés (obtained by blending or by bleeding the tanks), and can be produced from grapes grown in one or several villages. They can be labelled with the vintage date or not.

2. All wines have one thing in common: their acidity, which guarantees their freshness and their ability to age. The youngest wines have notes of great freshness: flowers and white fruits, citrus, mineral notes.

3. Mature wines offer a range of rounder aromas: yellow fruits, cooked fruits, spices.

4. The so-called wines of "plenitude" ("fullness": the apotheosis or ultimate development) wines, the most evolved, reveal deep tertiary aromas: candied fruit, forest floor and roasted, "smoky" notes.

5. The effervescence, the identity mark of Champagne, is sustained and persistent in young wines. With age, it decreases to become more delicate and creamier.

D) Causal interactions[16]:

1. The open landscape of the three cuestas on the plain and the valleys guarantees the vineyards sufficient light for the ripening of the grapes, even for the vineyards with northern exposures. This open landscape also helps keep air flowing and reduces the risk of frost.

2. The slope of the vineyard slopes ensures optimal natural drainage, which is also guaranteed by the different layers that allow a natural water management for the vine. Chalk, by its porosity and permeability, eliminates excess water, while ensuring the water supply of the soil in dry weather through the pores in the chalk. The other subsoils combine marl, which provide the water reserve, and either calcium bedrock or carbon-rich sand, which helps drain excess water during wet periods. This nature of the subsoil and the delicate climatic conditions have guided the establishment of grape varieties in the different regions of the vineyard.

3. The unique climatic situation of Champagne confers upon the grapes and thus the musts the ideal natural acidity for producing great sparkling wines. Indeed, the balance between this acidity - guarantee of essential freshness a) and the level of maturity of the grapes produces the best vintages and ensures a good aging potential.

4. A true mosaic, the diversity of natural factors is exploited at the scale of the parcel by the winegrower who employs all his grape-growing expertise to express the specificity of the grapes.

5. Keeping the grapes whole at harvest, gentle pressing and the separation of the pressing fractions makes it possible to avoid color in the must and thus to guarantee the limpidity of the wine, essential to the quality of the mousse. Separating the pressing fractions also brings additional complexity to the flavors.

6. The "cuvée" [commonly called "free run", but more properly, the first press juice], is rich in acidity, gives fresh and lively aromas; its use in the blends allows to the wines to fully reveal the tertiary aromas that develop during aging on the lees.

7. The "taille" [second press juice] is fruitier and has a greater tannic richness.

8. The reserve wines which come from preceding harvests (not used in vintage wines), bring to the blend more the riper character of evolved wines.

9. The talent of the producer in selecting the wines for the desired blend, expresses itself throughout the aging of the wine on the lees to give birth to champagne. This process of continuous maturation can, for wines of great substance, continue for several decades in Champagne cellars, their relative freshness ensuring a good bubble formation.

10. The technical elements in the development of champagne requires special and expensive infrastructure. The production, handling and bottling sites are located in villages close to the vineyards.

---

16   Between the natural factors and human factors listed above and how they impact the wine.

11. The existence of vineyards in Champagne dates back to the beginning of our era, but champagne has acquired its particular nobility, since the seventeenth century, with the gradual mastery of the *prise de mousse* by second fermentation in the bottle. At the end of the same century, the Champagne producers matured their wines in bottles rather than transporting them in barrels, in order to preserve all their quality and their characteristics. The mousse and fine bubbles enclosed in the flasks was revealed in the glass, and the success of the wine was immediate. The young nobles, eager for novelty, toast champagne, the poets sing of it, the writers give it a place in all their works. Champagne becomes the favorite of the court of the Regent, of Louis XV, and of Madame de Pompadour. Bankers and administrators imitate the nobles, the countryside copies the capital. Under Louis XV and Louis XVI, the wine industry flourished and the reputation of champagne increased considerably in France and abroad. Sparkling wine was in vogue wherever it was fashionable to follow French custom, and throughout eighteenth-century Europe, champagne was the ornament of feasts and dinners. This renown continues today. The vine growers, cooperatives and Champagne Houses are continuing their efforts by improving the collective rules to promote AOC Champagne, their common heritage, towards excellence and strive to uphold its name and her personality.

XI. Transitional measures

A) Method of planting:
1. The vineyard plots in place on 17 January 1978, which do not comply with the provisions relating to planting density, continue to benefit from the right to the controlled designation of origin until they are grubbed up, subject to the compliance with the rules for trellising and height of foliage laid down in these specifications.

B) Storage of part of the harvest as a reserve:
1. As a transitional measure, up to and including the 2018-2019 production year[17], the maximum volume of base wines that may be placed in the reserve set out in point 3 of section VIII above is governed by the following two-fold limit:
2. The cumulated volume of base wine placed in reserve may not exceed:
a) 10,000 kilograms of grapes per hectare for the 2015-2016 production year
b) 9,500 kilograms of grapes per hectare for the 2016-2017 production year
c) 9,000 kilograms of grapes per hectare for the 2017-2018 production year
d) 8,500 kilograms of grapes per hectare for the 2018-19 production year
3. As from the 2014 harvest, the cumulative volume of base wines placed in reserve from the 2011 and subsequent harvests may not exceed 8,000 kilograms of grapes per hectare.

---

17 i.e. from the harvest of 2018 until the bottling of those wines in 2019

XII. Rules of presentation and labeling

A) The wines for which the AOC is claimed under the terms of these specifications may not be offered to the public, shipped, put on sale or sold, unless
the Appellation is mentioned in any advertisements, prospectuses, labels,
invoices, containers, boxes or packaging.

B) The labeling of AOC wines may specify the name of a smaller geographical
unit, provided that:
1. that it is the name of a cadastral locality
2. that it appears on the harvest declaration.

C) The indication of a locality is authorized only if all the grapes used for
the development of the basic wines are grapes coming from the considered
locality.

D) The name of a registered locality may be printed in characters whose
dimensions, both in height and in width, may not exceed the size of the
characters composing the name of the registered AOC.

E) The grape variety may be indicated in characters the dimensions of
which, both in height and in width, are not greater than 3 mm and at half
the size of the characters making up the name of the registered AOC. The
indication of a grape variety is possible only if all the grapes used for the
preparation of the base wines are derived from that grape, with the exception of the volumes of wine or grape must used in the context of authorized
oenological practices and processes and products contained in the bottling
liqueur or in the shipping liqueur.

F) Where the vintage is indicated, it shall appear on the cork or, where
the nominal content of 0.20 liter or less is concerned, on another suitable
closure, and on the labeling. The indication of the vintage is also included on
the invoices and accompanying documents.

G) The bottles containing the wines are closed with a stopper bearing the
name of the registered AOC on the part contained in the neck of the bottle
or, in the case of a bottle of contents 0.20 liter or less, on another internal
part of the appropriate closure.

H) The name of the processor which appears on the labeling in clear and
legible lettering shall be supplemented by the name of the production commune in the case where the manufacturer's head office is located outside the
area referred to in section IV of these specifications.

I) No bottle may circulate, except between two sites of the same operator or between two operators, unless it is finished for sale and labeled in accordance with the regulations in force.

J) The labels and commercial documents shall include the registrations prescribed by the CIVC and permit the identification of the operators.

Chapter II

I. Reporting obligations:

A) Declaration of adaptation of the density of plantation according to the special provisions

B) Any operator adjusting the planting density of a parcel under the special planting provisions must file a declaration with the Syndicat Général des Vignerons[18] no later than 48 hours after the end of the works.

C) For each parcel concerned, the declaration shall specify in particular:
1. the cadastral references and the municipality;
2. area.

II. Declaration of plot development:

A) Before any development or work in the vineyard likely to change the terrain, the subsoil or any elements that ensure the integrity and sustainability of the soil of a parcel for the production of the AOC, excluding conventional tilling of the soil, the operator shall send a declaration to the Syndicat Général des Vignerons at least six weeks before the scheduled start date of the planned work.
B) The Syndicat Général des Vignerons shall immediately send a copy of this declaration to the INAO.

III. Declaration of intention to bottle:

A) The declaration of intention to bottle shall be sent to the approved inspection body and the local services of the DGDDI[19] at least 48 hours before the start of the operation.
1. It shall state in particular:
a) the appellation claimed and other specified claims (vintage, color, indication of a specified place...);
b) the projected volume of wine to be bottled;
c) the projected volume of sugar to be used;
d) the total volume to be bottled;
e) the date of bottling;

---

18   The Cahier de Charge refers to an ODG, which is an Organisme de Défense et de Gestion. This has been established as the Syndicat Général des Vignerons. (see footnote 19)
19   Direction générale des douanes et droits indirects, the Office of Customs and Indirect Taxes ("Les Douanes")

f) the place of bottling;
g) the EVV number[20];
h) the name and address of the applicant.
3. In addition, in the case of making rosé wines by blending red and white base wines before bottling:
a) the projected volume of red wine to be used;
b) the projected volume of white wine to be used.

IV. Declaration of Claim:

A) The declaration of claim, which is deemed to be a bottling declaration, shall be sent to the approved inspection body and to the local services of the DGDDI immediately after the end of the bottling operations.

B) It states in particular:
1. the appellation claimed and other specified claims (vintage, color, indication of a specified place...);
2. the volume of wine, expressed in number of bottles;
3. the end date of the bottling;
4. the EVV number or, for authorized dealers, the excise number;
5. the name and address of the applicant;
6. the place where the wine is stored.

V. Declaration of a circular return:

A) Any return to bulk storage of previously bottled wines is subject to a prior declaration at least forty-eight hours before the start of operations with the approved inspection body.

B) This prior declaration indicates in particular the nature, volume and, if applicable, the vintage of the products used.

VI. Record keeping:

A) Weighing register:
1. The pressing centers shall keep a weighing register separate from the press book.
2. This register indicates for each weighing:
a) the date and time of weighing;
b) the weight found;
c) specific claims (mentions, indication of specific locality...)
3. For centers performing pressing on behalf of third parties, the weighing register specifies, in addition to the above indications, the name of the operator supplying the grapes. A weighing ticket containing all these indications is issued to it.

---

20   Exploitation vitivinicole, a number for the vineyard assigned by FranceAgrimer and the INAO

B) Press register:
1. The maintenance of a press register is mandatory. It is filled as the pressing is conducted.
2. This notebook specifies, for each marc:
a) the date and time of the beginning of each operation;
b) the weight of the grapes used by grape variety;
c) the origin of the grapes, in the case of specific claims (mentions, indication of a name of specific locality ...);
d) the name of the operator who brought the grapes;
e) the volumes of musts obtained;
f) the actual alcoholic strength by volume;
g) the volumes of rebêches.
3. For red and rosé wines, the quantity of wine obtained is specified only at the end of pressing.
4. The volume of the gross lees are mentioned globally at the end of the settling operations.

VII. References concerning the mechanism of inspection:

A) National Institute of Origin and Quality (INAO), "TSA 30003", 93555 Montreuil-sous-Bois Cedex.

B) Verification of compliance with these specifications is carried out by a third-party body offering guarantees of competence, impartiality and independence, under the authority of the INAO, on the basis of an approved inspection plan.[21][22]

C) The inspection plan replicates the checks carried out by the operators themselves on their own activity and the internal controls carried out under the responsibility of the CIVC. It indicates the external controls performed by the third party as well as the analytical and organoleptic examinations. The complete set of inspections is performed by sampling.

---

21   Association de l'Inspection des Appellations de la Champagne
22   The document outlining the establishment of the SGV as the ODG, and of the AIAC as the Inspecting body can be found here : http://www.sgv-champagne.com/documentextranet/pichampagne.pdf

Principal Control Points	Method of Evaluation
Structural Rules	
A1. Ownership of parcels planted in the delimited area	Documentation (up-to-date CVI[23] form)
A2. Potential of claimable production (grape blend planted, density of plantation and trellising, start date of production for the vines)	Documentation and field visits
A3. Parcel layout	Documentation and field visits
A4. Production tools	
Reception and pressing, pressing facility	Site visit
Rules governing the production cycle	
B1. Vineyard management	
Pruning	Verification of the pruning method adopted, the number of buds per square meter (as counted), and the realization of pruning in the prescribed period
Maximum load per vine	Counting the bunches and estimating the load
State of the crop and other cultural practices	Inspection of the parcel
B2. Harvest, transport and grape ripeness	
Tracking the harvest date	Verification of exemptions, site visits
B3. Processing, winemaking, maturation, bottling and storage	
Pressing	Documentation and site visits (verification of compliance with rules governing pressing)
B4. Harvest declaration and declaration of claim	
Authorized yield	Documentation (verification of declarations)
Declaration of claim	Documentation and site visits verification of the amount of wine sold
Verification of Wines	
Wines after bottling and after the second fermentation in bottle	Chemical and organoleptic analysis

---

23   *Casier Viticole Informatisé*: Lit. "Computerized Winemaking Record"; a tool all EU member states must maintain. It contains all the information relating to wine-growing business, parcels planted or pulled up, levels of production and of stock.

Appendix II

ARTICLE D645-7 CODE RURAL ET DE LA PÊCHE MARITIME

[Hereafter referred to simply as the "Rural Code"]

[This appears in the Regulatory portion of the Rural Code in Book VI: Production and Markets, under Title IV: Valuation of agricultural, forestry or food and maritime products, in Chapter V: Special provisions relating to production conditions of AOC wine, spirits and other alcoholic beverages, in Section 1: General provisions applicable to AOC wines, Subsection 4: Yield of vineyards producing AOC wines.]

I. The yield fixed in the specifications of a registered AOC corresponds to the maximum quantity of grapes or the equivalent volume of wine or must harvested per hectare of vine for which the appellation can be claimed in the harvest declaration. It is expressed either in kilograms of grapes per hectare, or in hectoliters of must per hectare, or in hectoliters of wine per hectare.

In the latter two cases, this volume is understood after separation of lees and gross lees. The lees and gross lees are the by-products of winemaking as defined in the EU Regulations on the organization of the common wine market.

II. For a given harvest, taking into account in particular the characteristics of the harvest:

A) The return mentioned in section I above may be:
1. Decreased
2. Decreased, with possibility of individual claim for higher volume;
3. Increased within the limit of the target yield listed in the specifications of the controlled label of origin concerned;
4. Increased for certain operators, within the limits of the target yield listed in the specifications of the controlled label of origin concerned, on individual request duly justified with the services of the National Institute of Origin and Quality , and after investigation of said services.

B) An individual substitutable quantity, higher than the yield determined under section I or section IIa above, may be fixed within the limit of the maximum yield [Rendement Butoir] mentioned in the specifications of the AOC concerned.

C) For wines included in the list mentioned in Article D. 645-7-1 and in the absence of an individual substitutable volume, an individual additional volume may be fixed. This additional volume, added to the yield determined in application of sections I or II above, cannot, however, exceed the Rendement Butoir specified in the given AOC, or the maximum total individual volume of wine that may be stored by a given producer, fixed for each of them by the list mentioned in the third paragraph of section I of Article D. 645-7-1.

III. The modification of yield and of the individual substitutable volume mentioned in section II are fixed by decision of the INAO, taken upon the advice of the organization of defense and management of the AOC concerned.

A) The individual supplementary volume, mentioned in section IIc above, shall be fixed, at the request of the body responsible for the defense and management of the AOC concerned, by decision of the INAO, following the advice of the INAO regional committee concerned.

B) The request of the defense and management body includes a technical argument based on the characteristics of the harvest as well as the reasoned opinion of the competent interprofessional committee when it exists. This opinion is considered favorable if the interprofessional committee did not respond to the request of the defense and management organization within five weeks of its referral.

C) The decisions mentioned in the first two paragraphs are approved by joint decrees of the ministers concerned, in accordance with Article R. 642-7.

IV. For AOC liqueur wines that are obtained by the addition of spirits of wine or grape marc, the specifications may fix yields expressed in must for the elaboration of AOC wines and in liqueur wines that can benefit from the AOC label per hectare of vine planted.

V. When the irrigation of the vines is authorized pursuant to Article D. 645-5, the yield of the irrigated parcels corresponds to the yield fixed by the specifications of the AOC concerned in accordance with section I above. However, in the cases provided for in the first and second portions of section IIa above, the yield of the irrigated plots may not exceed the yield fixed for the AOC concerned for the specified harvest.

https://www.legifrance.gouv.fr/affichCodeArticle.do?cidTexte=LEGITEX-T000006071367&idArticle=LEGIARTI000023124713&dateTexte=&categorieLien=cid

Appendix III

ARTICLE D645-15 OF THE RURAL CODE

Amended by Decree No. 2013-1051 of November 22, 2013 - art. 6

[This appears in the Regulatory portion of the Rural Code in Book VI: Production and Markets, under Title IV: Valuation of agricultural, forestry or food and maritime products, in Chapter V: Special provisions relating to production conditions of AOC wine, spirits and other alcoholic beverages, in Section 1: General provisions applicable to AOC wines, Subsection 8: Provisions for the declaration of harvest for vineyards producing wines with controlled designation of origin.]

I. An operator can claim the right to the AOC label for a reserve wine authorized pursuant to II of the article D. 645-7 on the condition that an equivalent volume of wine is destroyed by sending for distillation for the industrial uses the same appellation and the same color of previous vintages, produced on the same property, before 31 July of the year following that of the harvest.

II. The proof of destruction is constituted by the certificate of delivery of the wines for industrial uses established by the processor and by the document accompanying the destruction of the volumes concerned.
In the "product description" section of the latter document, the vintage of the distilled controlled designation of origin appears immediately after the mention "VSI". These documents shall be made available to the approved inspection body in accordance with the procedures laid down in the control plan or the inspection plan.

https://www.legifrance.gouv.fr/affichCodeArticle.do;jsession-id=80911CE0A4D50CFE49E02D5F034683F1.tplgfr23s_2?cidTexte=LEG-ITEXT000006071367&idArticle=LEGIARTI000028240507&dateTex-te=20180927&categorieLien=cid

Appendix IV

ARTICLE D645-18 OF THE RURAL CODE

Created by Decree n ° 2010-1438 of November 22, 2010 - art. 2

[This appears in the Regulatory portion of the Rural Code in Book VI: Production and Markets, under Title IV: Valuation of agricultural, forestry or food and maritime products, in Chapter V: Special provisions relating to production conditions of AOC wine, spirits and other alcoholic beverages, in Section 1: General provisions applicable to AOC wines, Subsection 11: Packaging and storage.]

I. The preparation of the wine for sale in bulk to the consumer or the pre-packaging of wine in volumes less than or equal to 60 liters is considered as the preparation for sale.

II. The operators carrying out the packaging must keep at the disposal of the approved inspection bodies the information contained in the handling register provided for by Commission Regulation (EC) No 884/2001 of 24 April 2001 laying down detailed rules for the application of the provisions relating to documents accompanying the transport of wine products and the registers to be kept in the wine sector, as well as analyzes carried out before or after bottling under the conditions laid down in the specifications of the AOC concerned.

III. These operators shall retain representative samples of wine from the lot bottled under the conditions provided for in the control or inspection plan.

IV. Any operator exporting outside the territory of the European Union a wine with bulk AOC wine must require the recipient operator to make available the information provided for in point II and the transmission of the samples referred to in III and require the exporter to keep them.

https://www.legifrance.gouv.fr/affichCodeArticle.do?idArticle=LEGIAR-TI000023125336&cidTexte=LEGITEXT000022197698&dateTexte=20110101

Appendix V

DECREE OF 17 OCTOBER 1952: CONCERNING THE INDICATION OF THE VINTAGE OF AOC "CHAMPAGNE" WINES

Article I:
[Superseded by Decree n ° 2010-1441 of November 22, 2010 - art. 3 (V)]

A) Wine of AOC Champagne may carry the vintage date if it meets the following conditions:

1. Measures at least 11 ° ABV upon shipment from the cellars of the producer
2. Originates from existing supplies of wine from the year in question as they appear in the special account established by Article 4;
3. Does not exceed 80% of the total quantity of wine of the vintage concerned, bought or harvested by the merchant or shipper.

Article II:
[Amended by Decree of 18 April 1997 - art. 1, v. init., and superceded by Decree n ° 2010-1441 of November 22, 2010 - art. 3 (V)]

A) A vintage may only be used for the wine of Champagne wine from three years after the bottling.

Article III:
[Superceded by Decree n ° 2010-1441 of November 22, 2010 - art. 3 (V)]

A) The vintage must be noted on the cork and on the label or on the neck label, or on any other part of the packaging, except for any sticker that lacks the name of the producer or brand and their registration number with the CIVC. Mention of the vintage must also be made on sales invoices and shipping records.

Article IV:
[Superceded by Decree n ° 2010-1441 of November 22, 2010 - art. 3 (V)]

A) Each producer will keep a special account summarizing annually their outputs by vintage and establishing, at the end of the year, a breakdown of their stock by year of origin.

Article V:
[Superceded by Decree n ° 2010-1441 of November 22, 2010 - art. 3 (V)]

A) As a transitional measure, the wines held in cellars on the date of this decree must have been identified and approved by the CIVC in order to be sold under a vintage,

B) This organization will assess, by all the evidence presented to it and by any other means, including chemical analysis and tasting, if the wine fulfills the conditions defined in the article 1 above and deserves to be sold as vintage wine.

C) Refusal of the vintage will engender the remedies provided for by the texts governing the aforementioned Committee.

Appendix VI

Timeline of Champagne

1901: American rootstocks legalized in the Marne to combat phylloxera.

1902: André Simon becomes the London agent for Pommery et Greno.

1904: Fédération des Syndicats viticoles de la Champagne founded to defend the rights of growers.

Ruinart receives the royal warrant from the court of Spain.

1907: Roederer receives the royal warrant from the Russian imperial court.

Bertrand de Mun directs Veuve Clicquot, replacing his father-in-law, Alfred Werlé.

1908: Initial delimitation of the Champagne region.

1910: Joseph Krug succeeds his father, Paul.

1911: Champagne Riots

First Echelle des Crus, ranking villages from 46% to 100%

1912: Maurice Pol-Roger elected mayor of Epernay.

1914: Champagne A. Salon founded.

1918: Jacques Bollinger directs Renaudin Bollinger et Cie.

1920: The French government auctions off the confiscated assets of G.H. Mumm.

The average retail price of a bottle of Brut NV is equivalent to €21 – 25 in today's terms.

The échelle des crus is revised, with the lowest villages rated at 56%.

1922: Launch of Mumm Crémant de Cramant.

1923: Gaston Burtin arrives in Epernay.

Heidsieck et Cie. Monopole sold to grocer Edouard Mignot.

1924: Launch of the first vintage of Roederer Cristal released in Europe, the 1921.

Léon de Tassigny purchases Jacquesson.

1927: Vineyards of the Aube are officially re-integrated into Champagne production.

1929: Mailly cooperative founded.

1930: Direction of Moët & Chandon passes to Count Geoffroy d'Andigné.

1931: Pierre-Charles Taittinger acquires Forest-Fourneaux et Cie.

1932: Bertrand de Mun is joined by his son-in-law Bertrand de Vogüé at Veuve Clicquot.

Camille Olry-Roederer assumes the duties of her late husband, Léon, directing Roederer.

1934: Ayala sold to the English bank Guinness.

Production of sparkling wine from outside the region is forbidden in Champagne.

Louis Budin assumes direction of Perrier-Jouët.

1935: Pierre Philipponnat purchases the Clos des Goisses from several different owners.

Origins of Dom Pérignon: Moët 1926 shipped to clients of their English agent, Simon Brothers.

Establishment of Comité national des Appellations d'origine.

Establishment Commission de Châlons to set the minimum price of grapes each year.

1936: Dom Pérignon 1921 shipped to New York.

1938: Pruning and grape-growing regulations added to the legal definition of Champagne.

1939: Marie-Louise de Nonancourt assumes direction of Laurent-Perrier and Delamotte.

1940: Establishment of the Bureau National de Répartition du Champagne.

Otto Klaebisch « Weinführer du champagne » assumes his duties.

Germans name Godefroy Hermann de Mumm to run G.H. Mumm, displacing René Lalou.

1941: Bureau National de Répartition du Champagne becomes the CIVC.

Paul Chandon-Moët and Robert-Jean de Vogüé join Gislain de Maigret at the head of Moët.

Jacques' widow Lily Bollinger assumes the direction of Renaudin Bollinger et Cie.

1943: Arrest of Ghislain de Maigret and Robert-Jean de Vogüé for their work with the Resistance.

1945: Brut and Extra Dry champagne accounts for 50% of production throughout the region.

René Lalou re-installed at the head of G.H. Mumm.

1949: Bertrand de Nonancourt directs Laurent-Perrier.

Charles de Nonancourt directs Delmotte.

Michel Budin works alongside his father Louis at Perrier-Jouët.

1950: Creation of the cooperative La Goutte d'Or in Vertus.

1952: First vintage of Comtes de Champagne

The Princes Guy and Edmond de Polignac direct Pommery et Greno.

1955: Laurent-Perrier launches Grand Siècle.

Seagrams acquires acquires an interest in G.H. Mumm.

1956: Leclerc-Briant founded.

1958: Trouillard family buys de Venoge.

1959: G.H. Mumm acquires a majority stake in Perrier-Jouët.

Launch of the Cuvée William Deutz.

The first vintage of Dom Ruinart.

Dubonnet-Cinzano buys Besserat de Bellefon and Salon and is bought in turn by Pernod Ricard.

1960: Seagrams acquires Perrier-Jouët.

Renaudin Bollinger becomes Société Jacques Bollinger.

1961: Launch of the first vintage of Bollinger RD, the 1952.

1962: Paul Krug takes over from his father, Joseph.

Moët et Chandon listed on the stock exchange.

Besserat de Bellefon acquires Salon from Marcel Guillaume, grand son of Eugène-Aimé Salon.

Gilbey's merges with United Wine Traders to form International Distillers and Vintners.

1963: Ruinart merges with Moët & Chandon.

Michel Collard directs Philipponnat.

1966: Veuve Clicquot listed on the stock exchange

Introduction of Crown caps for the prise de mousse

First vintage of Dom Ruinart Rosé

1967: Creation of the Union Auboise co-operative.

Etienne Lanson directs Lanson.

1968: Moët & Chandon acquires an interest in Pommery et Greno.

Launch of Laurent-Perrier Rosé.

1969: Launch of Mumm René Lalou, the 1966.

Launch of Perrier-Jouët Belle Epoque, the 1964.

1970: Mercier merges with Moët & Chandon.

Launch of the first vintage of Dom Ruinart Rosé, the 1966.

1971: Piper-Heidsieck listed on the stock exchange.

Moët & Chandon merges with Hennessy Cognac.

Claude d'Hautefeuille directs Bollinger.

Krug acquires the Clos du Mesnil.

Creation of the appellation Rosé des Riceys.

1972: G.H. Mumm acquires a controlling interest in Heidsieck Monopole.

Launch of Veuve Clicquot La Grande Dame, the 1962.

Grand Metropolitan acquires International Distillers and Vintners.

1973: Introduction of the gyro-palette.

1974: Launch of the first vintage of Bollinger Vieilles Vignes Françaises, the 1966.

Vin Nature de Champagne becomes AOC Coteaux Champenois.

Jean Chiquet acquires Jacquesson.

1975: François Suarez d'Aulan directs Piper-Heidsieck.

1976: Pernod Ricard acquires Besserat de Bellefon and Salon.

1977: Henriot and Charles Heidsieck merge under the direction of Joseph Henriot.

Christian de Billy directs Pol Roger.

Clicquot acquires a controlling interest in Canard-Duchêne.

1978: Christian Bizot directs Bollinger.

1979: Jean-Claude Rouzaud directs Roederer.

The Gardinier family acquires Pommery et Greno.

Yves Benard directs Moët & Chandon.

1980: Launch of the first vintage of Cristal rosé, the 1974.

Gosset family acquires a majority stake in Philipponnat.

1981: Moët & Chandon acquires U.S. importer Schieffelin & Co.

Launch of Ultra-Brut by Laurent-Perrier.

Henriot-Charles Heidsieck acquires acquires a controlling interest in Trouillard and de Venoge.

1982: Jacques Trouillard acquires Château Malakoff and the brands Jeanmaire, Oudinot and Beaumet.

1983: Laurent-Perrier acquires de Castellane.

Six communes upgraded to grand cru and seven to premier cru.

Perrier-Jouët launches Belle Epoque rosé, first vintage 1978.

1984: Launch of the first vintage of Pol Roger Cuvée Sir Winston Churchill, the 1971.

Danon acquires Pommery et Greno and Lanson.

1985: Rémy-Martin acquires Charles Heidsieck.

Veuve Clicquot acquires Henriot.

1986: Louis Vuitton acquires Veuve Clicquot, Henriot, and Canard-Duchêne.

1987: Joseph Henriot directs Veuve Clicquot.

Marie Brizard acquires Philipponnat.

1988: Laurent-Perrier acquires Salon.

Rémy-Martin acquires Piper Heidsieck.

1989: Laurent-Perrier acquires Delamotte.

Bernard Arnault is President of LVMH.

1990 Leclerc-Briant trials biodynamic viticulture.

Bruno Paillard and Philippe Baijot form Paillard Baijot Investissement and revive Chanoine.

LVMH acquires Pommery et Greno.

Marne et Champagne acquires Besserat de Bellefon.

1991 Marne et Champagne acquires Lanson.

Carol Duval directs Duval-Leroy.

1993 Cointreau family acquires Gosset.

Rouzaud family acquires Deutz.

1994 Ghislain de Montgolfier directs Bollinger.

Yves Bénard directs champagne production across LVMH.

Joseph Henriot leaves LVMH, taking Champagne Henriot with him, minus the vineyards.

Paillard-Baijot merges with the Boizel family to become Boizel-Chanoine Champagne (BCC).

1995 Gosset launches the first vintage of Celebris, the 1990.

Veuve Clicquot launches the first vintage of La Grande Dame Rosé, the 1988.

1996 Rémy-Cointreau acquires de Venoge.

Thierry Budin directs Perrier-Jouët.

1997 Didier Depond directs Salon and Delamotte.

BCC acquires Philipponnat.

Guinness merges with Grand Metropolitan to form Diageo.

1998 Alain Thiénot acquires Joseph Perrier from Laurent-Perrier.

Moët & Chandon acquires de Venoge (and its vineyards) from Rémi-Cointreau.

Moët & Chandon sells de Venoge brand and inventory to BCC, retaining other assets.

BCC acquires Alexandre Bonnet.

Charles Heidsieck adds disgorgement date to the "mise en cave" series.

Discovery of the wreck of the Jönköping with its treasure of 1907 Heidsieck "Goût Américain" announced.

Creation of the Alliance Champagne by co-ops l'Union Auboise, COVAMA, and COGEVI.

1999 LVMH acquires Krug.

Laurent-Perrier listed on the stock exchange.

Launch of the first vintage of l'Amour de Deutz, the 1993.

Frey family acquires Ayala.

Charles Philipponnat directs Philipponnat.

Private equity firm Hicks, Muse acquires Mumm and Perrier-Jouët from Seagram's.

2000: Henkell acquires Alfred Gratien.

Allied Domecq acquires Mumm and Perrier-Jouët from Hicks, Muse.

Vranken acquires Pommery and 20 ha of vines from LVMH, who retains other assets.

2001: Cécile Bonnefond directs Veuve Clicquot.

2002 : Régis Camus appointed Chef de Caves at Piper-Heidsieck and Charles Heidsieck.

2003: Alain Thiénot acquires Canard Duchêne from Veuve Clicquot.

Moët & Chandon and Vranken divide the assets of Bricout-Delbeck following their bankruptcy.

2004: Caisse d'Epargne acquires 44% of Marne et Champagne, now called Lanson International

Frédéric Cuménal directs Moët & Chandon.

Stanislas Henriot named President of Henriot.

2005: Pernod Ricard acquires Allied Domecq, including champagne assets.

Starwood Capital acquires Taittinger.

Thierry Garnier named Chef de Cave at Philipponnat.

2006: BCC and Lanson merge.

Frédéric Rouzaud directs Roederer.

Stanislas Henriot takes over from his father Joseph.

Taittinger family re-acquires eponymous house with Crédit Agricole.

Dominique Demarville leaves G.H. Mumm for Veuve Clicquot, replaced by Didier Mariotti.

2007: Jérôme Philipon named president of Bollinger.

Frédéric Panaïotis named Chef de Caves of Ruinart.

2008: LVMH acquires Montaudon.

2010: Discovery of bottles of Veuve Clicquot and Juglar in a shipwreck near Åland in the Baltic sea.

LVMH sells Montaudon to co-op Champagne Allianc

2011: Guillaume Selosse joins his father Anselme at Jacques Selosse.

2013: Gilles Descôtes named Chef de Caves at Bollinger.

2014: Jay Z acquires sole ownership of Armand de Brignac brand from Sovereign Brands and Cattier.

2015: Gilles de Larouzière appointed president of Maisons et Domaines Henriot.

Cyril Brun named Chef de Caves at Charles Heidsieck.

Hervé Dantan named Chef de Caves at Lanson.

2017: Jérôme Philipon named Deputy Director General for Société Jacques Bollinger.

Charles-Armand de Belenet named managing director of Bollinger.

Christophe Juarez named managing director of Nicolas Feuillatte.

2018: Piper-Heidsieck launches Rare as a stand-alone brand; Régis Camus is Chef de Caves.

Séverine Frerson leaves Piper-Heidsieck for Perrier-Jouët, replaced by Emilien Boutillat.

Alexandre Ponnavoy appointed Chef de Caves at Taittinger.

Lanson launches "green label" organic Champagne.

Constellation Brands partners with Champagne Palmer.

2019: Vincent Chaperon replaces Richard Geoffroy as Chef de Caves for Dom Pérignon.

Krug announces the promotion of Julie Cavil as Chef de Caves replacing Eric Lebel.

Dominique Demarville announced as replacement of Michel Fauconnet at Laurent-Perrier.

Laurent Fresnet leaves Henriot for G.H. Mumm.

Didier Mariotti leaves G.H. Mumm for Veuve Clicquot.

Alice Tétienne named Chef de Caves at Henriot.

Vitalie Taittinger named president of Taittinger.

François Van Aal replaces Philippe Baijot at Lanson.

Jérôme Philipon leaves Société Jacques Bollinger.

2020: Demarville leaves Laurent-Perrier.

Guillaume Selosse directs Jacques Selosse.

Campari Group acquires Lallier.

Appendix VII

Champagne Villages

Village	Region	Terroir	Echelle
Avirey-Lingey	Côte des Bar	Barséquanais	80%
Bagneux-la-Fosse	Côte des Bar	Barséquanais	80%
Balnot-sur-Laignes	Côte des Bar	Barséquanais	80%
Bar-sur-Seine	Côte des Bar	Barséquanais	80%
Bertignolles	Côte des Bar	Barséquanais	80%
Bragelogne Beauvoir	Côte des Bar	Barséquanais	80%
Buxeuil	Côte des Bar	Barséquanais	80%
Buxières-sur-Arce	Côte des Bar	Barséquanais	80%
Celles-sur-Ource	Côte des Bar	Barséquanais	85%
Chacenay	Côte des Bar	Barséquanais	80%
Channes	Côte des Bar	Barséquanais	80%
Chervey	Côte des Bar	Barséquanais	80%
Courteron	Côte des Bar	Barséquanais	80%
Eguilly-sous-Bois	Côte des Bar	Barséquanais	80%
Essoyes	Côte des Bar	Barséquanais	80%
Fontette	Côte des Bar	Barséquanais	80%
Gyé-sur-Seine	Côte des Bar	Barséquanais	80%
Landreville	Côte des Bar	Barséquanais	80%
Les Riceys	Côte des Bar	Barséquanais	80%
Loches-sur-Ource	Côte des Bar	Barséquanais	80%
Merrey-sur-Arce	Côte des Bar	Barséquanais	80%
Mussy-sur-Seine	Côte des Bar	Barséquanais	80%
Neuville-sur-Seine	Côte des Bar	Barséquanais	80%
Noé-les-Mallets	Côte des Bar	Barséquanais	80%
Plaines-Saint-Lange	Côte des Bar	Barséquanais	80%
Polisot	Côte des Bar	Barséquanais	80%
Polisy	Côte des Bar	Barséquanais	80%
Saint-Usage	Côte des Bar	Barséquanais	80%
Verpillières-sur-Ource	Côte des Bar	Barséquanais	80%
Villenauxe la Grande	Côte des Bar	Barséquanais	87% [1]

Ville-sur-Arce	Côte des Bar	Barséquanais	80%
Vitry-le-Croisé	Côte des Bar	Barséquanais	80%
Viviers-sur-Artaud	Côte des Bar	Barséquanais	80%
Ailleville	Côte des Bar	Bar-sur-Aubois	80%
Arconville	Côte des Bar	Bar-sur-Aubois	80%
Argançon	Côte des Bar	Bar-sur-Aubois	80%
Arrentières	Côte des Bar	Bar-sur-Aubois	80%
Arsonval	Côte des Bar	Bar-sur-Aubois	80%
Baroville	Côte des Bar	Bar-sur-Aubois	80%
Bar-sur-Aube	Côte des Bar	Bar-sur-Aubois	80%
Bergères	Côte des Bar	Bar-sur-Aubois	80%
Bligny	Côte des Bar	Bar-sur-Aubois	80%
Champignol-lez-Mondeville	Côte des Bar	Bar-sur-Aubois	80%
Colombé-la-Fosse	Côte des Bar	Bar-sur-Aubois	80%
Colombé-le-Sec	Côte des Bar	Bar-sur-Aubois	80%
Colombey-les-Deux-Eglises[9] (Includes Argentolles)	Côte des Bar	Bar-sur-Aubois	80%
Couvignon (Includes Val Perdu)	Côte des Bar	Bar-sur-Aubois	80%
Cunfin	Côte des Bar	Bar-sur-Aubois	80%
Dolancourt	Côte des Bar	Bar-sur-Aubois	80%
Engente	Côte des Bar	Bar-sur-Aubois	80%
Fontaine	Côte des Bar	Bar-sur-Aubois	80%
Fravaux	Côte des Bar	Bar-sur-Aubois	80%
Jaucourt	Côte des Bar	Bar-sur-Aubois	80%
Lignol-le-Chateau	Côte des Bar	Bar-sur-Aubois	80%
Meurville	Côte des Bar	Bar-sur-Aubois	80%
Montier-en-l'Isle	Côte des Bar	Bar-sur-Aubois	80%
Proverville	Côte des Bar	Bar-sur-Aubois	80%
Rizaucourt-Buchey[9]	Côte des Bar	Bar-sur-Aubois	80%
Rouvres-les-Vignes	Côte des Bar	Bar-sur-Aubois	80%
Saulcy	Côte des Bar	Bar-sur-Aubois	80%
Spoy	Côte des Bar	Bar-sur-Aubois	80%
Trannes	Côte des Bar	Bar-sur-Aubois	80%
Urville	Côte des Bar	Bar-sur-Aubois	80%
Voigny	Côte des Bar	Bar-sur-Aubois	80%

Avize	Côte des Blancs	Côte des Blancs	100%
Bergères-les-Vertus	Côte des Blancs	Côte des Blancs	95%
Chouilly	Côte des Blancs	Côte des Blancs	100% [5]
Cramant	Côte des Blancs	Côte des Blancs	100%
Cuis	Côte des Blancs	Côte des Blancs	95% [5]
Grauves	Côte des Blancs	Côte des Blancs	95% [5]
Mesnil-sur-Oger (Le)	Côte des Blancs	Côte des Blancs	100%
Oger	Côte des Blancs	Côte des Blancs	100%
Oiry	Côte des Blancs	Côte des Blancs	100%
Vertus	Côte des Blancs	Côte des Blancs	95%
Voipreux	Côte des Blancs	Côte des Blancs	95%
Montgeux (Includes Grange l'Evêque, & Saint-Lyé	Côte des Blancs	Montgeux	80%
Allemant	Côte des Blancs	Sézannais	87% [1]
Barbonne-Fayel	Côte des Blancs	Sézannais	87% [1]
Bergères-sous-Montmirail	Côte des Blancs	Sézannais	82%
Bethon	Côte des Blancs	Sézannais	87% [1]
Broyes	Côte des Blancs	Sézannais	87% [1]
Celle-sous-Chantemerle (La)	Côte des Blancs	Sézannais	87% [1]
Chantemerle	Côte des Blancs	Sézannais	87% [1]
Fontaine-Denis-Nuisy	Côte des Blancs	Sézannais	87% [1]
Montgenost	Côte des Blancs	Sézannais	87% [1]
Saudoy (Includes Le Plessis)	Côte des Blancs	Sézannais	87% [1]
Sézanne	Côte des Blancs	Sézannais	87% [1]
Vindey	Côte des Blancs	Sézannais	87% [1]
Baye	Côte des Blancs	Val du Petit Morin	85%
Beaunay	Côte des Blancs	Val du Petit Morin	85%
Broussy-le-Grand	Côte des Blancs	Val du Petit Morin	84%
Coizard-Joches	Côte des Blancs	Val du Petit Morin	85%
Coligny (Val-des-Marais)	Côte des Blancs	Val du Petit Morin	90% [2]
Congy	Côte des Blancs	Val du Petit Morin	85%
Courjeonnet	Côte des Blancs	Val du Petit Morin	85%
Etoges	Côte des Blancs	Val du Petit Morin	85%
Etrechy	Côte des Blancs	Val du Petit Morin	90% [3]
Fèrebrianges	Côte des Blancs	Val du Petit Morin	85%

Givry-les-Loisy	Côte des Blancs	Val du Petit Morin	85%
Loisy en Brie	Côte des Blancs	Val du Petit Morin	85%
Mondement-Montgivroux	Côte des Blancs	Val du Petit Morin	84%
Oyes	Côte des Blancs	Val du Petit Morin	85%
Soulières	Côte des Blancs	Val du Petit Morin	85%
Talus-Saint-Prix	Côte des Blancs	Val du Petit Morin	85%
Vert-Toulon (Includes Vert-la-Gravelle)	Côte des Blancs	Val du Petit Morin	85%
Villeneuve-Renneville-Chevigny (Includes Chevigny)	Côte des Blancs	Val du Petit Morin	95%
Villevenard	Côte des Blancs	Val du Petit Morin	85%
Bassu	Côte des Blancs	Vitryat	85%
Bassuet	Côte des Blancs	Vitryat	85%
Changy	Côte des Blancs	Vitryat	84%
Couvrot	Côte des Blancs	Vitryat	84%
Glannes	Côte des Blancs	Vitryat	84%
Lisse-en-Champagne	Côte des Blancs	Vitryat	84%
Loisy-sur-Marne	Côte des Blancs	Vitryat	84%
Merlaut	Côte des Blancs	Vitryat	84%
Saint-Amand-sur-Fion	Côte des Blancs	Vitryat	84%
Saint-Lumier-en-Champagne	Côte des Blancs	Vitryat	85%
Val-de-Vière	Côte des Blancs	Vitryat	84%
Vanault-le-Chatel	Côte des Blancs	Vitryat	84%
Vavray-le-Grand	Côte des Blancs	Vitryat	84%
Vavray-le-Petit	Côte des Blancs	Vitryat	84%
Vitry-en-Perthois	Côte des Blancs	Vitryat	85%
Barzy-sur-Marne	Marne Valley	Condé	85%
Baulne-en-Brie (Now Vallées-en-Champagne)	Marne Valley	Condé	80%
Passy-sur-Marne	Marne Valley	Condé	85%
Trélou-sur-Marne	Marne Valley	Condé	85%
Brugny-Vaudancourt	Marne Valley	Coteaux Sud d'Epernay	86%
Chavot-Courcourt	Marne Valley	Coteaux Sud d'Epernay	88%
Epernay	Marne Valley	Coteaux Sud d'Epernay	88%
Mancy	Marne Valley	Coteaux Sud d'Epernay	88%

Monthelon	Marne Valley	Coteaux Sud d'Epernay	88%
Morangis	Marne Valley	Coteaux Sud d'Epernay	84%
Moslins	Marne Valley	Coteaux Sud d'Epernay	84%
Moussy	Marne Valley	Coteaux Sud d'Epernay	88%
Pierry	Marne Valley	Coteaux Sud d'Epernay	90%
Saint-Martin d'Ablois	Marne Valley	Coteaux Sud d'Epernay	86%
Vinay	Marne Valley	Coteaux Sud d'Epernay	86%
Avenay-Val-d'Or	Marne Valley	Grande Vallée	93%
Aÿ-Champagne [7]	Marne Valley	Grande Vallée	100%
Bisseuil	Marne Valley	Grande Vallée	95%
Champillon	Marne Valley	Grande Vallée	93%
Cumières	Marne Valley	Grande Vallée	93%
Dizy	Marne Valley	Grande Vallée	95%
Fontaine-sur-Aÿ	Marne Valley	Grande Vallée	80%
Germaine	Marne Valley	Grande Vallée	80%
Hautvillers	Marne Valley	Grande Vallée	93%
Mareuil-sur-Aÿ	Marne Valley	Grande Vallée	99%
Mutigny	Marne Valley	Grande Vallée	93%
Tours-sur-Marne	Marne Valley	Grande Vallée	100% [6]
Boursault (Includes Villesaint)	Marne Valley	Left Bank	84%
Courthiézy	Marne Valley	Left Bank	83%
Dormans (Includes Try, Vassieux. Vassy, Champaillé, Chavenay, & Soilly)	Marne Valley	Left Bank	83%
Festigny (Includes Le Mesnil-le-Huttier & La Rue)	Marne Valley	Left Bank	84%
Igny-Comblizy	Marne Valley	Left Bank	83%
Le Breuil	Marne Valley	Left Bank	83%
Leuvrigny	Marne Valley	Left Bank	84%
Mardeuil	Marne Valley	Left Bank	84%
Mareuil-le-Port (Includes Cerseuil & Port à Binson)	Marne Valley	Left Bank	84%
Nesle-le-Repons	Marne Valley	Left Bank	84%
Oeuilly	Marne Valley	Left Bank	84%
Orbais-l'Abbaye	Marne Valley	Left Bank	82%
Troissy (Includes Bouquigny)	Marne Valley	Left Bank	84%

Vauciennes	Marne Valley	Left Bank	84%
Baslieux-sous-Châtillon	Marne Valley	Right Bank	84%
Belval-sous-Châtillon Includes Paradis	Marne Valley	Right Bank	84%
Binson-et-Orquigny	Marne Valley	Right Bank	86%
Champlat-et-Boujacourt	Marne Valley	Right Bank	83%
Champvoisy	Marne Valley	Right Bank	84%
Châtillon-sur-Marn (Includes Montigny-sous-Châtillon)	Marne Valley	Right Bank	86%
Cormoyeux	Marne Valley	Right Bank	85%
Cuchery (Includes Orcourt)	Marne Valley	Right Bank	84%
Cuisles	Marne Valley	Right Bank	86%
Damery	Marne Valley	Right Bank	89%
Fleury-la-Rivière	Marne Valley	Right Bank	85%
Jonquery	Marne Valley	Right Bank	84%
La Neuville-aux-Larris	Marne Valley	Right Bank	84%
Olizy (Includes Olizy-Violaine)	Marne Valley	Right Bank	84%
Passy-Grigny	Marne Valley	Right Bank	84%
Reuil	Marne Valley	Right Bank	86%
Romery	Marne Valley	Right Bank	85%
Romigny	Marne Valley	Right Bank	82%
Sainte-Gemme	Marne Valley	Right Bank	84%
Vandières	Marne Valley	Right Bank	86%
Venteuil (Includes Arty)	Marne Valley	Right Bank	89%
Verneuil	Marne Valley	Right Bank	86%
Villers-sous-Châtillon	Marne Valley	Right Bank	86%
Vincelles	Marne Valley	Right Bank	86%
Azy-sur-Marne	Marne Valley	Western Marne	80%
Bézu-le-Guéry	Marne Valley	Western Marne	80%
Blesmes	Marne Valley	Western Marne	80%
Bonneil	Marne Valley	Western Marne	80%
Brasles	Marne Valley	Western Marne	80%
Celles-les-Condé	Marne Valley	Western Marne	83%
Charly-sur-Marne (Includes Drachy, Rudenoise, Ruvet, & Porteron)	Marne Valley	Western Marne	80%

Chartèves	Marne Valley	Western Marne	80%
Château Thiérry	Marne Valley	Western Marne	80%
Chézy-sur-Marne	Marne Valley	Western Marne	80%
Chierry	Marne Valley	Western Marne	80%
Citry-sur-Marne[s]	Marne Valley	Western Marne	80%
Connigis	Marne Valley	Western Marne	80%
Courtemont-Varennes	Marne Valley	Western Marne	80%
Crézancy	Marne Valley	Western Marne	80%
Crouttes-sur-Marne	Marne Valley	Western Marne	80%
Domptin	Marne Valley	Western Marne	80%
Essômes-sur-Marne Includes Aulnoy, Monneaux, Rouvroy, Vaux, & Crogis	Marne Valley	Western Marne	80%
Etampes-sur-Marne	Marne Valley	Western Marne	80%
Fossoy	Marne Valley	Western Marne	80%
Gland	Marne Valley	Western Marne	80%
Jaulgonne	Marne Valley	Western Marne	80%
La Chapelle-Monthodon (Now Vallées-en-Champagne)	Marne Valley	Western Marne	80%
Mézy-Moulins	Marne Valley	Western Marne	80%
Monthurel	Marne Valley	Western Marne	80%
Montreuil-aux-Lions	Marne Valley	Western Marne	80%
Mont-Saint Père	Marne Valley	Western Marne	80%
Nanteuil-sur-Marne[s]	Marne Valley	Western Marne	80%
Nesles-La Montagne	Marne Valley	Western Marne	80%
Nogentel	Marne Valley	Western Marne	80%
Nogent-l'Artaud	Marne Valley	Western Marne	80%
Pavant	Marne Valley	Western Marne	80%
Reuilly-Sauvigny	Marne Valley	Western Marne	80%
Romeny-sur-Marne	Marne Valley	Western Marne	80%
Saâcy-sur-Marne[s] (Includes Belle Ente & Changemanche)	Marne Valley	Western Marne	80%
Saint-Agnan (Now Vallées-en-Champagne)	Marne Valley	Western Marne	80%
Saulchery (Includes Le Pont)	Marne Valley	Western Marne	80%
Villiers-Saint-Denis	Marne Valley	Western Marne	80%

Arcis-le-Ponsart (Includes Igny)	Montagne de Reims	Ardre Valley	82%
Aubilly	Montagne de Reims	Ardre Valley	82%
Bligny	Montagne de Reims	Ardre Valley	83%
Bouleuse	Montagne de Reims	Ardre Valley	82%
Brouillet	Montagne de Reims	Ardre Valley	86%
Chambrecy	Montagne de Reims	Ardre Valley	83%
Chaumuzy	Montagne de Reims	Ardre Valley	83%
Courmas	Montagne de Reims	Ardre Valley	87%
Courtagnon	Montagne de Reims	Ardre Valley	82%
Courville	Montagne de Reims	Ardre Valley	82%
Crugny	Montagne de Reims	Ardre Valley	86%
Faverolles-et-Coëmy	Montagne de Reims	Ardre Valley	86%
Lagery	Montagne de Reims	Ardre Valley	86%
Lhery	Montagne de Reims	Ardre Valley	86%
Marfaux	Montagne de Reims	Ardre Valley	84%
Méry-Prémecy	Montagne de Reims	Ardre Valley	82%
Nanteuil-la-Forêt	Montagne de Reims	Ardre Valley	82%
Poilly	Montagne de Reims	Ardre Valley	83%
Pourcy	Montagne de Reims	Ardre Valley	84%
Saint-Euphraise-et-Clairizet	Montagne de Reims	Ardre Valley	86%
Saint-Gilles	Montagne de Reims	Ardre Valley	82%
Sarcy	Montagne de Reims	Ardre Valley	83%
Savigny-sur-Ardre	Montagne de Reims	Ardre Valley	86%
Serzy-et-Prin	Montagne de Reims	Ardre Valley	86%
Tramery	Montagne de Reims	Ardre Valley	86%
Treslon	Montagne de Reims	Ardre Valley	86%
Ville-en-Tardenois	Montagne de Reims	Ardre Valley	82%
Beaumont-sur-Vesle	Montagne de Reims	Grande Montagne North	100%
Chigny-les-Roses	Montagne de Reims	Grande Montagne North	94%
Ludes	Montagne de Reims	Grande Montagne North	94%
Mailly-Champagne	Montagne de Reims	Grande Montagne North	100%
Montbré	Montagne de Reims	Grande Montagne North	94%
Puisieulx	Montagne de Reims	Grande Montagne North	100%
Rilly-la-Montagne	Montagne de Reims	Grande Montagne North	94%

Sillery	Montagne de Reims	Grande Montagne North	100%
Taissy	Montagne de Reims	Grande Montagne North	94%
Trois-Puits	Montagne de Reims	Grande Montagne North	94%
Verzenay	Montagne de Reims	Grande Montagne North	100%
Verzy	Montagne de Reims	Grande Montagne North	100%
Villers-Allerand	Montagne de Reims	Grande Montagne North	90%
Ambonnay	Montagne de Reims	Grande Montagne South	100%
Bouzy	Montagne de Reims	Grande Montagne South	100%
Louvois (Now Val-de-Livre)	Montagne de Reims	Grande Montagne South	100%
Tauxières-Mutry (Now Val-de-Livre)	Montagne de Reims	Grande Montagne South	99%
Bouilly	Montagne de Reims	Massif de Saint-Thierry	86%
Brimont	Montagne de Reims	Massif de Saint-Thierry	83%
Cauroy-lès-Hermonville	Montagne de Reims	Massif de Saint-Thierry	83%
Châlons-sur-Vesle	Montagne de Reims	Massif de Saint-Thierry	84%
Chenay	Montagne de Reims	Massif de Saint-Thierry	84%
Cormicy	Montagne de Reims	Massif de Saint-Thierry	83%
Hermonville	Montagne de Reims	Massif de Saint-Thierry	84%
Merfy	Montagne de Reims	Massif de Saint-Thierry	84%
Montigny-sur-Vesle	Montagne de Reims	Massif de Saint-Thierry	84%
Pévy	Montagne de Reims	Massif de Saint-Thierry	84%
Pouillon	Montagne de Reims	Massif de Saint-Thierry	84%
Prouilly	Montagne de Reims	Massif de Saint-Thierry	84%
Saint-Thiérry	Montagne de Reims	Massif de Saint-Thierry	87%
Thil	Montagne de Reims	Massif de Saint-Thierry	84%
Trigny	Montagne de Reims	Massif de Saint-Thierry	84%
Villers-Franqueux	Montagne de Reims	Massif de Saint-Thierry	84%
Berru (Includes Witry-les-Reims)	Montagne de Reims	Monts de Berru	84%
Cernay-lès-Reims	Montagne de Reims	Monts de Berru	85%
Nogent-l'Abbesse	Montagne de Reims	Monts de Berru	87%
Pontfaverger-Moronvilliers	Montagne de Reims	Monts de Berru	84%
Selles	Montagne de Reims	Monts de Berru	84%
Billy-le-Grand	Montagne de Reims	Perle Blanche	95%
Trépail	Montagne de Reims	Perle Blanche	95%

Vaudemanges	Montagne de Reims	Perle Blanche	95%
Villers-Marmery	Montagne de Reims	Perle Blanche	95%
Bezannes	Montagne de Reims	Petite Montagne	90%
Chamery	Montagne de Reims	Petite Montagne	90%
Coulommes-la-Montagne	Montagne de Reims	Petite Montagne	90%
Ecueil	Montagne de Reims	Petite Montagne	90%
Gueux	Montagne de Reims	Petite Montagne	85%
Jouy-lès-Reims	Montagne de Reims	Petite Montagne	90%
Mesneux (Les)	Montagne de Reims	Petite Montagne	90%
Ormes	Montagne de Reims	Petite Montagne	85%
Pargny-lès-Reims	Montagne de Reims	Petite Montagne	90%
Sacy	Montagne de Reims	Petite Montagne	90%
Sermiers (Includes Courtaumont & Le Petit Fleury)	Montagne de Reims	Petite Montagne	90%
Villedommange	Montagne de Reims	Petite Montagne	90%
Villers-aux-Noeuds	Montagne de Reims	Petite Montagne	90%
Vrigny	Montagne de Reims	Petite Montagne	90%
Germigny	Montagne de Reims	Vesle Valley	85%
Janvry	Montagne de Reims	Vesle Valley	85%
Rosnay	Montagne de Reims	Vesle Valley	83%
Branscourt	Montagne de Reims	Vesle Valley	86%
Cormontreuil	Montagne de Reims	Vesle Valley	94%
Courcelles-Sapicourt	Montagne de Reims	Vesle Valley	83%
Hourges	Montagne de Reims	Vesle Valley	86%
Jonchery-sur-Vesle	Montagne de Reims	Vesle Valley	84%
Reims	Montagne de Reims	Vesle Valley	88%
Unchair	Montagne de Reims	Vesle Valley	86%
Vandeuil	Montagne de Reims	Vesle Valley	86%

[1] 85% for black grapes
[2] 87% for black grapes
[3] 87% for white grapes
[4] 90% for white grapes
[5] 90% for black grapes
[6] 90% for white grapes
[7] Aÿ-Champagne includes Bisseuil and Mareuil-sur-Aÿ since 2016, but this does not affect their ratings on the (defunct) échelle des crus
[8] Located in Seine-et-Marne
[9] Located in Haute-Marne

Bibliography

Books and Proceedings

Avellan, Essi. *Champagne : A Guide*. Helsinki : AvelVino Media, 2017.

Bidet, Nicolas. *Dissertation sur les Vins*. Paris : Dido Jeune, 1752. Online. Available : https://play.google.com/books/reader?id=L c86AAAAcAAJ&pg=GBS.PA1

Bonal, François. *Le Livre d'Or du Champagne*. Lausanne : Editions du Grand-Pont, 1984

Colin Georges. *Vignoble et vin de Champagne*. In: Travaux de l'Institut Géographique de Reims, n°15, 1973. Vignoble et vin de Champagne. pp. 3-92. https://www.persee.fr/doc/tigr_0048-7163_1973_num_15_1_966

Curien, Jean. *Guide Curien de la Champagne 2018/2019*. Paris : SPRED, 2018

Edwards, Michael. *The Finest Wines of Champagne*. Berkeley: University of California Press, 2009

Feuerheerd, H.L. *The Gentleman's Cellar and Butler's Guide*. London: Chatto & Windus, 1902. Online. Available :

Fradet, Dominique et al. *Un Siècle De Vendanges En Champagne*. Reims, Editions Fradet, 1998.

François, André. *Traité sur le Travail de Vins Blancs Mousseux*. Chalons-sur-Marne : Boniez-Lambert, 1837. Online. Available : https://gallica.bnf.fr/ark:/12148/bpt6k850205b.image

Godinot, Jean. *Manière de Cultiver la Vigne et de Faire le Vin en Champagne*. Reims : Multeau, 1718. Online. Available : https://www.youscribe.com/BookReader/Index/302491/?documentId=275165

Guyot, Dr. Jules. *Culture de la Vigne et Vinification*. Paris : Librarie Agricole de la Maison Rustique, 1861. Online. Available : https://books.google.com/books?id=sO9IAAAAIAAJ&printsec=frontcover&source=gbs_ge_summary_r&cad=0#v=onepage&q&f=false

Juhlin, Richard. *2000 Champagnes.* New York, M.T. Train, 1999

Juhlin, Richard. *A Scent of Champagne: 8,000 Champagnes Tested and Rated.* New York, Skyhorse Publishing. 2013

Liem, Peter. *Champagne: The Essential Guide to the Wines, Producers and Terroir of the Iconic Region.* New York: Ten Speed Press, 2017.

Redding, Cyrus. *A History and Description of Modern Wines.* London: George Bell & Sons, 1876. Online. Available: https://books.google.com/books?id=YjoNAAAAYAAJ&printsec=frontcover&source=gbs_ge_summary_r&cad=0#v=onepage&q&f=false

Saintsbury, George. *Notes on a Cellar-Book.* London: Macmillan & Co, 1920. Online. Available: https://play.google.com/books/reader?id=S9ZPAAAAYAAJ&hl=en&pg=GBS.PR3

Simon, André L. *History of the Champagne Trade in England.* London: Wyman and Sons, 1905. Online. Available: https://play.google.com/books/reader?id=qWAaAAAAYAAJ&hl=en&pg=GBS.PP9

Simon, André L. *The History of Champagne.* London: Octopus Books, 1971

Simon, André L. *Vintagewise.* London : Michael Joseph, 1945

Stevenson, Tom. *World Encyclopedia of Champagne and Sparkling Wine.* Bath: Absolute Press, 1998

Vizetelly, Henry. *Facts About Champagne and Other Sparkling Wines.* London: Ward, Lock and Co., 1879. Online. Available: http://www.gutenberg.org/files/20889/20889-h/20889-h.htm

Vizetelly, Henry. *A History of Champagne.* London: Vizetelly & Co., 1882. Online. Available: https://archive.org/details/historyofchampag00vize/page/n6

Wilson, James. *Terroir: The Role of Geology, Climate and Culture in the Making of French Wines.* Berkeley: University of California Press, 1998

French Government Publications

The most recent (2010) specification ("cahier de charges") for the production of Champagne:

Décret n° 2010-1441 du 22 novembre 2010 relatif à l'appellation d'origine contrôlée "Champagne": https://www.legifrance.gouv.fr/affichTexte. do;jsessionid=?cidTexte=JORFTEXT000023126020&dateTexte=&oldAction=rechJO&categorieLien=id

Increases the maximum possible yield to 15,500 kg/ha:

Décret n° 2007-1409 du 1er octobre 2007 modifiant la loi du 6 mai 1919 relative à la protection des appellations d'origine: https://www.legifrance. gouv.fr/affichTexte.do?cidTexte=JORFTEXT000000794000&dateTexte=&-categorieLien=id

Establishes a minimum aging of fifteen months after bottling and a minimum of twelve months on the lees:

Décret du 14 octobre 1997 relatif à l'appellation d'origine contrôlée "Champagne": https://www.legifrance.gouv.fr/affichTexte.do?cidTexte=-JORFTEXT000000568915&dateTexte=&categorieLien=id; JORF n°241 du 16 octobre 1997 page 15019

Reduces the amount that can be pressed from a given quantity of grapes:

Décret du 22 décembre 1994 relatif à l'appellation d'origine contrôlée "Champagne":https://www.legifrance.gouv.fr/affichTexte.do?cidTexte=JORF-TEXT000000185916&dateTexte=&categorieLien=id

Fixes the conditions of the use of a vintage date:

Le déret du 17 octobre 1952 concernant l'indication du millésime des vins à appellation d'origine contrôlée "Champagne": https://www.legifrance.gouv. fr/jo_pdf.do?id=JORFTEXT000000868803&pageCourante=09901

Creation of the INAO :

Décret-loi du 30 juillet 1935 sur la défense du marché des vins et le régime économique de l'alcool: https://www.legifrance.gouv.fr/affichTexte.do?cid-Texte=JORFTEXT000000667657&categorieLien=id

Creation of the AOC Champagne:

Décret du 29 juin 1936 relatif à l'appellation d'origine contrôlée
"Champagne":https://www.legifrance.gouv.fr/affichTexte.do?cidTexte=JORF-
TEXT000000664196&dateTexte=20101125

Prohibition of non-Champagne sparkling wine within the Champagne region:

Loi du 20 mars 1934 tendant à interdire la fabrication de vins mousseux
ordinaires à l'intérieur des territoires compris dans la Champagne viticole
délimitée par la loi du 27 juillet 1927: https://www.legifrance.gouv.fr/
affichTexteArticle.do;jsessionid=241FE7ACB280E19BBA675D44E2C36669.
tplgfr24s_1?idArticle=LEGIARTI000020213505&cidTexte=LEGITEX-
T000020213496&dateTexte=20180831

Inclusion of the Aube in AOC Champagne :

Loi du 22 juillet 1927 tendant à completer la loi du 6 mai 1919 relative à la
protection des appellations d'origine (Journal officiel du 27 juillet 1927.) In :
Rapport Sénat N° 21 : au nom de la Commission des Affaires économiques et
du Plan, sur le projet de loi modifiant la loi n° 55-1533 du 28 novembre 1955
relative aux appellations d'origine des fromages, (dépôt le 18 octobre 1973)
Avis présenté par M. Paul MALASSAGNE, annexe 2, p. 24. Online.
Available: https://www.senat.fr/rap/1973-1974/i1973_1974_0021.pdf

Protection of AOC Champagne specifically:

Loi du 6 mai 1919 modifiée relative à la protection des appellations d'origine,
notamment son article 17 relatif à l'appellation "Champagne" (Conditions de
production): https://www.inao.gouv.fr/show_texte/1005

Protection of geographic indications :

Loi du 6 mai 1919 relative à la protection des appellations d'origine:
https://www.legifrance.gouv.fr/affichTexte.do?cidTexte=LEGITEX-
T000006071952&dateTexte=20150730

First definition of AOC Champagne:

Decret du 17 décembre 1908 relatif à l'Appellation Régionale "Champagne":
https://gallica.bnf.fr/ark:/12148/bpt6k6250204d/f2.image

First modern French consumer protection legislation:

Loi du 1er août 1905 sur les fraudes et falsifications en matière de produits ou de services: https://www.legifrance.gouv.fr/affichTexte.do?cidTexte=-JORFTEXT000000508748&categorieLien=cid

Online Resources

Association des Champagnes Biologiques:
http://www.champagnesbiologiques.com/index.php

Chambre d'Agriculture Vignoble de Champagne:
https://vignoble-champenois.chambres-agriculture.fr/

Comité Champagne:
https://www.champagne.fr/en/homepage

Peter Liem Champagne Website:
https://www.champagneguide.net/

Richard Juhlin Champagne Club:
http://www.champagneclub.com/start.aspx

Syndicat Général des Vignerons de la Champagne:
http://www.sgv-champagne.fr/

Syndicat Professionnel des Courtiers en Vins de Champagne:
https://www.spcvc.com/

Union des Maisons de Champagne:
https://maisons-champagne.com/

VinTomas Blog:
https://winetomas.wordpress.com/

General Index

à la volée	459	Bottling liqueur	465
Agache-Willot-Boussac	374	Boues de ville	343, 409
Agrafe-et-liège	332, 451	Brut	453
Amont	455	Brut Nature	453
Ancien franc	282	Budbreak	453
Arab oil embargo	356	Bureau Veritas	469
Arbanne	331	Butte de Saran	456
Arce (river)	455	Cage	453
Ardre (river)	468	Cahier des charges	431
Arm	451	Carbon disulfide	278
Arrière-saison	451	Centre Vinicole de la Champagne	357
Association Viticole Champenoise	451	Certipaq Bio	469
Aube (river)	455	Chalk	453
Autolysis	451	Champagne Riots	288
Aval	455	Chaptalization	454
AVC	276	Chardonnay	331
Barriques	460	Chef de Caves	454
Barséquanais	455	Chef de Culture	454
Bar-sur-Aubois	455	Chlorosis	454
Belemnite	454	CIVC	318, 454
Belon	451	Clonal selection	342
Biodynamic	452	Club Trésors de Champagne	455
Biological pest control	410	Commission Appellation et Communication Champagne	455
Blanc	452		
Blanc de Blancs	452		
Blanc de Noirs	452	Commission de Châlons	309, 454
Blanc Vrai (Pinot Blanc)	331	Concrete Tanks	461
Blocage	391, 452	Coopérative de manipulation	455
Botrytis	453		

Coquard press	470	Extra Brut	453
Cork	455	Extra Dry (Extra Sec)	453
Côte des Bar	455	Fermentation vessel	460
Côte des Blancs	456	Filtration	462
Coteaux Sud d'Epernay	465	Fining	462
Coulure	457	Foudre	460
Crayères	457	French Resistance	318
Crown capsules	332, 457	Fromenteau (Pinot Gris)	331
Cru	457	Gluconic acid	276, 401
Cuvée	391, 470	Grande Charte Champenoise	290
Dannon	374		
Délimitation parcellaire	431	Grande Marque	462
Demi-muid	460	Great Depression	308
Demi-Sec	453	Grey rot	463
Département	458	Haute Valeur Environnementale	410, 463
Derogation	459		
Deuxième Zone	289, 300, 459	Hectare	463
		Hennessy Cognac	374
Disgorge (Dégorger)	459	Herrick, Myron	299
Domaine	460	House	460, 463
Dosage	458	Interprofessional contracts	332
Doux	453	ISO 14001	410
Dry (Sec)	453	Jetting	459
Echelle des crus	289, 431, 457	Kimmeridgian	464
		Laignes (river)	455
Ecocert	469	Late-disgorged	464
Eggs, concrete	461	Le Vigneron Champenois	279
En Foule	460	Lees	464
Epluchage	460	Left Bank (Marne Valley)	465
Epluché	312	Lieu-dit (Lieux-dits)	464
Estate	460	Liqueur de tirage	465
Expansion of appellation	430	Liqueur d'Expédition	464

Lutte Raisonnée	465	Parcellaire	469
LVMH	374	Paris Basin	453
Marc	465	Pectolytic enzymes	343
Marl	465	Perle Blanche	467
Marne Valley, river	465	Petit Meslier	331
Marque d'Acheteur	466	Petite Montagne	467
Massal selection	342	Phylloxera	277, 469
Massif de Saint-Thierry	468	Phytosanitary	470
Meunier	331	Pinot Noir	331
Micraster	454	Press, pressing	470
Mildew	466	Prise de mousse	471
Millerandage	466	Prix constaté	276
Millésime non-reclamé	467	Prix indicatif	276
Millésime non-revendiqué	467	Professional declaration	471
Millésime, Millésimé	467	CM (Coopérative de Manipulation)	471
Mont Aimé	456	MA (Marque d'Acheteur)	471
Montagne de Reims	467	ND (Négociant-Distributeur)	471
Montgueux	456	NM (Négociant-Manipulant)	471
Monts de Berru	468	RC (Récoltant-Coopérateur)	471
Moth	468	RM (Récoltant-Manipulant)	471
Mount Bernon	456	Prohibition	292
Mousse	468	Provinage	472
Must	468	Rebêches	472
"Natural" wine production	410	Récoltant-coopérateur	472
Négociant, Négociant-Manipulant	468	Récoltant-manipulant	472
Négociant-Distributeur	468	Reductive winemaking	472
North Face	467	Réserve perpetuelle	472
Oak casks	460	Retrousse	470
Organic Viticulture	469	Riddle, Remuage	473
Ource (river)	455	Right Bank (Marne Valley)	465
PAI press	470	Rosé	473

Rosé de Riceys 90

Rougeot (black rot) 473

Russian Revolution 291

Saignée 473

Sanitary condition 473

Sarce (river) 455

Saute-bouchon 474

Sauvage 474

Second (Secondary) 473
Fermentation

Seine (river) 455

Sexual confusion 474

Sézannais 456

Shipping liqueur 464

Société d'Intervention de 391
la Champagne Viticole

Société de Récoltants 474

Solera 474

Sorbic acid 343

Sous bois 474

South Face 467

Special Club (Club 474
Trésors de Champagne)

Stainless steel 356, 461

Subregions of Champagne 474

Sur pointes 473

Surmelin (river) 466

Sustainable viticulture 473

Syndicat d'Epernay 463

Syndicat Général des 290
Vignerons

Syndicat Général des 473
Vignerons de la
Champagne (SGV)

Syndicat Professionnel 276
des Courtiers

Syndicat Professionnel 473
des Courtiers en Vins de
Champagne

Taille 475

Terroir 473

Terroir de Condé 465

Tonneau 460

Ullage 476

Union des Maisons de 463
Champagne

Val du Petit Morin 456

Vaslin press 470

Veraison 476

Vesle (river) 468

Vigneron 432, 476

Vin clair 476

Vin Nature de Champagne 350

Vineux (vinous) 476

Vins mousseux ordinaires 300

Vins sur lattes 357

Viticulture Durable en 410, 465,
Champagne 477

Viticulture Raisonée 410

Vitriat 456

Volume Complémentaire 391
Indivduel

Western Marne Valley 465
(Aisne)

Woman's Harvest, The 295

World War I 291

World War II 318

Index of Producers & Cuvées

Agrapart	61
Complantée	61
Minéral	61
Avizoise	61
Vénus	61
Alexandre, Yann	202
Brut Vintage Blanc de Blancs	202
Sous les Roses	202
Aubry Fils, L.	203
Aubry de Humbert	203
Ivoire et Ebène	204
Le Nombre d'Or Campaniae Veteres Vitres	204
Le Nombre d'Or Sablé Blanc de Blancs	204
Ayala	205
Blanc de Blancs	205
Perle d'Ayala	205
Bara, Paul	206
Special Club	206
Special Club Rosé	207
Comtesse Marie de France	207
Beaumet	256
Bérêche et Fils	64
Le Cran	65
Rive Gauche	65
Les Chalois	65
Les Sablons	66
Beaux Regards	66

Campania Remensis	66
Coteaux Champenois	66
Coteaux Champenois Le Monts Fournois	67
Besserat de Bellefon	51
Billecart-Salmon	126
Brut Vintage Blanc de Blancs	126
Clos Saint-Hilaire	126
Cuvée Nicolas-François	127
Rosé Cuvée Elisabeth Salmon	127
Bollinger	32
Brut Vintage Grande Année	33
Brut Vintage RD	33
Brut Vintage Vieilles Vignes Françaises	33
Boulard et Fille, Francis	208
Petraea	208
Les Murgiers	208
Les Vieilles Vignes	209
Les Rachais	209
Les Rachais Rosé	209
Brochet, Emmanuel	68
Le Mont Benoit	68
Les Hauts Meuniers	68
Les Hauts Chardonnays	69
Calsac, Etienne	210
Clos des Maladries	210

Charlot, Vincent	211	
Fruit de ma Passion	211	
l'Or des Basses Ronces	211	
l'Extravagant	212	
l'Ecorché de la Genette	212	
Le Rubis de la Dune	212	
Clos des Futies	212	
Chartogne-Taillet	70	
Cuvée Fiacre	70	
Brut Millésime	71	
Orizeaux	71	
Chemin de Reims	71	
Les Barres	71	
Couarres Château	72	
Chevreux-Bournazel	213	
La Parcelle	213	
Chiquet, Gaston	119	
Or Millésime	119	
Special Club	119	
Bland de Blancs d'Aÿ	129	
Closerie, La	73	
Les Béguines	74	
d'Ailleurs	74	
Fac-simile	75	
Coessens	214	
Sens Boisés	214	
Brut Nature	214	
Rosé de Saignée	215	
Coteaux Champenois	215	
Collin, Ulysse	216	
Les Maillons	216	
Les Maillons Rosé	216	
Corbon	217	
Grand Cru Avize	217	
Couche, Vincent	218	
Millésime	218	
ADN Montgueux	218	
Courtin, Marie	76	
Resonance	76	
Efflorescence	76	
Concordance	76	
Eloquence	77	
Presence	77	
Indulgence	77	
Allégeance	77	
Coutier, R.H.	219	
Brut Vintage	219	
Coteaux Champenois	219	
de Castellane	256	
de Sousa	220	
Cuvée des Caudelies	220	
Dehours et Fils	130	
Côte en Bosses	131	
Maisoncelle	131	
Brisfer	131	
Les Genevraux	131	
La Croix Joly	132	
Déhu, Benoît	133	
Rue des Noyers	133	
l'Orme	133	
Coteaux Champanois	134	
Coteaux Champanois (Blanc de Noirs)	134	

Delamotte	135, 256
Brut Vintage Blanc de Blancs	135
Collection Rare	135
Deutz	221
Cuvée William Deutz	221
Amour de Deutz	221
Millésimé	221
Amour de Deutz Rosé	222
Dhondt, José	222
Mes Vieilles Vignes	222
Diebolt-Vallois	78
Brut Vintage	78
Fleur de Passion	79
Dom Perignon	37
Brut Vintage	38
Brut Vintage Rosé	39
Œnothèque	40
Brut Vintage P2	40
Brut Vintage P3	40
Doquet, Pascal	80
Vertus Cœur de Terroir	80
Mont Aimé Cœur de Terroir	81
Mesnil Cœur de Terroir	81
Doyard	223
Blanc de Blancs Grand Cru	223
Œil de Perdrix	224
Clos de l'Abbaye	224
Drappier	82
Brut Millésime Exception	82
Œnothèque	83
Grande Sendrée	83
Dubois Pere et Fils	46
Egly-Ouriet	84
Brut Grand Cru Millésime	85
Coteaux Champenois	85
Fallet-Dart	225
Brut Vintage	225
Les Hautes des Clos du Mont	225
Falmet, Nathalie	136
Brut Nature	136
Tentation Rosée	137
ZH 302	137
ZH 303	137
ZH 318	137
Fleury	226
Brut Vintage	226
Cuvée Robert Fleury	226
Sonate Opus 10	227
Forest-Fourneaux	57
Fourneaux, Jacques	57
Frison, Val	228
Goustan	228
Cuvée Lalore	228
Portlandia	228
Gatinois	229
Brut Vintage	229

Geoffroy	138		Gosset	233	
Terre Millésime	138		Grand Millésime	233	
Empreinte	139		Celebris	233	
Volupté	139		Gratien, Alfred	143	
Les Tiersaudes	139		Brut Vintage Blanc de Blancs	144	
Blanc de Rose	139		Brut Vintage	144	
Coteaux Champenois Cumières	140		Cuvée Paradis	144	
Gerbais, Pierre	141		Cuvée Paradis Rosé	144	
l'Osmose	142		Grumier, Maurice	145	
l'Originale	142		Les Plates Pierres	145	
l'Audace	142		Armand	146	
Coteaux Champenois	142		Guiborat	234	
Gimonnet, Pierre	86		Prisme	234	
Cuvée Gastronome	86		Le Mont Aigu	234	
Cuvée Fleuron	86		Millésime	235	
Cuvée Oenophile	87		Hébrart, Marc	147	
Special Club	87		Special Club	147	
Chouilly Grand Cru Special Club	87		Rive Gauche Rive Droite	147	
Oger Grand Cru Special Club	87		Noces de Craie	148	
Cuvée Millésime de Collection	88		Heidsieck Monopole	149, 182	
Glavier, Philippe	230		Goût Américain	285	
Emotion	230		Dry	307	
Folie de Cramant	230		Sec	345	
Gonet-Médeville	231		Heidsieck, Charles	149	
Champs d'Alouette	231		Brut Vintage	150	
Vintage Rosé	231		Collection Crayères	150	
Coteaux Champenois Rouge Cuvée Athenaïs	232		Champagne Charlie	150	
			Blanc des Millénaires	151	
			Heidsieck, Piper-	149	
			Brut Vintage	151	
			Rare	151	

Henriot	153
Brut Vintage	153
Cuvée des Enchanteleurs	154
Hemera	154
Horiot, Olivier	89
Rosé des Riceys En Barmont	90
Rosé des Riceys En Valingrin	90
Sève Rosé	90
5 Sens	90
Coteaux Champenois En Barmont	91
Coteaux Champenois En Valingrain	91
Huré Frères	155
Instantanée	156
4 éléments	156
Terre Natale	156
Jacquart, André	92
Millésime Experience	93
Jacquesson	27, 94
Grand Vin Signature	95
Corne Bautray	96
Champ Caïn	96
Vauzelle	96
Terme	96
Terres Rouges	96
Jeanmaire	256
Jeaunaux-Robin	236
Marnes Blanches	236
Rosé de Saignée	236
Les Grands Nots	236

Krug	26
Brut Vintage	28
Krug Collection	28
Krug Clos du Mesnil	29
Krug Clos d'Ambonnay	30
Lacourte-Godbillon	238
Brut Vintage	238
Les Chaillots	238
Lahaye, Benoît	157
Brut Vintage	157
Blanc de Noirs	158
Violaine	158
Le Jardin de la Grosse Pierre	158
Laherte Frères	162
Les Emprein tes	163
Vignes d'Autrefois	163
Les Longues Voyes	163
Les Grandes Crayères	164
Les Beaudiers	164
Lallement, Juillet-	159
Grand Tradition	159
Special Club	160
Belle de Juillet Blanc de Blancs	160
Belle de Juillet Blanc de Noirs	160
Belle de Juillet Meunier 100%	161
Lancelot, Philippe	239
Fine Fleur	239
Les Hauts d'Epernay	239
Ivresse	239

Lancelot-Pienne	240
Brut Vintage Marie Lancelot	240
Lanson	165
Brut Vintage Red Label	165
Brut Vintage Gold Label	166
Lanson Vintage Collection	166
Noble Cuvée	166
Larmandier Père et Fils	97
Larmandier, Guy	97
Larmandier-Bernier	97
Terre de Vertus	97
Vieilles Vignes du Levant	98
Chemins d'Avize	98
Lassaigne, Jacques	99
Brut Vintage	100
Acte I Scène II Haut Revers du Chutat	100
Acte III Scène I Autour de Minuit	101
Clos Sainte-Sophie	101
Acte IV Scène I Soprano	101
Acte IV Scène II Alto	101
Acte IV Scène III Tenor	101
Laurent-Perrier	51
Léclapart, David	102
Artiste	102
Astre	102
l'Apotre	103
Leclerc Briant	167
Brut Reserve	167
Extra Brut Premier Cru	168
Brut Rosé	168
Millésime	168
La Croisette	168
Le Clos des Trois Clochers	168
Les Basses Prières	169
Rosé de Saignée	169
Blanc de Meuniers	169
Grand Blanc	169
Ledru, Marie-Noëlle	170
Cuvée du Goulté	170
Legras, Pierre	171
Brut Vintage Monographie	171
Brut Nature Monographie	172
Brut Vintage	172
Idée de Voyage	172
Lenoble, A.R.	104
Grand Cru Blanc de Blancs	104
Blanc de Noirs	105
Gentilhomme	105
Collection Rare	105
Lilbert-Fils	106
Brut Vintage	106
Loriot-Pagel, Joseph	241
Cuvée de Reserve	241
Special Club	241
Cuvée No. 6	241

Maillart, Nicolas	173		Milan, Jean	251
Millésimé	173		Brut Nature	251
Les Chaillots Gillis	173		Symphorine	251
Mont Martin	174		Terres de Noël	251
Les Jolivettes	174		Moët & Chandon	37, 177
Les Francs de Pied	174		Grand Vintage	178
Mailly Grand Cru	165, 242		Grand Vintage Collection	178
l'Intemporelle	242			
Les Echansons	243		Imperial Dry Vintage	178
Malot, Sadi	244		Moncuit, Pierre	252
Coup de Foudre	244		Cuvée Pierre Moncuit-Delos	252
Margaine, A.	245			
Millésime	245		Vintage Grand Cru	252
Rosé de Saignée	245		Cuvée Nicole Vieille Vigne	252
Special Club	246			
Marguet	247		Moncuit, Robert	180
Les Crayères	247		Millésime Vieilles Vignes	180
Amboniacus	247			
Ambonnay	248		Chétillons	180
Sapience	248		Vozémieux	181
Mathieu, Serge	249		Moussé Fils	253
Brut Vintage	249		Terre d'Illite	253
Mercier	37		Special Club	253
Michel, José	175		Müller-Ruinart	32
Grand Vintage	175		Mumm, G.H.	182
Vintage Blanc de Blancs	175		Cordon Rouge	182
Special Club	175		Mumm de Cramant	183
Mignon, Christophe	250		RSRV Blanc de Blancs	183
Pur Meunier	250		RSRV Blanc de Noirs	183
Blanc de Blancs	250		RSRV Rosé	183
			Brut Vintage	184
			Cuvée René Lalou	184
			Oudinot	256

Paillard, Bruno	**186**	
Brut Vintage	187	
Brut Vintage Blanc de Blancs	187	
Nec Plus Ultra	188	
Paillard, Pierre	**108**	
Les Mottelettes	109	
Lai Maillerettes	109	
La Grande Recolte	109	
Coteaux Champenois	109	
Paulet, Hubert	**189**	
Risléus	189	
Brut Vintage Rosé	189	
Penet-Chardonnet	**254**	
Les Fervins	254	
Les Epinettes	254	
Les Blanches Voies	254	
Prestige	254	
Cuvée Diane Claire	254	
Perrier, Laurent-	**256**	
Grand Siècle	256	
Grand Vin Sans Sucre	256	
Millésimé	256	
Perrier-Jouët	**190**	
Belle Epoque	190	
Belle Epoque Blanc de Blancs	191	
Belle Epoque Rosé	192	
Perrier-Jouët Cramant	192	
Péters, Pierre	**110**	
l'Esprit	111	
Extra Brut	111	
Les Chétillons	111	

Philipponnat	**42**	
Brut Vintage Clos des Goisses	42	
Brut Vintage Blanc de Blancs	44	
Brut Vintage Blanc de Noirs	44	
Brut Vintage Cuvée 1522	44	
Brut Vintage Les Cintres	45	
Brut Vintage La Rémissonne	45	
Brut Vintage Le Léon	45	
Piollot Pere et Fils	**258**	
Colas Robin	258	
Mepetit	258	
Pol Roger	**112**	
Brut Vintage	112	
Brut Vintage Blanc de Blancs	112	
Brut Vintage Rosé	113	
Cuvée Sir Winston Churchill	113	
Pommery	**165**	
Pouillon, R.	**259**	
Les Valnons	259	
Les Blanchiens	259	
Chemin du Bois	260	
Les Chataigniers	260	
Coteaux Champenois	260	
Rare Champagne	**151**	

Rodez, Eric 114
    Cuvée Millésime 114
    Empreinte Blanche 114
    Empreinte Noire 114
    Les Beurys 115
    Les Beurys et Les Secs 115
    Les Genettes 115
    Les Fournettes 115
Roederer, Louis 46
    Brut Vintage 47
    Brut Vintage Rosé 47
    Brut Vintage Blanc de Blancs 47
    Brut Vintage Cristal 47
    Brut Vintage Cristal Rosé 47
Roses de Jeanne 116
    Côte de Val Vilaine 116
    Inflorescence 116
    Côte de Béchalin 116
    La Parcelle 116
    La Haut-Lemblé 117
    Creux d'Enfer 117
    Presle 117
Ruinart 118
    Dom Ruinart 119
    Dom Ruinart Rosé 120
Ruppert-Leroy 261
    Martin Fontaine 261
    Fosse Grely 261
    Les Cognaux 261
    Rosé de Saignée 261

Salomon, Denis 262
    Elegance 262
    Saignée de Meunier 262
    Brut Vintage 262
    Cuvée Vitalie 262
Salon 50, 256
Savart 121
    l'Année 122
    Dame de Cœur 122
    Mont des Chrétains 122
    Calliope 122
    Expression 122
Savès, Camille 263
    Brut Vintage 263
    Anaïs Jolicœur 263
    Coteaux Champenois 264
Sélèque, J.M. 265
    Soliste 265
    Partition 265
    Partition - 2ème Lecture 266
    Coteaux Champenois Dizy 266
    Coteaux Champenois Pierry 266
Selosse, Guillaume 54
    Au Dessous de Gros Mont 54
    Largillier 54
Selosse, Jacques 53
    Les Carelles 54
    Chemin de Chalons 54
    Les Chantereines 54

La Cote Faron	54
Bout du Clos	54
Sous le Mont	54
Brut Vintage	54
Substance	55
Soutiran	267
Brut Vintage	267
Brut Vintage Blanc de Blancs	267
Stroebel	268
Héraclite Sous Bois	268
Suenen	193
Les Robarts	193
La Cocluette	193
Le Mont Aigu	193
La Grande Vigne	194
Taittinger	57
Comtes de Champagne Blanc de Blancs	58
Comtes de Champagne Rosé	60
Brut Vintage	60
Tarlant	194
Brut Prestige	195
Vigne d'Or	195
l'Etincelante	195
La Matinale	195
Vazart-Coquart & Fils	196
Grand Bouquet	196
Special Club	196
Le Millésime	196

Velut, Jean	269
Temoinage	269
Vergnon, J.L.	270
Resonance	270
Msnl	270
Confidence	270
Les Hautes Mottes	270
Expression	270
OG	270
Veuve Clicquot	197
Brut Vintage Gold Label	198
Brut Vintage Rosé	198
Cave Privée	198
La Grande Dame	198
La Grande Dame Rosé	198
Clos Colin (still wine)	199
Veuve Fourney	271
Monts de Vertus	271
Clos Faubourg Notre Dame	271
Vilmart & Cie	200
Grand Cellier d'Or	200
Cœur de Cuvée	201
Vouette et Sorbée	123
Fidèle	124
Textures	124
Saignée de Sorbée	124
Extrait	125
Sobre	125